Empire State Railway Museum's 33rd Annual

Guide to Tourist Railroads and Museums

1998 Edition

Front cover: Virginia & Truckee Railroad Co., Virginia City, Nevada.
Photo by Kevin Franchak.

Copyright © 1998 Empire State Railway Museum, Inc., P.O. Box 455, Phoenicia, NY 12464. All Rights Reserved. Printed in the United States of America.

This book may not be reproduced in part or in whole without written permission from the publisher, except in the case of brief quotations used in reviews. Published by Kalmbach Publishing Co., 21027 Crossroads Circle, P.O. Box 1612, Waukesha, WI 53187-1612.

Cover Design: Kristi Ludwig   ISSN: 0081-542X

To the Museums and Tourist Railroads

Listings: We would like to consider for inclusion every tourist railroad, trolley operation, railroad museum, live-steam railroad, and toy train exhibit in the United States and Canada that is open to the public and has regular hours and about which reliable information is available. If you know of an operation that is not included in the book, please send information to the address below.

1999 *Directory*: To be published in February 1999. A packet that includes all pertinent information needed for inclusion in the 1999 Guide will be mailed to all organizations listed in this book. New listings are welcomed. For information, please write to:
   Editor—Guide to Tourist Railroads and Museums
   Books Division
   Kalmbach Publishing Co.
   P.O. Box 1612
   Waukesha, WI 53187–1612

Advertising: Advertising space for the 1999 Guide must be reserved by November 6, 1998. Please contact Mike Yuhas at 1-800-558-1544, extension 625.

Publisher's Cataloging in Publication
(Prepared by Quality Books, Inc.)

Guide to tourist railroads and museums : 33rd annual steam passenger service directory/ [editor, Julie LaFountain].
   p. cm.
   Includes index.
   ISBN: 0-89024-339-5

   1. Railroad museums—United States—Directories. 2. Railroad museums—Canada—Directories. I. LaFountain, Julie.

TF6.U5G85 1998   625.1'0075
                            QBI97-41481

Contents

To the Reader 3
Symbols 4
U.S. Railroads and Museums 5
Canadian Railroads and Museums .390
Coupons . . . . .after page 198
Index of Railroads and Museums 418

Advertising Contents

APPAREL
J-Bar Rail Boutique A-21
TrainGear A-7

CONSULTANTS
Centennial Rail, Ltd. A-20
Stone Consulting & Design, Inc. A-14

PUBLICATIONS
Kalmbach Publishing Co. .A-8, A-9, A-12

RAILROAD ASSOCIATIONS
Association of Railway Museums, Inc. A-13
Tourist Railway Association, Inc. A-4

RAILROAD EQUIPMENT REPAIR & SALES
Benson Mountain Co. A-6
D.F. Barnhardt & Associates A-17

RAILROAD INSURANCE
Hamman-Miller-Beauchamp-Deeble, Inc. A-18

RAILROADIANA
The Depot Attic A-19
Milepost 1 . . . . .Inside back cover
Native Ground Music A-5
Smith-Thompson A-20

TOURIST RAILROADS
California State Railroad Museum . . . . . . .Inside front cover, A-1
Colorado Railroad Museum A-16
Mid-Continent Railway A-14

TRAVEL
Trains Unlimited, Tours A-15

VIDEO
Golden Rail Video..................................A-3
Herron Rail Video A-10
Penn Valley Pictures A-11

WHOLESALERS
Britt Allcroft Inc....................................A-2
E&M Specialty Co. A-17
Railfan Specialties A-22

90 min. VHS - HiFi Stereo
Only **$19.95**

Almost 100 years ago...
a small railroad in Northern Arizona began operations to service mining and lumber companies near what was then the Grand Canyon Forest Reserve. The Santa Fe soon took over this railroad. They had other ideas.

★

Golden Rail Video presents a "marvelous" new railroad adventure…

THUNDER UNDER HEAVEN
The Complete Story of the Grand Canyon Ry.*

Fascinating history - Incredible action! An adventure not to be missed.

"…look no farther than this excellent offering from Golden Rail Video." - *Trains*

★

*Also available in the special
expanded edition
featuring exciting cab rides in both **4960** & the 1st generation **ALCO passenger diesels**. Both cab rides fully integrated into the story on two tapes. Like nothing else you may have seen.
$35.90 (160 min.) *plus* $4.00 S&H

also from Golden Rail Video

An action-packed look at an industrial survivor.

"Wonderful" - *Trains*

"Excellent" - *Modeltec*

"This is an outstanding video…Don't miss it."
Narrow Gauge & Shortline Gazette

"Spectacular…Watch it again and again."
Live Steam

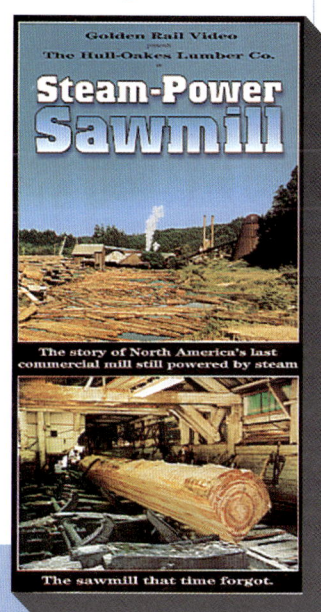

112 min. VHS - HiFi Stereo
$29.95

Call toll-free for additional titles & order info.
 **888-844-4449**
Golden Rail Video
Box 10474 • Glendale, CA 91209
CA add 8.25% sales tax - Foreign air-shipping add $8.00

A-3

You are invited to join TRAIN
THE TOURIST RAILWAY ASSOCIATION, INC.

TRAIN is the one trade association that is serving the growing needs of tourist rail lines, railroad museums, excursion operators, private car owners and suppliers - the multi-faceted groups that make up creative railroading.

With over 350 member organizations, and growing every month, our Roster is too long to print in the Steam Directory. Our members included in the *Guide to Tourist Railroads and Museums* may be identified by the **TRAIN** logo on their listing page.

TRAIN members receive our bi-monthly newsletter—*TRAINLINE,* filled with articles relating to the tourist railway industry.

TRAIN is an action association dealing decisively in the areas of
- Legislation
- Insurance
- Mechanical-steam
- Mechanical-electric
- Advertising
- Safety
- Operations
- Mechanical-diesel
- Mechanical-passenger cars
- Promotion

For further information on this important alliance of professionals write:

Tourist Railway Association, INc.
P.O. Box 28077
Denver, CO 80228-0010
1(800) 67-TRAIN
(303) 988-7764
FAX (303) 989-2192
http://www.train.org

BENSON MOUNTAIN

COMPANY

A company **DEDICATED** to the **REPAIR**, if possible,
the **REPLACEMENT**, if necessary,
and always the **PRESERVATION** of steam-powered equipment.

ASME CERTIFIED BOILER MANUFACTURERS

Capable to make replacement boilers for locomotives from 15" gauge to 56.5" gauge. We do some flanging and can weld on fake rivets for effect. Send us a good print, or the old boiler or hire us to blueprint your boiler on location.

NATIONAL BOARD & FRA BOILER REPAIRS/TESTING

Holder of National Board 'R' stamp for repairs of CODE/NON-CODE boilers. Ultrasonic testing to determine integrity of boiler in its present state. Repairs done in field as well as shop.

LOCOMOTIVE APPRAISALS & RESTORATION...OR BRAND NEW!

Before you purchase that locomotive, hire a Benson Mountain Company specialist to check it out. A complete package will include results of ultrasonic test, visual inspection, photographs and a written report of condition and may include cost to repair if required. We are capable of making a new locomotive in 15", 24" or 36" gauge if required.

TEAM EFFORT ON SOME REPAIRS

We realize that the cost of labor prevents many customers from doing the required repairs all at once. We will allow some of your volunteers/employees to assist us in working on your project in a non-skilled capacity, OR we will provide "clerk of the works" service and your personnel can do all the work (non-skilled or mechanical only).

INTERNET SERVICE NOW AVAILABLE

If you need to get some technical information or help, you may contact Benson Mountain Company by email at: benmtnco@tp.net or through our web page at: **BENMTNCO.TP.NET**

TRADE IN UNWANTED LOCOMOTIVES OR PARTS

We will consider all or part of a locomotive for a trade-in to offset the cost of a complete restoration. For details contact our office. We offer this service so that when time is available, we may be able to restore this equipment and offer it for sale/lease to another group needing a good running steam engine. We feel that there are some organizations which need a steam engine but do not have the resources to purchase & maintain one, so, therefore, we have entered the locomotive leasing field.

BENSON MOUNTAIN COMPANY
1555 WALLUM LAKE ROAD, PASCOAG, RI 02859-1818
TEL: (401) 567-0020   FAX: (401) 567-0021

Railroading Today

Hundreds of interesting historical and reference books, action-packed videos, exciting calendars, and other hobby products are available from Kalmbach Publishing Co.

Historical & Reference Books

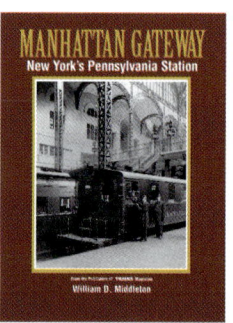

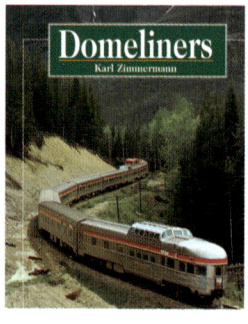

Look for these books at your favorite hobby shop or bookstore

Visit our on-line catalog at www.kalmbach.com

A-8

.And Yesterday!

Ask for your FREE catalog!

Railroad Videos

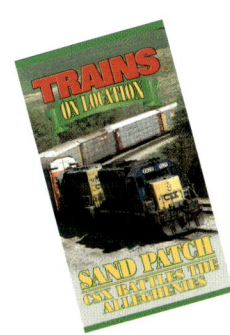

Calendars

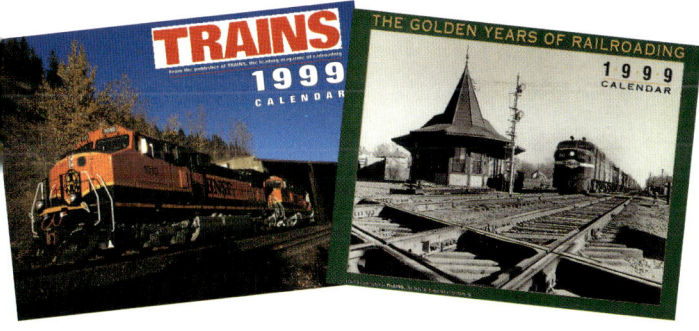

Call 1-800-533-6644, 24 hours a day.

For faster service call Monday-Friday 8:30am-5:00pm Central Time.
Outside the U.S. and Canada call 414-796-8776. Fax 414-796-1615.

E-mail: customerservice@kalmbach.com

KALMBACH BOOKS   21027 Crossroads Circle, P.O. Box 1612
Waukesha, WI 53187-1612   #Z072

Once upon a time......

𝒜merica was served by trains of classic design.

𝒯oday, they are largely only memories.

ℰxcept, at the museums in this directory where hard work and dedication of a few have preserved important examples from the glory days of railroading.

Visit them. Ride their trains. Patronize their efforts.

𝒜nd, for action programs of the glory days of railroading look for our videos in their gift shops for we're just as dedicated to preservation of the imagery of the classic trains as the museums are to their collections.

For new releases see our ads in leading railroad magazines
Download our catalog on the internet at http://www.rrhistorical.com/hrv

PENN VALLEY PICTURES

JUST RELEASED!

– VOLUME 6 –
UNDER THE CATENARY
Historical Features of the Pennsylvania Railroad
This all-color action packed video will take you back in time to the PRR's electric operations in the early sixties through the Penn Central era and beginnings of Amtrak in the early seventies. You will visit Harrisburg, Enola, Middletown, Safe Harbor, Havre de Grace, and Perryville to see a parade of passenger and freight trains pulled by E3B, P5A, GG-1, and E-44 electrics, and some Passenger E-7 and E-8 diesels. 45 minutes.

HISTORICAL FEATURES SERIES OF THE PENNSYLVANIA RAILROAD
RELIVED THROUGH THIS EXCITING 6-VOLUME COLOR VIDEO COLLECTION OF THE FILMS OF THE LATE CLARENCE WEAVER

PROFESSIONALLY NARRATED AND EDITED, SCRIPT BY DAN CUPPER OF TRAINS MAGAZINE

– VOLUME 1 –
THE ORE TRAIN
This video documentary follows steam-powered ore trains from the Northumberland Yards to Mt. Carmel, PA, via the PRR's Shamokin Branch in the early 50s. See 100-car 2-10-0 powered ore trains climbing 2% grades. 40 minutes.

– VOLUME 2 –
THE S & L STORY
Follow the daily trip of a steam-powered local freight as it travels through the rich farmlands of Snyder County, PA, over the PRR's Sunbury to Lewistown Branch. The H9 and H10 powered trains leave the Northumberland Yard and travel to McClure and back. 42 minutes.

– VOLUME 3 –
RAILFAN EXCURSION TO NORTHUMBERLAND, PA
Revisit a 1957 L1 powered steam excursion to the site of the PRR's historically preserved steam engine and equipment collection in Northumberland, PA. Also see K4's No. 1361 at Horseshoe Curve, and restored on an excursion in 1988. 35 minutes

– VOLUME 4 –
THE MIDDLE DIVISION – ROCKVILLE TO HORSESHOE CURVE
Revisit the glory days of the PRR in the 1950s. Featured are runby scenes of steam T1s, M1s, L1s, K4s, and J1s plus early EMD, Alco, Fairbanks Morse, and Baldwin diesels, and the Aerotrain. Original 16 mm film is 98% color and features an authentic PRR steam and diesel soundtrack. 40 minutes.

– VOLUME 5 –
THE SUSQUEHANNA DIVISION
See a parade of steam power: M1s, L1s, K4s, I1s, G5s, E6s, E5s, B6s, and early diesel locomotives. Visit the busy Northumberland roundhouse, and see freight and passenger trains (including the Bellefonte mixed train) in some of the best PRR runby scenes ever taken. 45 minutes.

Price of videos $39.95 each – 3 videos $110 – All 6 videos $210
Shipping instructions: 1 item add $3, additional items add $1 each • PA residents add 6% Sales Tax
Dealer inquiries invited

24 HOUR PHONE ORDER SERVICE 1-800-577-6003 • FAX 1-800-577-6004
PENN VALLEY PICTURES • PO BOX 429 • SUNBURY, PA 17801 • (717) 286-4618

Cross**TRAINING**

Model Railroader
The world's most popular railroading magazine. Each monthly issue covers all popular scales and includes challenging how-to projects and visits to remarkable layouts.

12 issues/$34.95 U.S.
Outside the U.S. $45.00*

Trains
The power, history and drama of America's railroads. Readers learn about great railroad empires, the newest high-tech locomotives and enjoy award-winning photography.

12 issues/$34.95 U.S.
Outside the U.S. $45.00*

Classic Toy Trains
A celebration of Lionel, American Flyer, Marx, and other vintage toy trains. Readers visit world-class collections, see new products, and get repair and restoration tips in each issue.

8 issues/$29.95 U.S.
Outside the U.S $38.00*

Garden Railways
Garden Railways celebrates the hobby of outdoor model railroading. Bimonthly issues offer layout plans, product reviews, planting tips and more.

6 issues/$22.50 U.S.
Outside the U.S. $28.00*

Start your subscription today!

To order call toll-free **1-800-533-6644**
24 hours a day. For faster service call
Monday-Friday 8:30am-5:00pm Central Time.
Please have your credit card ready. Payable in U.S. funds.
FAX 414-796-1615. Outside the U.S. and Canada call 414-796-8776.

*GST Included.

KALMBACH PUBLISHING CO.

Dept. *A81T*

Subscribe to the only publication devoted exclusively to railway museums and the preservation of railroad history. Published by the **Association of Railway Museums**, this quarterly publication carries the news of the Association and its member museums. It also provides other information on railway preservation including how-to articles and reports of government programs and agencies affecting railway museums.

One year subscriptions (four issues) cost $15. Send your payment and address to:

RAILWAY MUSEUM QUARTERLY
Association of Railway Museums
P. O. Box 3311 • City of Industry, CA 91744-0311

All railway museums and preservation societies are invited to join the more than 100 large and small, volunteer and professional, museums in the U. S. and Canada that recognize the value of membership in the Association of Railway Museums.

Since its founding in 1961, the Association of Railway Museums has been involved with helping and promoting the railway museum movement. Its publications and meetings serve this purpose.

The A.R.M. is a professional affiliate of the American Association of Museums. As such, it speaks to the larger museum community on behalf of railway museums. The Association also actively works to address the special regulatory problems of operating railway museums.

The Association offers full Memberships for non-profit museums displaying railway equipment on a regular schedule. Affiliations are available for other non-profits. Commercial supporters may join as commercial affiliates.

For information contact:
Association of Railway Museums, Inc.
P. O. Box 370 • Tujunga, CA 91043-0370
Telephone & Facsimile: (818) 951-9151

Stone Consulting & Design, Inc.

Serving Shortlines, Tourist Railroads, Trolley & Transit Systems, Rail Foundations and Museums

Planning & Studies
- Rail Freight Development & Planning
- Feasibility Studies
- Marketing, Ridership, & Financial Analysis
- Museum & Station Facilities

Design & Engineering Services
- Licensed for Engineering Services in __ states
- Canadian Services provided through Northwest Theil Rail Consultants, Ltd.
- Design/Build Capabilities
- Project Management & Inspection
- Track Inspection
- Full CAD Capabilities

Operations
- Shortline and Regional Rail Analysis
- For-Profit Operator Selection
- Ridership and Capacity Studies

Liaison
- Professional Rail Consultant for Community & Industrial Groups
- Class-1 Railroad Issues

Grantsmanship
- ISTEA Grant Preparation & Assistance
- Economic Development Grants & Foundation Fundings
- Historic Register Nominations

Harvey H. Stone, President - registered as a Professional Engineer in over 25 states
Randall D. Gustafson, Gary E. Landrio, Paul A. Jannotti
327 Pennsylvania Avenue West, P.O. Box 306, Warren, PA 16365 (814) 726-9870
e-mail: scdemail@stoneconsulting.com   Visit our web page at www.stoneconsulting.com!

Passage to the Past.

The weather is always beautiful for a steam train ride.

Take a seven-mile, 50-minute round trip on a former Chicago & North Western branch line built in 1903, and experience small town America in simpler times.

Smell the coal smoke and listen to the lonesome whistle against the wind.

Depart on a train from a restored 1894 C&NW depot. Then visit the museum with its nationally acclaimed, restored, turn-of-the-century wooden passenger and freight cars. North Freedom is near Baraboo and Wisconsin Dells in the heart of one of America's favorite tourist destination areas.

Mid-Continent Railway always welcomes members and volunteers. Call 608-522-4261, or write P.O. Box 358, North Freedom, WI 53951, for brochure and schedule materials; or member and volunteer information.

© 1996. Mid-Continent Railway Historical Society, Inc.

A-14

RAILROAD TOUR ADVENTURES

Our 14th Year Offering Railfan Tours
CALL US FOR OUR 24-PAGE BROCHURE
1-800-359-4870
(530) 836-1745 • Fax (530) 836-1748

STEAM IN THE ANDES: August 8-16 – To cover the Guayaquil & Quito in Ecuador with charter steam in the rugged Andes including the famous Devil's Nose Switchbacks plus railcars on the San Lorenzo line. This is the greatest mountain steam operation in South America. Steam all the way to Quito and beyond!

BEST OF SOUTH AMERICAN TRAINS '98: October 17 - November 8 – In Chile, Argentina, Paraguay, and Bolivia with 21 charters using steam, diesel, and railcars on 4 gauges and 12 railroads. Shorter options okay.

WHITE PASS & YUKON SPECTACULAR: September 17-20 – With charter steam, diesel, and railcar over this rugged narrow gauge line in Alaska, British Columbia & Yukon.

CUMBRES FALL COLORS SPECTACULAR: September 28-29 – With charter doubleheaded steam freight over the Cumbres & Toltic in the Rockies of Colorado and New Mexico.

NEVADA NORTHERN SPECTACULAR: October 3-4 – With charter steam including a doubleheader on the Nevada Northern Railroad.

NORTH AMERICAN RAILFAN SPECTACULAR: September 26 - October 10 – To cover current day railroading in Colorado, Utah, Nevada, and California. Includes the "Cumbres Fall Colors Spectacular" and "Nevada Northern Spectacular."

RUSSIAN STEAM: Three spectacular train tours using classic Russian steam will be operated in April, June and July including the famous Trans-Siberian.

AFRICA STEAM: September 13-20 – Charter steam excursion Victoria Falls, Zimbabwe to Cape Town, South Africa.

TRAINS UNLIMITED, TOURS

P.O. Box 1997
Portola, California 96122 USA

Discover the Fascination of Railroading at the
Colorado Railroad Museum

You can ring the bell on some of Colorado's oldest steam locomotives or climb into a red caboose. See over sixty cars and engines displayed in an authentic setting at the foot of the Rocky Mountains. The museum building, a replica of an 1880 style masonry depot, houses more than 50,000 rare old photographs, papers and artifacts. There's fun for the entire family!

Steam Train Runs	Open Every Day
June 6-7	9 a.m. - 5 p.m.
July 25-26	(to 6p.m. in June,
Sept 19-20	July, August)
October 24-25	
December 5-6	

Colorado Railroad Museum
Book Store and Gift Shop The Railroad Book Source

CALL US FIRST! 800-365-6263

Best Selection of Railroad Books
We stock over 1000 titles from throughout the country, hundreds of videos, calendars and gifts available *FAST PERSONAL SERVICE!*

Biggest & Best RR Book Catalog $2.00
(refundable with first purchase)

Members Receive Discounts!
Call for information about becoming a member, and charge to your Visa, Mastercard, or Discover today!

PURCHASE FROM US AND HELP TO PRESERVE RAILROAD HERITAGE!

Colorado Railroad Museum
P.O. Box 10, Golden, CO 80402-0010
17155 W. 44th Ave / 303-279-4591
800-365-6263 / fax 24 hours 303-279-4229
Email corrmus@aol.com

D.F. BARNHARDT & ASSOCIATES
Tourist Railroad Equipment Services

Established 1978

Equipment Appraisals & Sales

Telephone: (704) 436-9393   Fax: (704) 436-9399

FREE BROCHURE

8344 WEST FRANKLIN STREET
P.O. BOX 1088
MOUNT PLEASANT, NC 28124

"Gifts for Railroad Buffs"

E & M Specialty Co. *established 1964*

ATTENTION GIFT SHOP BUYERS
Increase your selection - Increase your sales

Large selection of costume Jewelry & Wrist Watches
Men's Ties, Hickory stripe Aprons & Hot pads,
Engineer Hats in adjustable sizes, Wall clocks,
Desk clocks & Alarm clocks, Keychains, Adult Puzzles.
Metal signs and Suncatchers. Children's Toys
and Books including Thomas the Tank Engine
merchandise.

P.O. Box 185 • Fremont, Ca 94536
1 800/701-5464 • FAX 510/796-0163

See our display at the Seattle & San Francisco gift shows   Member **TRAINS**

RAILROAD & TROLLEY TOURIST & MUSEUM INSURANCE

COMPREHENSIVE LIABILITY – RAILWAY OPERATIONS, ROLLING STOCK, VEHICLES, BUILDINGS, EQUIPMENT, GIFT SHOP INVENTORIES
RAILWAY EXCURSION LIABILITY & SHORTLINE FREIGHT INSURANCE

OUR CLIENTS ARE AMONG THE LEADING MUSEUM & TOURIST RAILWAYS

Tennessee Valley RR • Boone & Scenic Valley • Mt. Rainier Scenic • Portola RR Museum • Maine Narrow Gauge Co. • Virginia & Truckee RR Co. • Illinois RR Museum • Cooperstown & Marne RY • Kentucky RY Museum • Chehalis & Centralia RR Assoc. • Minnesota Transportation Museum • East Portland Traction & Molalla Western • Orange Empire RY Museum • Shoreline Trolley Museum • East Troy Electric RR • Niles Canyon RY • Walkersville Southern RY • Yolo Shortline/Scenic • Western RY Museum • Connecticut Valley RR Museum

I WANT TO INSURE YOUR MUSEUM!

Advantages:

- COMPETITIVE PREMIUMS
- ADMITTED A+ XIV BEST RATED
- NO LIABILITY DEDUCTIBLES
- MONTHLY PAY, NO FINANCE FEE
- NO TAXES or BROKERS FEES

Call or Fax Mike Deeble
Phone: 800-272-4594 • Fax: 310-439-4453

HAMMAN-MILLER-BEAUCHAMP-DEEBLE, INC. INSURANCE
3633 East Broadway, Long Beach, CA 90803

When you are in Strasburg, PA, be sure to visit

THE DEPOT ATTIC

**209 GAP ROAD, ROUTE 741
STRASBURG, PA 17579
PHONE (717) 687-9300**

Near the Railroad Museum of Pennsylvania, the Strasburg R.R. and the Toy Train Museum.

**THE LARGEST STORE IN AMERICA DEVOTED
TO AUTHENTIC RAILROAD AND TRANSPORTATION
BOOKS, ARTIFACTS AND MEMORABILIA**

- *Lanterns, Lamps, Timetables, Depot & Telegraph Items*
- *New, Used, Rare and Out-of-Print Books*
- *Chinaware & Silverware from Railroad, Ship and Air Lines*
- *Railroad & Transportation Posters, Prints & Graphics*
- *Signs from Railroad, Express & Transportation Companies*
- *Badges, Hats, Locks, Keys, Buttons & Postcards*
- *Bonds & Stock Certificates from Railroads & Industry*
- *Old Tickets, Passes, Guides, Brochures & Booklets*
- *Early Advertising, Pictorial Calendars & Original Art*

**MANY OTHER MISCELLANEOUS RAILROAD AND
TRANSPORTATION ITEMS TOO NUMEROUS TO MENTION!**

Catalogs are mailed approximately every 7 weeks.
Each catalog offers memorabilia and the latest new books.
Send $2.00 to receive the next 4 catalogs.

"America's foremost dealers in railroad memorabilia"
❂ Established 1956 ❂

Your best source for Custom Coins, Tokens and

RAILROAD GIFTS & COLLECTIBLES

RAILWAYMAN'S POCKET WATCH The Official Watch of the Russian State Railway. This beautiful 18-Jewel mechanical pocket watch is crafted by Molnija, Russia's leading military clock and watch maker. The dial features the famous "winged wheel" logo and 24-hour markings. The back cover features a Russian P36 4-8-4 steam locomotive. A FREE 14" chain is included.
$49.95 + $3 shipping

FREE CATALOG:
CALL 1-800-375-3943

Dealer Inquiries Welcome   P.O. Box 828, White River Jct., VT 05001

FROM A DREAM TO THE REALITY

PROFESSIONAL PLANNING
FEASIBILITY STUDIES
CAPITAL GENERATION
FUNDING & MARKETING
TOURIST RAILWAYS AND MUSEUMS

F.K. Minnich, President
J.E. Minnich, Executive Vice President

(303) 693-0664
FAX: (303) 680-6231

CENTENNIAL RAIL, LTD.
POST OFFICE BOX 460393
AURORA, COLORADO 80046-0393

J-BAR RAIL
SCREENPRINTING & DESIGN

"THE #1 SOURCE FOR FULL-COLOR RAILROAD APPAREL"

J-Bar Rail is an exclusive designer and screenprinter of railroad t-shirts, sweatshirts, and jackets. We can custom design a t-shirt just for you. We also have over 60 stock designs for you to pick from.

Trains is all we do,
and we can do them for you.

Special Custom Design Program

For more information,
or a copy of our catalog, contact:

J-BAR RAIL Worldwide

12832 Vivian Ct., Rockton, IL 61072

Production Shop

633 Progressive Lane #2, South Beloit, IL 61080
Phone 815.624.4015 Fax 815.624.2652
email: jbar@stateline-il.com
web site: www.stateline-il.com/jbar

J-BAR is a supplier to:

Cass Scenic Railway	Georgetown Loop Railroad
NP Historical Society	Minnesota Trans Museum
Santa Fe Southern RR	Ladysmith Rail Display
Norfolk Southern RR	Riverside & Great
North Dakota RR Museum	Northern Railway
National Railroad Museum	Illinois Railway Museum
Great Plains Museum of Transportation	Mad River & NKP Museum
Hoosier Valley RR Museum	Orville Historical Society
North Carolina Transportation Museum	Benton County Historical Society
South Carolina Railroad Museum	Galesburg RR Museum
	Lake Superior Museum of Transportation

plus many more

Railfan Specialties

Wholesale Supplier To Steam & Tourist R.R.'s

Specializing In:
NEW & UNIQUE R.R. GIFTS
CUSTOM SOUVENIRS
Exclusive Distributor:

TRAINOPOTAMUS T-SHIRTS CHILDREN'S COLORING T-SHIRTS
THOMAS THE TANK ITEMS & TRAVEL MUG FLASHING L.E.D. R.R
BUTTONS (We do Custom L.E.D. Flashing Buttons)

CALL OR WRITE FOR OUR CATALOG
P.O. Box 10245 Wilmington, N.C. 28405
Phone/Fax 910-686-2820
1-800-772-4532 *(Please specify wholesale or retail)*
SERVING OVER 200 R.R. ACCOUNTS IN THE UNITED STATES, CANADA & AUSTRALIA

NEW FOR 1998 – Thomas watches, audio tapes and t-shirts

Empire State Railway Museum's 33rd Annual

Guide to Tourist Railroads and Museums

To the Reader

In 1966, railroad enthusiasts Marvin Cohen and Steve Bogen produced, and the Empire State Railway Museum published, the first *Steam Passenger Service Directory*. At that time, tourist railroading was in its infancy, and the book featured 62 tourist railroads and steam excursion operations. Four years later, in 1970, the Museum and *Directory* sponsored a tourist railroad conference, and the Tourist Railroad Association, Inc. (TRAIN), was founded.

The tourist railroad industry has flourished over the past three decades, with local groups of rail enthusiasts and preservationists banding together to return to service locomotives and rolling stock that have sat dormant and neglected for too many years. The mission of these organizations includes educating and entertaining the general public. That's where the Empire State Railway Museum and this book fit in. Through the foresight and perseverance of the Museum, this book continues to be published so that rail enthusiasts, as well as those who are only casually interested in trains, can become aware of the hundreds of wonderful tourist railroads and railroad attractions available for them to enjoy and learn from. Kalmbach Publishing Co. is pleased and proud to be able to produce this book on behalf of the Empire State Railway Museum.

If you're an annual purchaser of the *Steam Passenger Service Directory* (this is the 33rd edition), you've probably noticed that the title has been changed to the Empire State Railway Museum's *Guide to Tourist Railroads and Museums*. We believe that by making the name more accurately reflect the content (diesel, electric, and other kinds of railroad-related attractions as well as steam railroads), we will be able to reach a wider audience and spread the word that trains are still out there. At the same time, we've made some format changes to make the book more attractive and easier to use.

Guest Coupons: The reduced-rate coupons provided by many operations in this edition of the *Guide to Tourist Railroads and Museums* will be honored by the museums. Be sure to present them when purchasing tickets.

Brochures: Many operations offer brochures and/or timetables. Please see the symbol sections in the listings for those operations that provide brochures.

Every effort has been made to ensure the accuracy of the contents. However, we depend on the information supplied by each operation. We cannot assume responsibility for errors, omissions, or fare and schedule changes. Internet addresses have not been verified and may be subject to change. Be sure to write or phone ahead to confirm hours and prices.

Symbols

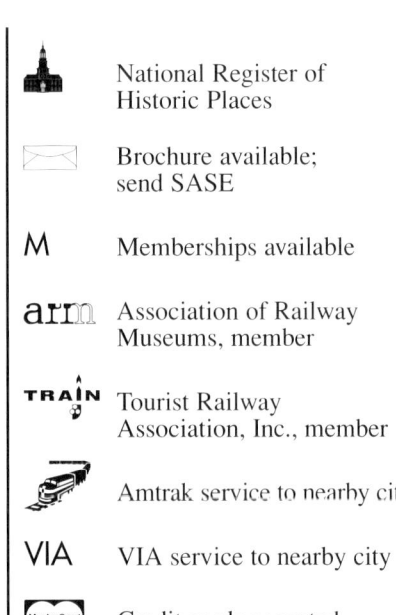

♿	Handicapped accessible
P	Parking
🚌	Bus/RV parking
🎁	Gift, book, or museum shop
☕	Refreshments
🍴	Restaurant
🤵	Dinner train/dining car
📷	Guided tours
⛱	Picnic area
🚂	Excursions
🎨	Arts and crafts
🏛	National Register of Historic Places
✉	Brochure available; send SASE
M	Memberships available
arm	Association of Railway Museums, member
TRAIN	Tourist Railway Association, Inc., member
🚆	Amtrak service to nearby city
VIA	VIA service to nearby city
MasterCard / VISA	Credit cards accepted

4

Alabama, Calera   **HEART OF DIXIE RAILROAD MUSEUM**
Diesel, scheduled
Standard gauge

NEIL SMART, JR.

Museum/Ride: Visitors can see a variety of railroad memorabilia in a 100-year-old depot and locomotives, cars, and equipment in the railroad yard. A 45-minute ride through scenic forests can be experienced on the museum's Calera and Shelby Railroad.

Schedule: Museum–year round: Saturdays, 9 a.m. to 4 p.m. April 18 through December 13: Sundays, 12 to 4:30 p.m. Train–April 18 through December 5: first and third Saturdays of each month.

Admission/Fare: Museum–donations appreciated. Train–adults $6.00; children $4.00.

Locomotive/Rolling Stock: 1951 U.S. Army EMD SW8 nos. 2019 and 2022; 1953 U.S. Army Fairbanks Morse H12-44 no. 1850, 1853, and 1861; 1910 Frisco coach no. 1062; and more.

Special Events: Halloween Train Ride, October 31. Santa Claus Train Ride, December 5, 6, 12, and 13. Spring and Fall Festivals to be announced.

Nearby Attractions/Accommodations: Brierfield Iron Works State Park, Oak Mountain State Park, Birmingham Zoo, Art Museum, Holiday Inn Express, Days Inn.

Location/Directions: I-65 to State 25 at exit no. 228, west to 9th Street South.

Site Address: 1919 9th Street, Calera, AL
Mailing Address: PO Box 727, Calera, AL 35040
Telephone: (205) 668-3435

Alabama, Huntsville **HISTORIC HUNTSVILLE DEPOT**
Railroad museum

HUNTSVILLE DEPOT

Museum: Built in 1860, the three-story structure is the only antebellum passenger depot in Alabama and one of few in the U.S. The museum exhibits include a 20-minute multimedia presentation and a ticket office brought to life through robotics. The museum operates a replica of a 1920s trolley on a 30-minute tour of downtown and the antebellum area.

Schedule: February through December: Monday through Saturday, 9 a.m. to 5 p.m. Last tour begins at 4 p.m.

Admission/Fare: Adults $6.00; seniors $5.00; students (6-18) $3.00.

Special Events: Vary throughout the year; call or write for details.

Nearby Attractions/Accommodations: Depot trolley rides through Historic District, Alabama Constitution Village, U.S. Space and Rocket Center, restaurants and lodging.

Location/Directions: I-565 east, exit 19, Washington/Jefferson Street exit, bear right to depot.

Site Address: 320 Church Street, Huntsville, AL
Mailing Address: 320 Church Street, Huntsville, AL 35801
Telephone: (205) 539-1860 or (205) 535-6526
Fax: (205) 535-6017

Alabama, Huntsville/Chase Community

NORTH ALABAMA RAILROAD MUSEUM, INC.
Diesel, scheduled
Standard gauge

NORTH ALABAMA RAILROAD MUSEUM, INC.

Museum/Ride: Headquartered in the Chase Depot, the smallest union station in the country, the focus is on telling the history of the railroads in North Alabama and South Central Tennessee. The story is told through old photographs, maps, an A/V presentation, and a walk through display train. Ride 1¼-hours on museum's Mercury & Chase Railroad, which follows the route of Nashville, Chattanooga & St. Louis Railway's 1887 Huntsville branch.

Schedule: Museum–April through October: Wednesdays and Saturdays, 9:30 a.m. to 2 p.m. Train–April through October: second and fourth weekends of each month.

Admission/Fare: Museum–adults $4.00; children 5-11 $2.00. Train–adults $8.00; children under 12 $4.00.

Locomotive/Rolling Stock: Alco S2; 1926 boxcab; 26 pieces passenger and freight equipment; maintenance way equipment; three motor cars.

Special Events: Mother's Day Special, Goblin Special, The Santa Train.

Nearby Attractions/Accommodations: Alabama Space and Rocket Center (home of Space Camp), The Huntsville Depot Museum, Twickenham Historic District, Dogwood Manor Bed & Breakfast.

Location/Directions: From east end I-565 in Huntsville, continue east on U.S. 72 for 2 miles, take left on Moores Mill Road for one mile, cross second railroad track, left on Chase Road for ½ mile to museum on left.

Site Address: 694 Chase Road, Chase Community, Huntsville, AL
Mailing Address: PO Box 4163, Huntsville, AL 35815-4163
Telephone: (205) 851-6276 (voice on Wed. and Sat., otherwise recording)
Fax: (205) 895-0222
E-mail: jlsims@hiwaay.net
Internet: www.suncompsvc.com/narm/

Alaska, Anchorage

ALASKA RAILROAD
Diesel, scheduled
Standard gauge

ALASKA RAILROAD

Ride/Display: The Alaska Railroad, established in 1914 with railroad equipment used in the construction of the Panama Canal, provides passenger service between Anchorage and Seward and between Anchorage, Denali National Park, and Fairbanks. Scenic rides on 469 miles of mainline track through state and national parks offer passengers an opportunity to view wildlife such as bear, moose, beavers, and birds. Spectacular mountain terrain and optional tours are also available at stops along the way. Potter Section House State Historic Park, 10 miles south of Anchorage, features rail cars depicting the history of the Alaska Railroad. Small gift shops.

Schedule: Call or write for information.

Admission/Fare: Call or write for information.

Locomotive/Rolling Stock: Four rail diesel cars; 48 locomotives of various types; three Vista-Dome cars; seven coaches; six new coaches constructed in 1990; five diners/food-service cars.

Special Events: Call or write for information.

Site Address: Anchorage, AK
Mailing Address: PO Box 107500, Anchorage, AK 99510
Telephone: (907) 265-2494 and (800) 544-0552

Alaska, Skagway

WHITE PASS & YUKON ROUTE
Steam, diesel, scheduled
36" gauge

GEORGE A. FORERO, JR.

Display/Ride: Built in 1898 to supply the Klondike Gold Rush, the White Pass Railroad is one of the most specitacular mountain railroads in the world. An International Historic Civil Engineering Landmark, the WP&YR offers round trip excursions from Skagway to the White Pass Summit and through rail/bus connections to Whitehorse, Yukon.

Schedule: May 15 through September 20: daily. Summit Excursion–depart Skagway 8:30 a.m. and 1 p.m., 3-hour round trip. Through service northbound–depart Skagway 12:40 p.m. (train); arr. Fraser, B.C., 2:00 p.m. (change to bus); arr. Whitehorse, Yukon, 6:30 p.m. Through service southbound–depart Whitehorse, Yukon, 8:15 a.m. (bus); arr. Fraser, B.C., 10:20 a.m. (change to train); arr. Skagway, Alaska, 12:00 p.m. Steam Train–June through August: every other Saturday, departs at 8:10 a.m.

Admission/Fare: Summit Excursion–adults $78.00; children $39.00. Through service–adults $95.00; children $47.50. Steam train–adults $150.00; children $75.00. Reservations recommended.

Locomotive/Rolling Stock: 1947 Baldwin no. 73 2-8-2, the last WP&WR steam engine; eleven GE 90 class boxcab diesel locomotives; more.

Special Events: WP&YR/Skagway Reunion, celebrate 100 years, May 6-9. Ceremony of the first spike driven on WP&YR, May 29.

Nearby Attractions/Accommodations: Klondike Gold Rush community.

Radio frequency: 160.325

Site Address: 2nd and Spring Street, Skagway, AK
Mailing Address: PO Box 435, Skagway, AK 99840
Telephone: (907) 983-2217 and (800) 343-7373
Fax: (907) 983-2734
E-mail: ngauge73@aol.com
Internet: www.whitepassrailroad.com

Alaska, Wasilla

MUSEUM OF ALASKA
TRANSPORTATION & INDUSTRY
Transportation museum
Standard gauge

PATRICK DURAND

Display: Alaska Railroad locomotives, five diesels, and 26 items of rolling stock, maintenance-of-way equipment. Also, planes, boats, and automobiles.

Schedule: May 1 through September 30: daily, 9 a.m. to 6 p.m. October 1 through April 30: Tuesdays through Saturdays, 9 a.m. to 5 p.m.

Admission/Fare: Adults $5.00; seniors and students $4.00; children under age 8 are free; families $12.00;

Locomotive/Rolling Stock: Alaska Railroad RS1 no. 1000; Chitina auto railer; EMD F7A no. 1500; USAF Baldwins nos. 1841 and 1842; Pullman McCord.

Special Events: Blast From the Past, July 4 weekend. Great Alaska Antique Power Show, third weekend in August.

Nearby Attractions/Accommodations: Alaska Live Steamers 1.5" scale railroad is next door.

Location/Directions: Follow signs at mile 47 of Parks Highway, north of Wasilla.

       M

Site Address: Mile 47, Parks Highway, Wasilla, AK
Mailing Address: PO Box 870646, Wasilla, AK 99687
Telephone: (907) 376-1211
Fax: (907) 376-3082
E-mail: sewtrain@alaska.net.com
Internet: www.alaska.net/~rmorris/mati1.htm

Arizona, Chandler

ARIZONA RAILWAY MUSEUM
Railway museum
Standard gauge

STEVE WHISEL

Display: The museum building, reminiscent of an early Southwestern railway depot, houses railroad memorabilia and artifacts from railways of the Southwest and elsewhere. The museum is expanding its trackage to exhibit additional equipment.

Schedule: Labor Day through Memorial Day: weekends, 12 to 4 p.m.

Admission/Fare: Donations appreciated.

Locomotive/Rolling Stock: Thirty pieces of rolling stock and locomotives.

Nearby Attractions/Accommodations: San Marco Golf Course, Phoenix Zoo.

Location/Directions: Thirty minutes from Phoenix.

     M arm

Site Address: 399 N. Delaware Street, Chandler, AZ
Mailing Address: PO Box 842, Chandler, AZ 85224
Telephone: (602) 821-1108

Arizona, Clarkdale

VERDE CANYON RAILROAD, LC
Diesel, scheduled
Standard gauge

TOM JOHNSON—RED ROCK STOCK

Ride: The Verde Canyon Railroad offers a panoramic rail experience into Arizona's other grand canyon, accessible only by rail. The flora, fauna, and rugged high desert rock faces are distinctive to this geological mecca. The train rolls past looming crimson cliffs, near ancient Indian ruins and passes through a 680-foot man-made tunnel.

Schedule: Year round: Tuesdays through Sundays, depart at 1 p.m. March, April, May, October, November: add Mondays. March, April, October, November: Saturdays, double trains depart 9 a.m. and 2:30 p.m.

Admission/Fare: Train–adult coach $35.95; senior coach $32.95; children under 12 coach $20.95. All first class $54.95. Mini-museum/depot are free.

Locomotive/Rolling Stock: FP7 engines nos. 1510 and 1512 pull five Pullman Standards and one Budd Stainless Steel which access five flatcars converted to open-air viewing cars with canopies.

Special Events: Starlight Trains, June through October. "Throw Mama on the Train," Mother's Day. Firecracker Barbecue, July 4. Early Bird New Year's Eve Party, December 31.

Nearby Attractions/Accommodations: Room, ride, meal packages with Sedona Super 8, Tuzigoot National Monument, historic Jerome.

Location/Directions: I-17 exit 260 to Cottonwood, 89A to Clarkdale.

Site Address: 300 N. Broadway, Clarkdale, AZ
Mailing Address: 300 N. Broadway, Clarkdale, AZ 86324
Telephone: (800) 293-7245
Fax: (520) 639-1253
E-mail: verdecanyonrr@verdenet.com
Internet: www.arizonaguide.com/verdecanyonrr

Arizona, Mesa

ARIZONA TRAIN DEPOT
G scale
Model railroad display

ARIZONA TRAIN DEPOT

Display: Display includes circus, mining, mountain. Relax in the hobo corner with videos and reading material.

Schedule: Year round: Mondays, Tuesdays, Thursdays, Fridays, Saturdays: 10 a.m. to 5 p.m.; Wednesdays, 1 to 8 p.m.; Sundays 10 a.m. to 3 p.m.

Admission/Fare: Free.

Locomotive/Rolling Stock: Four G scale.

Nearby Attractions/Accommodations: McCormick Ranch, Grand Canyon Railroad, Verde Canyon Railroad.

Location/Directions: Highway 60 to Mesa Drive exit north to McKellips, east to Horne, next to Napa Auto Parts.

[&] [P] [*] [☕] M

Site Address: 755 E. McKellips Road, Mesa, AR
Mailing Address: 755 E. McKellips Road, Mesa, AR
Telephone: (602) 833-9486
Fax: (602) 834-4644

Arizona, Tucson

OLD PUEBLO TROLLEY
Electric, scheduled
Standard gauge

Ride: Operating trolleys through historic business and residential areas.

Schedule: Year round: Fridays, 6 to 10 p.m.; Saturdays, 12 p.m. to 12 a.m.; Sundays 12 to 6 p.m.

Admission/Fare: Adults $1.00; children $ .50; special fares on Sundays. Local holidays and other special events operate with lower fares.

Locomotive/Rolling Stock: Historic trolleys in operation and undergoing restoration; historic buses under restoration.

Nearby Attractions/Accommodations: Hotels, bed & breakfasts, numerous restaurants, shopping.

Location/Directions: Car barn at 4th Avenue and 8th Street.

Site Address: 360 E. 8th Street, Tucson, AR
Mailing Address: PO Box 1373, Tucson, AR 85702
Telephone: (520) 791-1802 and (520) 791-0225
Fax: (520) 791-4964
Internet: www.azstarnet.com/~bnoon/opthome.html

Arizona, Williams

GRAND CANYON RAILWAY
Steam, scheduled
Standard gauge

Ride: Relive the excitement of the old west aboard a historic train to America's national treasure–the Grand Canyon. Grand Canyon Railway departs daily from a historic depot. Passengers choose from five classes of service featuring authentically restored coaches. During the 2.25 hour journey, passengers receive an interpretive program on the Grand Canyon region and are entertained by strolling musicians and antics of western characters. Arriving in the heart of Grand Canyon National Park's historic district at the 1910 log depot, guests have 3.5 hours to explore or spend the night in the park and return another day.

Schedule: Year round: daily. Williams departure–9:30 a.m. returning 5:30 p.m.

Admission/Fare: Adults $49.50; children under age 17 $19.50. Additional park entrance fee. Upgrades available.

Locomotive/Rolling Stock: Steam: Nos. 18 and 20, 1910 Alco SC-4 2-8-0s; no. 29, 1906 Alco SC-3 2-8-0; no. 4960, 1923 Baldwin O1A 2-8-2 Diesel; no. 2134 GP7 Electro-Motive Division of GM Corporation; more.

Nearby Attractions/Accommodations: Kaibab National Forest, historic Williams which has Route 66 running through the heart of town.

Location/Directions: I-40 exit 163 (Williams), Grand Canyon Blvd. ½ mile south to Williams depot.

*Coupon available, see coupon section.

Site Address: 235 N. Grand Canyon Blvd., Williams, AZ
Mailing Address: 123 N. San Francisco, Ste. 210, Flagstaff, AZ 86001
Telephone: (800) THE TRAIN (843-8724)
Fax: (520) 773-1610
Internet: www.thetrain.com

Arkansas, Eureka Springs

EUREKA SPRINGS & NORTH ARKANSAS RAILWAY
Steam, scheduled
Standard gauge

GEORGE A. FORERO, JR.

Ride/Display: A 4-mile, 45-minute round trip through a wooded valley next to a winding creek in the heart of the Ozarks. During the "turn-around" trip, the steam engine is turned on a turntable at one end of the line and on a wye at the other end. Visitors may also ride the train, then take the city-operated trolley through downtown Eureka Springs. The Eureka Springs depot was built in 1913 of locally cut limestone; the operating turntable came from the Frisco Lines.

Schedule: Call or write for information.

Admission/Fare: Call or write for information.

Locomotive/Rolling Stock: No. 1, 1906 Baldwin 2-6-0, former W.T. Carter; no. 201, 1906 Alco 2-6-0, former Moscow, Camden & San Augustine; no. 226, 1927 Baldwin 2-8-2, former Dierks For. & Coal; six commuter cars, former Rock Island; no. 4742, 1942 EMD SW1.

Location/Directions: Highway 23 north to the city limits. Site is located in northwest Arkansas, a short distance from the Missouri border.

Radio frequency: 151.655

Site Address: Eureka Springs, AR
Mailing Address: PO Box 310, 299 N. Main St., Eureka Springs, AR 72632
Telephone: (501) 253-9623

Arkansas, Eureka Springs **LIVINGSTON JUNCTION CABOOSES**

Display: Unique tourist lodging romantically secluded, nestled in the countryside.
Schedule: Year round: daily. Closed January 1 to February 14.
Admission/Fare: $95.00 per night.
Locomotive/Rolling Stock: Two Burlington cabooses.
Nearby Attractions/Accommodations: Eureka Springs.
Location/Directions: Two miles north on Highway 23 after crossing over the highway bridge on the upper gravel road.

Site Address: Highway 23N, Eureka Springs, AR
Mailing Address: 1473 CR 222, Eureka Springs, AR
Telephone: (501) 253-7143 and (501) 253-8292

Arkansas, Flippin

WHITE RIVER RAILWAY
Diesel, scheduled
Standard gauge

WHITE RIVER RAILWAY

Ride: Enjoy breathtaking vistas, historical sights and engineering landmarks accessible by no other form of transportation. Recapture the romance and nostalgia of an era lost to our modern times and the scenery of the ancient Ozark mountains. Multiple routes and boarding locations to choose from.

Schedule: April through November: Wednesday through Sunday, two trips daily. Call for departure times and reservations. Available for birthdays, reunions, meetings, or any special occasion.

Admission/Fare: Adults $23.50, first class $30, dome car $35; seniors $22.50; children 4-12 $17.50.

Locomotive/Rolling Stock: Alco RSX-4 (MRS-1) 1953, 1600 hp; one dome; two coaches; two table cars; one power car; one platform lounge.

Nearby Attractions/Accommodations: Shoals Lake, White River, Ozark Folk Center State Park, Blanchard Springs Caverns.

Location/Directions: Highway 5.

P 🚌 ✳ ☕ 🚂

Site Address: 14029 Highway 5 South, Norfolk, AR
Mailing Address: PO Box 306, Norfolk, AR 72658
Telephone: (870) 499-5700 and (800) 305-6527
Fax: (870) 499-5959

Arkansas, Pine Bluff

ARKANSAS RAILROAD MUSEUM
Railway museum

BARRY ROBINSON

Museum: Located on 1.5 acres in a former cotton belt erecting and machine shop. It contains the last two SSW steam locomotives and other railroad equipment and artifacts.

Schedule: Year round: Mondays through Saturdays, 9 a.m. to 3 p.m. Closed during periods of extremely cold weather.

Admission/Fare: Donations appreciated.

Locomotive/Rolling Stock: SSW 4-8-4 no. 819; SSW 2-6-0 no. 336; GP 30; SSW relief crane and outfit; cabooses; passenger cars.

Special Events: Annual Model Train Show and Sale. Mainline steam excursions with SSW 819.

Nearby Attractions/Accommodations: Jefferson County Museum in Old Union Station.

Location/Directions: Highway 65 exit Port Road.

Site Address: 1700 Port Road, Pine Bluff, AR
Mailing Address: PO Box 2044, Pine Bluff, AR 71613
Telephone: (870) 541-1819

Arkansas, Springdale

ARKANSAS & MISSOURI RAILROAD
Diesel, scheduled
Standard gauge

ARKANSAS & MISSOURI RAILROAD

Ride: Visitors can choose either a 134-mile round trip journey from Springdale or a 70-mile round trip journey from Van Buren. Both rides cross the Boston range of the Ozark Mountains.

Schedule: April through September, early November: Wednesdays and Saturdays. October: Tuesdays, Wednesdays, Fridays and Saturdays. Springdale–8 a.m. to 4 p.m. Van Buren– 10:30 a.m. to 1:15 p.m.

Admission/Fare: April through September, November: Springdale $25.00; Van Buren $17.00; Saturdays add $5.00; October add $10.00.

Locomotive/Rolling Stock: 1899 B&M combine no. 102; 1917 DL&W (Pullman) coach no. 104; 1925 CNJ (Harlen & Hollingsworth) coaches no. 105 and 106.; all Alco.

Special Events: Please write or call for information.

Nearby Attractions/Accommodations: Numerous hotels in Springdale and Fayetteville, historic district in Van Buren. Devil's Den State Park near Winslow.

Location/Directions: U.S. 71 exit 52. AR route 412 east to U.S. 71B. Routwe 71B north to Emma Street. East on Emma to tracks.

*Coupon available, see coupon section.

Site Address: 306 E. Emma Street, Springdale, AR
Mailing Address: 306 E. Emma Street, Springdale, AR 72764
Telephone: (501) 751-8600 and (800) 687-8600
Fax: (501) 751-2225

California, Alpine

DESCANSO, ALPINE & PACIFIC RAILWAY
Gasoline mechanical, scheduled
24" gauge

WEBB PHOTOGRAPHY

Ride: Passengers ride an industrial 2-foot-gauge railway to yesteryear among 100-year-old Engelman oaks in San Diego County's foothills. The train leaves Shade Depot and makes a ½-mile round trip, climbing the 6½-percent grade to High Pass/Lookout and crossing a spectacular 100-foot-long wooden trestle, giving passengers magnificent views of the surrounding area. At Shade Depot and Freight Shed is a display of railroad artifacts, including those of the DA&P. Mail service with mailer's postmark permit canceling is available.

Schedule: June through August: Sundays, 1 to 3 p.m., every half hour. September through May: Intermittent Sunday operation. Rides and tours may be scheduled at other times with advance notice; please call to arrange.

Admission/Fare: Free.

Locomotive/Rolling Stock: No. 2, 1935 2½-ton Brookville, SN 2003, powered by original McCormick-Deering 22½-horsepower P-12 gasoline engine, former Carthage (Missouri) Crushed Limestone Company.

Location/Directions: Thirty miles east of San Diego. I-8 exit Tavern Road, travel south on Tavern 1.9 miles, turn right on South Grade Road and travel .6 mile, turn left onto Alpine Heights Road; the DA&P is the fifth driveway on the right.

Site Address: Alpine, CA
Mailing Address: 1266 Alpine Heights Road, Alpine, CA 91901
Telephone: (619) 445-4781

California, Anaheim **DISNEYLAND RAILROAD**
Steam, scheduled
36" gauge

DISNEYLAND RAILROAD

Ride: All aboad an old-fashioned steam train for a grand circle tour of Disneyland! Passengers can depart at any of the four station stops within the theme park.

Schedule: Year round: daily.

Admission/Fare: Fare included with park admission.

Locomotive/Rolling Stock: 1954 4-4-0 "CK Holiday" Walt Disney Imagineering; 1954 4-4-0 "EP Riley" Walt Disney Imagineering; 1894/1968 Baldwin 2-4-4T "Fred Gurley"; 1925/1959 Baldwin 2-4-0 "Ernest S. Marsh"; replicas of various train cars, cattle cars, excursion cars; caboose converted to transport passengers.

Location/Directions: Disneyland Theme Park.

Site Address: 1313 Harbor Blvd., Anaheim, CA
Mailing Address: PO Box 3232, Anaheim, CA 92803
Telephone: (714) 999-4565
Internet: Numerous sites.

California, Berkeley

GOLDEN GATE LIVE STEAMERS, INC.
Steam, scheduled
2½", 3¼", 4¾", 7½" gauges

Display: Operating live steam club since 1936. GGLS is the oldest live steam club in the U.S.

Schedule: Year round: Sundays, weather permitting.

Admission/Fare: Donations appreciated.

Locomotive/Rolling Stock: Two steam locomotives 1½" gauge plus various club members' locomotives.

Special Events: Spring Meet, May 9, 10. Fall Meet, October 10, 11.

Nearby Attractions/Accommodations: Redwood Valley Railway 15" gauge next door.

Location/Directions: Tilden Park, East Oakland Hills.

[P] [⊼] ✉ M

Site Address: Berkeley, CA
Mailing Address: 130 Pereira Avenue, Tracy, CA 95367
Telephone: (510) 540-9264 and (209) 835-0263

California, Berkeley

REDWOOD VALLEY RAILWAY CORP.
Steam, scheduled
15" gauge

REDWOOD VALLEY RAILWAY

Display: A 1¼-mile, 12-minute ride through redwoods, laurels, and the scenic wilds of Tilden Park, passing through a tunnel, over a trestle, up and down grades, and around many curves. The operation re-creates an old-time narrow-gauge atmosphere with authentically designed locomotives, wooden cars, realistic trackwork, and scale buildings.

Schedule: Year round: weekends and holidays, 11 a.m. to 6 p.m., weather permitting (no trains after dark). Weekdays, Easter and summer vacations, 12 to 5 p.m. Closed Thanksgiving Day, Christmas Day.

Admission/Fare: Single-ride ticket $1.50, five-ride ticket $6.00, under age two ride free.

Locomotive/Rolling Stock: 0-4-0 no. 2, "Juniper," internal-combustion switcher; 2-4-2 no. 4, "Laurel"; 4-4-0 no. 5, "Fern"; 4-6-0 no. 11, "Sequoia"; freight-type cars with wood bodies, truss rods, and archbar trucks; Denver & Rio Grande Western-style eight-wheel caboose; nine four-wheel work "Jimmies"; weed-spray car; tie-inserter car; ballast-regulator car; push car.

Location/Directions: Tilden Regional Park.

P TRAIN

Site Address: Berkeley, CA
Mailing Address: 2950 Magnolia Street, Berkeley, CA 94705
Telephone: (510) 548-6100
Fax: (510) 841-3609
Internet: members.aol.com/rvrytrain/index.html

California, Bishop

LAWS RAILROAD MUSEUM & HISTORICAL SITE
Railway museum
Narrow gauge

LAWS RAILROAD MUSEUM & HISTORICAL SITE

Display: Original 1883 depot and agent's house, including over 20 other historic buildings with exhibits, and 11 acres of mining, farming, and railroad equipment. Located on the original location of the Carson-Colorado and later the Southern Pacific site.

Schedule: Year round: daily, 10 a.m. to 4 p.m. except Thanksgiving and Christmas.

Admission/Fare: Donations appreciated, suggested $2 per person.

Locomotive/Rolling Stock: 1909 Baldwin engine; no. 9 tender, cars, and caboose. Brill self-powered car.

Location/Directions: From Bishop follow Highway 6 north 4.5 miles, then turn right on Silver Canyon Road.

Site Address: Silver Canyon Road, Bishop, CA
Mailing Address: Box 363, Bishop, CA 93515
Telephone: (760) 873-5950
Internet: www.mammothweb.com/SierraWeb/bishop/laws/

California, Eureka

NORTHERN COUNTIES LOGGING MUSEUM
Steam, scheduled
Standard gauge

EILEEN FAHEY

Museum/Ride: Fort Humbolt's State Historic Park includes a logging museum. The exhibit emphasizes historic steam logging equipment used in redwood logging. Several artifacts have been restored to operating condition and are demonstrated on occasion by the Northern Counties Logging Interpretive Association. Two small steam locomotives provide short rides on a recently reconfigured right-of-way once a month during the summer.

Schedule: Museum–year round: daily, 9 a.m. to 5 p.m. Steam trains and equipment operate April 25, 26, May 16, June 20, July 18, August 15, September 19.

Admission/Fare: Museum–free. Train–adults $1.00; children $ .50.

Locomotive/Rolling Stock: No. 1 "Gypsy" 1892 Marshutz & Cantrell, 12-ton 0-4-0, former Bear Harbor Lumber Co.; no. 1 "Falk" 1884 Marshutz & Cantrell, 9-ton 0-4-0, former Elk River Mill and Lumber Co.; no. 2 1898 Baldwin 2-4-2T, former Bear Harbor Lumber Co.; no. 7 1918 LIma 2-truck Shay, former Arcata & Mad River Railroad; more.

Special Events: Dolbeer Steam Donkey Days, April 25, 26; demonstration of steam locomotives and other equipment.

Location/Directions: Off Highway 101 at the southern end of Eureka, opposite Bayshore Mall.

[P] [bus] [*] [π] [train]

Site Address: 3431 Fort Avenue, Eureka, CA
Mailing Address: 3431 Fort Avenue, Eureka, CA 95503
Telephone: (707) 445-6567

California, Felton

SANTA CRUZ, BIG TREES & PACIFIC RAILWAY
Diesel, scheduled
Standard gauge

GEORGE A. FORERO, JR.

Ride: Our Santa Cruz, Big Trees & Pacific Railway carries passengers from Roaring Camp, through Henry Cowell Redwood State Park, then proceeds down the spectacular San Lorenzo River Canyon. After leaving the forest, this turn-of-the-century passenger train rolls sedately through a beautiful "gingerbread" residential section of downtown Santa Cruz. The train then stops in front of the Carousel at the Beach/Boardwalk in Santa Cruz.

Schedule: Call or write for information.

Admission/Fare: Call or write for information.

Locomotive/Rolling Stock: Nos. 2600 & 2641, CF7 1500-horsepower diesels, former Santa Fe; no. 20, 50-ton center-cab Whitcomb; three 1900-era wooden passenger coaches; two 1920s-era steel coaches; four open-air cars; restored 1895 caboose, former Lake Superior & Ishpeming.

Location/Directions: Six miles inland from Santa Cruz on Graham Hill Road.

Site Address: Graham Hill Road, Felton, CA
Mailing Address: PO Box G-1, Felton, CA 95018
Telephone: (408) 335-4484
Fax: (408) 335-3509
Internet: www.furryfriends.org/roaringcamp/roaring1.htm

California, Fish Camp

YOSEMITE MOUNTAIN-SUGAR PINE RAILROAD
Steam, scheduled
36" gauge

JOSEPH T. BISPO

Museum/Ride: A museum housed in an 1856 log cabin displays railroad artifacts, antique Yosemite photos, and many relics of sawmill life. Steam donkey engine and assorted rolling stock on display. The YM-SP operates a narrated, four-mile, 45-minute round trip over the restored line of the Madera Sugar Pine Lumber Company. Track runs through the scenic Sierra Nevada at an elevation of 5,000 feet, winds down a 4-percent grade into Lewis Creek Canyon, passes Horseshoe Curve, crosses Cold Spring Crossing, and stops at Lewis Creep Loop.

Schedule: Railcars: April through October: daily. Steam train: May 11 through September: daily. Early May and October: weekends.

Admission/Fare: Railcars: adults $6.75; children (3-12) $3.75. Steam train: adults $10.50; children (3-12) $5.75.

Locomotive/Rolling Stock: 1928 Lima 3-truck Shay, no. 10; 1913 Lima 3-truck Shay, no. 15; logging cars; covered and open converted flatcars; wedge snowplow, oil tank car, refrigerator cars, parts car, and more.

Special Events: Moonlight Special with steak barbecue and music every Saturday night in summer; reservations advised.

Nearby Attractions/Accommodations: Location/Directions: Operating in the Sierra National Forest, 4 miles south of Yosemite National Park on Highway 41.

Site Address: 56001 Yosemite Highway 41, Fish Camp, CA
Mailing Address: 56001 Yosemite Highway 41, Fish Camp, CA 93623
Telephone: (209) 683-7273

California, Folsom
(Folsom City Zoo)

FOLSOM VALLEY RAILWAY
DIV. OF GOLDEN SPIKE ENTERPRISES
Steam, scheduled
12" Narrow gauge

Ride/Display: A ¾-mile ride through a 50 acre city park features vintage wooden freight cars drawn by a ⅓-scale coal buring locomotive representative of late nineteenth century steam motive power.

Schedule: February through November: Tuesdays through Fridays, 11 a.m. to 2 p.m.; weekends and holidays, 11 a.m. to 5 p.m. December through January: weekends and school holidays. All are weather permitting.

Admission/Fare: Call or write for information.

Locomotive/Rolling Stock: 1950 Ottaway old-time wooder; truss rod-style freight car; cattle car; hopper car; five open gondola cars; bobber caboose.

Special Events: Train will operate all day until 10 p.m., week of July 4.

Location/Directions: Folsom is 25 miles east of Sacramento off U.S. 50.

Site Address: Folsom City Zoo, Folsom, CA
Mailing Address: 121 Dunstable Way, Folsom, CA 95630
Telephone: (916) 983-1873
Fax: (916) 983-1873 call first
Internet: members.aol.com/steampark

California, Fort Bragg-Willits　　**CALIFORNIA WESTERN RAILROAD**
　　　　　　　　　　　　　　　　　　　　　　　THE SKUNK TRAIN
　　　　　　　　　　　　　　　　　　　　　　　　Diesel, steam, scheduled
　　　　　　　　　　　　　　　　　　　　　　　　　　　　Standard gauge

GARY RICHARDS

Ride: A 40-mile scenic ride through the redwoods.

Schedule: Year round: call or write for information.

Admission/Fare: Full day–adults $26.00; children 5-11 $12.00. Half day–adults $21.00; children $10.00.

Locomotive/Rolling Stock: 1924 steam no. 45 Baldwin; 1955 EMD GP9 nos. 64, 65; 1955 Alco RS11 no. 62; 1925 M100; 1935 M300; coaches nos. 655, 656, 657, 658, 696, 697, 698, 699.

Nearby Attractions/Accommodations: Fort Bragg.

Location/Directions: Highway 1 in Fort Bragg or Highway 101 in Willits.

*Coupon available, see coupon section.

Radio frequency: 160.650

Site Address: Fort Bragg and Willits, CA
Mailing Address: PO Box 907, Fort Bragg, CA 95437
Telephone: (800) 77-SKUNK and (707) 964-6371
Fax: (707) 964-6754
Email: skunk@mcn.org

California, Fremont   **NILES DEPOT MUSEUM**
                                         Railway museum

Display: Located at the mouth of Niles Canyon where the Central Pacific Railroad's transcontinental route entered the San Francisco Bay Area is the small town of Niles. The Niles Depot was built in 1904 by the Southern Pacific Railroad, replacing an earlier Central Pacific depot. The building served the railroad as a passenger station into the 1950s and later as a freight station into the 1960s. Today the depot is home to HO scale and N scale model railroads and a museum of artifacts from area railroads. Restoration of the depot building and development of the grounds are ongoing projects.

Schedule: Year round: first and third Sundays of each month, 10 a.m. to 4 p.m. Work on displays and model railroads, Tuesdays and Fridays, 7:30 to 10:30 p.m. Group visits by appointment.

Admission/Fare: Free.

Locomotive/Rolling Stock: Western Pacific steel bay window caboose no. 467.

Nearby Attractions/Accommodations: Historic downtown Niles.

Location/Directions: US Route 880, Mowry Avenue exit, east to Mission Blvd. (State Route 238) and turn left. Museum is located between Sullivan Underpass and Nursery Avenue, approximately ¾ mile north of Niles Canyon Road (State Route 84).

Fremont (Centerville)

Site Address: 36997 Mission Blvd., Fremont, CA
Mailing Address: PO Box 2716, Fremont, CA 94536
Telephone: (510) 797-4449
Internet: www.wenet.net/~oldtraff/tcme.html

California, Fremont

SOCIETY FOR THE PRESERVATION OF CARTER RAILROAD RESOURCES

Horse, scheduled
36" gauge

BRUCE MAC GREGOR

Museum: This group is dedicated to acquiring and restoring railroad cars constructed by Carter Brothers of Newark, California in the late 1800s. The society currently has seven Carter cars and three other cars. The cars are restored using appropriate hand tools, following the techniques used in the original construction. The 1½-mile ride is powered by a draft horse, making this the only regularly scheduled horse-drawn railroad in the U.S.

Schedule: April through October: Thursdays and Fridays, 10:30 a.m. to 3 p.m. and weekends, 10:30 a.m. to 4 p.m.

Admission/Fare: Park admission–adults $5.00; seniors $4.00; children 4-17 $3.50; special events $1.00 more.

Locomotive/Rolling Stock: "Tucker" and "Jiggs" 1989 Belgians, 0-2-2-0T hay burners; 1940 Whitcomb no. 2 14-ton, former ASARCO; 1922 Plymouth DL 7-ton, former Old Mission Cement Company.

Special Events: Transportation Fair, Spring. Harvest Festival, early October.

Nearby Attractions/Accommodations: The museum is located in the Ardenwood Historic Farm, which demonstrates life on a farm at the turn of the century. It consists of a historic farmhouse, blacksmith shop, farmyard, and operating Best steam tractor.

Location/Directions: Fifteen miles south of Oakland at the intersection of I-880 and Highway 84.

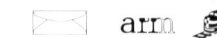

Site Address: 34600 Ardenwood Blvd., Fremont, CA
Mailing Address: SPCRR, PO Box 783, Newark, CA 94560
Telephone: (408) 370-3555
E-mail: hill@optivision.com

California, Goleta

SOUTH COAST RAILROAD MUSEUM
Railway museum
Standard gauge

DAVID HIETER

Museum: The centerpiece is the historic Goleta Depot, a victorian styled Southern Pacific country station. The museum features refurnished rooms and station grounds, and a variety of informative displays, inlcuding a 300 square foot HO scale model railroad exhibit. Other attractions include miniature train and handcar rides, Gandy Dancer Theater, picnic grounds, and a museum store and gift shop.

Schedule: Museum–Wednesdays through Sundays, 1 to 4 p.m. Miniature train–Wednesdays and Fridays, 2 to 3:30 p.m.; weekends, 1 to 3:45 p.m. Handcar–third Saturday of each month, 1 to 3:45 p.m.

Admission/Fare: Museum–donations appreciated. Handcar–free. Miniature train–$1.00.

Locomotive/Rolling Stock: 1960s Southern Pacific bay window caboose no. 4023.

Special Events: Depot Day, September 27, 11 a.m. to 4 p.m.

Location/Directions: Goleta is seven miles west of Santa Barbara, U.S. 101 north exit Los Carneros Road.

Site Address: 300 N. Los Carneros Road, Goleta, CA
Mailing Address: 300 N. Los Carneros Road, Goleta, CA 93117-1502
Telephone: (805) 964-3540
Fax: (805) 964-3549
E-mail: scrm@silcom.com
Internet: www.silcom.com/~scrm/

California, Jamestown

RAILTOWN 1897
SIERRA RAILWAY COMPANY
Steam, diesel, scheduled
Standard gauge

TED BENSON

Ride/Display: Operated by the California State Railroad Museum, Railtown 1897 Historic Sierra Railway Shops is enjoying its Centennial Year as a continuously operated steam locomotive maintenance complex established in 1897, now a California State Historic Park. Railtown 1897 and the Sierra Railway is also one of Hollywood's most popular feature film and television locations. Over 200 movies, television programs and commercials have been filmed at Railtown, including *The Unforgiven, Back to the Future III, High Noon, The Virginian, Petticoat Junction,* and *Wild, Wild West.*

Schedule: Park–Year round: daily, 9:30 a.m. to 4:30 p.m. Trains–April through October: weekends, 11 a.m. to 3 p.m. on the hour. November: Saturdays only. Closed Thanksgiving, Christmas, New Year's.

Admission/Fare: Roundhouse tour–adults $2.00; youth 6-12 $1.00. Train–adults $6.00; youth $3.00; age five and under are free.

Locomotive/Rolling Stock: 1922 no. 2 Shay; 1891 no. 3 Rogers 4-6-0; no. 5 combine; no. 6 coach.

Special Events: School Daze, Living History programs, holiday specials.

Nearby Attractions/Accommodations: Gold rush towns of Jamestown, Sonora, Columbia. Yosemite National Park.

Location/Directions: Located at 5th Avenue & Reservoir Road, five blocks off Highway 49/108.

Site Address: 5th Avenue & Reservoir Road, Jamestown, CA
Mailing Address: PO Box 1250, Janestown, CA 95327
Telephone: (209) 984-3953 and (209) 984-1600
Fax: (209) 984-4936
E-mail: csrmf@csrmf.org
Internet: www.csrnf.org

California, Lomita

LOMITA RAILROAD MUSEUM
Railway museum
Standard gauge

LOMITA RAILROAD MUSEUM

Museum: This museum is a replica of the Boston & Maine station at Wakefield, MA. On display are lanterns of the steam era, chinaware and silverware of the period, scale model live steam engines, spikes, tie date nails, insulators, prints, photographs, postcards, clocks, and more.

Schedule: Year round: Wednesdays through Sundays, 10 a.m. to 5 p.m. Closed Thanksgiving and Christmas.

Admission/Fare: Adults $1.00; children under age 12 $ .50.

Locomotive/Rolling Stock: 1902 Baldwin 2-6-0 (Mogul) no. 1765 with a whale-back tender, former Southern Pacific; 1910 yellow caboose, UP OWR&N; 1913 UP boxcar; 1923 oil tank car, Union Oil Co.; Santa Fe red caboose.

Special Events: Founders Days, call or write for details.

Nearby Attractions/Accommodations: So. Bay Botanical Gardens, Torrance, Cabrillo Museum, San Pedro, Banning House and Drum Barracks, Wilmington.

Location/Directions: Take 110 (Harbor) Freeway South to Pacific Coast Highway off ramp. Turn right going west to Narbonne Avenue. Turn right going east one block. Parking lot on 250th Street.

*Coupon available, see coupon section.

[♿] [P] [✳] [📷] [⛩] [✉] M

Site Address: 250th & Woodward Avenue, Lomita, CA
Mailing Address: 2137 W. 250th Street, Lomita, CA 90717
Telephone: (310) 326-6255

California, Long Beach ELDORADO EXPRESS RAILROAD
18" gauge

Ride: Experience a scenic one-mile round trip through the park while viewing a 150-year-old lake that features paddle boats.

Schedule: Year round: Wednesday through Sunday, 10:30 a.m. to 4:30 p.m. Closed for one week in mid-October.

Admission/Fare: Adults $1.75; children $1.25. Parking: autos $3.00 weekdays and $5.00 weekends and holidays; buses $10.00.

Locomotive/Rolling Stock: Gas-powered locomotive 4-6-2, former live steamer; tender; three open-air passenger cars.

Special Events: Birthday parties, anniversaries, family festival, first weekend in June.

Nearby Attractions/Accommodations: Queen Mary, Long Beach, Knotts Berry Farm, Eldorado Park, featuring pony rides, boat rides, archery, golf, nature center.

Location/Directions: South on 605 Freeway, exit Spring. Eldorado Regional Park in Long Beach.

*Coupon available, see coupon section.

Site Address: 605 Freeway and Spring Streets
Mailing Address: 4943 Lincoln Avenue, Cypress, CA 90630
Telephone: (562) 514-5067

California, Los Angeles

CRYSTAL SPRINGS & CAHUENGA VALLEY RAILROAD
Diesel, scheduled
Standard gauge

ED SIKORA

Ride: The first section of a planned railroad through Griffith Park. A diesel locomotive pulls caboose train on available track at the Travel Town Museum.

Schedule: First Sunday of every month, 10 a.m. to 4 p.m.

Admission/Fare: Donations appreciated.

Locomotive/Rolling Stock: EMD model 40, CS&CV no. 1; California Western Railroad RS12; St&SSF caboose no. 999110; SP caboose no. 4049.

Nearby Attractions/Accommodations: Griffith Park, Griffith Observatory, LA Zoo, Autry Museum of Western Heritage, Universal, Warner Brothers, and NBC studios.

Location/Directions: Ventura Freeway exit 134 (Forest Lawn Drive) located at Griffith Park and Zoo Drive in the Travel Town Museum.

P 🚌 ✳ 🅓 🎪 ✉ M TRAIN 🚂

Site Address: 5200 Zoo Drive, Los Angeles, CA
Mailing Address: 3900 W. Chevy Chase Drive, Los Angeles, CA 90039
Telephone: (213) 662-5874 and (213) 485-5520
Fax: (818) 247-4740
Internet: www.ci.la.ca.us/dept/RAP/grifmet/tt/index.htm *or*
www.scsra.org/~scsra

California, Los Angeles

TRAVEL TOWN MUSEUM
Railway museum
Standard gauge

DALE L. BROWN, JR.

Museum: One of the oldest displays of pre-World War II passenger cars and steam locomotives in the United State, concentrating on railroads in the west, specifically California.

Schedule: Year round: daily, 10 a.m. to 4 p.m. Closed Christmas Day.

Admission/Fare: Museum–free. Train–adults $1.75; children age 12 and under $1.25.

Locomotive/Rolling Stock: No. 1, 1864 Norris-Lancaster 4-4-0, former Stockton Terminal & Eastern; no. 664, 1899 Baldwin 2-8-0, former Santa Fe; no. 3025, 1904 Alco 4-4-2, former Southern Pacific; no. 1544, 1902 steeple-cab electric, former Pacific Electric; 1955 Baldwin RS-12, former McCloud River no. 33, later California Western No. 56; "The Little Nugget," club-dorm no. 701 from the Union Pacific Streamliner *City of Los Angeles,* and sleeping cars "Rose Bowl" (1937) and "Hunters Points" (1940), both originally on *City of San Francisco;* others.

Special Events: Pullman car tours, third Sunday of every month.

Nearby Attractions/Accommodations: Griffith Park, Griffith Observatory, LA Zoo, Autry Museum of Western Heritage, Universal, Warner Brothers, and NBC studios.

Location/Directions: Ventura Freeway exit 134 (Forest Lawn Drive), located at Griffith Park and Zoo Drives.

P 🚌 ✳ 🍴 🚻 ✉ M TRAIN 🚂

Site Address: 5200 Zoo Drive, Los Angeles, CA
Mailing Address: 3900 W. Chevy Chase Drive, Los Angeles, CA 90039
Telephone: (213) 662-5874 and (213) 485-5520
Fax: (818) 247-4740
Internet: www.ci.la.ca.us/dept/RAP/grifmet/tt/index.htm

California, Napa

NAPA VALLEY WINE TRAIN
Diesel, scheduled
Standard gauge

NAPA VALLEY WINE TRAIN

Ride: When you enter the Wine Train's Station, you will begin a threefold adventure: a return to the gracious era of elegant rail travel and distinguished service; a deliciously crafted culinary and wine experience—champagne brunch, gourmet lunch or exquisite full-course dinner; and an enjoyable and relaxing journey through California's historic and scenic wine country. Enter the restored 1917 Pullman Dining Car replete with etched glass, polished brass, fine fabrics and rich mahogany, where you will be pampered with superb meals served with all the accoutrements of fine dining including damask linens, bone china, silver flatware, lead crystalware. Our luxury lounge cars and elegant dining cars have been painstakingly restored to their former unmatched opulence. Every brunch, lunch, and dinner excursion is a 36-mile, 3-hour adventure through the heart of the Napa Valley Wine Country.

Schedule: Year round. Call or write for information.

Admission/Fare: Call or write for information. Reservations and deposit.

Locomotive/Rolling Stock: Four 1951 Alco diesel engines.

Special Events: Wine Tasting Seminars, Vintners Luncheons, and more.

Location/Directions: Located 54 miles north of San Francisco. Call, write, or see web page for directions.

Site Address: 1275 McKinstry Street, Napa, CA
Mailing Address: 1275 McKinstry Street, Napa, CA 94559
Telephone: (707) 253-2111 and (800) 427-4124
Internet: www.napavalley.com/napavalley/outdoor/nvwinetr/nvwinetr.html

California, Orange   **IRVINE PARK RAILROAD**
                                                       Propane, scheduled
                                                       24" gauge

JOHN FORD

Ride: Irvine Park Railroad is located on 500 acres in Irvine Regional Park, the oldest county park in the state of California. The train departs from an old fashioned depot, where railroad folk songs fill the air. The locomotive will make a scenic one-mile journey around the park during which riders can view two lakes complete with waterfalls and fountains, a grove of oak trees, and the Orange County Zoo. The ride is narrated by the engineer and lasts approximately 12 minutes.

Schedule: Winter–daily, 10 a.m. to 4 p.m. Summer–daily, 10 a.m. to 4:30 p.m. Closed Thanksgiving and Christmas.

Admission/Fare: $2.00; children under age one are free. School group rates available.

Special Events: Christmas train two weeks prior to Christmas.

Nearby Attractions/Accommodations: Bicycle and paddleboat rentals.

Locomotive/Rolling Stock: A ⅓ scale replica of the 1863 C.P. Huntington; four coaches.

Location/Directions: From State Highway 55 take the Chapman Avenue exit and drive east to Jamboree Road. Turn left into the park entrance.

*Coupon available, see coupon section.

Site Address: 1 Irvine Park Road, Orange, CA
Mailing Address: 1 Irvine Park Road, Orange, CA 92669
Telephone: (714) 997-3968
Fax: (714) 997-0459

California, Orland

ORLAND, NEWVILLE & PACIFIC RAILROAD
Steam, scheduled
15" gauge

ONP RR

Ride/Display: The ON&P is an all-volunteer railroad operating in the Glenn County Fairgrounds. A 1-mile ride takes visitors past the original Orland Southern Pacific depot, the picnic site, and the demonstration orchard, then through a tunnel and along Heritage Trail. The train is normally pulled by a magnificent 5/12th-scale live-steam model of the North Pacific Coast's 1875 Baldwin narrow-gauge locomotive "Sonoma." The picnic grounds at Deadowl Station are open whenever the train is running. Former Orland Southern Pacific depot, 1918 Southern Pacific 2-8-0 No. 2852, caboose, schoolhouse, blacksmith shop, print shop, 1920s gas station, miscellaneous steam machinery, old farm equipment. Livestock is also exhibited at fair time, during May and October.

Schedule: April 11-12, 18-19, 25-26, May 2-3, 9-10, 23-24, 30-31, June 14, July 4, August 29-31, September 5-6, 12-13, 19-20, 26-27, October 3-4, 10-11.

Admission/Fare: $1.00; under age two are free.

Locomotive/Rolling Stock: No. 12 replica of 1876 Baldwin 4-4-0; no. 2 4-4-0 amusement park type; four open gondolas; covered car.

Special Events: Glenn County Fair, May 13-17. Harvest Festival, October 17-18. Spook Train, October 31.

Location/Directions: Glenn County Fairgrounds. Orland is 100 miles

Site Address: 221 E. Yolo Street, Orland, CA
Mailing Address: 221 E. Yolo Street, Orland, CA 95963
Telephone: (916) 865-1168 and (916) 865-9747
Fax: (916) 865-1197

California, Perris **ORANGE EMPIRE RAILWAY MUSEUM**
Electric, diesel, steam, scheduled
Standard, 36", and 42" gauge

JIM WALKER, JR.

Museum: More than 200 streetcars, interurbans, locomotives (electric, diesel, and steam), passenger and freight cars, work cars, and cabooses. Trains run on 1½-mile right-of-way, streetcars on 0.7-mile loop within museum.

Schedule: Demonstration railroad–year round: weekends and some holidays, 11 a.m. to 5 p.m. Museum grounds–daily: 9 a.m. to 5 p.m. Closed Thanksgiving and Christmas.

Admission/Fare: Free admission. All day ride pass–adults $7.00; children 5-11 $5.00; under age 5 are free. Special events have additional fees.

Locomotive/Rolling Stock: VC Ry 2 Prairie; GF 2 Mogul; UP 2564 Mikado; SP 1474 S4; SP 3100 U25B; UP 942 E8A; and more.

Special Events: Rail Festival, April and October. Railroadiana Swap Meets, spring and fall. Pumpkin Trains, October. Santa's Christmas Trains, December. Trains to March Field Air Museum, May and November.

Nearby Attractions/Accommodations: Perris Valley Skydiving Center, Perris Auto Speedway, Lake Perris Recreation Area, March Field Air Museum, Temecula Wineries; Best Western Perris Inn, Mission Inn in Riverside.

Location/Directions: I-215, exit west onto 4th Street/Route 74, left on "A" Street to museum.

*Coupon available, see coupon section.

P 🚌 ✳ ☕ 📷 ⛩ ⛪ ✉ arm TRAIN 🚆
M MasterCard VISA

Site Address: 2201 South "A" Street, Perris, CA
Mailing Address: PO Box 548, Perris, CA 92572-0548
Telephone: (909) 657-2605 and (909) 943-3020
Fax: (909) 943-2676
E-mail: oerm@juno.com
Internet: www.oerm.mus.ca.us

California, Portola

PORTOLA RAILROAD MUSEUM
Diesel, scheduled
Standard gauge

Ride/Display: A one-mile ride around a balloon turning track through pine forest. On display are more than 70 freight cars representing nearly every car type of the Western Pacific Railroad; several passenger cars; other rolling stock; railroad artifacts in the diesel shop building.

Schedule: Displays–year round: daily, 10 a.m. to 5 p.m. Train–late May through early September: weekends, 11 a.m. to 4 p.m., departs every half hour.

Admission/Fare: Call or write for information.

Locomotive/Rolling Stock: One electric locomotive and 35 diesels of all types: 14 Electro-Motive Division engines, including a former Western Pacific SW1, an NW2, a GP7, an F7, a former Union Pacific GP30, a DDA40X, a GP9, and a former Southern Pacific SD9; 9 Alcos, including a former Western Pacific S-1, a former Southern Pacific RS-32, a former VIA FPA-4 & FBB-4, and a former Kennecott Copper RS-3; 5 Baldwins, including a former Oregon & North Western AS616 and a former U.S. Steel S-12; 5 General Electrics, including a former Western Pacific U30B and a former Milwaukee Road U25B; a Fairbanks Morse, former U.S. Army H-12-44; more.

Location/Directions: From state route 70, travel one mile south on county road A-15 (Gulling) across the river and through town. Follow signs to the museum.

Site Address: Portola, CA
Mailing Address: PO Box 608, Portola, CA 96122
Telephone: (916) 832-4131

California, Sacramento

CALIFORNIA STATE RAILROAD MUSEUM
Railway museum
Standard and 36" gauge

CALIFORNIA STATE RAILROAD MUSEUM

Museums: One of the finest interpretive railroad museums in North America, CSRM's 11 acre facilities in Old Sacramento include the 100,000 square feet museum of railroad history, a reconstructed 1870s Central Pacific passenger station, and an extensive library and archive.

Schedule: Year round: daily, 10 a.m to 5 p.m. Closed Thanksgiving, Christmas, New Year's Day.

Admission/Fare: Adults $6.00; youth 6-12 $3.00; children under age six are free.

Locomotive/Rolling Stock: More than 30 meticulously restored locomotives and cars on display dating from the 1860s to present.

Special Events: Rail Days, Father's Day weekend, National Railway Preservation Symposium, March. U.S. National Handcar Races, September.

Nearby Attractions/Accommodations: Old Sacramento State Historic Park, state capitol, Sutter's Fort, dining, shopping, and lodging.

Location/Directions: In Old Sacramento, adjacent to I-5 exit J Street.

Radio frequencies: 160.335 and 160.440

Site Address: Corner of 2nd and "I" Streets, Old Sacramento, CA
Mailing Address: 111 "I" Street, Sacramento, CA 95814
Telephone: (916) 552-5252 ext. 7245
Fax: (916) 327-5655
E-mail: csrmf@csrmf.org
Internet: www.csrmf.org/

California, Sacramento

CALIFORNIA STATE RAILROAD MUSEUM
SACRAMENTO SOUTHERN RAILROAD

Steam, diesel, scheduled
Standard gauge

CALIFORNIA STATE RAILROAD MUSEUM

Display: The Sacramento Southern is the excursion railroad of the California State Railroad Museum. The line was built as a subsidiary of the Southern Pacific at the turn of the century; museum trains have been in regular service since 1984. A 6-mile, 40-minute round trip takes passengers along the historic Sacramento River. Extension of the line is planned to the towns of Freeport and Hood, 17 miles down the river.

Schedule: Steam–April through September: weekends, 10 a.m. to 5 p.m., departures hourly. Diesel–October: weekends, 11 a.m. to 4 p.m. departures hourly.

Admission/Fare: Adults $6.00; youth 6-12 $3.00; children under age six ride free.

Locomotive/Rolling Stock: No. 10 1942 Porter 0-6-0T, former Granite Rock Company; no. 4466, 1920 Lima 0-6-0, former Union Pacific; more.

Special Events: Rail Days, Father's Day weekend. Harvest Haunt & Goosebump Express, October weekends. Holiday Festival & Santa Claus, December.

Nearby Attractions/Accommodations: State capitol, Sutter's Fort.

Location/Directions: Northern terminus is the reconstructed Central Pacific Railroad Freight Depot at Front and "K" Streets in Old Sacramento.

*See advertisement on inside cover and page A-1.

Radio frequencies: 160.335 and 160.440

Site Address: Front and "K" Streets, Sacramento, CA
Mailing Address: 111 "I" Street, Sacramento, CA 95814
Telephone: (916) 552-5252 ext. 7245
Fax: (916) 327-5655
Email: csrmf@csrmf.org
Internet: www.csrmf.org/

45

California, San Diego

SAN DIEGO MODEL RAILROAD MUSEUM
Model railroad

T. J. WEGMANN

Display: The world's largest indoor model railroad museum includes four large model railroad exhibits, toy trains, educational displays, and a railroad-themed gift shop. Cabrillo Southwestern O-scale layout, San Diego & Arizona Eastern and Southern Pacific/Santa Fe Tehachapi Pass HO-scale layouts, and Pacific Desert Lines N-scale layout; the HO exhibits are of railroads that run through southern California. On the SD&AE, trains leave San Diego heading east and descend into the desert over the huge wooden trestle in spectacular Carriso Gorge. A narrow-gauge railroad connects with the standard-gauge trains on the final leg of the journey. The SP/SF layout models southern California's busiest rail artery—nearly all north-south rail traffic passes through this notch in the Tehachapi mountains northeast of Los Angeles. Leaving the yards in Bakersfield, trains roll through California's Central Valley to the Caliente Creek, where a steep, winding climb begins.

Schedule: Year round: Tuesday through Friday, 11 a.m. to 4 p.m.; Saturday through Sunday, 11 a.m. to 5 p.m.

Admission/Fare: Adults $3.00; discounts for senior citizens, military personnel, and students; children under 15 admitted free.

Location/Directions: Off I-5 or California route 163. Take Park Blvd. to Space Theater Way; museum is located in the Casa de Balboa Building.

Site Address: 1649 El Prado, San Diego, CA
Mailing Address: 1649 El Prado, San Diego, CA 92101
Telephone: (619) 696-0199 and (800) 446-8738
E-mail: sdmodrailm.com
Internet: www.globalinfo.com/noncomm/SDMRM/sdmrm.html

46

California, San Diego   **SAN DIEGO RAILROAD MUSEUM**
Railroad museum

BILL SCHNEIDER

Display: Over 80 pieces of rail equipment of display and regularly scheduled train trips featuring trips to Mexico.

Schedule: Year round: weekends and some holidays.

Admission/Fare: Adults $10.00; children 6-12 $3.00; ages five and under are free.

Locomotive/Rolling Stock: No. 2353 4-6-0 Baldwin steam; 1950s vintage diesels; variety of cars.

Special Events: Ticket to Tecate rail trips, Starlight Express, Dinner Train, Wine Train.

Nearby Attractions/Accommodations: Viejas Indian Casino, Stone Store Museum.

Location/Directions: Highway 94 and Campo in east San Diego County.

Site Address: Highway 94 & Campo, San Diego, CA
Mailing Address: 1050 Kettner Blvd., San Diego, CA 92101
Telephone: (619) 595-3030 amd (888) 228-9246
Fax: (619) 595-3034
Internet: www.sdrm.com

California, San Francisco **GOLDEN GATE RAILROAD MUSEUM**
Railway museum

Museum: Dedicated to the preservation and restoration of steam trains. This site owns and operates a vintage P8 class locomotive as well as a variety of railcars and antiques.

Schedule: Year round: weekends, 10 a.m. to 4 p.m. and by appointment only.

Admission/Fare: Donations appreciated.

Locomotive/Rolling Stock: SP Baldwin P8 4-6-2 no. 2472.

Special Events: Annual Garlic Train takes attendees to the Gilroy Garlic Festival, July 26.

Nearby Attractions/Accommodations: 3-Comm Park.

Location/Directions: Highway 101 to Cesar Chavez Street to Evans Street to Hunter's Pt., Shipyard Building no. 809.

Site Address: Hunter's Point Naval Shipyard Bldg. 809, Evans St., San Francisco, CA
Mailing Address: PO Box 881686, San Francisco, CA 94188
Telephone: (415) 363-2472 and (415) 822-1883
Fax: (415) 822-8739
E-mail: info@ggrm.org
Internet: www.ggrm.org

California, San Francisco   **SAN FRANCISCO CABLE CAR MUSEUM**
Railway museum

Display: This museum, located in the historic San Francisco cable car barn and powerhouse, allows visitors to view the actual cable winding machinery as well as the path of the cable entering the building and leaving under the street. Included in the displays are three antique cable cars, a Sutter street dummy and trailer, and the first cable car built in 1873. Historic information gives visitors a peek at the cable cars' glorious past. Also on display is a photo narration of the 1981-84 reconstruction effort, as well as various mechanical devices, such as grips, track, trucks, cable, and brake mechanisms, with corresponding explanations.

Schedule: Call or write for information.
Admission/Fare: Free.
Location/Directions: Corner of Mason and Washington Streets.

Site Address: 1201 Mason Street, San Francisco, CA
Mailing Address: 1201 Mason Street, San Francisco, CA 94108
Telephone: (415) 474-1887

California, San Francisco   **SAN FRANCISCO MUNICIPAL RAILWAY**
F-MARKET carline
Electric, regular
Standard gauge

Ride: The F MARKET is a regular Municipal Railway line, operating between the Transbay Terminal at 1st & Mission Streets and Castro & Market Streets via Market Street. Most service is with rehabilitated ex-Philadelphia PCC cars painted to represent US cities where PCCs served. Occasionally, a car from the historic fleet takes the place of a PCC.

Schedule: Year round: daily, 5:45 a.m. to 12:30 a.m. Headways are from 9 to 15 minutes, 20 minutes on Sunday morning and evening.

Admission/Fare: Adults $1.00; seniors and youth 5-17 $ .35. Free transfers. Passports accepted, call for details.

Locomotive/Rolling Stock: Cars are rehabilitated P.C.C.s from Philadelphia, each painted in the color scheme of a city where P.C.C.s ran.

Nearby Attractions/Accommodations: San Francisco.

Location/Directions: The F operates on Market Street, the central thoroughfare. Stop in at the volunteers' site at Market & Duboce (near the new U.S. Mint).

Site Address: Along Market Street, San Francisco, CA
Mailing Address: 949 Presidio Avenue, San Francisco, CA 94115
Telephone: (415) 6-SF-MUNI

California, San Jose

KELLEY PARK TROLLEY
Electric, scheduled
Standard gauge

FRED BENNETT

Ride: Car nos. 129 and 168 operate on 1,200 feet of track on Museum Street.

Schedule: Year round: weekends, 12 to 4 p.m. except Thanksgiving, Christmas, and New Year's Day.

Admission/Fare: Included with admission to San Jose Historical Museum.

Locomotive/Rolling Stock: Operational trolley no. 168, former Porto, Portugal no. 154; no. 129, former Sacramento no. 35; no. 143, former Fresno 68.

Special Events: Civil War Days, Chinese Festival, Victorian Christmas.

Location/Directions: Museum is located in Kelley Park, which is a short distance from intersection of Highways 280, 680, and 101.

Site Address: 1600 Senter Road, San Jose, CA
Mailing Address: 1600 Senter Road, San Jose, CA 95112
Telephone: (408) 293-2276 and (408) 287-2290
Fax: (408) 277-3890
E-mail: mccanley@sgi.com

California, Sonoma

TRAIN TOWN
Steam, scheduled
15" gauge

TRAIN TOWN

Ride/Display: Train Town is a 10-acre railroad park filled with thousands of trees, animals, lakes, bridges, tunnels, waterfalls, and historic replica structures. Fifteen-inch-gauge live-steam locomotives and diesel replicas pull long passenger trains through the park. Railroad shops and a complete miniature town, built to the same ¼ scale as the railroad. Full-sized rail equipment includes Santa Fe caboose No. 999648; Union Pacific caboose No. 25155; and Southern Pacific's first steel caboose, No. 11.

Schedule: June 1 through September 30: daily. Year round: Fridays through Sundays. 10:30 a.m. to 5 p.m. Closed Christmas and Thanksgiving.

Admission/Fare: Adults $3.50; seniors and children 16 months-16 $2.50.

Locomotive/Rolling Stock: Replica of No. 5212, 1937 Alco J-1a 4-6-4, former New York Central; no. 1, 1960 Winton Engineering 2-6-0; SW 1200, 1992 custom locomotive; no. 401, 1975 gas-electric motor car.

Location/Directions: Sonoma is in wine country, less than an hour north of San Francisco. Train Town is on Broadway, one mile south of the Sonoma Town Square.

Site Address: 20264 Broadway, Highway 12, Sonoma, CA
Mailing Address: PO Box 656, Sonoma, CA 95476
Telephone: (707) 996-2559
Fax: (707) 966-6344
Internet: www.traintown.com

California, Sunol **NILES CANYON RAILWAY**
Steam, diesel, scheduled
Standard gauge

ALAN FRANK

Display: A 12-mile ride through scenic Niles Canyon over original transcontinental railroad route built in the 1860s.

Schedule: Year round: first and third Sunday of every month, 10 a.m. to 4 p.m.

Admission/Fare: Donation: adults $6.00; children 3-12 $3.00.

Locomotive/Rolling Stock: Ten steam locomotives; eight diesel locomotives; vintage rolling stock.

Special Events: Christmas trains, December; Wildflower excursions.

Nearby Attractions/Accommodations: Marine World, regional wilderness parks.

Location/Directions: One mile west of I-680 between Pleasanton and Freemont, California.

P 🚌 ✳ ☕ ⛩ 🔔 🏛 ✉ arm TRAIN 🚂
M Radio frequency: 160.695

Site Address: Sunol Depot, Sunol, CA
Mailing Address: PO Box 2247, Niles Station, Fremont, CA 94536-0247
Telephone: (510) 862-9063
Fax: (510) 582-8840
E-mail: cliffow@aol.com
Internet: www.digisource.com/ncry/

53

California, Tuolumne   **SONORA SHORT LINE RAILWAY**
12" gauge
Steam, scheduled

JAMES HOBACK

Display: Scenic ten-minute steam powered train ride through a working apple ranch in the foothills of California's Sierra Nevada Mountains. Train is ⅓ full size, 12" gauge.

Display/Exhibits: Apple ranch has farm animals on display.

Schedule: Mid-Februrary through Thanksgiving: weekends and holidays, 11 a.m. to 5 p.m.

Admission/Fare: $1.50 single ticket, $6.25 for a 5-ride ticket. Children under one year are free.

Locomotive/Rolling Stock: ⅓ scale: 4-4-0 steam locomotive, oil fired, 1910 era Baldwin narrow gauge styling; Plymouth, 1927, diesel powered. (Locomotives are 12 inch gauge); five Hurlbut-built excursion cars

Special Events: September through October, apple harvest season.

Location/Directions: Five miles east of Sonora, CA.

Riverbank

Site Address: Sonka's Apple Ranch, 19200 Cherokee Road, Tuolumne, CA
Mailing Address: 19720 Tuolumne Road, North Tuolumne, CA 95379
Telephone: (209) 928-4689

California, Woodland

YOLO SHORTLINE RAILROAD COMPANY
Steam, diesel, scheduled
Standard gauge

RICHARD JONES

Ride: A 28-mile, two-hour round trip between Woodland and West Sacramento over former Sacramento Northern Interurban track. Crosses 8,000 foot Fremont Trestle and offers views of the Sacramento River and scenic Yolo County farmlands and wetlands. Also specials to Clarksburg.

Schedule: Mid-May through October: Sundays and holidays. Specials on selected Saturdays. Charters available year round.

Admission/Fare: Adults $13.00; seniors $11.00; children $8.00; children age 3 and under are free.

Locomotive/Rolling Stock: No. 1233, former Southern Pacific 0-6-0 switcher; nos. 131, 132, 133 GP-9 EMD diesels, former Southern Pacific.

Special Events: Great Train Robberies; BBQ trains; Beer & Salsa trains on selected Saturdays; Santa Train, December.

Nearby Attractions/Accommodations: Hayes Truck and Tractor Museum, Southern Pacific Depot (under restoration), Woodland Opera House.

Location/Directions: I-5, Main Street exit, one mile west to East Main and Thomas Streets. Twenty minutes from Sacramento.

Radio Frequency: 160.260

Site Address: East Main and Thomas, Woodland, CA
Mailing Address: 1965 East Main Street, Woodland, CA 95776
Telephone: (916) 666-9646 and (800) 942-6387
Fax: (916) 666-2919
E-mail: dmagaw@worldnet.att.net
Internet: http://www.ysrr.com

California, Yreka

YREKA WESTERN RAILROAD
Steam, scheduled
Standard gauge

YREKA WESTERN RAILROAD

Display/Ride: Constructed in 1888 as the Yreka Railroad Company, this line began operations on January 8, 1889, providing rail service between the city of Yreka and the newly constructed California & Oregon Railroad 7.4 miles to the east at the cattle town of Montague, California. Today's YWR offers a 15-mile, 3-hour round trip between Yreka and Montague, including a one-hour stopover at Montague. The train travels through local lumber mills and across the scenic Shasta Valley, where passengers see panoramic views of 14,162-foot Mount Shasta.

Schedule: May through October. Call or write for information.

Admission/Fare: Adults $12; children 3-12 $5.00.

Locomotive/Rolling Stock: 1915 Baldwin 2-8-2; two 1948 Milwaukee Hiawatha cars; two Southern Pacific cars.

Special Events: Dinner trains, call for information. Great Wild Goose Chase, 10k race, August.

Nearby Attractions/Accommodations: Located in the center of the Shasta-Cascade Wonderland.

Location/Directions: I-5, east side of Central exit.

Site Address: 300 E. Miner Street, Yreka, CA
Mailing Address: PO Box 660, Yreka, CA 96097
Telephone: (916) 842-4148 and (800) YREKA RR
Fax: (916) 842-4148

Colorado, Canon City

ROYAL GORGE SCENIC RAILWAY AND MUSEUM
Diesel, scheduled
15" gauge

Ride: Established in 1959, this railway operates from a depot west of Canon City. The train of open cars runs 1½-miles to the rim of Royal Gorge Canyon at Point Alta Vista, then returns. Royal Gorge Bridge, 1053 feet above the Arkansas River, is the world's highest suspension bridge. Narration is provided during the 30-minute round trip. Also on the grounds is the Steam Train and Antique Car Museum, which features 3-inch scale working steam engines and a diesel switcher. Other displays include 22 steam whistles and mint-condition antique and classic automobiles.

Schedule: Call or write for information.

Admission/Fare: Call or write for information.

Locomotive/Rolling Stock: Four diesel outline; open cars.

Nearby Attractions/Accommodations: Rafting, horseback riding, Buckskin Joe (old western town).

Location/Directions: Located one mile off Highway 50, Royal Gorge Road, eight miles west of Canon City.

Site Address: Royal Gorge Road, Canon City, CO
Mailing Address: PO Box 8, Canon City, CO 81215
Telephone: (719) 275-5485

Colorado, Colorado Springs

PIKE'S PEAK HISTORICAL STREET RAILWAY FOUNDATION, INC.
Electric, PCC streetcar, scheduled
Standard gauge

PIKES PEAK HISTORICAL STREET RAILWAY FOUNDATION, INC.

Display/Ride: Interpretive center displaying street railway history with a strong emphasis on Colorado Springs street railway history. Also lecture on history and return of streetcars to Colorado Springs. Several trips over 500' test track. Operation and history of car explained during ride. Visit a working car house (former Rock Island Engine House) built in 1888. See cars under restoration. Guided tour of cars on hand and shop area.

Schedule: Saturday, 10:00 a.m.-4:00 p.m., year round except Thanksgiving, Christmas and New Year's week. Other times please write or call. Group tours, please call ahead for special showing.

Admission/Fare: Adults $2.00, children (12 and under) $1.00.

Locomotive/Rolling Stock: Nine Southeastern Pennsylvania Transportation Authority PCC's (Philadelphia) 1947; Los Angeles Railways PCC 1943; Colorado Springs double truck, 1901 Laclede Car Co.; Ft. Collins Municipal Railway, single truck, 1919 Birney, American Car Co.

Location/Directions: I-25, exit Fillmore Street east, south on Cascade, west on Polk Street. When forced to turn south, you will automatically be on Steel Dr. Site is located at the end of Steel Drive.

arm M

Site Address: 2333 Steel Drive, Colorado Springs, CO
Mailing Address: PO Box 544, Colorado Springs, CO 80901
Telephone: (719) 475-9508
Fax: (719) 475-2814

Colorado, Denver

FORNEY HISTORIC TRANSPORTATION MUSEUM
Transportation museum
Standard gauge

JACK FORNEY

Museum: This museum features four steam locomotives, railroad exhibits, antique automobiles, and transporation displays.

Schedule: Mondays through Saturdays, 10 a.m. to 5 p.m.; Sundays, 11 a.m. to 5 p.m. Closed major holidays.

Admission/Fare: Adults $4.00; youth (12-18) $2.00; children (5-11) $1.00. Group rates available.

Locomotive/Rolling Stock: Big Boy no. 4005; 1897 Forney 0-4-4T; C&NW 4-6-0; 0-4-0T from Germany.

Nearby Attractions/Accommodations: Union Station; Elitch Gardens Amuseument Park; Plat Valley Trolley.

Location/Directions: I-25, exit 211 (23rd Avenue), east on Water Street to Platte Street.

*Coupon available, see coupon section.

Site Address: 1416 Platte Street, Denver, CO
Mailing Address: 1416 Platte Street, Denver, CO 80202-1120
Telephone: (303) 433-3643

Colorado, Denver

THE SKI TRAIN
Diesel, scheduled
Standard gauge

THE SKI TRAIN

Ride: The Ski Train, a Colorado tradition since 1940, offers a 120-mile round trip from Denver's Union Station over the main line of the Rio Grande, passing through the famous Moffat Tunnel and stopping at West Portal, the location of Winter Park Resort.

Schedule: Call or write for information.

Admission/Fare: Call or write for information.

Locomotive/Rolling Stock: Varies.

Location/Directions: Train departs from Denver Union Station.

Site Address: Denver Union Station, Denver, CO
Mailing Address: 555 17th Street, Suite 2400, Denver, CO 80202
Telephone: (303) 296-4754

Colorado, Durango

DURANGO & SILVERTON NARROW-GAUGE RAILROAD
Steam, scheduled
36" gauge

AMOS CORDOVA

Ride: The Durango & Silverton was established in 1881 to transport miners to and from Silverton and to haul precious metals to smelters. Today, a coal-fired, steam-powered, narrow-gauge train travels through the wilderness of the two-million-acre San Juan National Forest, following the Animas River through breathtaking Rocky Mountain scenery. The 90-mile round trip, which originates at Durango, takes approximately nine hours, including a 2¼-hour layover at Silverton for lunch and sightseeing. A half-day winter trip to Cascade Canyon is also offered.

Schedule: April 26 through October 8: daily. Leave Durango 8:30 a.m.; May 13 through October 25, 9:15 a.m. train added; June 2 through August 14 & August 30 through September 28, 10:10 a.m. train added; June 17 through August 14, 7:30 a.m. train added but will run Monday-Friday only. Consult timetable for exact schedule on day of your visit. Winter Train: November 28 through April 25, except Christmas Day, 10:00 a.m.

Admission/Fare: Silverton: Adults $42.70; children 5-11 $21.45; parlor car $73.40; caboose $67.85. Cascade Canyon: Adults $36.15; children 5-11 $18.00. Yard Tours: Adults $5.00; children 5-11 $2.50.

Locomotive/Rolling Stock: Nos. 473, 476 & 478, 1923 Alco class K-28 2-8-2s; Nos. 480, 481 & 482, 1925 Baldwin class K-36 2-8-2s; Nos. 493, 498 & 499, 1930 Burnham Shops class K-37 2-8-2s; all former Denver & Rio Grande Western.

Site Address: 479 Main Avenue, Durango, CO
Mailing Address: 479 Main Avenue, Durango, CO 81301
Telephone: (888) TRAIN-07

Colorado, Georgetown

GEORGETOWN LOOP RAILROAD
Tourist railroad
Steam, scheduled
36" gauge

GEORGE A. FORERO, JR.

Ride: A 6.5-mile, 70-minute round trip over the right-of-way of the former Colorado & Southern. The train travels through highly scenic, mountainous terrain and over the reconstructed Devil's Gate Viaduct, a spectacular 96-foot high curved trestle. Stop at the Old Georgetown Station Railroad Headquarters for train tickets. Baggage Cart Gifts, and the Depot Express Cafe with its operating LGB model. The Georgetown Loop Railroad is a project of the Colorado Historical Society.

Schedule: Memorial Day weekend through first weekend in October: daily. Silver Plume–9:20 and 10:40 a.m., 12, 1:20, 2:40, and 4 p.m. Devil's Gate–10 and 11:20 a.m., 12:40, 2:40, and 3:20 p.m. Limited schedule weekdays in September. No mine tours after Labor Day.

Admission/Fare: Train–adults $11.95; children $7.50; under age three ride free. Mine–adults $4.00; children $2.00. Charters and groups rates available.

Locomotive/Rolling Stock: No. 40, 1920 Baldwin 2-8-0 & No. 44, 1921 Baldwin 2-8-0, both former International Railways of Central America; No. 8, 1922 Lima 3-truck Shay, No. 12, 1926 Lima 3-truck Shay; more.

Nearby Attractions/Accommodations: Trails and Rails Downhill Mountain Bike Tours, reservations can be made with Georgetown Loop RR.

Location/Directions: I-70 exit 228 for Devil's Gate or exit 226 for Silver Plume. Tickets available only at Old Georgetown Station.

Site Address: 1106 Rose Street, Georgetown, CO
Mailing Address: PO Box 217, Georgetown, CO 80444
Telephone: (303) 569-2403 and (303) 670-1686 Denver Metro
Fax: (303) 569-2894
E-mail: markg@gtownloop.com
Internet: www.gtownloop.com

Colorado, Golden

COLORADO RAILROAD MUSEUM
Railway museum
Standard gauge, 36" gauge

COLORADO RAILROAD MUSEUM

Ride: This 38-year old museum, oldest and largest in the Rocky Mountain area, houses an extensive collection of Colorado railroad memorabilia as well as the layout of the Denver HO Model Railroad Club. On outdoor trackage are more than 50 cars and locomotives, both narrow- and standard-gauge, including the oldest locomotives and cars in the state. No. 346, an 1881 Baldwin 2-8-0, and a Rio Grande "Galloping Geese" operate on selected weekends.

Schedule: Museum–June through August, daily, 9 a.m. to 6 p.m.; September through May, 9 a.m. to 5 p.m. Train–call, fax, or write for schedule. HO Model Railroad–first Thursday of every month, 7:30 to 9:30 p.m.

Admission/Fare: Adults $4.00; seniors $3.50; children under age 16 $2.00; families (parents and children under age 16) $9.50.

Locomotive/Rolling Stock: No. 20 4-6-0 Schenectady 1899, former Rio Grande Southern; 2-8-0 no. 583 Baldwin 1890, former Denver & Rio Grande—the only surviving D&RG standard gauge steam locomotive; no. 5629 4-8-4 West Burlington 1940, former Chicago, Burlington & Quincy; more.

Nearby Attractions/Accommodations: Coors Brewery, Buffalo Bill Museum, Georgetown Loop Railroad, Colorado Rockies baseball.

Location/Directions: Twelve miles west of downtown Denver. I-70 westbound exit 265 or eastbound exit 266 to West 44th Avenue.

*See advertisement on page A-16.

Site Address: 17155 West 44th Avenue, Golden, CO
Mailing Address: PO Box 10, Golden, CO 80402
Telephone: (303) 279-4591 and (800) 365-6263
Fax: (303) 279-4229
Email: corrmus@aol.com
Internet: www.nyx.net/~dpitts/crrm.html

Colorado, Grand Junction

RIO GRANDE CHAPTER NRHS
Museum preservation site
Narrow gauge

HENRY FILIP

Museum: Uintah Railroad narrow gauge equipment under restoration and rebuilt trestle. Reference and photo library. Garden railway under construction.

Schedule: May through October: daily, 9 a.m. to 5 p.m. October through December: reduced hours, call for information. January through April: by appointment only.

Admission/Fare: Adults $4.00; seniors $3.50; children $2.00. Includes entire Cross Orchards Historic Site.

Locomotive/Rolling Stock: Uintah and D&RGW narrow gauge freight and passenger cars.

Nearby Attractions/Accommodations: Site includes agricultural and cultural displays including farm and construction equipment.

Location/Directions: I-70 exit 31, south one mile to Patterson Road (F) and travel east three miles.

Site Address: 3070 Patterson Road (F), Grand Junction, CO
Mailing Address: PO Box 3381, Grand Junction, CO 81504
Telephone: (970) 434-9814 and (970) 434-6393

Colorado, Leadville

LEADVILLE, COLORADO & SOUTHERN RAILROAD
Diesel, scheduled
Standard gauge

LEADVILLE, COLORADO & SOUTHERN RAILROAD

Display/Ride: The 22½-mile, 2½-hour train trip follows the headwaters of the Arkansas River to an elevation of 11,120 feet, over an old narrow-gauge roadbed converted to standard gauge in the 1940s. The train leaves from the restored 1894 railroad depot (formerly Colorado & Southern, built originally for the Denver, South Park & Pacific) in Leadville, the highest incorporated city in the United States.

Schedule: Memorial Day weekend through September.

Admission/Fare: Adults $22.50; children 4-12 $12.50; age 3 and under are free.

Locomotive/Rolling Stock: 1955 EMD GP9 no. 1714, former Burlington Northern; six excursion cars; boxcar; caboose.

Nearby Attractions/Accommodations: National mining district. Leadville historical district.

Site Address: 326 E. 7th Street, Leadville, CO
Mailing Address: Box 916, Leadville, CO 80461
Telephone: (719) 486-3936
Fax: (719) 486-0671

Colorado, Manitou Springs

MANITOU & PIKE'S PEAK RAILWAY
Diesel, scheduled
Standard gauge (cog)

MANITOU & PIKE'S PEAK RAILWAY

Ride: The M&PP, the highest cog railway in the world, was established in 1889 and has been operating continuously since 1891; it celebrated its centennial of passenger operations in June 1991. A 3¼-hour round trip takes passengers to the summit of Pike's Peak (elevation 14,110 feet) from Manitou Springs (elevation 6,575 feet) and includes a 40-minute stop at the summit.

Schedule: Daily; May-mid June, September & October, 9:20 a.m. & 1:20 p.m.; mid June-August, every 80 minutes, 8:00 a.m.-5:20 p.m.

Admission/Fare: Adults $21.50; children 5-11 $10.00. July through August 15: adults $22.50; children $10.50.

Locomotive/Rolling Stock: Twin-unit diesel hydraulic railcars and single unit diesel electric railcars.

Special Events: Occasional steam-up of former M&PP steam locomotive No. 4, built by Baldwin in 1896.

Location/Directions: Six miles west of Colorado Springs.

Radio frequency: 161.55 and 160.23

Site Address: 515 Ruxton Avenue, Manitou Springs, CO
Mailing Address: PO Box 351, Manitou Springs, CO 80829
Telephone: (719) 685-5401

Colorado, Montrose

DENVER & RIO GRANDE
U.S. NATIONAL PARK SERVICE
Railroad exhibit
36" gauge

LISA LYNCH

Display: At Cimarron, 20 miles east of Montrose, a historic narrow gauge railroad exhibit with engine no. 278, its coal tender, a boxcar, and a caboose sit on a stone and steel trestle one mile into the Cimarron River Canyon. At the Cimmaron Visitor Center, a cattle car, sheep car, outfit car, hoist car, livestock corral, and interpretive panels illustrate early mountain railroad operations of the Denver & Rio Grande.

Schedule: Year round.

Admission/Fare: Free.

Locomotive/Rolling Stock: 1882 Baldwin locomotive no. 278.

Nearby Attractions/Accommodations: Morrow Point Dam. Black Canyon, New Mexico has hiking, fishing, camping, biking, cross country skiing, snowshoeing. Cimarron has campgrounds, motels, and restaurants.

Location/Directions: Cimarron is 20 miles west of Montrose on U.S. highway 50. Exhibit can be seen from the highway. Follow Curecanti National Recreation Area signs.

[&] [P] [🚌] [*] [🏓] [✉]

Site Address: U.S. Highway 59, Cimarron, CO
Mailing Address: Curecanti NRA, 102 Elk Creek, Gunnison, CO 81230
Telephone: (970) 249-1915 and (970) 641-2337 ext. 205
Fax: (970) 240-0504 and (970) 641-3127
E-mail: cure_vis_mail@nps.gov
Internet: www.nps.gov/cure *or* www.nps.gov/blca

Colorado, Morrison

TINY TOWN RAILROAD
Steam, scheduled
15" gauge

HAROLD ARNOLD

Display/Ride: Tiny Town Railroad, a ⅓-scale live steam railroad, takes passengers from its full sized station on a one mile loop around Tiny Town. Started in 1915, Tiny Town is the oldest miniature town in the United States. It features more than 100 hand crafted, ⅙-sized structures laid out in the configuration of a real town, rural and mountain area.

Schedule: Memorial Day through Labor Day: daily. May, September, and October: weekends. 10 a.m. to 5 p.m. Train runs continuously.

Admission/Fare: Display–adults $2.50; children 3-12 $1.50; children under age three are free. Train–$1.00.

Locomotive/Rolling Stock: 1970 standard-gauge 4-6-2 "Occasional Rose" propane-fired; 1970 narrow-gauge 2-6-0 "Cinderbell" coal-fired; 1954 F-unit "Molly," gas-powered; 1952 A- and B-unit "Betsy" gas-powered. Open amusement park style cars, propane tank car and caboose.

Nearby Attractions/Accommodations: Red Rocks Park and Dinosaur Ridge.

Location/Directions: Approximately 30 minutes southwest of Denver, off Highway 285.

Site Address: 6249 S. Turkey Creek Road, Morrison, CO
Mailing Address: 6249 S. Turkey Creek Road, Morrison, CO 80465
Telephone: (303) 697-6829
Fax: (303) 674-4238

Connecticut, Danbury

DANBURY RAILWAY MUSEUM
Diesel, irregular
Standard gauge

BILL GUIDER

Ride/Museum: Excursions over Metro-North commuter routes, or the seldom traveled Beacon branch (former New Haven Maybrook line), connecting with Hudson River cruises or other attractions. Displays consist of a locomotive, RDC's, FCD railbus, coaches, caboose, freight and maintenance of way cars in ex-New Haven yard. Exhibits in Danbury Union Station.

Schedule: January through March: Thursdays through Saturdays, 10 a.m. to 4 p.m.; Sundays, 12 to 4 p.m. April through December: Wednesdays through Saturdays, 10 a.m. to 4 p.m.; Sundays, 12 to 4 p.m. Closed holidays.

Admission/Fare: Adults $3.00; children 5-15 $2.00.

Locomotive/Rolling Stock: NH RS1 0673; NYC E9 4096; NH RDCs 32, 47; NH FCD II 15; NH caboose C627; more.

Special Events: Easter Bunny Trains, April 4. Spring Train Show, May 16-17. Fall Train Show, October 17-18. Haunted Rail Yard, October 23-25. Holiday Express, December 5. Santa Trains, December 12-13.

Nearby Attractions/Accommodations: Military Museum of Southern New England.

Location/Directions: I-84 exit 5, right on Main Street, left on White Street.

  [&]   [P]   ✳   ⛪   ✉   TRAIN

Site Address: 120 White Street, Danbury, CT
Mailing Address: PO Box 90, Danbury, CT 06813
Telephone: (203) 778-8337
Fax: (203) 778-1836
E-mail: wguider@ibm.net
Internet: www.danbury.org/org/drm

Connecticut, East Haven **SHORE LINE TROLLEY MUSEUM**
Electric, scheduled
Standard gauge

G. BOUCHER

Display: The Shore Line Trolley Museum operates the sole remaining segment of the historic 98-year old Branford Electric Railway. The three mile ride passes woods, salt marshes, and meadows along the scenic Connecticut shore.

Schedule: Memorial Day through Labor Day: daily. May, September, and October: weekends and holidays. April and November: Sundays.

Admission/Fare: Unlimited rides and guided tours–adults $5.00; seniors $4.00; children 2-11 $2.00; under age two are free.

Locomotive/Rolling Stock: Connecticut Co. suburban no. 775; Montreal no. 2001; Brooklyn (NY) convertible no. 4573; 3rd Avenue no. 629; Atlanta no. 948; New Orleans no. 850.

Special Events: Santa Days, Thanksgiving to Christmas on weekends.

Nearby Attractions/Accommodations: Holiday Inn Express, East Haven. Yale University. Foxwoods Casino.

Location/Directions: I-95 exits 51 north or 52 south and follow signs.

Site Address: 17 River Street, East Haven, CT
Mailing Address: 17 River Street, East Haven, CT 06512-2519
Telephone: (203) 467-6927 and (203) 467-7635 group sales
E-mail: BERASLTM@aol.com
Internet: www.panix.com/~christos/trolleypage.html

Connecticut, East Windsor

CONNECTICUT TROLLEY MUSEUM
Electric, scheduled
Standard gauge

SCOTT R. BECKER

Display/Ride: More than 60 pieces of rolling stock, including streetcars, interurbans, rapid-transit cars, electric freight equipment, work cars, steam and diesel locomotives, wooden passenger cars from the 1890s, and freight cars. A 3-mile, 25-minute round trip through scenic woodlands over a rebuilt portion of the former Rockville branch of the Hartford & Springfield Street Railway, originally built in 1906. The ride often includes meets with other trolleys, and the line features a historic working semaphore signal system. Trolleys leave from the "Isle of Safety" trolley-stop shelter built in 1913 for downtown Hartford, Connecticut, and from the CTM North Road terminal.

Schedule: March 15 through Memorial Day and Labor Day through Thanksgiving: Saturdays, 10 a.m. to 5 p.m.; Memorial Day through Labor Day, Mondays through Saturdays, 10 a.m. to 5 p.m. Sundays, 12 to 5 p.m.

Admission/Fare: Adults $6.00; seniors $5.00; children (5-12) $3.00; under age 5 are free. Group rates are available.

Trolleys: Nos. 65, 355, 840 and 1326, former Connecticut Co. and more.

Special Events: Call or write for information.

Location/Directions: Between Hartford, Connecticut, and Springfield, Massachusetts. I-91, exit 45, ¾ mile east on Route 140.

*Coupon available, see coupon section.

Site Address: East Windsor, CT
Mailing Address: PO Box 360, East Windsor, CT 06088-0360
Telephone: (860) 627-6540 and (860) 623-2372
Fax: (860) 627-6540

Connecticut, Essex

ESSEX STEAM TRAIN AND RIVERBOAT RIDE
Steam, scheduled
Standard gauge

Display: A 2½-hour excursion along the scenic banks of the Connecticut River on restored 1920s vintage cars. All trains except the last of the day connect with a riverboat cruise at Deep River.

Schedule: May through October: daily. November through December: weekends for North Pole Express. Call or write for departure times.

Admission/Fare: Train and boat–adults $15.00; children 3-11 $7.50; under age three ride free. Train only–adults $10.00; children 3-11 $5.00. Parlor car–extra fare. Senior discounts and group rates for 25 or more available.

Locomotive/Rolling Stock: No. 97, 1926 Alco 2-8-2, former Birmingham & Southeastern; no. 40, 1920 Alco 2-8-2, former Aberdeen & Rockfish; 44-ton diesel no. 0800; 80-ton diesel no. 0900.

Special Events: Presidents' Weekend Special, February. Spring Special, March. Easter Eggspress, April. Antique Machinery and Transportation Day, May. Working on the Railroad Days, September. Hot Steamed Music Festival, June. Ghost Train, October. North Pole Express, November, December. Tuba Concert, December. Call or write for more information.

Location/Directions: From shoreline, take exit 69 off I-95, then travel north on state route 9 to exit 3. From Hartford, take exit 22 off I-91, then travel south on state route 9 to exit 3. Valley Railroad is a half-mile west of route 9 on state route 154.

Site Address: Essex, CT
Mailing Address: PO Box 452, Essex, CT 06426
Telephone: (860) 767-0103
Internet: www.valleyrr.com

Connecticut, Essex   **THE NORTH COVE EXPRESS DINNER TRAIN**

Ride: Dinner excursions along the scenic Connecticut River.

Schedule: May through October: Thursdays through Saturdays, 7 p.m. departure.

Admission/Fare: $34.95 to $49.95; children eight and under are half fare.

Locomotive/Rolling Stock: 40 ton GE diesel; 1955 Korean War kitchen car; 1924 Pullman dining car; 1928 Pullman dining car.

Special Events: Romantic Dinner Runs, Murder Mysteries, Barber Shoppe Quartet Nights, Rail to River Rendevous.

Nearby Attractions/Accommodations: CT Valley Railroad, Waters Edge Inn.

Site Address: 1 Railroad Avenue, Essex, CT
Mailing Address: 176 Laning Street, Southington, CT 06489
Telephone: (800) 398-7427 and (860) 629-9311
Fax: (860) 628-0803

Connecticut, Kent

CONNECTICUT ANTIQUE MACHINERY ASSOCIATION, INC.
Railway exhibit
36" gauge

CONNECTICUT ANTIQUE MACHINERY

Display/Ride: A wide range of exhibits showing the development of the country's agricultural and industrial technology from the mid 1800s to the present, including a collection of large stationary steam engines in the Industrial Hall; a display of large gas-engines; a tractor and farm-implement display in the large tractor barn; and the reconstrucrted Cream Hill Agricultural School buildings, which housed an early agricultural school that was the forerunner of the University of Connecticut, and a large engine-pumping exhibit. A stretch of three-foot-gauge track is in operation during this group's popular Fall Festival.

Schedule: Memorial Day through September: weekends and by appointment.

Admission/Fare: Adults $3.00; children 5-12 $1.50; under age five are free.

Locomotive/Rolling Stock: No. 4 1908 Porter 2-8-0, former Argent Lumber Co.; no. 16 1921 Plymouth D1, former Hutton Brick Co.; no. 18 1917 Vulcan limited clearance 0-4-0T, former American Steel & Wire Co.; no. 111 caboose, former Tionesta Valley Railway; no. 6 coach, former Waynesburg & Washington Railroad; misc. ore cars.

Special Events: Spring Gas Up, May 3. Fall Festival, September 26-27.

Nearby Attractions/Accommodations: Sloane-Stanley Museum.

Location/Directions: One mile north of village on route 7 adjacent to Housatonic Railroad.

Site Address: Kent, CT
Mailing Address: PO Box 1467, New Milford, CT 06776
Telephone: (860) 927-0050

Connecticut, Waterbury

NAUGATUCK RAILROAD
RAILROAD MUSEUM OF NEW ENGLAND
Diesel, scheduled
Standard gauge

HOWARD PINCUS

Ride: A 17½-mile round trip over a former New Haven Railroad line from the brass mills of Waterbury, along the scenic Naugatuck River, on to face of the Thomaston Dam. The original Naugatuck Railroad opened this route in 1849. The Naugatuck Railroad is operated by the Railroad Museum of New England, a non-profit historical organization.

Schedule: May through October: Tuesdays, Saturdays, Sundays, and holidays. Schedule varies, write or call for information. Christmas trains operate in December.

Admission/Fare: Adults $9.00; seniors and children 3-12 $8.00. Group rates and charters available.

Locomotive/Rolling Stock: New Haven RS3 no. 529; NH U25B no. 2525; Naugatuck GP9 no. 1732; Canadian National open window heavyweight coaches from 1920s.

Special Events: Occasional excursions over entire 19.6 mile route between Waterbury and Torrington.

Nearby Attractions/Accommodations: Amusement parks, vineyards, state parks.

Location/Directions: Located in Waterville section of Waterbury. I-84 exit 20 to route 8, travel north 1.5 miles to exit 36.

Site Address: 175 Chase River Road, Waterbury, CT
Mailing Address: PO Box 4658, Waterbury, CT 06704
Telephone: (203) 575-1931
Fax: (203) 269-3364
E-mail: allanlgalanty@snet.net
Internet: www.rmne.org

D.C., Washington	SMITHSONIAN INSTITUTION
	Museum, railway displays

SMITHSONIAN INSTITUTION

Display: The Smithsonian's Railroad Hall symbolizes the achievements of railroads and rail transit in the United States from the 1820s to about 1965. On display are original pieces of the "Stourbridge Lion" and the "Dewitt Clinton," a complete Winton 201-A engine from the Pioneer Zephyr, a series of ½-inch-scale models showing locomotive development from the earliest steam engine to present-day diesels, and many other exhibits. Information leaflet no. 455, available on request, describes the railroad exhibits. (Extensive research inquiries cannot be answered.)

Schedule: Year round: daily, 10 a.m. to 5:30 p.m.

Admission/Fare: Free.

Locomotive/Rolling Stock: No. 1401, 1926 Alco 4-6-2, former Southern Railway; "John Bull," 1831 Stephenson 4-2-0, former Camden & Amboy Railroad. "Pioneer," 1851 Wilmarth 2-2-2, former Cumberland Valley Railroad; "Olomana," 1883 Baldwin 2-4-2T, former plantation locomotive; "Jupiter," 1876 Baldwin narrow gauge 4-4-0 (in Arts & Industries Building).

Site Address: 14th Street and Constitution Avenue, Washington, D.C.
Mailing Address: National Museum of American History, Washington, D.C. 20560

Delaware, Lewes

QUEEN ANNE'S RAILROAD
Steam, diesel, scheduled
Standard gauge

QARR

Display: The Queen Anne's Railroad travels through the southern Delaware countryside on the former Pennsylvania Railroad Lewes-Georgetown line. The passengers ride aboard the *Royal Zephyr* Dinner Train enjoying a full dinner reflecting the opulence of the 1940s. A live Murder Mystery or musical entertainment is provided to complete a pleasurable evening. A cash bar and cash raw bar are on board. Luncheon trains and one-hour excursion trains may be scheduled.

Schedule: Dinner trains–May through October: Saturdays, 6 p.m. Special trains through December.

Admission/Fare: Call or write for information.

Locomotive/Rolling Stock: 1943 no. 3 Vulcan locomotive 0-6-0T, former U.S. Navy; 1959 Alco T-6 no. 19, former PRR; 1947 Pullman standard coaches, former New Haven; MP-54 coach, former PRR; coach, former New York Central; heavy combine, former Norfolk & Western baggage car.

Site Address: 730 Kings Highway, Lewes, DE
Mailing Address: 730 Kings Highway, Lewes, DE 19958
Telephone: (302) 644-1720 and (888) 456-TOOT
Fax: (302) 644-9212

Delaware, Wilmington

WILMINGTON & WESTERN RAILROAD
Steam, scheduled
Standard gauge

EDWARD J. FEATHERS

Museum/Ride: A ten-mile, 1¼-hour round trip over a portion of former Baltimore & Ohio Landenberg Branch from Greenbank Station to Mt. Cuba. Occasional trips to Yorklyn and Hockessin are also offered.

Schedule: April through October: Saturdays and/or Sundays, one- and two-hour excursions along the Red Clay Valley. Call or write for timetable.

Admission/Fare: Call or write for information. Caboose rentals, group rates, and private charters are available.

Locomotive/Rolling Stock: 1909 Alco no. 98, former Mississippi Central; 1942 EMD SW1 no. 8408, former B&O.

Special Events: Easter Bunny Special, Santa Claus Special, Wild West Robbery, Dinner-Murder Mystery Train.

Nearby Attractions/Accommodations: Longwood Gardens, Hagley Museum, Winterthur Museum.

Location/Directions: I-95, exit 5, follow route 141 north to route 2 west, then follow route 41 north. Greenbank Station is on route 41 just north of route 2, 4 miles southwest of Wilmington.

Radio frequency: 160.755

Site Address: Route 41 North, Newport Gap Pike, Wilmington, DE
Mailing Address: PO Box 5787, Wilmington, DE 19808
Telephone: (302) 998-1930
Fax: (302) 998-7408

Florida, Fort Myers

**RAILROAD MUSEUM OF
SOUTH FLORIDA—DISPLAYS**

JEANNE HICKAM

Museum: Historical exhibits featuring, but not limited to, railroads that operated in South Florida, historic locomotives, stations, and more.

Schedule: Call or write for information.

Admission/Fare: Call or write for information.

Special Events: Open House when new major exhibits go on display.

Nearby Attractions/Accommodations: Spring training facilities for Red Sox and Twins. Many motels, hotels, campgrounds, and restaurants.

Location/Directions: Museum is within the Shell Factory complex, just north of Fort Myers.

Site Address: 2787 N. Tamiami Trail, North Fort Myers, FL
Mailing Address: PO Box 7372, Fort Myers, FL 33911-7273
Telephone: (941) 997-2457
Fax: (941) 997-7673

Florida, Fort Myers

RAILROAD MUSEUM OF SOUTH FLORIDA—TRAIN VILLAGE
Steam, diesel, scheduled
7½" gauge

JEANNE HICKAM

Ride: A 15-minute, 1⅛-mile ride in country park with tunnel, bridges, gardens, and miniature villages along the right-of-way.

Schedule: Year round: daily, Mondays through Fridays, 10 a.m. to 2 p.m. Saturdays, 10 a.m. to 4 p.m. Sundays 12 to 4 p.m. Closed Christmas.

Admission/Fare: $2.50; children under age 5, 50 cents. Park charges for parking–75 cents per hour with $3.00 maximum.

Locomotive/Rolling Stock: FP7A diesels nos. 1994, 1995, 1996; 7½" gauge 0-6-0 no. 143 gasoline w/steam sound; GP50 diesel with 3-5 riding cars; 1905 Baldwin 0-6-0 no. 143, former Atlantic Coast Line (awaiting restoration).

Special Events: Easter Bunny Express– Good Friday, Saturday, Easter Sunday. Halloween Express. Holiday Express. Call for information.

Nearby Attractions/Accommodations: Shell Factory, Edison Winter Home, many motels, hotels, and campgrounds.

Location/Directions: Located in Lakes Park/Lee County Park, which is ⅛ mile west of route 41 (Cleveland Ave.) at the south end of Fort Myers.

Site Address: 7330 Gladiolus Drive, Fort Myers, FL
Mailing Address: PO Box 7372, Fort Myers, FL 33911-7372
Telephone: (941) 267-1905

Florida, Fort Myers

SEMINOLE GULF RAILWAY
Diesel, scheduled
Standard gauge

SEMINOLE GULF RAILWAY

Ride: Daytime excursion trains can be boarded at Colonial Station or at Bonita Springs for a two-hour round trip or for trips that include the scenic Caloosahatchee River bridge crossing. All dinner trains depart from Colonial Station in Fort Myers. They stop during the trip on the Caloosahatchee Bridge for the scenic view or a sunset before continuting the ride north. Special holiday trains are popular, such as the Rail/Boat Christmas train to Punta Gorda featuring a tour by boat, viewing decorated homes and boats along the canals of Punta Gorda Isles.

Schedule: Excursion trains–Year round: Wednesdays and weekends. Dinner train–Fridays and Saturdays, 6:30 p.m.; Sundays, 5:30 p.m.

Admission/Fare: Excursion train–adults $7.00 and up; children 3-12 $4.00 and up. Dinner trains–$29.75 to $54.75.

Locomotive/Rolling Stock: Eight GP9s; three RDCs; four dining cars; Sanibel and Captiva, former CN; kitchen and dining car Marco, former Budd Southern RR diner; Gasparilla, former Pullman RF&P.

Special Events: Easter, Mother's Day, Father's Day, Thanksgiving, Christmas, and New Year's Eve dinner trips.

Location/Directions: Excursion and dinner trains depart from Colonial Station near the Colonial Boulevard (SR 884) and Metro Parkway intersection in Fort Myers, three miles west of I-75 exit 22.

Site Address: Fort Myers, FL
Mailing Address: 4410 Centerpointe Drive, Fort Myers, FL 33916
Telephone: (941) 275-8487 and (800) SEM-GULF
Fax: (941) 275-0581
E-mail: information@semgulf.com
Internet: www.semgulf.com

Florida, Miami

GOLD COAST RAILROAD MUSEUM
Diesel, scheduled
Standard and narrow gauge

GOLD COAST RAILROAD EXHIBIT

Ride: The Gold Coast Railroad Museum, a non-profit, volunteer organization, has been in existence for over 35 years. Located on approximately 60 acres, which formerly housed the N.A.S. Richmond base in World War II, the museum has over 30 pieces of rolling stock on display, hundreds of railroad memorabilia, and a 20-minute train ride into a scenic pineland on both standard and narrow gauge trains. Self-guided tours of railroad cars and engines dating from the 1920s to 1950s are available. Railroad artifacts are displayed in one of the baggage cars, while exhibits of N.A.S. Richmond and the early lumbering industry in South Florida, as well as several layouts of model railroads, including one that visitors can operate are displayed in the buildings.

Schedule: Call or write for information.

Admission/Fare: Call or write for information.

Locomotive/Rolling Stock: Nos. 113 and 153 Florida East Coast steam engines. Ferdinand Magellan, also known as U.S. Presidential Car No. 1, and the only Pullman car ever custom built for the President of the U.S. The Silver Crescent built in 1948 for the *California Zephyr*.

Location/Directions: Florida Turnpike or U.S. 1 to SW 152nd Street, heading west to the Metrozoo entrance, follow signs to Gold Coast Railroad Museum.

P 🚌 ✻ ☕ 🎡 🏛 ✉ M arm TRAIN

Miami Airport, Hialeah

Site Address: 12450 SW 152nd Street, Miami, FL
Mailing Address: 12450 SW 152nd Street, Miami, FL 33177
Telephone: (305) 253-0063
Fax: (305) 233-4641

Florida, Mount Dora

MOUNT DORA, TAVARES & EUSTIS RAILROAD

DAVE MINER

Ride: The Mount Dora Scenic Railway operates on the 11-mile Sorrento Branch of the Florida Central Railroad. The line was built in 1889 as the Sanford & Lake Eustis Railroad. It was merged into the "Plant System" and became the Atlantic Coast Line by 1902. The route travels through orange groves, rural Florida, and skirts around Lake Dora.

Schedule: Year round: daily, approximately six trips per day.

Admission/Fare: Adults $9.00; seniors $8.00; children 12 and under $5.00.

Locomotive/Rolling Stock: 1926 Edwards Railway Motor Car Company "Doodlebug" (steam operation planned for the future).

Special Events: Art festival, craft shows, bicycle festival, antique car meet, vintage boat festival, antique extravaganzas, and sailboat regatta.

Nearby Attractions/Accommodations: Walt Disney World, Universal Studios, historic downtown with antiquing, shopping, walking, dining, bed and breakfasts, inns, restaurants, lodging.

Location/Directions: Located 30 miles north of Orlando on U.S. highway 441.

Site Address: Caboose located at corner of 3rd and Alexander Streets.
Mailing Address: PO Box 6412, Mount Dora, FL 32756
Telephone: (800) 625-4307

Florida, Orlando

FLORIDA CENTRAL RAILROAD ADVENTURE DINNER TRAIN
Diesel, scheduled
Standard gauge

Ride: A 2- to 3-hour ride through Central Florida on former ACL and SAL trackage. Lunch and dinner trains available.

Schedule: Year round: Saturdays, 12 to 2 p.m. and 7 to 10 p.m. Sundays, 12:30 to 3:30 p.m.

Admission/Fare: Excursions–adults $19.95; children age 12 and under $12.00. Dinner trains–adults $45.95 and $49.95 or lunch $25.95.

Locomotive/Rolling Stock: CF7 locomotives; 1952 dining cars nos. 300 and 301; and more.

Special Events: Mystery Night–one Friday night per month, New Year's Eve Train, Mystery Adventure Train, Fourth of July Special, Jazz Train.

Nearby Attractions/Accommodations: Disney World, Universal Studios, Trainland.

Location/Directions: Depot located in Altamonte Springs on Highway 434, ¼ mile south of Highway 436, approximately 6 miles from downtown Orlando.

Site Address: Orlando, FL
Mailing Address: PO Box 967, Plymouth, FL 32768
Telephone: (407) 889-7005
Fax: (407) 880-7748

Florida, Orlando

TRAINLAND EXPRESS
Steam, scheduled
24" gauge

TRAINLAND EXPRESS

Display/Ride: One of the largest indoor G gauge train displays featuring interactive scavenger hunt and prize. Museum cabinets with trains from 1920s to present. Train ride lasts 20 minutes.

Schedule: Year round: daily, 10 a.m. to 9 p.m.. Sundays, 12 to 4 p.m.

Admission/Fare: Display, museum, ride–adults $8.95; seniors $7.95; children $5.95. Train only–adults $3.00; children $2.00.

Locomotive/Rolling Stock: No. 15 Mason Bogey replica; two excursion passenger cars.

Nearby Attractions/Accommodations: Disney World, Universal Studios, Sea World, numerous hotels and restaurants.

Location/Directions: I-4 exit 29 (Sand Lake Rd.), east one block to International Drive, turn south ½ mile to Goodings Plaza, on left next to Ripleys.

*Coupon available, see coupon section.

Site Address: 8255 International Drive, Orlando, FL
Mailing Address: 8255 International Drive, Orlando, FL 32819
Telephone: (407) 363-9002
Fax: (407) 363-0496
E-mail: wolcy@aol.com

Florida, Palm Beach

THE HENRY MORRISON FLAGLER MUSEUM

THE HENRY MORRISON FLAGLER MUSEUM

Display: Whitehall, a 55-room Gilded Age estate, was the winter home of Henry M. Flagler, developer of the Florida East Coast Railway that linked the entire east coast of Florida. Visitors to the Flagler Museum experience life during America's Gilded Age through the eyes of one of its most important citizens, Henry Flagler. Flagler, with partners John D. Rockefeller and Samuel Andrews, founded Standard Oil. Displays and exhibits focus on the contributions Flagler made to the state of Florida by building the Florida East Coast Railway and developing tourism and agriculture as the state's major industries.

Schedule: Year round: Tuesdays through Saturdays, 10 a.m. to 5 p.m. Sundays 12 to 5p.m. Museum is closed Thanksgiving, Christmas Day and New Year's Day.

Admission/Fare: Adults $7.00; children 6-12 $3.00.

Locomotive/Rolling Stock: Henry Flagler's private railcar, built in 1886.

Location/Directions: I-95 to exit 52A (Okeechobee Blvd. E.). Cross bridge onto island of Palm Beach. Turn left at first light on Cocoanut Row. Left turn on Whitehall Way.

Site Address: One Whitehall Way, Palm Beach, FL
Mailing Address: PO Box 969, Palm Beach, FL 33480
Telephone: (561) 655-2833
Fax: (561) 655-2826
E-mail: flagler@emi.net
Internet: www.flagler.org

Florida, Parrish

FLORIDA GULF COAST RAILROAD MUSEUM, INC.
Diesel, scheduled
Standard gauge

FLORIDA GULF COAST RAILROAD MUSEUM, INC.

Ride: A 12-mile, 1½-hour ride through rural Florida on pre-1950s and 1950s passenger equipment—a museum where you ride the exhibits.

Schedule: Call or write for information.

Admission/Fare: Adults $8.00; children $5.00.

Locomotive/Rolling Stock: Alco RS-3 diesel. EMD GP7 diesel. Open-window coach, caboose, air-conditioned lounge car.

Location/Directions: I-75 exit 45 (Moccasin Wallow Road) to U.S. 301, turn south ¼ mile to the Parrish Post Office, turn east to the train.

[P] 🚌 ✳ ☕ 🎫 M arm TRAIN 🚂 Tampa

Site Address: Parrish, FL
Mailing Address: PO Box 355, Parrish, FL 34219
Telephone: (941) 722-4272
Internet: www.past-and-present-auto.com/sp_ent/train/fgcrr.html

Florida, Winter Haven   **CYPRESS GARDENS**

CYPRESS GARDENS, INC.

Schedule: Year round: daily, 9:30 a.m. to 5:30 p.m. Extended hours during special seasons.

Admission/Fare: Adults $29.95; seniors $24.50; children 6-12 $19.50; under age 6 are free.

Locomotive/Rolling Stock: Great Northern no. 707; Santa Fe no. 3571; Atlantic Coast Line no. 963; CSX no. 2704.

Nearby Attractions/Accommodations: Admiral's Inn Best Western, Bok Tower Gardens, Fantasy of Flight, Sea World, Disney World.

Location/Directions: I-4 to US 27 south to 540 west.

*Coupon available, see coupon section.

Site Address: Winter Haven, FL
Mailing Address: PO Box 1, Cypress Gardens, FL 33884
Telephone: (941) 324-2111 and (800) 282-2123
Fax: (941) 324-7946
Internet: www.cypressgardens.com

Georgia, Duluth

SOUTHEASTERN RAILWAY MUSEUM
Steam, diesel, scheduled
Standard gauge

Museum/Ride: Visitors meet rail history "hands on" through the display of over 90 pieces of retired railway rolling stock, including a WWII troop kitchen railway post office, the 1911 Pullman "Superb" used by Pres. Warren Harding, a modern office car, vintage steam locomotives, restored wooden cabooses. Ride on ¾-mile loop track aboard vintage cabooses.

Schedule: April through November: Saturdays 9 a.m. to 5 p.m. Sundays, on third full weekend, 12 to 5 p.m. Train rides included with admission. Miniature trains operated by North Georgia Live Steamers on third full weekend of each month. Exhibits only–December through March: Saturdays, 9 a.m. to 5 p.m.

Admission/Fare: Adults $5.00; seniors and children 2-12 $3.00; under age 2 are free.

Locomotive/Rolling Stock: 1950 and 1941 HRT GE 44-ton nos. 2 and 5; 1943 Georgia Power Porter 0-6-0T no. 97; 1954 CRR caboose no. 1064; SOU caboose XC7871; SCL caboose no. 01077.

Location/Directions: I-85 NW of Atlanta to west on exit 40 (Pleasant Hill Rd.) for 3.5 miles to US 23 (Buford Highway). South ¼ mile at railroad crossing.

Site Address: Buford Highway at May Road, Duluth, GA
Mailing Address: PO Box 1267, Duluth, GA 30096
Telephone: (770) 476-2013
Fax: (770) 908-8322
E-mail: 71045.2202@compuserve.com

Georgia, Kennesaw

KENNESAW CIVIL WAR MUSEUM
Railway museum
Standard gauge

KENNESAW CIVIL WAR MUSEUM

Display: The Andrews Raid and the Great Locomotive Chase, one of the unusual episodes of the Civil War, has been much publicized over the years. The "General," now one of the most famous locomotives in American history, is enshrined in a museum within 100 yards of the spot where it was stolen on April 12, 1862. The old engine, still operable, last ran in 1962. The Kennesaw Civil War Museum was officially opened on April 12, 1972, 110 years after the historic seizure of the "General."

Schedule: April through September: Mondays through Saturdays, 9:30 a.m. to 5:30 p.m. and Sundays, 12 to 5:30 p.m. October through March: Monday through Saturdays, 10 a.m. to 4 p.m. and Sundays, 12 to 4 p.m.

Admission/Fare: Adults $3.00; seniors $2.50; children 7-15 $1.50; age 6 and under are free.

Locomotive/Rolling Stock: Rodgers Ketchum & Grosvenor 4-4-0; Western & Atlantic General.

Special Events: Big Shanty Festival, April.

Nearby Attractions/Accommodations: Kennesaw Mountain.

Location/Directions: I-75 north (from Atlanta) exit 118 (Wade Green Rd.), west 2.3 miles. Museum is on right.

*Coupon available, see coupon section.

  [&] [P] 🚌 ✳ ⛪ ✉ M [MasterCard] [VISA]

Site Address: 2829 Cherokee Street, Kennesaw, GA
Mailing Address: 2829 Cherokee Street, Kennesaw, GA 30144
Telephone: (770) 427-2117 and (800) 742-6897
Fax: (770) 429-4559
E-mail: kcwm@juno.com
Internet: www.ngeorgia.com/history/kcwm.html

Georgia, Savannah

HISTORIC RAILROAD SHOPS
Railway museum

HISTORIC RAILROAD SHOPS

Display: Savannah's Historic Railroad Shops are an antebellum railroad manufacturing and repair facility. Construction of the site was begun in 1845 and 13 of the original structures are still standing. Included in these structures are the massive roundhouse and operating turntable, and the 125-foot smokestack. The Railroad Shops make up the oldest and most complete railroad repair and manufacturing facility still standing in the United States, and are a National Historic Landmark. The site, owned by the City of Savannah, was used for the filming of the motion picture "Glory" in 1988. On August 1, 1989, operation of the Railroad Shops was taken over by the Coastal Heritage Society. The goal of the site is to present a resource that protects its structures and its history, including artifacts and written history. The site is a multiple-use facility and therefore dedicates its mission to serving as wide a range of public and private use as possible. Permanent exhibits in five of the structures on the site. The Shops are open for self-guided tours.

Schedule: Self-guided tours daily, 10 a.m. to 4 p.m. Group tours and special daytime functions are available at the Shops as well as "After Hours" functions and dinner programs. Groups are welcomed to enjoy a variety of menus and historic programs. Please call for more information or reservations.

*Coupon available, see coupon section.

Site Address: 601 West Harris Street, Savannah, GA
Mailing Address: 601 West Harris Street, Savannah, GA 31402
Telephone: (912) 651-6823
Fax: (921) 651-3691

Georgia, Stone Mountain

STONE MOUNTAIN SCENIC RAILROAD
Diesel, scheduled
Standard gauge

Ride: A 25-minute narrated trip around Stone Mountain, behind a diesel locomotive. Occasionally a steam locomotive is used as a remote control for the diesel.

Schedule: March through May: 10 a.m. to 5:20 p.m. Memorial Day through Labor Day: 10 a.m. to 8 p.m. Extended weekend hours.

Admission/Fare: Adults $3.50; seniors $3.00; children 3-11 $2.50; discount for AAA and military.

Locomotive/Rolling Stock: Two FP7s; GP9; GP7; two Baldwin 4-4-0s; Vulcan 2-6-2 on display.

Special Events: Christmas Train, late November and December. Ghost Mountain Hayrides, October weekends. Call or write for information.

Nearby Attractions/Accommodations: Stone Mountain Park, skylift, riverboat, auto museum, plantation, Confederate memorial carving, wildlife preserve.

Location/Directions: Site is 16 miles east of Atlanta off Stone Mountain freeway, U.S. 78, and into Stone Mountain Park.

Site Address: Stone Mountain Park, Stone Mountain, GA
Mailing Address: PO Box 778, Stone Mountain, GA 30086
Telephone: (770) 498-5616 and (770) 498-5615

Hawaii, Ewa

HAWAIIAN RAILWAY SOCIETY
Diesel, scheduled
36" gauge

MARK D. BRUESHABER

Ride: A 6½-mile, 90-minute, ride along OR&L track from Ewa to Kahe Point where passengers can witness the surf crashing against the rocks. The train passes Barbers Point Naval Air Station, Ko'Olina Golf Course, and more. Fully narrated trip provides railroading history of the area.

Schedule: Every Sunday except major holidays. Weekdays by reservation. Weather permitting. Call for schedule.

Admission/Fare: Adults $8.00; seniors and children (2-12) $5.00.

Locomotive/Rolling Stock: Two Whitcomb diesel-electrics, nos. 302 and 423; converted U.S. Army flatcars, parlor car no. 64.

Nearby Attractions/Accommodations: Ihilani Resort; Ko'Olina Golf Course; Paradise Cover Luau.

Location/Directions: Freeway H-1, exit 5A, south on Weaver Road to Renton Road, right to Fleming Road.

Site Address: 91-1001 Renton Road, Ewa, HI
Mailing Address: PO Box 1208, Ewa Station, Ewa Beach, HI 96706
Telephone: (808) 681-5461
Fax: (808) 681-4860

Hawaii, Lahaina (Maui)

LAHAINA, KAANAPALI & PACIFIC RAILROAD
Steam, scheduled
36" gauge

LAHAINA, KAANAPALI & PACIFIC RAILROAD

Ride: The "Sugar Cane Train" chugs its way through the colorful history and breath-taking scenes of Maui by bringing back memories, sounds, and experiences of turn-of-the-century sugar plantation life. The sugar trains of the past were used to transport sugar cane from the fields to the mills and was a popular means of transportation for sugar workers in the early 1900s. Passengers are taken on an entertaining and historical tour by one of our singing conductors. The train stations are designed to resemble turn-of-the-century boarding platforms and are a delightful glimpse at Hawaii's historical and cultural past.

Schedule: Year round: daily, 8:55 a.m. to 5:30 p.m.

Admission/Fare: Round trip–adults $13.50, children $7.00. One-way–adults $9.50, children $5.00.

Locomotive/Rolling Stock: No. 1, "Anaka," 1943 Porter 2-4-0 & no. 3, "Myrtle," 1943 Porter 2-4-0, both former Carbon Limestone Co.; no. 45, "Oahu," 1959 Plymouth diesel, former Oahu Railway and more.

Nearby Attractions/Accommodations: Historic town of Lahaina, Maui.

Location/Directions: Lahaina Station located near Pioneer Mill, turn off Highway 30 at Hinau Street, turn right at Limahana Street.

Site Address: 975 Limahana Place, Lahaina, Maui, HI
Mailing Address: 975 Limahana Place, Lahaina, Maui, HI 96761
Telephone: (808) 667-6851 and (808) 661-0089
Fax: (808) 661-8389

Illinois, Chicago

HISTORIC PULLMAN FOUNDATION
Railway displays

HISTORIC PULLMAN FOUNDATION

Display: This organization offers guided tours of the historic Pullman district. The tour begins with an introductory video and a view of the interior of the HPF Visitor Center and the Greenstone Church; it then continues with the visitor's choice of a walk or a bus trip through the area, taking in the Pullman Suite at the Hotel Florence (once reserved for George M. Pullman), a Victorian furniture display room, and a "wood display" room containing actual pieces from Pullman's home on Prairie Avenue.

Schedule: Restaurant and museum–year round: Mondays through Fridays, 11 a.m. to 2 p.m.; Saturdays, 10 a.m. to 2 p.m.; Sundays 10 a.m. to 3 p.m. Visitor Center exhibit and video–Saturdays, 11 a.m. to 2 p.m.; Sundays, 12 to 3 p.m. Guided walking tour–May through October: adults $4.00; seniors $3.00; students $2.50. Rates subject to change.

Admission/Fare: Museum–donations appreciated. Visitor center: adults $3.00; students $1.00; children free.

Special Events: Annual House Tour, second weekend in October.

Nearby Attractions/Accommodations: Downtown Chicago, Sandridge Nature Center, riverboat casinos.

Location/Directions: Four blocks west of I-94 exit 66A (111th St.). Easy access to Metra trains.

*Coupon available, see coupon section.

Site Address: 11111 S. Forrestville Avenue, Chicago, IL
Mailing Address: 11111 S. Forrestville Avenue, Chicago, IL 60628-4649
Telephone: (773) 785-8181 and (773) 785-8900
Fax: (773) 785-8182

Illinois, Chicago

MUSEUM OF SCIENCE AND INDUSTRY
Railroad display, model railroad display

ALEX TREML

Display: The Museum of Science and Industry's model railroad exhibit was originally installed in 1941. The layout is approximately 3,000 square feet. Features include an O gauge track that is 1/48 the actual size, totaling 1,200 feet, in addition to 10,000 feet of switchboard wire, 350 relays, 5,500 trees, 150 telegraph poles, as well as a host of freight cars.

Schedule: Call or write for information.

Admission/Fare: Call or write for information.

Locomotive/Rolling Stock: Engine 999 was the first vehicle to go over 100 mph. The *Pioneer Zephyr* was the first streamlined diesel-electric train *Zephyr* exhibit opens in December 1997.

Location/Directions: From the north, proceed south on Lake Shore Drive past 57th Street and turn right at a new traffic signal at Science Drive. From south, follow Cornell Drive north to 57th Street and enter Museum grounds by making a right turn at Everett Drive.

[&] [P] [✳] [⓪]

Site Address: 57th Street & Lake Shore Drive, Chicago, IL
Mailing Address: 57th Street & Lake Shore Drive, Chicago, IL 60637
Telephone: (773) 684-1414
Fax: (773) 684-2907
Internet: www.msichicago.org

Illinois, Freeport **SILVER CREEK & STEPHENSON RAILROAD**
Steam, scheduled
Standard gauge

GEORGE A. FORERO, JR

Display/Ride: The "Turn-of-the-Century" Silver Creek Depot is a tribute to an important part of our country's transportation history. On display are lanterns, locks and keys, whistles, sounders, tickets, couplers, and more, representing railroads from across the country. The 4-mile train trip travels through Illinois farmland and stands of virgin timer known as "Indian Gardens," crossing Yellow Creek on a 30-foot high cement and stone pier bridge.

Schedule: May 24, 25; June 20, 21; July 4, 24, 25, 26; September 7, 26, 27; October 10, 11, 24, 25: 11 a.m. to 5 p.m.

Admission/Fare: Adults $4.00; children (under 10) $1.50.

Locomotive/Rolling Stock: 1912, 36-ton Heisler; 1941 bay-window caboose, former Chicago, Milwaukee, St. Paul & Pacific; 1889 wooden caboose with cupola, former Hannibal & St. Joseph, reported to be the oldest running caboose in Illinois; 1948 caboose, former Illinois Central Gulf; covered flatcar; 14-ton Brookville switch engine; 12-ton Plymouth switch engine; and work cars.

Location/Directions: Intersection of Walnut and Lamm Roads, one-half mile south of Stephenson County Fairgrounds.

Site Address: 2954 W. Walnut Road, Freeport, IL
Mailing Address: PO Box 255, Freeport, IL 61032
Telephone: (800) 369-2955 and (815) 232-2306

Illinois, Galesburg

GALESBURG RAILROAD MUSEUM
Railroad museum

GALESBURG RAILROAD MUSEUM

Museum: As you visit the Galesburg Railroad Museum, you will experience railroading of the early 1900s. The Museum has restored an engine and three cars built in the 20s and 30s and maintains an extensive collection of railroad memorabilia.

Schedule: Memorial Day through Labor Day: daily except Mondays, 12 to 5 p.m. Group tours by appointment.

Admission/Fare: Adults $1.00; youth over age 12 $ .50.

Locomotive/Rolling Stock: Steam engine CB&Q 300b Hudson 54; BCB&Q 2645 Pullman parlor car; CB&Q 1945 RPO baggage car; CB&Q 13501 caboose.

Special Events: Railroad Days city-wide celebration, last full weekend in June.

Nearby Attractions/Accommodations: Carl Sandburg birthsite, Knox College, site of Lincoln-Douglas debate, camping, amusement parks.

Location/Directions: I-74 exit 48, west to downtown Galesburg.

Site Address: 423 Mulberry Street, Galesburg, IL
Mailing Address: PO Box 947, Galesburg, IL 61402-0947
Telephone: (309) 342-9400

Illinois, Mendota UNION DEPOT RAILROAD MUSEUM

ALICE ZEMAN

Display: This restored 1940s station features an operating HO layout replica of downtown Mendota in the 1940s during its heyday as a railroad center with the Milwaukee, Illinois Central, and Burlington Railroads. Also see the old time telegraphy office, railroad memorabilia, and more.

Schedule: May through September: daily except Monday, 12 to 5 p.m. October through April: Fridays, Saturdays, Sundays, 12 to 5 p.m.

Admission/Fare: $2.00; members are free.

Locomotive/Rolling Stock: Burlington O-1A Mikado-type locomotive 2-8-2 no. 4978; tender; Burlington waycar no. 14451.

Special Events: Mendota Sweet Corn Festival, second week in August.

Nearby Attractions/Accommodations: Hume-Carnegie Historical Museum, Breaking the Prairie Agricultural Museum, restaurants, lodging, campgrounds.

Location/Directions: I-39/51 and route 34, approximately 100 miles west of Chicago, and 50 miles south of Rockford.

  [♿] [P] 🚌 ✱ [📷] ✉ M 🚂

Site Address: 783 Main Street, Mendota, IL
Mailing Address: PO Box 433, Mendota, IL 61342
Telephone: (815) 538-3800

Illinois, Monticello

MONTICELLO RAILWAY MUSEUM
Diesel, scheduled
Standard gauge

PAUL YOOS

Ride/Display: This museum, incorporated in 1966, offers a 50-minute round trip over former Illinois Central and Illinois Terminal trackage. Passengers board at the Illinois Central Depot at the museum or at the 1899 Wabash Depot in downtown Monticello. Displays of the following are on site: 1907 Baldwin 2-8-0, former Southern Railway no. 401; Shedd Aquarium's "Nautilus" (fish car); Nickel Plate RPO; Santa Fe Pullman "Pleasant Valley"; 1931 Alco 0-4-0 tank engine no. 1; 1944 Industrial Brownhoist; freight equipment; cabooses.

Schedule: May 4 through October 31: weekends and holidays, 1, 2, 3, and 4 p.m. at museum site; 1:30, 2:30 and 3:30 p.m. in town. Charters, private cars, birthday caboose on request. Throttle times available.

Admission/Fare: Call or write for information.

Locomotive/Rolling Stock: No. 1, 1930 Alco 0-4-0, former Montezuma Gravel Co.; no. 191, 1916 Alco 0-6-0, former Republic Steel Corp.; no. 301, 1955 Alco RS-3, former Long Island Railroad; no. 401, 1907 Baldwin 2-8-0, former Southern Railway; no. 44, 1940 Davenport 44-ton diesel; no. 1189, 1953 GMD F7A, former Wabash no. 725; more.

Special Events: Numerous. Call or write for information.

Location/Directions: I-72 exit 166. Site is located 20 miles southwest of Champaign; 20 miles northeast of Decatur.

[P] [bus] [*] [coffee] [picnic] [ ] M arm TRAIN

Champaign   Radio frequency: 160.635

Site Address: Monticello, IL
Mailing Address: PO Box 401, Monticello, IL 61856-0401
Telephone: (217) 762-9011 and (800) 952-3396

Illinois, Monticello

RAYVILLE RAILROAD MUSEUM
(PIATT COUNTY MUSEUM)
Model railroad
HO gauge

RAYVILLE RAILROAD MUSEM

Display: Rayville is a 10 x 36 foot miniature town hand crafted by and named after the museum's curator, Ray McIntyre. The town of Rayville, which opened in 1966, is an HO scale community that features a ball park, a drive-in movie, a race track, a circus, a lake and a collection of railroad memorabilia.

Schedule: Weekends. Call first.

Admission/Fare: Adults $2.00; children $ .50.

Location/Directions: Off I-72, Decatur/Champaign, half block off square. Twenty miles southeast of Champaign.

[P] 🚌 M 🚆

Site Address: 217 Washington, Monticello, IL
Mailing Address: 315 W. Main Street, Monticello, IL 61856
Telephone: (217) 762-2793

Illinois, Peoria (Dunlap)   **WHEELS O' TIME MUSEUM**
Railway museum

Museum: Steam locomotive with combo car, caboose, and switcher. Antique autos, fire trucks, clocks, tools, toys, farm equipment, and more.

Schedule: Year round: Wednesdays through Sundays and holidays, 12 to 5 p.m. and other times by appointment. Group tours available.

Admission/Fare: Adults $4.00; children $1.50. Group rates available.

Locomotive/Rolling Stock: Rock Island Pacific no. 886; Milwaukee Road combine no. 2716; TP&W caboose no. 508; Plymouth switcher.

Nearby Attractions/Accommodations: Wildlife Prairie Park, Lakeview Museum.

Location/Directions: On route 40, north of Peoria.

Site Address: 11923 N. Knoxville, Dunlap, IL
Mailing Address: PO Box 9636, Peoria, IL 61612-9636
Telephone: (309) 243-9020 and (309) 691-3470
E-mail: wotmuseum@aol.com
Internet: members.aol.com/wotmuseum

Illinois, Rockford

TROLLEY CAR 36
Propane, scheduled

Ride: All aboard! Departing from downtown Rockford, you will discover interesting tidbits about the history of Rockford while enjoying a ride on the trolley.

Schedule: June through August: Tuesdays, Thursdays, Saturdays, and Sundays September: weekends only. 12 to 4 p.m. Forty-five minute rides run hourly.

Admission/Fare: Adults $2.50; children 5-17 $2.00; ages four and under are free.

Special Events: On the Waterfront Festival, Labor Day weekend, downtown Rockford.

Nearby Attractions/Accommodations: Magic Waters Waterpark, Forest City Queen, Clock Tower Resort.

Location/Directions: I-90 to Business 20/E. State Street, to Madison to trolley station.

Site Address: 324 N. Madison Street, Rockford, IL
Mailing Address: 324 N. Madison Street, Rockford, IL 61107
Telephone: (815) 987-8894

Illinois, Rossville

DANVILLE JUNCTION CHAPTER, NRHS
Railroad museum, model railroad display

RICHARD M. SCHROEDER

Display: Displays show the history of former Chicago & Eastern Illinois and other area railroads. The Baggage Room contains an HO model railroad. The Depot Museum preserves the railroads history of east Central Illinois and western Indiana in a former C&EI Railroad Depot.

Schedule: Memorial Day through Labor Day: weekends, noon to 4 p.m. and by appointment.

Admission/Fare: Free. Donations are appreciated.

Nearby Attractions/Accommodations: Rossville Historical Society Museum, Mann's Chapel, Vermilion County Museum.

Location/Directions: In Rossville, one block north on Illinois Route 1 to Benton Street, east three block to CSX transportation tracks.

[&] [P] [*] [=] M

Site Address: East Benton Street, Rossville, IL
Mailing Address: PO Box 1013, Danville, IL 61834-1013
Telephone: (217) 748-6615 and (217) 442-1374
E-mail: djcnrhs@prairienet.org or rickshro@aol.com
Internet: http://www.prairienet.org/djc-nrhs/

Illinois, South Elgin **FOX RIVER TROLLEY MUSEUM**
Electric, scheduled
Standard gauge

FRED LONNES

Display: Ride the historic 102-year-old remnant of an interurban railroad aboard Chicago-area interurban and "el" equipment. Includes the oldest surviving American interurban, Chicago, Aurora & Elgin no. 20 (shown above).

Schedule: May 9 through November 1: Sundays and holidays, 11 a.m. to 5 p.m.; June 27 through August 29: Saturdays, Sundays, and holidays.

Admission/Fare: Adults $2.50; seniors $2.00; children 3-11 $1.50.

Locomotive/Rolling Stock: Historic Chicago interurban and "L" equipment including CA&E no. 20; North Shore nos. 715 and 756; CTA 4451; CRT 5001; CSL S-202.

Special Events: Mother's Day; Father's Day; Trolleyfest, June 27 and 28; Old Time Commuter Day, August 23; Folkfest, September 13; Haunted Trolley, October 24, 25, and 31.

Nearby Attractions/Accommodations: Grand Victoria Casino, Elgin; historic towns of St. Charles and Geneva; Blackhawk Forest Preserve.

Location/Directions: Illinois 31 south from I-90 or US 20, or north from I-88. Site is located 3 blocks south of State Street stoplight in South Elgin.

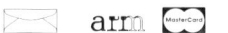

Site Address: 365 S. LaFox Street, South Elgin, IL
Mailing Address: 365 S. LaFox Street, South Elgin, IL 60177
Telephone: (847) 697-4676

Illinois, Union (McHenry County) **ILLINOIS RAILWAY MUSEUM**
Steam, electric, diesel, scheduled
Standard gauge

STAN KISTLER

Museum/Ride: I.R.M. is America's largest railroad museum with the most comprehensive collection in the nation. A collection of over 25 steam locomotives and more than 300 pieces of rail equipment of all types. The museum also has a C&NW depot built in 1851, a signal tower, and a restored Chicago "el" station. A 5-mile, 25-minute round trip over the reconstructed right-of-way of the former Elgin & Belvedere, featuring steam and/or diesel trains and electric interurban on weekends and streetcars on weekdays.

Schedule: May 26 through September 7: daily. April, May, September, and October: weekends.

Admission/Fare: Weekends: adults $8.00; children 5-11 $6.00. Weekdays: adults $6.00; children 5-11 $3.50. Maximum family admission $30.00.

Locomotive/Rolling Stock: No. 2903 Santa Fe 4-8-4; no. 2050 N&W 2-8-8-2; no. 9911A CB&Q EMC E5; no. 6930 UP DDA 40X; Electroliner; many more.

Special Events: Scout Day, May 26; Chicago Weekend, June 20, 21; Trolley Pageant, July 4; Diesel Days, July 18, 19; Vintage Transport Extravaganza, August 2; Zephyr Weekend, August 15, 16; Railfan Weekend, September 5, 6, and 7; Members Weekend, September 26, 27.

Location/Directions: One mile east of Union off U.S. Route 20.

*Coupon available, see coupon section.

Site Address: 7000 Olson Road, Union, IL
Mailing Address: PO Box 427, Union, IL 60108
Telephone: (815) 923-4391 or (815) 923-4000 recorded message
Fax: (815) 923-2006

Illinois, Union (McHenry County)

VALLEY VIEW MODEL RAILROAD
Model railroad

VALLEY VIEW MODEL RAILROAD

Display: This display is modeled after the Chicago & North Western's Northwest line, with accurate track layouts of some of the towns modeled. Three to four trains operate simultaneously over the railroad which has eight scale miles of track, 16 ever changing trains, 250 buildings, 64 turnouts, 250 vehicles, 450 people, 84 operating signal lights, 250 pieces of rolling stock, and operating grade crossings with flashers and gates. Extra equipment is on static display in the gift shop.

Schedule: Memorial Day through Labor Day: Wednesdays, Saturdays, and Sundays.

Admission/Fare: Adults $4.00; seniors $3.50; children $2.00; age five and under are free.

Nearby Attractions/Accommodations: Illinois Railway Museum.

Location/Directions: Travel north ¾ mile on Olson Road to Highbridge.

Site Address: 17108 Highbridge Road, Union, IL
Mailing Address: 17108 Highbridge Road, Union, IL 60180
Telephone: (815) 923-4135

Illinois, Waterman

WATERMAN & WESTERN RAILROAD
Diesel, irregular
15" gauge

Ride: A one-mile ride around and through Lions Park in downtown Waterman.

Schedule: Mother's Day through Labor Day: Sundays, 1 to 4 p.m.

Admission/Fare: $1.00; under age 3 are free.

Locomotive/Rolling Stock: F3 model diesel.

Special Events: Pumpkin Train/Haunted Train Ride, free pumpkins to children: mid-October through Halloween, weekends. Holiday Lights Train: Thanksgiving through Christmas, weekends.

Nearby Attractions/Accommodations: Shabbon State Park, many antique shops.

Location/Directions: One block south of U.S. 30. One mile west of route 23.

[P] [bus] [picnic]

Site Address: 200 S. Birch Street, Waterman, IL
Mailing Address: PO Box 217, Waterman, IL 60556
Telephone: (815) 264-7800 and (815) 264-7753
Fax: (815) 264-3230
E-mail: wwrr@watermannet.com
Internet: wwrr@watermannet.com

Indiana, Connersville

WHITEWATER VALLEY RAILROAD
Diesel, scheduled
Standard gauge

WHITEWATER VALLEY RAILROAD

Ride: This line offers a 32-mile, 5½-hour round trip to Metamora, Indiana, a restored canal town that features 100 shops and a working grist mill. A 2-hour stopover at Metamora give passengers a change to tour the town.

Schedule: Year round: Saturday, Sundays, and holidays, 12:01 p.m.; May and October: additional trips added.

Admission/Fare: Adults $12.00; children 2-12 $6.00.

Locomotive/Rolling Stock: No. 6, 1907 Baldwin 0-6-0, former East Broad Top; no. 8, 1946 General Electric, former Muncie & Western; no. 11, 1924 Vulcan 0-4-0T; no. 100, 1919 Baldwin 2-6-2; no. 25, 1951 Lima SW7.5; no. 210, 1946 General Electric 70-ton; no. 709, 1950 Lima SW10; no. 2561, 1931 Plymouth 32-ton gas engine; no. 9339, 1948 Alco S1; no. 9376, 1950 Lima SW12, former Baltimore & Ohio.

Special Events: Metamora Canal Days, first weekend in October; Christmas Trains, December.

Nearby Attractions/Accommodations: Whitewater State Park, Brookville Lake, Mary Gray Bird Sanctuary.

*Coupon available, see coupon section.

Radio Frequency: 160.650

Site Address: 5th Street and Grand Avenue, Connersville, IN
Mailing Address: PO Box 406, Connersville, IN 47331
Telephone: (765) 825-2054
Fax: (765) 825-4550
Internet: http://www.inetdirect.net/railline/WVRR.html

Indiana, Corydon

CORYDON SCENIC RAILROAD
Diesel, scheduled
Standard gauge

CORYDON SCENIC RAILROAD

Ride: A 1½-hour, 16-mile ride over part of the 114 year old Louisville, New Albany & Corydon Railroad from Corydon (the state's first capitol) to Corydon Junction. Air conditioned trains with guides aboard to answer passengers' questions as the train travels along Big Indiana Creek into the southern Indiana woods and hills, crossing two major bridges and passing many sink holes.

Schedule: May: Saturdays and Sundays. June, September through November 15: Fridays, Saturdays, Sundays. July, August: Wednesdays through Sundays. Fridays, 1 p.m.; Saturdays and Sundays, 1 and 3 p.m.

Admission/Fare: Adults $9.00; seniors $8.00; children $5.00; age three and under are free.

Locomotive/Rolling Stock: Two 44-ton GE center cab diesels; two Alco 1000 horsepower RS1s.

Location/Directions: One mile south of I-64 in downtown Corydon, Walnut and Water Streets.

Site Address: 210 W. Walnut Street, Corydon, IN
Mailing Address: PO Box 10, Corydon, IN 47112
Telephone: (812) 738-8000
Fax: (812) 738-3101

Indiana, Elkhart

NATIONAL NEW YORK CENTRAL RAILROAD MUSEUM
Railway museum

NATIONAL NEW YORK CENTRAL RAILROAD MUSEUM

Museum: The museum traces the rich history of the New York Central and its impact on Elkhart and the nation. Extensive hands-on exhibits bring railroading alive!

Schedule: Year round: Tuesdays through Fridays, 10 a.m. to 2 p.m.; weekends 10 a.m. to 3 p.m. Closed Mondays and major holidays.

Admission/Fare: Adults $2.00; seniors and students 6-14 $1.00; children age five and under are free.

Locomotive/Rolling Stock: NYC 3001 L3a Mohawk Alco 1940; NYC 4085 E8 LaGrange 1951; PRR 4-8-8-2 GG1; freight and passenger equipment.

Nearby Attractions/Accommodations: Northern Indiana Amish Country, Midwest Museum of American Art, S. Ray Miller Auto Museum, Ruthmere.

Location/Directions: Indiana Toll Road exit 92. Main Street in downtown Elkhart, next to the tracks.

Site Address: 721 S. Main Street, Elkhart, IN
Mailing Address: PO Box 1043, Elkhart, IN 46515
Telephone: (219) 294-3001
Fax: (219) 295-9434

Indiana, Fort Wayne

FORT WAYNE RAILROAD HISTORICAL SOCIETY
Steam, irregular
Standard gauge

WAYNE YORK

Ride: The FWRHS is America's most successful all-volunteer mainline steam operator. Since 1979 the Society has operated over 300 mainline excursions carrying 250,000 passengers over 50,000 miles on over a dozen different railroads.

Schedule: Various excursions in Indiana, Ohio, Michigan, Kentucky, Tennessee, West Virginia, Pennsylvania, and Illinois.

Admission/Fare: Varies according to excursion sponsor.

Locomotive/Rolling Stock: NKP 2-8-4 Berkshire steam locomotive no. 765.

Location/Directions: The shop is in the Casao Industrial Park, which is east of New Haven, Indiana.

[P] TRAIN M [MasterCard] [VISA]

Mailing Address: Box 11017, Fort Wayne, IN 46855
Telephone: (219) 493-0765
E-mail: info@steamloco765.org
Internet: www.steamloco765.org

Indiana, French Lick

FRENCH LICK, WEST BADEN & SOUTHERN RAILWAY
Diesel, electric, scheduled
Standard gauge

ALAN BARNETT

Museum/Ride: A 20-mile, 1¾-mile round trip between the resort town of French Lick and Cuzco, site of Patoka Lake. The train traverses wooded Indiana limestone country and passes through one of the state's longest railroad tunnels.

Schedule: April through October: weekends and May 25 and September 7: 10 a.m., 1 and 4 p.m. November: 1 p.m. June through October: Tuesdays, 1 p.m.

Admission/Fare: Adults $8.00; children 3-11 $4.00; under 3 ride free.

Locomotive/Rolling Stock: 1947 General Electric 80-ton diesel no. 3; 1947 Alco RS-1 no. 4; open window Rock Island coaches.

Special Events: Wild West holdups are scheduled for many holiday weekends. Call or write for dates and times.

Nearby Attractions/Accommodations: French Lick Springs Resort.

Location/Directions: Trains depart the old Monon Passenger Depot on Highway 56 in French Lick.

Site Address: 1 Monon Street, French Lick, IN
Mailing Address: 1 Monon Street, French Lick, IN 47432
Telephone: (812) 936-2405 and (800) 74-TRAIN
Fax: (812) 936-2904

Indiana, Hesston

HESSTON STEAM MUSEUM
Steam, unscheduled
Various gauges

Museum: Features antique steam train rides, steam sawmill, steam crane, traction engines, and static displays.

Ride: Explore the world of the steam engine and ride behind a genuine coal-fired steam locomotive through 155 acres of rolling meadows and deep forests on a 2-mile railway line.

Schedule: Memorial Day weekend through Labor Day: Saturdays and Sundays. September through October: Sundays. Noon to 5 p.m.

Admission/Fare: Free admission except Labor Day weekend. Train rides, $3.00.

Locomotives/Rolling Stock: Darjeeling & Himalayan built by Atlas Works; New Mexico Lumber Shay built by Lima Locomotive.

Special Events: Hesston Steam and Power Show, Labor Day weekend.

Nearby Attractions/Accommodations: Lighthouse Mall, Dunes National Lakeshore, Washington Park Beach/Zoo.

Location/Directions: South of Indiana-Michigan state line. Four miles east of State Road 39 on County Road 1000 North.

*Coupon available, see coupon section.

[P] 🚌 ✳ ☕ 🍴 ✉ M

Site Address: County Road 1000 North
Mailing Address: 2946 Mt. Clair Way, Michigan City, IN 46360
Telephone: (219) 872-7405 or (219) 778-2783

Indiana, Indianapolis

THE CHILDREN'S MUSEUM OF INDIANAPOLIS
Railway museum
Toy trains

ED LACEY

Museum: The 356,000-square-foot facility is home to ten major galleries, including the newest addition of a large format CineDome theater and outdoor Festival Park area. Programs explore the physical and natural sciences, history, foreign cultures and the arts. Whenever possible, exhibits are "hands-on" or participatory in nature. The world's largest children's museum invites you to view the world from a seat in our CineDome theater, dig for fossils, try your skill at a rock-climbing wall, hop a ride on our turn-of-the-century carousel and sail through the cosmos in our SpaceQuest Planetarium.

Schedule: September through February: Tuesdays through Sundays. March through Labor Day: first Thursday of every month. 10 a.m. to 5 p.m. Closed Thanksgiving and Christmas.

Admission/Fare: Museum–adults $7.00; seniors $6.00; children 2-17 $3.50. Additional fees for CineDome, SpaceQuest, and Lilly Theater.

Locomotive/Rolling Stock: Rueben Wells, a 35-foot long, 55-ton steam engine. It was used to push five to eight cars and freight up Madison Hill, the steepest U.S. railroad grade in 1868, in 15 minutes.

Location/Directions: Museum is located five minutes north of downtown at 30th and Meridian Streets. Free parking available in the museum lot on Illinois Street (one street west of Meridian).

    [♿] [P] 🚌 ✼ ☕ 🎟 ⛩ M

Site Address: 3000 N. Meridian Street, Indianapolis, IN
Mailing Address: PO Box 3000, Indianapolis, IN 46206-3000
Telephone: (317) 924-5431
Fax: (317) 921-4000
E-mail: tcmi@childrensmuseum.org
Internet: www.childrensmuseum.org

Indiana, Knightstown

CARTHAGE, KNIGHTSTOWN & SHIRLEY RAILROAD
Diesel, scheduled
Standard gauge

CARTHAGE, KNIGHTSTOWN & SHIRLEY RAILROAD

Ride: A ten mile, 1.25 hour round trip over the former Cleveland, Cincinnati, Chicago & St. Louis Michigan Division through scenic country, crosssing the Big Blue River into Carthage, Indiana. Train leaves from the former NYC freight house in Knightstown.

Schedule: May through October: weekends and holidays, 11 a.m., 1, and 3 p.m. Fridays, 1 p.m.

Admission/Fare: Adults $6.00; children 3-11 $4.00; under age three ride free. Group rates available.

Locomotive/Rolling Stock: No. 215 45-ton GE, former Air Force no. 1215.

Location/Directions: Thirty three miles east of Indianapolis on U.S. 40; three miles outh of I-70 on state route 109.

Site Address: 112 W. Carey Street, Knightstown, IN
Mailing Address: 112 W. Carey Street, Knightstown, IN 46148
Telephone: (317) 345-5561

Indiana, Linden

LINDEN RAILROAD MUSEUM
Railway museum

LINDEN RAILROAD MUSEUM

Display: Operated by the Linden-Madison Township Historical Society, this museum is housed in the former Linden depot built by the Chicago, Indianapolis & Louisville Railway and the Toledo, St. Louis & Western Railroad in 1908. Restored to its 1950s appearance, the depot houses a collection of railroadiana from the Nickel Plate and Monon railroads. The Monon agent's room houses the E.E. Kaukffman Monon collection, including a ¾-inch scale model of the Louisville, New Albany & Chicago "Admiral" locomotive and cars and a ¾-inch live steam model of Monon Pacific no. 440 and the observation car "Babe."

Schedule: April through October: Wednesday through Sunday, 1 to 5 p.m. Group tours by appointment.

Admission/Fare: Adults $2.00, teens 13-17 $1.00, children 6-12 $.50, under age 6 are free.

Locomotive/Rolling Stock: Former Nickel Plate caboose no. 497; Fairmont A-3 motor car.

Nearby Attractions/Accommodations: Old jail museum, Crawfordsville, Indiana.

Location/Directions: South of Lafayette on U.S. 231 and is 7.9 miles north of the Crawfordsville exit off I-74. The depot museum is across from Jane Stoddard Park in Linden.

*Coupon available, see coupon section.

[♿] [P] [🚌] [✳] [📷] [⛩] [⛪] [✉] M

Site Address: 514 N. Main Street, Linden, IN
Mailing Address: PO Box 154, Linden, IN 47955
Telephone: (705) 339-7245 or (800) 866-3973
E-mail: weaver@tctc.com
Internet: http://www.tctc.com/~weaver/depot.htm

Indiana, Noblesville

INDIANA TRANSPORTATION MUSEUM
Steam, electric, diesel, scheduled
Standard gauge

JIM VAWTER

Display/Ride: Many railroad cars on display. Henry M. Flagler private car open on special occasions. Train rides through rural Hamilton county available weekends.

Schedule: April, May, September, and October: weekends, 10 a.m. to 5 p.m. Memorial Day through Labor Day: Tuesday through Sunday, 10 a.m. to 5 p.m. Trains run each weekend at 1:30 p.m.

Admission/Fare: Museum: adults $3.00; children 4-12 $2.00. Train: adults $7.00; children 4-12 $5.00. Children under 3 are free.

Locomotive/Rolling Stock: EMD F7 and FP7 diesels; 1918 Baldwin steam engine no. 587, former NKP; 8 stainless steel coaches from 1937 Santa Fe Scout.

Special Events: Fair Train during Indiana State Fair, August. Train rides to Atlanta New Earth Festival, September. Hamiltonian to restaurants in Cicero and Atlanta, Friday evenings.

Nearby Attractions/Accommodations: Conner Prairie Museum in Fishers, Children's Museum in Indianapolis, Motel 8 in Noblesville.

Location/Directions: Located 20 miles north of Indianapolis in Forest Park/Noblesville on State Road 19 just north of the intersection with State Road 32.

*Coupon available, see coupon section.

Site Address: 325 Cicero Road, Noblesville, IN
Mailing Address: PO Box 83, Noblesville, IN 46061-0083
Telephone: (317) 773-6000 and (317) 776-7881
Fax: (317) 773-5530

Indiana, North Judson

HOOSIER VALLEY RAILROAD MUSEUM, INC.
Museum and ride, unscheduled
Standard gauge

BRUCE EMMONS

Museum: Established in North Judson since 1988. The organization has been in the process of building the physical plant for a working railroad museum. The collection today consists of 30 pieces of railroad rolling stock. This includes the former 2-8-4 Chesapeake & Ohio steam locomotive no. 2789, which is under roof and being restored.

Schedule: Year round: Saturdays, 8 a.m. to 5 p.m.

Admission/Fare: No charge.

Locomotive/Rolling Stock: C&O 1947 Alco K-4 2-8-4 no. 2789; Erie 1947 Alco S-1 switcher no. 310; EL caboose no. C345; 30 pieces rolling stock.

Special Events: Appreciation Day/Open House, Annual Dinner. Dates to be announced.

Nearby Attractions/Accommodations: Tippecanoe River State Park, Bass Lake State Beach, Kersting's Cycle Center & Museum, Oak View Motel.

Location/Directions: Seventy miles southeast of downtown Chicago, Indiana 10 and 39.

Site Address: 507 Mulberry Street, North Judson, IN
Mailing Address: PO Box 75, North Judson, IN 46366
Telephone: (219) 223-3834 and (219) 946-6499 eves

Iowa, Boone

BOONE & SCENIC VALLEY RAILROAD
IOWA RAILROAD HISTORICAL SOCIETY
Steam, electric, scheduled
Standard gauge

IOWA RAILROAD HISTORICAL SOCIETY

Ride/Display: A 14-mile, 1½-hour trip through the Des Moines River Valley crossing a 156 foot high trestle and the "Y" camp river bridge. Displays a growing collection of electric and vintage equipment.

Schedule: May: weekends, 1:30 p.m. May 23 through October 31: weekdays, 1:30 p.m., weekends, 11 a.m., 1:30, and 4 p.m. Electric trolleys–weekends, on demand.

Admission/Fare: Diesel (weekdays)–adults $10.00; children 5-12 $5.00; under age four and under are free. Steam (weekends)–adults $12.00. Trolleys–$2.00. "Wolfe Train" first class–$25.00.

Locomotive/Rolling Stock: JS 8419 Chinese steam locomotive, Datong, China; C&NW 1003; CCW no. 50; CO&E no. 17.

Special Events: Pufferbilly Days, September 10-13; Thomas the Tank rides, mid-summer.

Nearby Attractions/Accommodations: Mamie Eisenhower's birth place, Union Pacific 186 foot high double-track bridge.

Location/Directions: I-35 to Ames, U.S. 30 West to Boone. Travel north on Story street to 11th Street, turn west for 6 blocks.

Site Address: 11th and Division Streets, Boone, IA
Mailing Address: Box 603, Boone, IA 50036
Telephone: (515) 432-4249 and (800) 626-0319
Fax: (515) 432-4253

Iowa, Clear Lake

MASON CITY & CLEAR LAKE ELECTRIC RAILWAY HISTORICAL SOCIETY
Electric, scheduled
Standard gauge

MASON CITY & CLEAR LAKE RAILWAY

Museum/Display/Ride: We are adjacent to the nation's oldest continuously operating, electrical freight railroad (private property). Opportunities to view and photograph the railroad in operation occur almost daily. One mile of electric travel from our carbarn and collection of historic trolley equipment/cars. Historic Baldwin-Westinghouse steeple cab power.

Schedule: Memorial Day through Labor Day: weekends, 12:30 to 4:30 p.m. Charters available April through October.

Admission/Fare: Adults $3.50; children under age 12 $2.00.

Locomotive/Rolling Stock: 1927 Chicago North Shore and Milwaukee Interurban no. 727; 1948 PCC trolley car; wooden trolley car (circa 1890s); 1900 electric sweeper car; Fairmont motor car.

Location/Directions: One-half mile east of I-35. East end of Main Street, Clear Lake, Iowa.

P 🚌 ✳ 📷 🚂 ✉ M

Site Address: East Main Street, Clear Lake, IA
Mailing Address: PO Box 956, Clear Lake, IA 50428
Telephone: (515) 357-7433

Iowa, Colfax **TRAINLAND U.S.A.**
Model railroad display

OREGON LOGGING OPERATIONS

Display: Operating O gauge toy train museum.

Schedule: Memorial Day to Labor Day: daily, 10 a.m. to 6 p.m.

Admission/Fare: Adults $4.50; seniors $4.00; children 4-12 $2.00; age three and under are free.

Locomotive/Rolling Stock: O gauge Lionel.

Nearby Attractions/Accommodations: Newton Air Show, Knoxville Spring Car Nationals, Pella Tulip Time, Walnut Creek.

Location/Directions: I-80 exit 155, north of Colfax to Prairie Preserve, 2.5 miles on Highway 117.

[♿] [P] [🚌] [✻] [⛱]

Site Address: 3135 Highway 117N, Colfax, IA
Mailing Address: 3135 Highway 117N, Colfax, IA 50054
Telephone: (515) 674-3813

Iowa, Council Bluffs

RAILSWEST RAILROAD MUSEUM
Railway museum
Model railroad

RAILSWEST RAILROAD MUSEUM

Museum: The RailsWest Railroad Museum and HO model railroad are housed in a former 1899 Rock Island depot. The museum contains displays of historic photos, dining car memorabilia, uniforms, and many other items used during the steam era. The 22 x 33 foot model railroad depicts scenery of the Council Bluffs/Omaha area, featuring train lines that served the heartland: Union Pacific; Chicago & Northwestern; Wabash; Chicago Great Western; Wabash, Rock Island; Milwaukee Road; Chicago, Burlington & Quincy.

Schedule: Memorial Day through Labor Day: Mondays, Tuesdays, Thursdays through Saturdays, 10 a.m. to 4 p.m.; Sundays, 1 to 5 p.m.

Locomotive/Rolling Stock: Burlington Route handcar; 1963 Budd RPO no. 903690, former UP no. 5908; 1967 caboose no. 24548; Rock Island no. 17130; 1969 UP boxcar no. 462536.

Special Events: Depot Days, last weekend in September. Christmas at the Depot, Thanksgiving through New Year's, weekends 1 to 5 p.m.

Location/Directions: I-80 exit 3 or I-29 exit Manawa.

Omaha, NE

Site Address: 1512 S. Main Street, Council Bluffs, IA
Mailing Address: 72 Bellevue Avenue, Council Bluffs, IA 51503
Telephone: (712) 323-5182 depot and (712) 322-0612

Iowa, Donnellson

FORT MADISON, FARMINGTON & WESTERN RAILROAD
Diesel, scheduled

FORT MADISON, FARMINGTON & WESTERN RAILROAD

Museum/Ride: An authentic re-creation of a pre-World War II branchline terminus. A country village, enginehouse with displays, an extensive collection of hand and motor cars, and the yard are on display. A wye is demonstrated and there are many restored pieces of rolling stock. The FMF&W is one of the most authentically operated and appearing railroads in the country. The ride is two miles through woods, up grade, and over a trestle.

Schedule: Memorial Day weekend through October: weekends and holidays, 12 to 5 p.m. Trains depart hourly on the half hour.

Admission/Fare: Adults $5.00; students $4.00; under age 5 are free. Price includes admission and ride.

Locomotive/Rolling Stock: Davenport diesel mechanical no. 348; 8-ton Vulcan nbo. 1; 1913 Baldwin no. 4; Edward Doodlebug no. 507; 30-ton steam crane no. 3; more.

Special Events: Antique Machinery Show, September 26, 27. Santa Train, December 6, 13, 20.

Nearby Attractions/Accommodations: Old Fort Madison, Catfish Bend Riverboat Casino, motels.

Location/Directions: Off Highway 2 between Fort Madison and Donnellson.

Radio frequency: 464.9750

Site Address: 2208 220th Street, Donnellson, IA
Mailing Address: 2208 220th Street, Donnellson, IA 52625
Telephone: (319) 837-6689
Fax: (319) 837-6080

Iowa, Fairfield

ANDERSON STEEL FLANGE
Railroad Equipment Company
Rail Merchants International

D.J. THEBODO

Display: We are rail merchants specializing in saving railroad rolling stock and other vintage transportation equipment from being destroyed. We are connected to the U.S. Rail system through our own siding and yard located in southeastern Iowa and serviced by Burlington Northern Santa Fe Railroad. The company is located on the site of the former Rock Island Railroad freight yard (the Golden State route) in Fairfield, Iowa.

Schedule: Year round: viewing by appointment.

Admission/Fare: Free.

Locomotive/Rolling Stock: Inventory includes cabooses, passenger cars, equipment, tools, and railroadiana.

Nearby Attractions/Accommodations: Midwest Central Railroad, Old Threshers Trolley Museum.

Location/Directions: I-80, Iowa City exit to route 1, south to Fairfield. Site is located 75 miles south of Cedar Rapids, Iowa.

*Coupon available, see coupon section.

[P] 🚌 ✳ 📷 ⍜ M TRAIN 🚂

Site Address: 700 W. Grimes, Fairfield, IA
Mailing Address: 700 W. Grimes, Fairfield, IA 52556
Telephone: (515) 472-2020
Fax: (515) 472-6510
Internet: www.sover.net/~cthebodo/Caboose.html

Iowa, Mt. Pleasant

MIDWEST CENTRAL RAILROAD
Steam, irregular
36" gauge

SCOTT A. WILEY

Ride/Display: A one-mile steam train ride encircling the grounds of the Midwest Old Threshers Reunion. The all volunteere Midwest Central is a non-profit, educational organization dedicated to the preservation and operation of narrow gauge steam railroad equipment. The Midwest Old Threshers Reunion is the world's largest steam show, featuring over 100 acres of exhinits including steam and gas tractors, antique cars, stationary steam, gas engines, horse power, recreated villages, working craft shows, and more.

Schedule: May 24-25 and July 4-5: 10 a.m. to 5 p.m. September 3-7, 8:30 a.m. to 9:30 p.m.

Admission/Fare: Adults $2.00; children $1.00. Reunion–one day $7.00; five days $15.00.

Locomotive/Rolling Stock: 1891 Baldwin 2-6-0 Surrey, Sussex & Southhampton Railway no. 6; 1923 Lima three truck Shay, West Side Lumber no. 9; 1951 Henschel 0-4-0T no. 16; 1935 Vulcan gas mechanical switcher; three vintage speeders; five wooden coaches; wooden caboose; White Pass & Yukon steel caboose no. 903.

Special Events: Midwest Old Thresher's Reunion, September 3-7.

Location/Directions: Southeast Iowa.

Site Address: Mt. Pleasant, IA
Mailing Address: Box 102, Mt. Pleasant, IA 52641
Telephone: (319) 385-2912

Kansas, Abilene

ABILENE & SMOKY VALLEY RAILROAD
Diesel, scheduled
Standard gauge

Ride: A 1½-hour, 10-mile round trip through Smoky Hill River Valley from historic Abilene to Enterprise, Kansas. Crosses the Smoky Hill River on high steel span bridge.

Schedule: Memorial Day through Labor Day: Tuesdays through Sundays. May, September through October: weekends. Dinner train specials. Call or write for more information.

Admission/Fare: Adults $7.50; children 3-11 $5.50. Dinner train prices vary. All prices subject to change without notice.

Locomotive/Rolling Stock: 1945 Alco S1; 1945 GE 44-ton; 1945 Whitcomb 45-ton side-rod; more.

Special Events: Abilene–Chisholm Trail Day, Saturday of first full weekend in October. Enterprise–Old Settlers Day, first weekend in May. Easter Bunny Train. Santa Claus Train. Call or write for details.

Nearby Attractions/Accommodations: Eisenhower Center Dickinson County Heritage Center, C.W. Parker Carousel, Greyhound Hall of Fame, Great Plains Theater Festival, Abilene Community Theater.

Location/Directions: I-70 exit 275, south 2 miles on K-15 (Buckeye Street). Park in lot west of Eisenhower Center. (Shared lot with Greyhound HF).

*Coupon available, see coupon section.

Site Address: 417 S. Buckeye, Abilene, KS
Mailing Address: PO Box 744, Abilene, KS 67410
Telephone: (785) 263-1077 and (888) 426-6687
Fax: (785) 263-1066
Internet: www.ukans.edu/heritage/abilene/asvra.html

Kansas, Baldwin City

MIDLAND RAILWAY
Diesel, scheduled
Standard gauge

E. N. GRIFFIN

Ride: This line was constructed in 1867 as the Leavenworth, Lawrence & Galveston, the first railroad south of the Kansas River. The Midland Railway, which began service in 1987 as Kansas's first excursion railway, is an intrastate common-carrier railroad. The 7-mile round trip to "Nowhere" passes through scenic eastern Kansas rolling farmland and woods and crosses a 250-foot wooden trestle.

Displays/Exhibits: Railroad equipment, photos, and memorabilia, including photographs of two U.S. presidents arriving in Baldwin.

Schedule: May 17-October 26: weekends and holidays, 11:30 a.m., 1:30 & 3:00 p.m. (subject to change).

Admission/Fare: Adults $5.50, children (4-12) $2.50, children under 4 ride free. All-day fare, $8.00 (4 and older). Discounts for groups of 25 or more.

Locomotives/Rolling Stock: No. 524, 1946 EMD NW2, former Chicago, Burlington & Quincy; No. 142, 1950/59 Alco/EMD RS-3, former Missouri-Kansas-Texas; and more.

Special Events: Hobo Days, August 16-17. Maple Leaf Festival, October 18-19. Halloween Train, October 24, 25, 26. Railfans Weekend, TBA.

Location/Directions: About 30 miles southwest of Kansas City on U.S. 56 at the 1906 former AT&SF depot, 1515 High Street, 7 blocks west of downtown.

Lawrence   **Radio Freqency:** 161.055

Site Address: Baldwin City, Kansas
Mailing Address: PO Box 412, Baldwin City, KS 66006
Telephone: (785) 594-6982

Kansas, Ellis　　　　　　　　　　　　　　　　**ELLIS RAILROAD MUSEUM**

Museum: A museum of railroad memorabilia and an HO gauge model railroad layout 22 x 24 feet. Also, a miniature railroad train ride covering about 1¼-miles.

Schedule: Year round: Mondays through Fridays, 9 a.m. to 5 p.m. Saturdays, 11 a.m. to 5 p.m. Sundays, 1 to 5 p.m.

Admission/Fare: Adults $2.00; children 5-12 $1.00; under age 4 are free with adult.

Special Events: Railroad Days, August.

Nearby Attractions/Accommodations: Union Pacific Depot, Union Pacific Caboose.

Location/Directions: I-70 exit 145, south to museum.

Site Address: 911 Washington, Ellis, KS
Mailing Address: Box 82, Ellis, KS 67637
Telephone: (785) 726-4493
Fax: (785) 726-3294

Kansas, Wichita

GREAT PLAINS TRANSPORTATION MUSEUM, INC.
Railway museum

L. L. CLERICO

Museum: The museum was established in 1985 with the help of the local National Railway Historical Society chapter to preserve and display transportation history as it relates to Kansas. The museum is one of the sponsors of the annual Air Capital Train Show. A former ATSF 3768 is the highlight of our outdoor display. The indoor display is housed in a former railroad hotel that is currently being remodeled.

Schedule: Year round: Saturdays, 9 a.m. to 4 p.m. April through October: Sundays, 1 to 4 p.m. Closed Christmas and New Year's Day.

Admission/Fare: Adults $2.50; children 5-12 $1.50. Group rates available.

Locomotive/Rolling Stock: 4-8-4 No. 3768, former Atchison, Topeka & Santa Fe; electric No. 603, former Kansas Gas & Electric; NW2 diesel-electric No. 421, former Burlington Northern; Whitcomb 30-ton No. 3819, former Mobil Oil; heavyweight baggage car, former AT&SF.

Location/Directions: Union Station Complex, upper level.

Site Address: 700 E. Douglas Avenue, Wichita, KS (upper level)
Mailing Address: Box 2017C, Wichita, KS 67201
Telephone: (316) 263-0944

Kentucky, Bardstown   **MY OLD KENTUCKY DINNER TRAIN**
Diesel, electric, scheduled

Ride: Travel 35 miles in another era on board a 1940s dining car while enjoying delicious meals at lunch or dinner.

Schedule: Year round: schedule varies, call or write for details.

Admission/Fare: Varies/seasonal.

Locomotive/Rolling Stock: Two FP7A units; GP7 locomotive; three Budd dining cars; Budd kitchen car.

Special Events: Valentine's Day, Mother's Day, Thanksgiving, New Year's Eve, Mardi Gras.

Nearby Attractions/Accommodations: My Old Kentucky Home, Stephen Foster–The Musical, Jim Beam, several bed & breakfasts and hotels.

Location/Directions: Site is 32 miles from Louisville via I-65 and 60 miles from Lexington via Bluegrass Parkway.

Site Address: 602 N. Third Street, Bardstown, KY
Mailing Address: PO Box 279, Bardstown, KY 40004
Telephone: (502) 348-7300
Fax: (502) 348-7780

Kentucky, Hardin
HARDIN SOUTHERN RAILROAD
Diesel, scheduled

HARDIN SOUTHERN RAILROAD

Ride: This line is a working common-carrier railroad offering seasonal *Nostalgia Train* passenger service for a 2-hour, 18-mile journey to the past. Built in 1890, the railroad was once a portion of the Nashville, Chattanooga & St. Louis Railway's Paducah main line through the Jackson Purchase in western Kentucky. The railroad is a designated Kentucky State Landmark. Today's trip features the rural farms and lush forests of the Clarks River Valley.

Schedule: May 25 through October 31: weekends, midday and late afternoon.

Admission/Fare: Adults $9.75; children 3-12 $6.00. Tour, group, and charter rates available.

Locomotive/Rolling Stock: No. 863, 1940 Electro-Motive Corporation SW1, former Milwaukee Road; one of the oldest examples of this model still in common-carrier service.

Special Events: Easter, Mother's Day, Halloween, Christmas.

Nearby Attractions/Accommodations: Land Between the Lakes National Recreation Area.

Location/Directions: In western Kentucky, southeast of Paducah via I-24 and state route 641; 6 miles from the Tennessee Valley Authority's Land Between the Lakes National Recreation Area. Hardin is located at juction of routes 641/80. Depot is on route 80 in the center of town.

Site Address: Hardin, KY
Mailing Address: PO Box 20, Hardin, KY 42048
Telephone: (502) 437-4555
E-mail: office@hsrr.com
Internet: www.hsrr.com

Kentucky, New Haven

KENTUCKY RAILWAY MUSEUM
Railway museum
Standard gauge

ELMER KAPPELL

Museum/Ride: Steam alternates weekends with diesel on a 20-mile, 1½-hour round trip through scenic Rolling Fork River Valley, from nostalgic New Haven to Boston, Kentucky. Ride over former Louisville & Nashville trackage. Our new brick depot is a replica of the original NH depot complete with station master's office, from the 1930s. See more than 5,000 square feet of artifacts depicting Kentucky's railroad history.

Schedule: Museum–year round: daily. Train–April, May, September through November: weekends. June through August: Tuesdays through Sundays. Call or write for hours. Group tours by appointment.

Admission/Fare: Call or write for information.

Locomotive/Rolling Stock: No. 152, 1905 Rogers 4-6-2 no. 152, EMD E3 no. 770 (first diesel for the *Pan-American*), and 1925 Alco 0-8-0 no. 2152, all former L&N; former L&N and other open and closed window cars; diner "Kentucky Colonel," former Southern Pacific; Pullman solarium-lounge "Mt. Broderick"; 1910 Jackson & Sharp, "Itsuitsme," former Bangor & Aroostook no. 100.

Special Events: Kentucky Home Coming Festival, May 30-June 6. Murder Mystery Weekend, fall. Rolling Fork Iron Horse Festival, September 12. Kentucky Bourbon Festival, September 19. Halloween. Christmas.

Location/Directions: I-65 exit 112 to Bardstown, then U.S. 31E south.

Site Address: 136 South Main Street, New Haven, KY
Mailing Address: PO Box 240, New Haven, KY 40051
Telephone: (502) 549-5470 and (800) 272-0152
Fax: (502) 549-5472
Internet: www.rrhistorical.com/krm/

Kentucky, Paris

KENTUCKY CENTRAL RAILWAY
Steam, unscheduled
Standard gauge

RUTH ANN COMBS

Display/Ride: The Kentucky Central Railway is operated by the Kentucky Central Chapter of the National Railway Historical Society. Trips typically originate in Paris and run to Carlisle, Ewing, or Maysville. The 50-mile "Bluegrass Route," now operated by the Transkentucky Transportation Railroad, was part of the original Kentucky Central Railway, which later became part of the Louisville & Nashville Railroad. It passes through some of Kentucky's most beautiful horse farms and through two tunnels.

Schedule: Call or write for information.

Admission/Fare: To be announced.

Locomotive/Rolling Stock: 1925 Baldwin 2-6-2, former Reader no. 11; no. 9, VO, 1000 Baldwin diesel, former LaSalle & Bureau County Railroad; three coaches, former Erie Lackawanna; KCR no. 1, former Southern Railway concession/observation car; bay-window caboose no. 225, former Southern Railway; caboose no. 904055, former Baltimore & Ohio.

Special Events: To be announced.

Nearby Attractions/Accommodations: Kentucky Horse Park, Claiborn Farm.

Location/Directions: U.S. 460 E (North Middletown Rd.)

[P] 🚌 ✳ 👤 ⬜ M TRAIN

Site Address: U.S. 460 East, North Middletown Rd., Paris, KY
Mailing Address: 1749 Bahama Rd., Lexington, KY 40509
Telephone: (606) 293-0807

Kentucky, Stearns **BIG SOUTH FORK SCENIC RAILWAY**
Diesel, scheduled
Standard gauge

BIG SOUTH FORK SCENIC RAILWAY

Display/Ride: Interpretive exhibits at the Blue Heron Mining Community tell the stories of miners and their families living and working in the mining camp. Passengers enjoy a trip reminiscent of rail travel in the early 1900s as the Big South Fork Scenic takes them through the gorge area near Roaring Paunch Creek. The 3-hour ride features a 1½-hour stop at the restored mining community of Blue Heron, where oral interpretations are offered.

Schedule: May 1 through October 31: Wednesday through Friday, 10 a.m.; weekends, 10 a.m. and 2 p.m.

Admission/Fare: Adults $10.00; seniors $9.50; children $5.00.

Locomotive/Rolling Stock: Nos. 102 and 105, 1942 Alcos; open cars; caboose.

Special Events: To be announced.

Location/Directions: U.S. 460 East (North Middletown Road).

Cincinnati, OH and Maysville, KY

Site Address: Stearns, KY
Mailing Address: Box 68, Stearns, KY 42647
Telephone: (606) 376-5330 and (800) GO-ALONG
Fax: (606) 376-5332

Kentucky, Versailles

BLUEGRASS RAILROAD MUSEUM
Diesel, scheduled
Standard gauge

BLUEGRASS RAILROAD MUSEUM

Display/Ride: The museum was founded in 1976 and includes displays of limestone sills from the Lexington & Ohio Railroad, built 1831-1835; an air-conditioned display car housing railroad artifacts; "Duncan Tavern" diner car; baggage express car; and caboose, former Southern Railway. The ride offers a 1½-hour, 11½-mile round trip through Kentucky's famed horse country. The trip includes a stop to view the Kentucky River Palisades and the 104-year-old Louisville Southern Railroad's "Young High Bridge," which is 281 feet high and 1,659 feet long.

Schedule: Early May through late October: Saturdays, 10:30 a.m., 1:30 and 3:30 p.m. Sundays, 1:30 and 3:30 p.m.

Admission/Fare: Adults $7.00; seniors $6.00; children 2-12 $4.00; under age 2 ride free unless occupying a seat. Prices may increase during special events.

Locomotive/Rolling Stock: 1953 Alco MRS-1s nos. 2043, 2086, and 1849; Fairbanks Morse H12-44, former U.S Army.

Special Events: Halloween Ghost Train, Santa Express, Hobo Days, Clown Days, and train robberies. Write for complete listing.

Location/Directions: Woodford County Park, U.S. 62 (Tyrone Pike).

P 🚌 ❄ ☕ 🚻 ✉ M arm TRAIN
Radio frequency: 160.275

Site Address: Versailles, Kentucky
Mailing Address: PO Box 27, Versailles, KY 40383
Telephone: (606) 873-2476

Louisiana, DeQuincy

DEQUINCY RAILROAD MUSEUM
Railway museum

DEQUINCY RAILROAD MUEUM

Display: Nestled among tall pines at the beginning of Louisiana's foothills in north Calcasieu County, the city of DeQuincy was at the intersection of two major railroads in 1895. Its turn-of-the-century beginnings have been preserved, including two major historical landmarks—the All Saints Episcopal Church and the Kansas City Southern Railroad Depot. Both structures are on the National Register of Historic Places, and the depot now houses the railroad museum. A 1913 steam locomotive; vintage caboose; passenger coach; a host of railroad artifacts.

Schedule: Year round: Mondays through Fridays, 9 a.m. to 4 p.m. and weekends, 1 to 4 p.m.

Admission/Fare: $10.00.

Locomotive/Rolling Stock: Vintage caboose; steam engine no. 124; passenger coach.

Special Events: Louisiana Railroad Days, second weekend of April.

Nearby Attractions/Accommodations: Lake Charles, Casino gambling boats.

Location/Directions: I-10 exit at DeQuincy, Louisana 12, Louisiana 27 (27 runs parallel to I-10).

Site Address: Lake Charles Avenue and Main Street, DeQuincy, LA
Mailing Address: PO Box 997, DeQuincy, LA 70633
Telephone: (318) 786-2823 and (318) 786-7113

Louisiana, Gretna   **LOUISIANA STATE RAILROAD MUSEUM**

GRETNA HISTORICAL SOCIETY

Museum: Railroad artifacts, library, an HO layout and coin-operated HO. The Gretna Station was the starting point of all Texas-Pacific rails going west and northwest of the Mississippi River. Passengers boarded in New Orleans, the cars were ferried across the river and assembled into the train at Gretna Station. The station is restored to its 1905 appearance.

Schedule: Year round: Mondays through Fridays, 10 a.m. to 3 p.m. and usually on Saturdays. Call to confirm.

Admission/Fare: Adults $1.50; seniors, students, children $1.00; family $5.00 maxium.

Locomotive/Rolling Stock: In Mel Ott Park (½ mile away): Porter compressed air compound locomotive and box-cab electric locomotive; special-built cradle car to deliver canisters of ammonia used to manufacture ice.

Special Events: Louisiana Railroad Festival, November. Mardi Gras celebration. Call or write for information.

Nearby Attractions/Accommodations: New Orlean Vieux Carre, Cabildo, Museum of Art.

Location/Directions: Fifteen minutes from downtown New Orleans. Over bridge on Bus. 90 west, exit 7 (Lafayette St.), continue two blocks past light, right on Huey P. Long Avenue to 3rd Street.

New Orleans

Site Address: 3rd Street & Huey P. Long Avenue, Gretna, LA
Mailing Address: PO Box 8412, New Orleans, LA 70182
Telephone: (504) 283-8091

**Maine, Alna
(Sheepscot Station)**

**WISCASSET, WATERVILLE &
FARMINGTON RAILWAY MUSEUM**
*Diesel, scheduled
24" gauge*

BRUCE N. WILSON

Museum/Ride: Ride a restored flatcar hauled by Brookville gas-mechanical 1½-ton engine, formerly SR&RL. Model T inspection car operates on special occassions. Museum of the narrow gauge railway.

Schedule: Year round: Saturdays, 9 a.m. to 5 p.m. Memorial Day through Labor Day: Sundays, 12 to 5 p.m.

Admission/Fare: Donations appreciated.

Locomotive/Rolling Stock: 1891 Portland Co. steam locomotive no. 9; boxcar no. 309; flatcar no. 118.

Special Events: Annual picnic, second Saturday in August.

Nearby Attractions/Accommodations: Maine Coast Railroad, Boothbay Railway Village, Maine Narrow Gauge Railroad Co. and Museum.

Location/Directions: Four miles north of Wiscasset on route 218, left to Crossroad.

Site Address: 97 Crossroad, Alna, ME
Mailing Address: 103 Crossroad, Alna, ME 04535-3401
Telephone: (207) 882-6897

Maine, Boothbay

BOOTHBAY RAILWAY VILLAGE
Steam, scheduled
24" gauge

ROSS EDWARDS

Museum/Ride: Ride a coal-fired, narrow gauge train through woods and a covered bridge, around a recreated village. View an exceptional antique vehicle exhibit and restored railroad structures and other buildings.

Schedule: June 13 through October 11: daily, 9:30 a.m. to 5 p.m. Train rides every half hour. September through October, train runs hourly.

Admission/Fare: Adults $6.00; children $3.00; under age 2 are free. Group rates.

Locomotive/Rolling Stock: Locomotives: 1913, 1934, 1938 Henschels; Baldwin Plymouth locomotive; Ford Model T inspection car; rolling stock.

Special Events: Antique Engine Meet, first weekend in July. Antique Auto Days and Auction, third weekend in July. Maine Narrow Gauge Day, third Sunday in September. Columbus Day Weekend Craft Fair.

Nearby Attractions/Accommodations: Boothbay Harbor, restaurants, lodging, boat rides.

Location/Directions: On State Route 27, 8 miles from route 1.

Site Address: Route 27, Boothbay, ME
Mailing Address: PO Box 123, Boothbay, ME 04538
Telephone: (207) 633-4727
Fax: (207) 633-4733 (call first)
E-mail: railvill@lincoln.midcoast.com
Internet: lincoln.midcoast.com/~railvill

Maine, Fort Fairfield

FORT FAIRFIELD RAILROAD MUSEUM
Motor car, railroad display, museum, irregular
Standard gauge

BRUCE NETT

Ride/Display: An 8-mile, 25-minute round trip. Motor car rides on former Bangor & Aroostook tracks. Former CP station a CP caboose with numerous artifacts. Mockup of CP diesel locomotive cab. ½ mile away at former BAR station we have a former CP sleeping car built in 1921 and converted to an outfit car in 1965. We restored it to a dining car open only for special occasions. Also a CP diesel, a boxcar and a BAR reefer.

Schedule: Weekends and other times by appointment.

Admission/Fare: Call or write for information.

Locomotive/Rolling Stock: CP RS-23 diesel (shell); CN caboose; BAR reefer; CAR/CP boxcar.

Special Events: Maine Potato Blossom Festival 3rd weekend in July.

Location/Directions: Along Main Street in town.

  [&] [P] ✱ ✉ M

Site Address: Fort Fairfield, MA
Mailing Address: Box 269, Fort Fairfield, MA 04742
Telephone: (207) 473-4045

Maine, Kennebunkport

SEASHORE TROLLEY MUSEUM
Electric, scheduled
Standard gauge

CHARLES WOOLNOUGH

Display: A 3¾-mile round trip takes passengers over the former Atlantic Shore Line interurban right-of-way, where they can experience the trolley era through the "National Collection" spanning a century of mass-transit vehicles.

Schedule: Times indicated are: opening time/time of last ride. Museum store open one hour past last departure. May 1-24: weekdays, 12/1:30 p.m.; weekends, 11 a.m./3:30 p.m. May 25-27 (Memorial Day Weekend): daily 11 a.m./4:30 p.m. May 28-June 30: weekdays, 11 a.m./3:30 p.m.; weekends, 11 a.m./4:30 p.m. July 1-September 2: daily, 10 a.m./5:30 p.m. July 24-August 28 (Wed. only):Ice Cream Night at 7:30 p.m. September 3-October 14: weekdays, 10 a.m./3:30 p.m.; weekends, 10 a.m./4:30 p.m. October 15-November 15 (weather permitting): weekdays, by chance or appointment; weekends, 11 a.m./3:30 p.m. Other times by appointment.

Admission/Fare: Adults $7.00; seniors $5.00; children (6-16) $4.00; family pass $25.00. Group rates: Adult $4.50; children (6-16) $3.00. Special admission prices, special events, call for specific information.

Location/Directions: 1.5 miles off U.S. Route 1, 3 miles north of Kennebunkport, and 20 miles south of Portland. Short distance from exits 3 and 4 of the Maine Turnpike.

*Coupon available, see coupon section.

Site Address: 195 Log Cabin Road, Kennebunkport, ME
Mailing Address: PO Box A, Kennebunkport, ME 04046-1690
Telephone: (207) 967-2800 and (207) 967-2712
Internet: http://www.biddeford.com/trolley

Maine, Phillips

SANDY RIVER RAIL ROAD MUSEUM DIVISION
PHILLIPS HISTORICAL SOCIETY

Railway museum, gas replica of steam
24" gauge

CHRIS COYLE

Display: Ride on original roadbed in a restored coach and caboose powered by a replica of SR&RL no. 4. Take a trip back in time as you visit our roundhouse and view our roster.

Schedule: Train–June through September: first and third Sundays. October: first Sunday. 10 a.m. to 3 p.m. Museum–tours by appointment.

Admission/Fare: Train–adults $3.00; seniors and children to age 12 $2.00; under age 5 are free with adult.

Locomotive/Rolling Stock: No. 4 replica; coaches nos. 5 and 6; five boxcars; two cabooses nos. 556 and 558; flatcar; toolcar; flanger; two Brookvilles; Plymouth.

Special Events: Old Home Days, August 15-17. Fall Foliage Days.

Nearby Attractions/Accommodations: Stanley Museum Kingfield, Eastman Park and Small Falls. The Elcourt Bed and Breakfast.

Location/Directions: Located 18 miles north of Farmington on route 4.

Site Address: Bridge Hill Road, Phillips, ME
Mailing Address: PO Box B, Phillips, ME 04966
Telephone: (207) 639-3352
Fax: (207) 639-2553

Maine, Portland

MAINE NARROW GAUGE RAILROAD COMPANY AND MUSEUM
Steam, diesel, scheduled
24" gauge

J.E. LANCASTER

Museum/Ride: A two-foot gauge train takes passengers on a 3-mile round trip along Casco Bay.

Schedule: February 15 through May 15 and October 15 through December 11: weekends. May 16 through October 14 and December 11 through January 1: daily. Also all Maine and New Hampshire school vacation weeks.

Admission/Fare: Train–adults $5.00; children $3.00. Museum–free.

Locomotive/Rolling Stock: No. 3, 1913 Vulcan 0-4-4T; no. 4, 1918 Vulcan 0-4-4T, former Monson; no. 8, 1924 Baldwin 2-4-4T, former B&SR; no. 1, 1949 General Electric B-B diesel; circa 1890 coaches nos. 4, 19 & 20 and Combine no. 14, former SR&RL; coaches nos. 15, 16 & 18, former B&SR; replica coaches, excursion cars, former Edaville; railbus no. 4, Model T track car and cabooses nos. 551, 553 & 557, former SR&RL; tank cars nos. 21 & 22, flanger no. 40; snowplow no. 2, boxcars, all former B&SR.

Special Events: Railfair, Father's Day. Call or write for others.

Nearby Attractions/Accommodations: Old Port shopping area, tour boats, ferry terminal, restaurants.

Location/Directions: Off Franklin Arterial, U.S. route 1A.

Site Address: 58 Fore Street, Portland, ME
Mailing Address: 58 Fore Street, Portland, ME 04101
Telephone: (207) 828-0814
Fax: (207) 774-7835

Maryland, Baltimore	THE B&O RAILROAD MUSEUM
	Railway museum
	Steam scheduled, irregular
	Standard gauge

THE B&O RAILROAD MUSEUM

Museum/Ride: The B&O Railroad Museum's collection of locomotives, cars, artifacts, and archives originated as an exhibit at the 1893 Columbian Exposition in Chicago. A variety of equipment and interpretive exhibits, model railroads, toy-train exhibits, railroad artifacts are displayed, including 48 locomotives, 146 cars and 20 miscellaneous vehicles. Buildings include the 1851 Mt. Clare Station, the 1884 Annex Building, the 1884 covered passenger-car roundhouse, and a large 1870 car shop currently used for equipment storage. Excursion trains depart Mt. Clare Station for a 3-mile round trip over the first mainline in America.

Schedule: Museum: daily, 10 a.m. to 5 p.m. Closed major holidays. Train: weekends.

Admission/Fare: Museum admission: adults $6.50; seniors $5.50; students 3-12 $4.00; children age 2 and under are free. Train fare: $2.00; children 2 and under are free. Group rates are available.

Locomotive/Rolling Stock: Numerous; call or write for information.

Special Events: All Aboard Days, April and September.

Nearby Attractions/Accommodations: Oriole Park, Babe Ruth Museum.

Location/Directions: Pratt and Poppleton Streets, 10 blocks west of the Inner Harbor.

*Coupon available, see coupon section.

Site Address: 901 W. Pratt Street, Baltimore, MD
Mailing Address: 901 W. Pratt Street, Baltimore, MD 21223-2699
Telephone: (410) 752-2490
Fax: (410) 752-2499
E-mail: webinfo@borail.org
Internet: www.borail.org

Maryland, Baltimore

BALTIMORE STREETCAR MUSEUM
Electric, scheduled
5'4½" gauge

ANDREW S. BLUMBERG

Museum: Re-live rail transit in the city of Baltimore from 1859 to 1963 through a 13-car collection (11 electric, 2 horse-drawn). Cars operate over 1¼-mile round trip package. The Vistor Center contains displays and a video presentation.

Schedule: June 1 thorugh October 31: weekends. November 1 through May 31: Sundays. 12 to 5 p.m.

Admission/Fare: Adults $5.00; seniors and children 4-11 $2.50; family $15.00 maximum.

Locomotive/Rolling Stock: No. 554, 1896 single-truck summer car, no. 1050, 1898 single-truck closed car and no. 264, 1900 convertible car, all Brownell Car Co.; no. 1164, 1902 double-truck summer car, no. 3828, 1902 double-truck closed car and no. 6119, 1930 Peter Witt car, all J.G. Brill Co.; no. 7407, 1944 Pullman-Standard PCC car.

Special Events: Mother's, Father's, and Grandparent's Days. Museum Birthday Celebration. Antique Auto Meets. Dixieland Concert. Tinsel Trolley, December. Call or write for more information.

Nearby Attractions/Accommodations: B&O Railroad Museum, Baltimore Museum of Industry, Maryland Science Center, National Aquarium.

Location/Directions: From Maryland and LaFayette Avenues, one block west on LaFayette to Falls.

Site Address: 1901 Falls Road, Baltimore, MD
Mailing Address: PO Box 4881, Baltimore, MD 21211
Telephone: (410) 547-0264 and (410) 298-5034 (Groups only)
Fax: (410) 547-0264
Internet: www.baltimor@news.com/streetcar/

Maryland, Chesapeake Beach

CHESAPEAKE BEACH RAILWAY MUSEUM
Railway museum
Standard gauge

CHESAPEAKE BEACH RAILWAY MUSEUM

Museum: The CBRM preserves and interprets the history of the Chesapeake Beach Railway, which brought people from Washington, D.C. to the resorts of Chesapeake Beach and North Beach from 1900 until 1935. The museum exhibits photographs and artifacts from the days of the railroad and resort, including photos of the steamships that brought visitors from Baltimore.

Schedule: May 1 through September 30: daily, 1 to 4 p.m. April and October: weekends only. By appointment at all other times.

Admission/Fare: Free.

Locomotive/Rolling Stock: The CBR chair car "Dolores" is undergoing restoration by the museum staff and volunteers. Only one half of "Dolores" survives; it is the only known CBR rolling stock to survive.

Special Events: Annual Right of Way Hike, April 4 or raindate of April 11. Antique Vehicle Show, May, 17. Bay Breeze Summer Program Series, June through mid-August, second Thursdays. Children's Summer Program Series, June through mid-August, Thursdays. Christmas Open House, December 6.

Nearby Attractions/Accommodations: Chesapeake Beach Water Park, Breezy Point Beach & Campground, restaurants, antique/arts & crafts.

Location/Directions: From Washington's Capital Beltway–I-95 to route 4 south. From Baltimore Beltway–I-695 to route 301 south to route 4 south. Left on route 260, right on route 261 to museum.

Site Address: 4155 Mears Avenue, Chesapeake Beach, MD
Mailing Address: PO Box 783, Chesapeake Beach, MD 20732
Telephone: (410) 257-3892

Maryland, Cumberland

WESTERN MARYLAND SCENIC RAILROAD
Steam, diesel, scheduled
Standard gauge

Ride: Take a 32-mile roundtrip from Cumberland to Frostburg, climbing 1,300 feet with grades of 2.8 percent through three horseshoe curves and a 900-foot tunnel. Layover at historic C&P Rail Depot.

Schedule: May through December: Tuesday through Sunday. May through September departs at 11:30 a.m. October departs at 11 a.m. and 4 p.m. on Friday through Sunday.

Admission/Fare: May through September: adults $16.00; seniors $14.50; children 12 and under $9.75. October through December: adults $18.00; seniors $17.50; children $10.75. Group rates available.

Locomotive/Rolling Stock: Atlantic Coastline no. 850; Florida East Coast no. 851; Pennsylvania Railroad diner no. 1155; Central of Georgia combine no. 726; Norfolk & Western coach no. 540; two Southern coaches nos. 844 and 845; Seaboard coach no. 846; Union Pacific coach no. 2001; Santa Fe coach no. 1504; two Long Island coaches nos. 876 and 880; miscellaneous coaches and freight cars.

Special Events: Maryland Rail Fest, first weekend in October; Murder Mystery Train; Dinner Trains; Santa Express.

Nearby Attractions/Accommodations: Holiday Inn, Best Western, Comfort Inn, several bed & breakfasts, Rocky Gap State Park.

Location/Directions: I-68, exit 43C to Harrison Street to station.

Site Address: Cumberland, MD
Mailing Address: 13 Canal Street, Cumberland, MD 21502
Telephone: (301) 759-4400 or (800) 872-4650
Fax: (301) 759-1329
E-mail: trainmaster@miworld
Internet: www.wmsr.com

Maryland, Union Bridge

WESTERN MARYLAND RAILWAY HISTORICAL SOCIETY, INC.
Railroad museum

WESTERN MARYLAND AND RAILWAY HISTORICAL SOCIETY, INC.

Display: The Western Maryland Railway Historical Society was founded in 1967 to preserve the heritage of the WM, now part of CSX. It has established a museum in the former general office building of the railway at Union Bridge, next to the Maryland Midland station. On exhibit are Western Maryland artifacts and an N scale model railroad. The museum includes a library and an archives collection which are available for research by appointment.

Schedule: Call or write for information.

Admission/Fare: Donations appreciated.

Location/Directions: On Main Street (State Route 75) at railroad tracks.

Site Address: Main Street, Union Bridge, MD
Mailing Address: 8600 Midi Avenue, Baltimore, MD 21234-4011
Telephone: (410) 668-4349

Maryland, Walkersville

WALKERSVILLE SOUTHERN RAILROAD
Diesel & gasoline, scheduled
Standard gauge

PAUL J. BERGDOLT

Ride: An 8-mile, one-hour round trip through the woods and rural farm country north of Frederick, Maryland.

Schedule: May through October: Saturdays and Sundays, departs at 11 a.m., 1 and 3 p.m. Also Memorial Day, July 4th, and Labor Day.

Admission/Fare: Adults $7.00; children 3-12 $3.50; under age 3 ride free unless occupying a seat.

Locomotive/Rolling Stock: Plymouth 0-4-0 no. 1; Davenport 0-4-0 no. 2; converted flatcar no. 11; coach no. 12, former troop sleeper; caboose no. 2827, former Wabash.

Special Events: Saturday Evening Mystery Trains, Father's and Mother's Day special, Zoo Choo Trains, Nature Trains, Ghost Trains, Santa Claus Specials. Call for details.

Nearby Attractions/Accommodations: Catoctin Mountain Zoological Park in Thurmont, Maryland.

Location/Directions: Two miles east on Biggs Ford Road, off U.S. Route 15, three miles north of Frederick. Located 50 miles west of Baltimore and 50 miles northwest of Washington, D.C.

*Coupon available, see coupon section.

Radio frequency: 160.650 and 160.725

Site Address: 34 W. Pennsylvania Avenue, Walkersville, MD
Mailing Address: PO Box 651, Walkersville, MD 21793-0651
Telephone: (301) 898-0899
Fax: (703) 533-0433
Internet: www.angelfire.com/md/wsrr/index.html

Maryland, Wheaton

NATIONAL CAPITAL TROLLEY MUSEUM
Electric, scheduled
Standard gauge

LARRY VELTE

Museum/Ride: Visit "From Streetcars to Light Rail," a computer-based exhibit and "Radio Theater," recalling Glen Echo Amusement Park. Take a 1¼-mile, 20-minute round trip in Northwest Branch Park on cars selected from the museum's collection of 15 streetcars. Passengers board the trolleys at the Visitors Center Station.

Schedule: January 2 through November 30, Memorial Day, July 4, and Labor Day: weekends, 12 to 5 p.m. July and August: Wednesdays, 11 a.m. to 3 p.m. December 5-6, 12-13, 19-20, 26-27: 5 to 9 p.m.

Admission/Fare: Adults $2.50/5 rides $6.25; children 2-17 $2.00/5 rides $5.00; under age 2 are free.

Locomotive/Rolling Stock: DCTS 1101; CTCo 1053; TTC 4603; European trains; Washington work cars.

Special Events: Snow Sweeper Day, March 21. Trolley Spectacular, April 19. Fall Open House, October 18. Holly Trolley Fest, December.

Nearby Attractions/Accommodations: Brookside Gardens, Sandy Spring Museum, Marriott Courtyard.

Location/Directions: On Bonifant Road between Layhill Road (route 182) and New Hampshire Avenue (route 650), north of Wheaton.

*Coupon available, see coupon section.

Site Address: 1313 Bonifant Road, Silver Spring, MD
Mailing Address: 1313 Bonifant Road, Silver Spring, MD 20905
Telephone: (301) 384-6088
Fax: (301) 384-6352

Massachusetts, Beverly

WALKER TRANSPORTATION COLLECTION BEVERLY HISTORICAL SOCIETY & MUSEUM

Railway museum

WALKER TRANSPORTATION COLLECTION—O. C. LEONARD

Museum: A collection of over 100,000 photographs depicting all forms of transportation in New England. The majority of the collection is railroad and streetcar related. There are also models, memorabilia, library, videos, and oral history transcripts to view and browse.

Schedule: Year round: Wednesdays, 7 to 10 p.m. or by appointment. Closed the week between Christmas and New Year's.

Admission/Fare: $2.00.

Nearby Attractions/Accommodations: Balch House, Beverly. House of Seven Gables, Salem. Numerous hotels and motels.

Location/Directions: I-95 north or south to route 128 north, exit 22 onto route 62 east, to Cabot Street for one mile.

[♿] [P] [✷] [✉] M

Site Address: 117 Cabot Street, Beverly, MA
Mailing Address: 117 Cabot Street, Beverly, MA 01915
Telephone: (508) 922-1186
E-mail: fletcher@tiac.com
Internet: www.tiac.net/users/fletcher

Massachusetts, Fall River

OLD COLONY AND FALL RIVER RAILROAD MUSEUM
Railway museum
Standard gauge

DAVID SOUZA

Museum: The museum, located in railroad cars that include a renovated Pennsylvania Railroad coach, features artifacts of the Old Colony, New Haven, Penn Central, Conrail, and other New England lines.

Schedule: April 25 through June 20 and September 5 through December 5, weekends only: Saturdays, 10 a.m. to 4 p.m.; Sundays, 10 a.m. to 3 p.m. June 27 through September 4, daily: Sundays through Fridays, noon to 5 p.m.; Saturdays, 10 a.m. to 4 p.m.

Admission/Fare: Adults $2.00; seniors $1.50; children (5-12) $1.00; under age 5 are free. Group rates available.

Rolling Stock: Pennsylvania P-70 coach; No. 42 New Haven R.D.C. "Firestone"; New Haven 40' boxcar; New York City N7B caboose.

Special Events: Annual Railroad Show, third weekend in January; Fall River Celebrates America, mid-August.

Nearby Attractions/Accommodations: Battleship Cove (six warships on display), Marine Museum at Fall River, Heritage State Park, Fall River Carousel.

Location/Directions: The museum is located in a railroad yard at the corner of Central and Water Streets, across from the entrance to Battleship Cove.

*Coupon available, see coupon section.

Site Address: 2 Water Street, Fall River, MA
Mailing Address: PO Box 3455, Fall River, MA 02724
Telephone: (508) 674-9340
E-mail: railroadjc@aol.com

Massachusetts, Holyoke

HOLYOKE HERITAGE PARK RAILROAD, INC.
Diesel, scheduled
Standard gauge

Ride: Board restored antique coaches for a 20-mile trip through Holyoke's mill and canal district and scenic countryside.

Schedule: June through December: Sundays. Call or write for schedule.

Admission/Fare: Regular trips $7.00 to $10.00. Short trips $5.00 to $7.00. Special events $10.00 to $18.00.

Locomotive/Rolling Stock: CF7 diesel; two restored Erie Lackawanna coaches, 1915 and 1924.

Special Events: Narration on board, theme trips, musical and theatrical events, railfan trips.

Nearby Attractions/Accommodations: Holyoke Heritage State Park, Merry-Go-Round, Children's Museum, Volleyball Hall of Fame, Heritage Crafts.

Location/Directions: From Mass Pike, exit 4 (W. Springfield) to route 91 north, to exit 16; route 202 north to Appleton Street at ninth traffic lights, right on Appleton, through two lights to Heritage State Park on left.

Site Address: 221 Appleton Street, Holyoke, MA
Mailing Address: 221 Appleton Street, Holyoke, MA
Telephone: (413) 534-1723
Fax: (413) 534-1723
E-mail: lotspeic@javanet.com

Massachusetts, Hyannis

CAPE COD RAILROAD
Diesel, scheduled
Standard gauge

CAPE COD

Ride: The Cape Cod Railroad offers two-hour scenic excursions through the beauty of hidden Cape Cod. Trains depart from Hyannis Depot as well as Sandwich Station. The Cape Cod Dinner Train departs Hyannis Depot for a three-hour dining experience.

Schedule: April through May: weekends. June through October: Tuesdays through Sundays. 10 a.m., 12:30, and 3 p.m. Dinner Trains–February through December, evenings.

Admission/Fare: Adults $11.50; children $7.50; under age 3 are free. Dinner train–$41.86, reservation required. Senior discount. Group rates.

Locomotive/Rolling Stock: 1947 EMD F7 and F10, nos. 1100 and 1114, former Gulf, Mobile, Alabama; 1955 EMD GP9 no. 1789, former Burlington Northern.

Location/Directions: Hyannis Depot–corner of Main and Center Streets, Hyannis. Sandwich Station–Jarves Street off route 6A, Sandwich.

*Coupon available, see coupon section.

Site Address: 252 Main Street, Hyannis, MA
Mailing Address: 252 Main Street, Hyannis, MA 02601
Telephone: (508) 771-3788

Massachusetts, Lenox

BERKSHIRE SCENIC RAILWAY
Diesel, scheduled
Standard gauge

Ride/Museum: Fifteen-minute short shuttle train ride within Lenox Station yard, with narrative of Berkshire railroading and Lenox Station history. Locomotive cab tours for youngsters. The museum is in the restored Lenox station. Restored former New York, New Haven & Hartford NE-5 caboose; Fairmont speeder and track-gang train; displays about Berkshire railroading history; railroad videos; two model railroads.

Schedule: May through October: weekends and holidays, 10 a.m. to 4 p.m. Lenox local shuttle trains operate half-hourly.

Admission/Fare: Adults $2.00; seniors and children under age 14 $1.50.

Locomotive/Rolling Stock: Diesel engines; passenger cars.

Nearby Attractions/Accommodations: Tanglewood, summer home of the Boston Symphony Orchestra.

Location/Directions: U.S. 7/20 to Housatonic Street, travel east 1½ miles.

Site Address: Willow Creek Road, Lenox, MA
Mailing Address: PO Box 2195, Lenox, MA 01240
Telephone: (413) 637-2210
E-mail: W1sexton@taconic.net

Massachusetts, Lowell

LOWELL NATIONAL HISTORICAL PARK
Electric, scheduled
Standard gauge

JAMES HIGGINS

Ride: Three turn-of-the-century replica trolleys transport visitors to Park sites including museums, exhibits, and canal boat tours.

Schedule: Year round: 9 a.m. to 5 p.m. Closed Thanksgiving, Christmas, and New Year's Day.

Admission/Fare: Free. Selected Park sites have admission fees.

Locomotive/Rolling Stock: Two open-car trolleys are reproductions of the 1597-1600 series J.G. Brill Co. trolleys; one closed reproduction of 4100 series St. Louis Car Co.

Special Events: Lowell Folk Festival, last full weekend in July. Numerous concerts and other special events.

Nearby Attractions/Accommodations: American Textile History Museum, New England Quilt Museum, New England Sports Museum.

Location/Directions: Take the Lowell Connector from either Route 495 (exit 35C) or Route 3 (exit 30N) to Thorndike Street (exit 5B). Follow signs.

Site Address: 246 Market Street, Lowell, MA
Mailing Address: 67 Kirk Street, Lowell, MA 01852
Telephone: (978) 970-5000 and (978) 970-5002 (TDD)
Fax: (978) 275-1762
Internet: www.nps.gov/lowe

Michigan, Blissfield	**ADRIAN & BLISSFIELD RAILROAD**
	Diesel, scheduled
	Standard gauge

ADRIAN & BLISSFIELD RAILROAD

Ride: This working, common-carrier freight and passenger railroad offers 14-mile, 1½-hour round trips from Blissfield to Lenawee Junction over a former New York Central line—the first railroad built west of the Allegheny Mountains and the oldest in the former Northwest Territory. The train travels through the village of Blissfield, crosses the River Raisin, and runs through Lenawee County farmland to Lenawee Junction. The "Old Road Dinner Train" is a 2- to 3-hour round trip featuring traditional, impeccable dining-car service including an elegant four-course dinner.

Schedule: Year round: call for information.

Admission/Fare: Adults $8.00; seniors $7.00; children 3-12 $5.00. Additional fare for dinner train. Group rates and charters available.

Locomotive/Rolling Stock: Nos. 1751 & 1752, 1957 EMD GP9s, former Grand Trunk Western/Central Vermont; no. 5197, 1937 *Canadian Flyer* coach, former Canadian National; no. 721; no. 3370, 1949 diner, former Union Pacific.

Special Events: Murder Mystery, Fall Color Tours, Ghost Train, and Santa Train.

Nearby Attractions/Accommodations: Michigan Speedway, Super 8, and Carlton Lodge.

Location/Directions: U.S. 223 and Depot Street. Ten miles west of exit 5 off U.S. 23 and 20 miles northwest of Toledo.

Site Address: 301 E. Adrian Street, Blissfield, MI
Mailing Address: PO Box 95, Blissfield, MI 49228
Telephone: (888) GO RAIL 1
Fax: (517) 263-2511
E-mail: abrrdp@tc3net.com
Internet: lenaweb.com/railroad

Michigan, Bridgeport | **JUNCTION VALLEY RAILROAD**
Diesel, scheduled
14 1/8" gauge

JUNCTION VALLEY RAILROAD

Ride/Display: The ride, more than 2 miles long, travels 22 feet down into a valley around a lake, over several bridges and trestles, through a 100-foot tunnel, playground, and a picnic area. Junction Valley Railroad is the "Largest Quarter-Size Railroad in the World." Railroad shops; 10-stall roundhouse with turntable; 17 railroad and 6 highway bridges; 30 buildings and stations; more than 865 feet of bridges and trestles; 100-foot tunnel; the only diamond-crossing trestle in the world.

Schedule: Mid-May through Labor Day: Mondays through Saturdays, 10 a.m. to 6 p.m. Sundays, 1 to 6 p.m. September through October 15: weekends, 1 to 5 p.m.

Admission/Fare: Adults $4.50; seniors $4.25; children $3.75. Special events fares are higher. Group rates available.

Locomotive/Rolling Stock: No. 1177 GP45; no. 333 SW1500; no. 4 Plymouth; no. 300 SW1500 booster unit; no. 5000 WS4A; no. 7000 WS4A; no. 6000 WS4B; no. 555 MP15. All are built ¼ size of their models.

Special Events: Opening Day balloon launch. Valley of Flags, July 4. Railroad Days, June 20-21, July 18-19, August 15-16. Halloween Spook Ride, October. Fantasyland Train Ride, December. Much more.

Location/Directions: Junction Valley Railroad is located just off I-75. Two miles south of Bridgeport exit, 5 miles west of historic Frankenmuth.

Site Address: 7065 Dixie Hwy., Bridgeport, MI
Mailing Address: 7065 Dixie Hwy., Bridgeport, MI 48722
Telephone: (517) 777-3480

Michigan, Clinton

SOUTHERN MICHIGAN RAILROAD SOCIETY
Diesel, scheduled
Standard gauge

Ride/Museum: Rides are offered over two portions of the former Clinton Branch of the New York Central. An indoor museum is open during passenger operations.

Schedule: June through September: roundtrips between Clinton and Tecumseh, Sundays, depart Clinton 11 a.m., 1 and 3 p.m. and depart Tecumseh noon and 2 p.m. September 26-27: shuttle trips between Clinton and Tecumseh for Clinton Fall Festival. October: Fall Color Tour weekends, depart Tecumseh 11 a.m., 1:30 and 4 p.m.

Admission/Fare: Adults $7.00; seniors $6.00; children 2-12 $4.00. Fall Tours: adults $10.00; seniors $8.00; children 2-12 $6.00. Children under 2 are free.

Locomotive/Rolling Stock: 1938 Plymouth no. 1, former Hayes Albion Corp.; Alco RS-1 diesel, former Ann Arbor; 1943 General Electric no. 75.

Special Events: Fall Color Tours, October. Call or write for brochure.

Nearby Attractions/Accommodations: Historic downtowns with many gift and antique shops, Clinton Inn Hotel, Tecumseh Inn, Stacy Mansion Bed & Breakfast, Hidden Lake Gardens, W.J. Hayes State Park.

Location/Directions: On U.S. 12, 25 miles southwest of Ann Arbor and 45 miles northwest of Toledo, Ohio. Museum: in Clinton on corner of Clark and Division Streets. Train: in Tecumseh board train at corner of Evan and Chicago Streets.

P 🚌 ✳ ☕ ✉ arm TRAIN 🚂 Ann Arbor M

Site Address: 320 S. Division Street, Clinton, MI
Mailing Address: PO Box K, Clinton, MI 49236-0009
Telephone: (517) 456-7677

Michigan, Coldwater and White Pigeon　　　**LITTLE RIVER RAILROAD**
Steam, scheduled
Standard gauge

LITTLE RIVER RAILROAD

Display: The Little River Railroad offers two round trips: a 10-mile, 80-minute ride from Coldwater to Batavia, and a 24-mile, 2½-hour ride from White Pigeon to Sturgis. Both trips run over tracks of the Michigan Southern Railroad.

Schedule: Call or write for information.

Admission/Fare: Call or write for information.

Locomotive/Rolling Stock: No. 110, 1911 Baldwin 4-6-2, former Little River Railroad—the smallest standard-gauge Pacific locomotive ever built; combination car no. 2594, former Chicago & Alton; *Hiawatha* coaches, former Milwaukee Road; open-air cars; World War II troop car; cabooses, former Baltimore & Ohio.

[P]

Site Address: 13187 SR 120, Middlebury, IN
Mailing Address: 13187 SR 120, Middlebury, IN 46540
Telephone: (219) 825-9182

Michigan, Dearborn

HENRY FORD MUSEUM AND GREENFIELD VILLAGE RAILROAD
Steam, scheduled
Standard gauge

E.J. GULASH

Ride/Display: The Greenfield Village Railroad offers a 2½-mile, 35-minute narrated circuit of the world-famous Greenfield Village in open-air passenger cars. Rides are also now offered in an authentic 75-year old caboose. While riding you will hear interpretations of the history of the village, its occupants and the railroad. The Henry Ford Museum, a general museum of American history occupying about 12 acres under one roof, contains a huge transportation collection, including the widely acclaimed "Automobile in American Life" exhibit. Greenfield Village is an 81-acre outdoor museum comprising more than 80 historic structures. Also at the site are 1941 Lima 2-6-6-6 No. 1601; a 1902 Schenectady 4-4-2; an 1858 Rogers 4-4-0; an 1893 replica of the "DeWitt Clinton"; 1909 Baldwin 2-8-0, former Bessemer & Lake Erie No. 154; a 1923 Canadian Pacific snowplow; a 1924 FGE reefer; and a 1925 Detroit, Toledo & Ironton caboose.

Schedule: Call or write for information.

Admission/Fare: Call or write for information.

Locomotive/Rolling Stock: No. 1, 1876 Ford Motor Co. 4-4-0 (rebuilt 1920s); no. 3, 1873 Mason-Fairlie 0-6-4T, former Calumet & Hecla Mining; no. 8, 1914 Baldwin 0-6-0, former Michigan Alkali Co.

Location/Directions: One-half mile south of U.S. 12 (Michigan Avenue) between Southfield Road and Oakwood Boulevard.

Dearborn

Site Address: Dearborn, MI
Mailing Address: PO Box 1970, Dearborn, MI 48121
Telephone: (313) 271-1620
Internet: www.hfmgv.org/index.html

Michigan, Detroit

DEPT. OF TRANSPORTATION VINTAGE TROLLEYS
Electric, scheduled

GAIL JONES

Ride: Operates along Washington Blvd. and Jefferson Ave. between the Renaissance Center and Grand Circus Park in downtown Detroit's central business district.

Schedule: Memorial Day through Labor Day: daily, 7:30 a.m. to 5:30 p.m.

Admission/Fare: 50 cents.

Locomotive/Rolling Stock: Seven closed; one open-air; one open-air double-decker; built 1895 to 1925 in England, Germany, Portugal, and the United States.

Special Events: Sports events, conventions, and festivals.

Nearby Attractions/Accommodations: New Tigers and Lions stadiums, theater district, lodging.

Location/Directions: I-75 to I-375 (Civic Center) to Jefferson and Washington Blvd.

P ✉

Site Address: 1551 Washington Blvd., Detroit, MI
Mailing Address: 1301 E. Warren Ave., Detroit, MI 48207
Telephone: (313) 933-1300 and (888) DDOT BUS
Fax: (313) 833-5523

Michigan, Durand

MICHIGAN RAILROAD HISTORY MUSEUM AT DURAND UNION STATION, INC.
Museum

JIM KNEER

Musuem: A preserved Union Station, historic displays, library, archives, gift shop, active Amtrak station, busy railroad junction.

Schedule: Year round: Tuesdays through Sundays, 1 to 5 p.m. except Easter, Thanksgiving, and Christmas.

Admission: Donations appreciated.

Locomotive/Rolling Stock: GTW caboose.

Special Events: Durand Railroad Days, model railroad flea market. Call or write for dates.

Nearby Attractions/Accommodations: Crossroads Village & Huckleberry Railroad in Flint.

Location/Directions: I-69 exit 118 between Flint and Lansing.

M

Site Address: 200 Railroad Street, Durand, MI
Mailing Address: PO Box 106, Durand, MI 48429
Telephone: (517) 288-3561
Fax: (517) 288-4114

Michigan, Elberta

SOCIETY FOR THE PRESERVATION OF THE S.S. *CITY OF MILWAUKEE*
Railway display

SOCIETY FOR THE PRESERVATION OF THE S.S. CITY OF MILWAUKEE

Display: The society was founded to preserve the last remaining railroad-car ferry in Betsie Bay. These ferries were an integral part of the community between 1892 and 1982, hauling railroad cars and passengers across Lake Michigan. SS *City of Milwaukee* represents the classic design created by the Manitowoc Shipbuilding Company; ships of the same class served the Ann Arbor, Pere Marquette/Chesapeake and Ohio, and Grand Trunk Western railroads.

Schedule: Tours are available by appointment. Call or write for information.

Admission/Fare: $5.00 for one day (special events; $10.00 individual annual membership; $25.00 family annual membership.

Locomotive/Rolling Stock: Car ferry; 1931 triple expansion steamer, capacity 22 50-foot railroad cars and 50 passengers and crew, former Ann Arbor, former Grand Trunk Western; five steel boxcars; more.

Special Events: Fireworks, July 4. Annual Meeting and Volunteer work sessions.

Nearby Attractions/Accommodations: SS *Badger* car ferry operating between Ludington, Michigan and Manitowoc, Wisconsin.

Location/Directions: Elberta is across Lake Betsie from Frankfort. From Manistee take M-22 North to Elberta. Follow M-168 West to the scenic overlook and railroad-car ferry historical marker.

[P] [✹] [◉] [⛪] [✉] M

Site Address: West terminus of M-168 at Elberta
Mailing Address: PO Box 506, Beulah, MI 49617
Telephone: (616) 882-9688
Fax: (616) 882-4600
E-mail: sscitymilw@aol.com
Internet: www.t-one.net/~msh/spcm

Michigan, Fairview

MICHIGAN AUSABLE VALLEY RAILROAD
Steam & diesel, scheduled
16" Gauge

Ride: A 1½-mile, 20-minute scenic ride on a ¼ scale passenger train that runs through a jackpine forest, part of the Huron National Forest, and overlooks beautiful AuSable Valley. You will pass through a 115-foot wooden tunnel and over two wooden trestles, one over 220 feet long to view the wooded valley below. The MAV RR is also home to Schrader's Railroad Gift Catalog for railroad enthusiasts. You will find many one-of-a-kind items in the quaintly designed Railroad Depot Gift Shop from past and present catalogs.

Schedule: Memorial Day through Labor Day: weekends and holidays, 10 a.m to 5 p.m. Fall Color Tours–last weekend in September and first two weekends in October. Steam on Sundays and holidays only. Diesels on Saturdays.

Admission/Fare: $3.00; children 2 and under are free.

Locomotive/Rolling Stock: Hudson steam locomotive 4-6-4 no. 5661, built by E.C. Eddy of Fairview and formerly run on the Pinconning & Blind River Railroad; two F7 diesel hydraulic locomotives.

Nearby Attractions/Accommodations: Huron National Forest, canoe ride National Scenic AuSable River, campgrounds, nature hikes.

Location/Directions: North on I-75 exit 202 on to M-33. Head north to Fairview and turn south at blinker light in Fairview and go 3.5 miles south on Abbe Road.

*Coupon available, see coupon section.

Site Address: 230 S. Abbe Road, Fairview, MI
Mailing Address: 230 S. Abbe Road, Fairview, MI 48621
Telephone: (517) 848-2229
Fax: (517) 848-2240

Michigan, Flint **HUCKLEBERRY RAILROAD**
Steam, scheduled
Narrow gauge

Ride: This eight-mile ride departs from the 1860s Crossroads Village Depot and travels through the scenic Genesee Recreation Area. The track borders Mott Lake and crosses a 26-foot trestle. Steam equipment and historic coaches in service.

Schedule: Mid-May through Labor Day: daily.

Admission/Fare: Adults $8.75; seniors $7.75; children (4-12) $5.75; under age 3 are free. (Subject to change.)

Locomotive/Rolling Stock: No. 2 Baldwin 4-6-0 steam locomotive in service; 15 vintage wooden coaches.

Special Events: Christmas at Crossroads, begins November 27; Halloween Ghost Train, October; Bunny Train, April; Railfans Weekend, call for information.

Nearby Attractions/Accommodations: Crossroads Village, Genesee Belle Riverboat, outlet shopping, camping, many area motels and restaurants.

Location/Directions: North of Flint. I-475, exit 13, north on Saginaw Street, east on Stanley Road, south on Bray Road to Crossroads Village and Huckleberry Railroad.

*Coupon available, see coupon section.

Site Address: 6140 Bray Road, Flint, MI
Mailing Address: 5045 Stanley Road, Flint, MI 48506
Telephone: (810) 736-7100 and (800) 648-7275
Fax: (810) 736-7220
E-mail: gencopks@concentric.net
Internet: http://genesee.freenet.org/vil/

Michigan, Iron Mountain

IRON MOUNTAIN IRON MINE
Electric, scheduled
24" gauge

IRON MOUNTAIN IRON MINE

Ride: Designated a Michigan Historical Site, the Iron Mountain Iron Mine offers guided underground tours by mine train. Visitors travel 2,600 feet into the mine to see mining demonstrations and the history of iron mining in Michigan's Upper Peninsula. Mining equipment dating from the 1870s is shown and explained.

Schedule: June 1 through October 15: daily, 9 a.m. to 5 p.m.

Admission/Fare: Adults $6.00; children 6-12 $5.00; children under 6 are free. Group rates available.

Locomotive/Rolling Stock: Electric locomotive and five cars.

Location/Directions: Nine miles east of Iron Mountain on U.S. 2.

*Coupon available, see coupon section.

Site Address: Iron Mountain, MI
Mailing Address: PO Box 177, Iron Mountain, MI 49801
Telephone: (906) 563-8077

Michigan, Mt. Clemens

MICHIGAN TRANSIT MUSEUM
Electric, diesel, scheduled
Standard gauge

GARY J. MICHAELS

Ride: This unique train ride is a 6-mile, 40-minute trip through farmlands and a park on trackage of the Selfridge Air National Guard Base. Eastbound, the train is controlled from "el" cars, with a diesel locomotive providing electricity. Westbound, the locomotive powers the train. Located on the route is the Selfridge Military Air Museum, with more than 20 military aircraft, plus photos, models, and memorabilia. A small donation for the museum is collected with the train fare. The group leases the Mt. Clemens Grand Trunk Railroad station, built in 1859, and operates it as a museum. The station is located at the Cass Avenue crossing of the Grand Trunk in Mt. Clemens.

Schedule: Train–late May through September: Sundays, 1, 2, 3, and 4 p.m.

Admission/Fare: Train–adults $6.00; children 4-12 $3.00. Museum–donations appreciated.

Locomotive/Rolling Stock: No. 1807, Alco S-1, former Alco plant switcher; no. 761, 1929 interurban, former Chicago, North Shore & Milwaukee; PCC No. 268, former Detroit Street Railway: more.

Special Events: Museums of Mt. Clemens Weekend, first weekend in April.

Location/Directions: Train–northbound Gratiot (M-3), ¾ mile north of Mt. Clemens. Museum–Cass Ave. ¾ mile west of downtown Mt. Clemens.

*Coupon available, see coupon section.

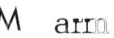

Site Address: 200 Grand Avenue, Mt. Clemens, MI
Mailing Address: PO Box 12, Mt. Clemens, MI 48046
Telephone: (810) 463-1863

Michigan, Owosso

MICHIGAN STATE TRUST FOR RAILWAY PRESERVATION
Steam, irregular
Standard gauge

AARNE FROBOM

Display/Ride: 1941 steam locomotive in 1887 locomotive shop. Occasional events, exhibits, and excursions.

Schedule: Saturdays, 10 a.m. to 5 p.m. Occasional events as announced.

Admission/Fare: Free. Event prices as announced.

Locomotive/Rolling Stock: Pere Marquette 2-8-4 no. 1225 (Lima, 1941).

Special Events: Engineer-for-an-Hour program permits MSTRP members to operate Locomotive 1225.

Nearby Attractions/Accommodations: Durand Depot Museum, Historic Crossroads Village.

Location/Directions: Located in Tuscola and Saginaw Bay Railway Yard on South Oakwood Street, off Highway M-71 in southeast Owosso.

Site Address: 600 South Oakwood Street, Owosso, MI
Mailing Address: PO Box 665, Owosso, MI 48867-0665
Telephone: (517) 725-9464
Internet: http://www.shianet.org/~twelve25

Michigan, Soo Junction

TOONERVILLE TROLLEY AND RIVERBOAT TRIPS
24" gauge

Ride: Enjoy a 6½-hour round trip on a 5½-mile ride on a narrow gauge train and a 21 mile riverboat trip to Tahquamenon Falls.

Schedule: June 15 through October 6: one trip daily, departs at 10:30 a.m. and return at 5 p.m.

Admission/Fare: Adults $18.00; children 6-15 $9.00; under age 6 are free.

Locomotive/Rolling Stock: Three Plymouth 5-ton locomotives; 11 passenger cars; one flatcar; one fuel car; three gondola cars.

Nearby Attractions/Accommodations: Twenty minutes from Newberry, which offers lodging, dining, 9-hole golf course, logging museum.

Location/Directions: Two minutes off Highway M-28 in Michigan's Upper Peninsula, one hour from Mackinaw Bridge.

*Coupon available, see coupon section.

Site Address: Soo Junction, MI
Mailing Address: RR 2 Box 938, Newberry, MI 49868
Telephone: (888) 77TRAIN and (906) 876-2311

Michigan, Traverse City

CITY OF TRAVERSE CITY PARKS & RECREATION
Steam, scheduled
15" gauge

LAUREN VAUGHN

Ride: No. 400, the "Spirit of Traverse City," is an oil-fired, ¼-scale replica of a 4-4-2 steam locomotive, which takes passengers around a ⁹⁄₁₀-mile loop at the Clinch Park Zoo and Marina on West Bay in Traverse City. The ride provides views of West Grand Traverse Bay, the marina, the beach, and the zoo, which features native Michigan wildlife and the Con Foster Museum.

Schedule: May 23 through September 7: Daily, 10 a.m. to 4:30 p.m. and September 12-13, 19-20.

Admission/Fare: Adults $1.00; children 5-12 $ .50; under age 5 are free.

Locomotive/Rolling Stock: "Spirit of Traverse City" no. 400 oil-fired 4-4-2 steam locomotive; three open-air passenger cars.

Special Events: Family Fun Day, June 7.

Nearby Attractions/Accommodations: Clinch Park Zoo, Clinch Park Beach, Con Foster Museum.

Location/Directions: On U.S. 30 in downtown Traverse City on Grand Traverse Bay.

*Coupon available, see coupon section.

Site Address: 100 East Grandview Parkway, Traverse City, MI
Mailing Address: 625 Woodmere Avenue, Traverse City, MI 49686
Telephone: (616) 922-4910
Fax: (616) 941-7716

Michigan, Walled Lake

**MICHIGAN STAR CLIPPER
DINNER TRAIN COE RAIL**
Diesel, scheduled
Standard gauge

MICHIGAN STAR CLIPPER

Ride: The *Star Clipper* offers a 3-hour scenic excursion throughout southeastern Michigan while passengers dine on a five-course meal reminiscent of years gone by. Live entertainment featuring Murder Mysteries or Musical Revues are performed nightly. The lunch excursion is two hours long and a three-course meal is served. On the *Star Clipper Overnight B&Bs*, passengers can relax and sleep aboard two fabulous cars that feature a 50-foot all-mahogany drawing room, a dance floor at the opposite end, and eight suites in between. The *Coe Rail Vintage Tourist Train* offers one hour rides with full commentary and optional puppet show. The newly remodeled 1884 depot offers check-in area along with a gift shop.

Schedule: Year-round: call or write for information.

Admission/Fare: Call or write for information.

Locomotive/Rolling Stock: 1945 Whitcomb, gasoline; 1945 Alco S1; 1947 Alco S1; 1952 Alco S1; *Michigan Star Clipper*–1952 Pennsylvania Railroad Keystone dining cars; kitchen car; power car; 1950s-vintage stainless steel sleepers; more.

Special Events: Call or write for information.

Location/Directions: On Pontiac Trail just north of Maple Road, eight minutes north of Novi/Walled Lake exit off I-96.

*Coupon available, see coupon section.

Site Address: Walled Lake, MI
Mailing Address: 840 N. Pontiac Trail, Walled Lake, MI 48390
Telephone: (810) 960-9440
Fax: (810) 960-9444

Minnesota, Chisholm

IRONWORLD DISCOVERY CENTER
Electric trolley
Scheduled

Display/Ride: A vintage electric trolley transports visitors to Mesaba Junction where a "location" house and mining equipment are on display.

Schedule: Daily: 10 a.m. to 4:30 p.m., departures every half-hour.

Admission/Fare: Included in park gate admission.

Special Events: Polkafest, Minnesota Ethnic Days, International Button Box Festival. Call or write for dates.

Nearby Attractions/Accommodations: Minnesota Museum of Mining, Kahler Park Inn, Hull Rust Mine Overview.

Location/Directions: Highway 169, five miles east of Hibbing.

*Coupon available, see coupon section.

Site Address: Chisholm, MN
Mailing Address: PO Box 392, Chisholm, MN 55719
Telephone: (218) 254-3321 and (800) 372-6437
Fax: (218) 254-5235

Minnesota, Currie

END-O-LINE RAILROAD PARK AND MUSEUM
Railway museum

END-O-LINE RAILROAD PARK AND MUSEUM

Ride: Rides on a manually operated turntable are given to all visitors. For the children, rides are also given on a 3½ gauge Hilfers Train. A working railroad yard including a rebuilt enginehouse on its original foundation, an original four-room depot, a water tower, an 1899 section-foreman's house, and an outhouse. The turntable, built in 1901 by the American Bridge Company and still operable, is the only one left in Minnesota on its original site. The section-foreman's house, a general store, and one-room schoolhouse can also be seen. A replica of the coal bunker was built in the fall of 1995 and will be used for a picnic shelter and gift shop. The enginehouse has been lengthened to its original 90 feet. It contains various exhibits and displays of railroad artifacts, photographs, memorabilia and equipment. The freight room in the depot has an HO scale model train layout of the railroad yards in Currie. A bicycle/pedestrian paved pathway connects the railroad park to Lake Shetek State Park (approximately 6 miles round trip).

Schedule: May 26 through September 1: Mondays through Fridays, 10 a.m. to 12 p.m. and 1 to 5 p.m.; weekends, 1 to 5 p.m.; and by appointment. Last tour 4 p.m.

Admission/Fare: Adults $2.00; students $1.00; families $5.00.

Locomotive/Rolling Stock: 1923 Georgia Northern steam locomotive; and more.

Location/Directions: Highway 30 to Currie, travel ¾ mile north on Cty. Road 38.

Site Address: 440 North Mill Street, Currie, MN
Mailing Address: 440 North Mill Street, Currie, MN 56123
Telephone: (507) 763-3708 and (507) 763-3113 (off season)

Minnesota, Dassel

THE OLD DEPOT RAILROAD MUSEUM
Railway museum

THE OLD DEPOT RAILROAD MUSEUM

Display: A former Great Northern depot built in 1913 is filled with railroad memorabilia and pictures. This 33-foot by 100-foot country depot has two waiting rooms, an agent's office, and a large freight room, as well as a full basement. Authentic recorded sounds of steam locomotives and the clicking of the telegraph key create the realistic feel of an old small-town depot. Items displayed include lanterns, telegraph equipment, semaphores, and other signals; section crew cars, a hand pump car, and a velocipede; tools and oil cans; depot and crossing signs; buttons, badges, service pins, and caps; a large date-nail collection; and many baggage carts. Also included are children's toy trains, an HO scale model railroad, and many railroad advertising items. Interpretation of the items is provided. Static ½-scale train on display.

Schedule: Memorial Day through October 1: Daily, 10 a.m. to 4:30 p.m.

Admission/Fare: Adults $2.50; children under age 12 $1.00.

Locomotive/Rolling Stock: Two cabooses, two boxcars.

Location/Directions: Fifty miles west of Minneapolis.

Site Address: 651 W. Highway 12, Dassel, MN
Mailing Address: 651 W. Highway 12, Dassel, MN 55325
Telephone: (320) 275-3876

Minnesota, Duluth

LAKE SUPERIOR & MISSISSIPPI RAILROAD
Diesel, scheduled
Standard gauge

DAVE SCHAUER

Ride: A historic 90-minute rail journey along the scenic St. Louis River. The railroad uses vintage equipment as well as on open safari car on its excursions.

Schedule: June 13 through August 30: weekends. Charters available seven days a week during season.

Admission/Fare: Adults $6.00; seniors $5.00; children $4.00.

Locomotive/Rolling Stock: GE 44-ton no. 46 diesel locomotive; restored full coach no. 85 and solarium coach no. 29, former DM&IR; safari car no. 100, rebuilt flatcar with railing and seating.

Nearby Attractions/Accommodations: Many hotels, restaurants, and attractions in the Duluth area.

Location/Directions: Six miles southwest of downtown Duluth on Grand Avenue, route 23, across from the Duluth Zoo and the Lake Superior Zoological Gardens. Train leaves from the Western Waterfront Trail; park in Western Waterfront Trail lot.

*Coupon available, see coupon section.

[P] [bus] [handicap] [camera] [picnic] [locomotive] [mail]   M

Site Address: Western Waterfront Trail parking lot, Duluth, MN
Mailing Address: 506 W. Michigan Street, Duluth, MN 55802
Telephone: (218) 624-7549 and (218) 728-2262
Fax: (218) 728-6303
E-mail: captkatt@aol

Minnesota, Duluth

LAKE SUPERIOR MUSEUM OF TRANSPORTATION
Railway museum
Standard gauge

BRUCE OJARD PHOTOGRAPHY

Display: A number of interesting and historic locomotives and cars, including the Great Northern's famous "William Crooks" locomotive and cars of 1861; Northern Pacific Railway #1, The "Minnetonka" built in 1870; the Soo line's first passenger diesel, FP7 No. 2500A; Duluth, Missabe & Iron Range 2-8-8-4 No. 227, displayed with revolving drive wheels and recorded sound; Great Northern No. 400, the first production-model SD45 diesel; an 1887 steam rotary snowplow; other steam, diesel, and electric engines; a Railway Post Office car; a dining-car china exhibit; freight cars; work equipment; an operating electric single-truck streetcar; and much railroadiana.

Schedule: Museum–year round. Train/trolley–May through September. Call or write for information.

Admission/Fare: Combo tickets (museum and train)–$6.00 to $20.00.

Special Events: Steam train weekends.

Location/Directions: I-35 exit downtown Duluth/Michigan Street.

Site Address: 506 W. Michigan Street, Duluth, MN
Mailing Address: 506 W. Michigan Street, Duluth, MN 55802
Telephone: (218) 733-7590
Fax: (218) 733-7596

Minnesota, Duluth	**NORTH SHORE SCENIC RAILROAD**
	Diesel, steam, scheduled
	Standard gauge

TIM SCHANDEL

Display: Formerly the Duluth Missabe & Iron Range Railway's Lake Front Line, this railroad's 26 miles of track run between the Depot in downtown Duluth, along the Lake Superior waterfront, and through the residential areas and scenic woodlands of northeastern Minnesota to the Two Harbors Depot, adjacent to DM&IR's active taconite yard and shiploading facility. The line offers 1½-, 2½-, and 6-hour round trips with departures from Duluth and Two Harbors.

Schedule: June through September: to Lester River–Mondays through Fridays, 12:30 and 3 p.m., Saturdays 10 a.m. Pizza train–Wednesdays through Saturdays, 6:30 p.m. Two Harbors–Fridays and Saturdays, 10:30 a.m.

Admission/Fare: Lester River–adults $9.00; children $5.00. Pizza train–adults $16.00; children $11.00. Two Harbors–adults $17.00; children $8.00.

Locomotive/Rolling Stock: FP7 Soo Line; SD45 Great Northern; NW5 Great Northern; 1918 OM&IN coach; dinner car "Silver Pheasant."

Special Events: Steam excursion weekends, elegant dinner trains, Grandma's Marathon Train.

Location/Directions: Duluth–Duluth Depot, Michigan Street, downtown. Two Harbors–Lake County Historical Society, 7th and Waterfront.

Site Address: 506 W. Michigan Street, Duluth, MN
Mailing Address: 506 W. Michigan Street, Duluth, MN 55802
Telephone: (218) 722-1273 and (800) 423-1273
Email: nssr1@aol.com

Minnesota, Minneapolis **MINNESOTA TRANSPORTATION MUSEUM COMO-HARRIET STREETCAR LINE**
Electric, scheduled
Standard gauge

LOUIS HOFFMAN

Ride: A 2-mile, 15-minute round trip on a restored portion of the former Twin City Rapid Transit Company's historic Como-Harriet route. Streetcars operate over a scenic line through a wooded area between Lakes Harriet and Calhoun. This is the last operating portion of the 523-mile Twin City Lines system, abandoned in 1954. The Linden Hills Depot, a re-creation of the 1900 depot located at the site, houses changing historical displays about electric railways in Minnesota.

Schedule: May 22 through September 7: weekends, holidays, 12:30 p.m. to dusk. Mondays through Fridays, 6:30 p.m. to dusk. May before Memorial weekend, September after Labor Day, and October: weekends, 12:30 p.m. to dusk.

Admission/Fare: $1.00; children under age 5 are free. Chartered streetcars–$45.00 per one-half hour.

Locomotive/Rolling Stock: No. 10, 1912 Mesaba Railway Co. (Niles Car Co.); No. 78, 1893 DSR (Laclede Car Co.); no. 265, 1915 Duluth Street Railway (TCRT Snelling Shops, St. Paul); and more.

Special Events: Linden Hills Neighborhood Fair, May 16-17.

Nearby Attractions/Accommodations: Lake Harriet Rock and Rose Gardens.

Location/Directions: I-35W, 46th Street west to Lake Harriet Parkway, follow parkway to west shore of lake.

*Coupon available, see coupon section.

  ♿ P 🚌 ✻ ☕ ⛩ ⛪ ✉ arm TRAIN

🚂 St. Paul

Site Address: 2330 West 42nd Street, Minneapolis, MN
Mailing Address: PO Box 17240, Nokomis Station, Minneapolis, MN 55417
Telephone: (612) 228-0263 and (800) 711-2591
Internet: www.mtmuseum.org/

Minnesota, Minneapolis **MINNESOTA TRANSPORTATION MUSEUM**
MINNEHAHA DEPOT
Railway museum

LOUIS HOFFMAN

Display/Museum: Built in 1875, the Minnehaha Depot replaced an even smaller Milwaukee Road depot on the same site. Milwaukee Road agents quickly nicknamed the depot the "Princess" because of its intricate architectural details. Until Twin City Rapid Transit Company streetcars connected Minnehaha Falls Park to the city, as many as 13 passenger trains per day served the depot. It remained in service, primarily handling freight, for many years. Located at the south end of CP Rail System's South Minneapolis branch, once a through route to the south, the depot sees occasional freight movements and often hosts visiting private cars. Visitors may tour the depot, which appears much as it did when in service as a typical suburban station. Exhibits include telegraphy demonstrations and historic photographs of the depot and its environs.

Schedule: May 24 through September 7: Sundays and holidays, 12:30 to 4:30 p.m.

Admission/Fare: Donations appreciated.

Special Events: Annual Open House, May 18.

Nearby Attractions/Accommodations: Fort Snelling State Park. Historic Fort Snelling. Mall of America.

Location/Directions: In Minnehaha Falls Park just off State Highway 55 (Hiawatha Avenue).

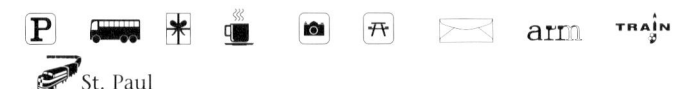

St. Paul

Site Address: 4926 Minnehaha Avenue, Minneapolis, MN
Mailing Address: PO Box 17240, Nokomis Station, Minneapolis, MN 55417
Telephone: (612) 228-0263 and (800) 711-2591
E-mail: corbin@solon.com
Internet: www.mtmuseum.org/

Minnesota, Minneapolis **NORTH STAR RAIL, INC.**
Steam, irregular
Standard gauge

VICTOR HAND

Ride: North Star Rail, Inc. operates a day-long steam powered excursion over various Class 1 railroads.

Schedule: Varies with trip. Call or write for information.

Admission/Fare: Varies. Reservations recommended.

Locomotive/Rolling Stock: No. 261 1944 Alco 4-8-4, former Milwaukee Road class S3, leased to North Star Rail by the National Railroad Museum in Green Bay, Wisconsin.

Site Address: Minneapolis, MN
Mailing Address: 1418 Rocky Lane, St. Paul, MN 55122
Telephone: (612) 688-7320
Fax: (612) 688-7282
E-mail: friends261aol.com

SAVE with TRAINS!

The most popular magazine among railfans

One Year (12 issues) only $34.95 ■ 26% OFF!

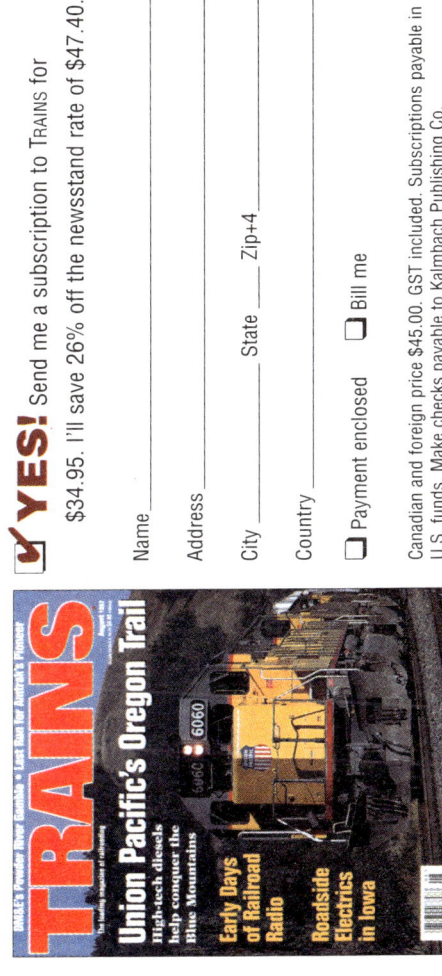

✓ YES! Send me a subscription to TRAINS for $34.95. I'll save 26% off the newsstand rate of $47.40.

Name _____

Address _____

City _____ State _____ Zip+4 _____

Country _____

❏ Payment enclosed   ❏ Bill me

Canadian and foreign price $45.00. GST included. Subscriptions payable in U.S. funds. Make checks payable to Kalmbach Publishing Co. Offer expires December, 1999.

L2381T

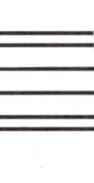

BUSINESS REPLY MAIL

FIRST-CLASS MAIL   PERMIT NO. 16   WAUKESHA, WI

POSTAGE WILL BE PAID BY ADDRESSEE

TRAINS
PO BOX 1612
WAUKESHA WI 53187-9950

NO POSTAGE
NECESSARY
IF MAILED
IN THE
UNITED STATES

Guide to Tourist Railroads and Museums
1998 GUEST COUPONS

ABILENE & SMOKY VALLEY RR
With coupon: $1 off admission
Valid April 1998 through March 1999
Maximum discount 4 persons per coupon

AMERICA'S RAILROADS ON PARADE
Regular price: Adults $5, seniors $5, children $2.50
With coupon: Adults $4, seniors $3.50, children $2
Valid April 1998 through March 1999
Maximum discount 10 persons per coupon

ANDERSON STEEL FLANGE RAILROAD EQUIPMENT CO.
Free caboose logo key chain and
$8 caboose logo ball cap for $5
Valid April 1998 through March 1999

ARKANSAS & MISSOURI RAILROAD
10% off regular fare
Valid April 1998 through March 1999
Maximum discount 4 persons per coupon

B&O RAILROAD MUSEUM
With coupon: Buy one admission get
equal admission free
Valid April 1998 through March 1999

BIG BEAR FARM
With coupon: $1 off admission
Valid April 1998 through March 1999
Maximum discount 1 person per coupon

BONANZAVILLE, U.S.A.
Regular price: Adults $6, seniors $6, children $3
With coupon: Adults $5, seniors $5, children $2
Valid April 1998 through March 1999

BRANDYWINE SCENIC RAILWAY CO.
Regular price: Adults $8, seniors $7, children $6
With coupon: Adults $7, seniors $6, children $5
Valid April 1998 through March 1999
Maximum discount 1 person per coupon

C.P. HUNTINGTON RAILROAD HISTORICAL SOCIETY
Regular price: Adults $99, children $69
With coupon: Adults $89, children $62
Valid April 1998 through March 1999

CAFE LAFAYETTE DINNER TRAIN
Regular price: Adults $38.95, children $19.95
With coupon: Adults $36.95, children $18.95
Valid April 1998 through March 1999

CALIFORNIA WESTERN RAILROAD
With coupon: Buy one admission get
equal price admission free
Valid April 1998 through March 1999
Maximum discount 2 persons per coupon

CAMP FIVE MUSUEM FOUNDATION, INC.
Regular price: Adults $14, children $4.75
With coupon: Adults $13, children $3.75
Valid April 1998 through March 1999
Maximum discount 1 person per coupon

AMERICA'S RAILROADS ON PARADE WILLIAMSBURG, VA GUIDE TO TOURIST RAILROADS AND MUSEUMS 1998 GUEST COUPON	**ABILENE & SMOKY VALLEY RR** ABILENE, KS GUIDE TO TOURIST RAILROADS AND MUSEUMS 1998 GUEST COUPON
ARKANSAS & MISSOURI RAILROAD SPRINGDALE, AR GUIDE TO TOURIST RAILROADS AND MUSEUMS 1998 GUEST COUPON	**ANDERSON STEEL FLANGE RAILROAD EQUIPMENT CO.** FAIRFIELD, IA GUIDE TO TOURIST RAILROADS AND MUSEUMS 1998 GUEST COUPON
BIG BEAR FARM HONESDALE, PA GUIDE TO TOURIST RAILROADS AND MUSEUMS 1998 GUEST COUPON	**B&O RAILROAD MUSEUM** BALTIMORE, MD GUIDE TO TOURIST RAILROADS AND MUSEUMS 1998 GUEST COUPON
BRANDYWINE SCENIC RAILWAY CO. NORTHBROOK, PA GUIDE TO TOURIST RAILROADS AND MUSEUMS 1998 GUEST COUPON	**BONANZAVILLE, U.S.A.** WEST FARGO, ND GUIDE TO TOURIST RAILROADS AND MUSEUMS 1998 GUEST COUPON
CAFE LAFAYETTE DINNER TRAIN MEREDITH, NH GUIDE TO TOURIST RAILROADS AND MUSEUMS 1998 GUEST COUPON	**C.P. HUNTINGTON RAILROAD HISTORICAL SOCIETY** HUNTINGTON, WV GUIDE TO TOURIST RAILROADS AND MUSEUMS 1998 GUEST COUPON
CAMP FIVE MUSEUM FOUNDATION, INC. LAONA, WI GUIDE TO TOURIST RAILROADS AND MUSEUMS 1998 GUEST COUPON	**CALIFORNIA WESTERN RAILROAD** FORT BRAGG, CA GUIDE TO TOURIST RAILROADS AND MUSEUMS 1998 GUEST COUPON

Guide to Tourist Railroads and Museums
1998 GUEST COUPONS

CAPE COD RAILROAD
Regular price: Adults $11.50, seniors $10.50, children $7.50
With coupon: Adults $9.50, seniors $8.50, children $5.50
Valid April 1998 through March 1999

CASS SCENIC RAILROAD STATE PARK
With coupon: $1 off regular admission
Valid April 1998 through March 1999
Maximum discount 1 person per coupon

PIONEER VILLAGE AND MUSEUM
CHELAN COUNTY HISTORICAL SOCIETY
Regular price: Adults $3, seniors $2, children $2
With coupon: Adults $2, seniors $1, children $1
Valid April 1998 through March 1999
Maximum discount 1 person per coupon

CHOO CHOO BARN
TRAINTOWN U.S.A
Regular price: Adults $64 children $2
With coupon: Adults $3, children $1.50
Valid April 1998 through March 1999

CLOVIS DEPOT MODEL TRAIN MUSEUM
Regular price: Adults $3, children $1
With coupon: Adults $1.50, children $.50
Valid April 1998 through March 1999

COMO-HARRIET STREETCAR LINE
Regular price: $1
With coupon: $ .50
Valid April 1998 through March 1999
Maximum discount 4 persons per coupon

CONNECTICUT TROLLEY MUSEUM
Regular price: Adults $6, seniors $5, children $3
With coupon: Adults $5, seniors $4, children $2.50
Valid April 1998 through March 1999
Maximum discount 2 persons per coupon

CONWAY SCENIC RAILROAD
With coupon: $1 off Notch Train or $ .50 off Valley Train
Valid April 1998 through March 1999
Maximum discount 6 persons per coupon

CORYDON SCENIC RAILROAD
Regular price: Adults $9, seniors $8, children $5
With coupon: Adults $8, seniors $7, children $4
Valid April 1998 through March 1999

CROOKED RIVER RAILROAD COMPANY
Regular price: Adults $69, seniors $62, children $32
With coupon: Adults $64, seniors $57, children $27
Valid April 1998 through March 1999

CUMBRES & TOLTEC SCENIC RAILROAD
Regular price: Adults $34, seniors $30.60, children $17
With coupon: Adults $30.60, seniors $27.20, children $15.30
Valid April 1998 through March 1999
Maximum discount 6 persons per coupon

CYPRESS GARDENS
Regular price: Adults $31.27, seniors $25.97, children $10.55
With coupon: Adults $28.02, seniors $22.72, children $7.30
Valid April 1998 through March 1999
Maximum discount 2 persons per coupon
PLU 969

CASS SCENIC RAILROAD STATE PARK CASS, WV GUIDE TO TOURIST RAILROADS AND MUSEUMS 1998 GUEST COUPON	**CAPE COD RAILROAD** HYANNIS, MA GUIDE TO TOURIST RAILROADS AND MUSEUMS 1998 GUEST COUPON
CHOO CHOO BARN TRAINTOWN U.S.A. STRASBURG, PA GUIDE TO TOURIST RAILROADS AND MUSEUMS 1998 GUEST COUPON	**PIONEER VILLAGE AND MUSEUM CHELAN COUNTY HISTORICAL SOCIETY** CASHMERE, WA GUIDE TO TOURIST RAILROADS AND MUSEUMS 1998 GUEST COUPON
COMO-HARRIET STREETCAR LINE MINNEAPOLIS, MN GUIDE TO TOURIST RAILROADS AND MUSEUMS 1998 GUEST COUPON	**CLOVIS DEPOT MODEL TRAIN MUSEUM** CLOVIS, NM GUIDE TO TOURIST RAILROADS AND MUSEUMS 1998 GUEST COUPON
CONWAY SCENIC RAILROAD NORTH CONWAY, NH GUIDE TO TOURIST RAILROADS AND MUSEUMS 1998 GUEST COUPON	**CONNECTICUT TROLLEY MUSEUM** EAST WINDSOR, CT GUIDE TO TOURIST RAILROADS AND MUSEUMS 1998 GUEST COUPON
CROOKED RIVER RAILROAD COMPANY REDMOND, OR GUIDE TO TOURIST RAILROADS AND MUSEUMS 1998 GUEST COUPON	**CORYDON SCENIC RAILROAD** CORYDON, IN GUIDE TO TOURIST RAILROADS AND MUSEUMS 1998 GUEST COUPON
CYPRESS GARDENS WINTER HAVEN, FL GUIDE TO TOURIST RAILROADS AND MUSEUMS 1998 GUEST COUPON	**CUMBRES & TOLTEC SCENIC RAILROAD** CHAMA, NM GUIDE TO TOURIST RAILROADS AND MUSEUMS 1998 GUEST COUPON

Guide to Tourist Railroads and Museums
1998 GUEST COUPONS

DENNISON RAILROAD
With coupon: Buy one admission get equal price admission free
Valid April 1998 through March 1999
Maximum discount $3 per person per coupon

DURBIN & GREENBRIER
Regular price: Adults $5, seniors and children $4
With coupon: Adults $4, seniors and children $3
Valid April 1998 through March 1999
Maximum discount 2 persons per coupon

ELDORADO EXPRESS RAILROAD
Regular price: Adults $1.75, children $1.25
With coupon: Adults $1, children $ .75
Valid April 1998 through March 1999
Maximum discount 4 persons per coupon

FAIRFAX STATION RAILROAD MUSEUM
With coupon: free admission
Valid April 1998 through March 1999

FLORIDA CENTRAL RAILROAD
With coupon: 10% off fare
Valid April 1998 through March 1999

FORNEY TRANSPORTATION MUSEUM
With coupon: Buy one admission get equal price addmission free
Valid April 1998 through March 1999
Maximum discount 1 person per coupon

FORT GEORGE RAILWAY SOCIETY
With coupon: Free admission
Valid April 1998 through March 1999

GRAND CANYON RAILWAY
Regular price: Adults $49.50, children $19.50
With coupon: Adults $44.55, children $17.55
Valid April 1998 through March 1999

GREEN MOUNTAIN RAILROAD
Regular price: Adults $11, children $7
With coupon: Adults $10, children $6
Valid April 1998 through March 1999
Maximum discount 2 persons per coupon

HALTON COUNTY RADIAL RAILWAY
With coupon: Buy one admission get equal price admission free
Valid April 1998 through March 1999
Maximum discount 1 persons per coupon

HARMAR STATION
With coupon: Buy one admission get equal price admission free
Valid April 1998 through March 1999

HARPER'S FERRY TOY TRAIN MUSEUM AND JOY LINE RAILROAD
Regular price: $1
With coupon: $ .75
Valid April 1998 through March 1999
Maximum discount 2 persons per coupon

DURBIN & GREENBRIER DURBIN, WV GUIDE TO TOURIST RAILROADS AND MUSEUMS 1998 GUEST COUPON	**DENNISON RAILROAD** DENNISON, OH GUIDE TO TOURIST RAILROADS AND MUSEUMS 1998 GUEST COUPON
FAIRFAX STATION RAILROAD MUSEUM FAIRFAX STATION, VA GUIDE TO TOURIST RAILROADS AND MUSEUMS 1998 GUEST COUPON	**ELDORADO EXPRESS RAILROAD** LONG BEACH, CA GUIDE TO TOURIST RAILROADS AND MUSEUMS 1998 GUEST COUPON
FORNEY TRANSPORTATION MUSEUM DENVER, CO GUIDE TO TOURIST RAILROADS AND MUSEUMS 1998 GUEST COUPON	**FLORIDA CENTRAL RAILROAD** ALTAMONTE SPRINGS, FL GUIDE TO TOURIST RAILROADS AND MUSEUMS 1998 GUEST COUPON
GRAND CANYON RAILWAY WILLIAMS, AZ GUIDE TO TOURIST RAILROADS AND MUSEUMS 1998 GUEST COUPON	**FORT GEORGE RAILWAY SOCIETY** PRINCE GEORGE, BC, CANADA GUIDE TO TOURIST RAILROADS AND MUSEUMS 1998 GUEST COUPON
HALTON COUNTY RADIAL RAILWAY MILTON, ON, CANADA GUIDE TO TOURIST RAILROADS AND MUSEUMS 1998 GUEST COUPON	**GREEN MOUNTAIN RAILROAD** BELLOWS FALLS, VT GUIDE TO TOURIST RAILROADS AND MUSEUMS 1998 GUEST COUPON
HARPER'S FERRY TOY TRAIN MUSEUM AND JOY LINE RAILROAD HARPER'S FERRY, WV GUIDE TO TOURIST RAILROADS AND MUSEUMS 1998 GUEST COUPON	**HARMAR STATION** MARIETTA, OH GUIDE TO TOURIST RAILROADS AND MUSEUMS 1998 GUEST COUPON

Guide to Tourist Railroads and Museums
1998 GUEST COUPONS

HERBER VALLEY RAILROAD
Regular price: Adults $17, seniors $15, children $10
With coupon: Adults $14, seniors $13, children $8
Valid April 1998 through March 1999
Maximum discount 6 persons per coupon

HESSTON STEAM MUSEUM
With coupon: $1 off admission
Valid April 1998 through March 1999
Maximum discount 6 persons per coupon

HISTORIC PULLMAN FOUNDATION
With coupon: Buy one admission get equal price admission free
Valid April 1998 through March 1999
Maximum discount 2 persons per coupon

HISTORIC RAILROAD SHOPS
Regular price: Adults $2.50
With coupon: Adults $2
Valid April 1998 through March 1999
Maximum discount 2 persons per coupon

HISTORIC STEWARTSTOWN RAILROAD
With coupon: $1 off admission
Maximum discount 2 persons per coupon

HUCKLEBERRY RAILROAD
With coupon: $1 off admission
Valid April 1998 through March 1999
Maximum discount 6 persons per coupon

ILLINOIS RAILWAY MUSEUM
With coupon: $1 off admission
Valid April 1998 through March 1999
Maximum discount 8 persons per coupon

INDIANA TRANSPORTATION MUSEUM
With coupon: $1 off fare for any regularly scheduled train
Valid April 1998 through March 1999
Maximum discount 4 persons per coupon

IRON MOUNTAIN IRON MINE
With coupon: $1 off admission
Valid April 1998 through March 1999

IRONWORLD DISCOVERY CENTER
With coupon: 50 cents off admission
Valid April 1998 through March 1999
Maximum discount 1 person per coupon

IRVINE PARK RAILROAD
With coupon: Buy one admission get equal price admission free on weekdays only
Valid April 1998 through March 1999
Maximum discount 1 person per coupon

JEFFERSON DEPOT
With coupon: Buy one admission get equal price admission free
Valid April 1998 through March 1999
Maximum discount 1 person per coupon

HESSTON STEAM MUSEUM HESSTON, IN GUIDE TO TOURIST RAILROADS AND MUSEUMS 1998 GUEST COUPON	**HERBER VALLEY RAILROAD** HERBER CITY, UT GUIDE TO TOURIST RAILROADS AND MUSEUMS 1998 GUEST COUPON
HISTORIC RAILROAD SHOPS SAVANNAH, GA GUIDE TO TOURIST RAILROADS AND MUSEUMS 1998 GUEST COUPON	**HISTORIC PULLMAN FOUNDATION** CHICAGO, IL GUIDE TO TOURIST RAILROADS AND MUSEUMS 1998 GUEST COUPON
HUCKLEBERRY RAILROAD FLINT, MI GUIDE TO TOURIST RAILROADS AND MUSEUMS 1998 GUEST COUPON	**HISTORIC STEWARTSTOWN RAILROAD** STEWARTSTOWN, PA GUIDE TO TOURIST RAILROADS AND MUSEUMS 1998 GUEST COUPON
INDIANA TRANSPORTATION MUSEUM NOBLESVILLE, IN GUIDE TO TOURIST RAILROADS AND MUSEUMS 1998 GUEST COUPON	**ILLINOIS RAILWAY MUSEUM** UNION, IL (MCHENRY COUNTY) GUIDE TO TOURIST RAILROADS AND MUSEUMS 1998 GUEST COUPON
IRONWORLD DISCOVERY CENTER CHISHOLM, MN GUIDE TO TOURIST RAILROADS AND MUSEUMS 1998 GUEST COUPON	**IRON MOUNTAIN IRON MINE** IRON MOUNTAIN, MI GUIDE TO TOURIST RAILROADS AND MUSEUMS 1998 GUEST COUPON
JEFFERSON DEPOT JEFFERSON, OH GUIDE TO TOURIST RAILROADS AND MUSEUMS 1998 GUEST COUPON	**IRVINE PARK RAILROAD** ORANGE, CA GUIDE TO TOURIST RAILROADS AND MUSEUMS 1998 GUEST COUPON

Guide to Tourist Railroads and Museums
1998 GUEST COUPONS

KENNESAW CIVIL WAR MUSEUM
With coupon: Buy one admission get
equal admission free
Valid April 1998 through March 1999
Maximum discount 1 person per coupon

LAKE SUPERIOR & MISSISSIPPI RAILROAD
With coupon: $1 off admission
Valid April 1998 through March 1999
Maximum discount 10 persons per coupon

LINDEN RAILROAD MUSEUM
Regular price: Adults $2, children $1
With coupon: Adults $1, children $.50
Valid April 1998 through March 1999
Maximum discount 1 person per coupon

**LITTLE RIVER RAILROAD
AND LUMBER CO. MUSEUM**
With coupon: Free admission
Valid April 1998 through March 1999

LOMITA RAILROAD MUSEUM
Regular price: Adults $1, children $.50
With coupon: Adults $.50, children $.25
Valid April 1998 through March 1999
Maximum discount 1 person per coupon

**LYCOMING COUNTY
HISTORICAL SOCIETY AND MUSEUM**
With coupon: Buy one admission get
equal price admission free
Valid April 1998 through March 1999
Maximum discount 1 person per coupon

MICHIGAN AUSABLE VALLEY RAILROAD
With coupon: $1 off admission
Maximum discount 2 persons per coupon

MICHIGAN STAR CLIPPER DINNER TRAIN
Regular price: Adults $68.50
With coupon: Adults $58.50
Valid April 1998 through March 1999
Tuesday, Wednesday, Thursday only.
Not valid month of December, on holidays, or with any other offer.

MICHIGAN TRANSIT MUSEUM
Regular price: Adults $6, children $3
With coupon: Adults $5, children $2.50
Valid April 1998 through March 1999
Maximum discount 4 persons per coupon

MOUNT RAINIER SCENIC RAILROAD
With coupon: $1 off admission
Valid April 1998 through March 1999
Maximum discount 4 persons per coupon

MOUNTAIN STATE MYSTERY TOURS
With coupon: Buy one adult ticket get
second ticket at half price
Valid April 1998 through March 1999
Maximum discount 1 persons per coupon

NATIONAL CAPITAL TROLLEY MUSEUM
With coupon: Buy one admission get
equal price admission free
Valid April 1998 through March 1999
Maximum discount 1 person per coupon

LAKE SUPERIOR & MISSISSIPPI RAILROAD DULUTH, MN GUIDE TO TOURIST RAILROADS AND MUSEUMS 1998 GUEST COUPON	**KENNESAW CIVIL WAR MUSEUM** KENNESAW, GA GUIDE TO TOURIST RAILROADS AND MUSEUMS 1998 GUEST COUPON
LITTLE RIVER RAILROAD AND LUMBER CO. MUSEUM TOWNSEND, TN GUIDE TO TOURIST RAILROADS AND MUSEUMS 1998 GUEST COUPON	**LINDEN RAILROAD MUSEUM** LINDEN, IN GUIDE TO TOURIST RAILROADS AND MUSEUMS 1998 GUEST COUPON
LYCOMING COUNTY HISTORICAL SOCIETY AND MUSEUM WILLIAMSPORT, PA GUIDE TO TOURIST RAILROADS AND MUSEUMS 1998 GUEST COUPON	**LOMITA RAILROAD MUSEUM** LOMITA, CA GUIDE TO TOURIST RAILROADS AND MUSEUMS 1998 GUEST COUPON
MICHIGAN STAR CLIPPER DINNER TRAIN WALLED LAKE, MI GUIDE TO TOURIST RAILROADS AND MUSEUMS 1998 GUEST COUPON	**MICHIGAN AUSABLE VALLEY RAILROAD** FAIRVIEW, MI GUIDE TO TOURIST RAILROADS AND MUSEUMS 1998 GUEST COUPON
MOUNT RAINIER SCENIC RAILROAD ELBE, WA GUIDE TO TOURIST RAILROADS AND MUSEUMS 1998 GUEST COUPON	**MICHIGAN TRANSIT MUSEUM** MT. CLEMENS, MI GUIDE TO TOURIST RAILROADS AND MUSEUMS 1998 GUEST COUPON
NATIONAL CAPITAL TROLLEY MUSEUM WHEATON, MD GUIDE TO TOURIST RAILROADS AND MUSEUMS 1998 GUEST COUPON	**MOUNTAIN STATE MYSTERY TOURS** HUNTINGTON, WV GUIDE TO TOURIST RAILROADS AND MUSEUMS 1998 GUEST COUPON

Guide to Tourist Railroads and Museums
1998 GUEST COUPONS

NATIONAL RAILROAD MUSEUM
With coupon: Buy one admission get
equal price admission free
Valid April 1998 through March 1999

NEW HOPE & IVYLAND RAILROAD
Regular price: Adults $8.50, seniors $7.50, children $4.50
With coupon: Adults $7, seniors $5, children $3
Valid April 1998 through March 1999

NORTH CAROLINA TRANSPORTATION MUSEUM
With coupon: $ .50 off admission
Valid April 1998 through March 1999
Maximum discount 4 persons per coupon

OIL CREEK & TITUSVILLE RAILROAD
With coupon: $1 off admission
Valid April 1998 through March 1999
Maximum discount 6 persons per coupon

OLD COLONY & FALL RIVER RAILROAD MUSEUM
With coupon: $ .50 off admission
Valid April 1998 through March 1999
Maximum discount 4 persons per coupon

ORANGE EMPIRE RAILWAY MUSEUM
With coupon: $1 off admission
Valid April 1998 through March 1999

OSCEOLA & ST. CROIX VALLEY RAILWAY
With coupon: $1 off admission
Valid April 1998 through March 1999
Maximum discount 4 persons per coupon

PHOENIX & HOLLY RAILROAD
With coupon: Buy one admission get
equal price admission free
Valid April 1998 through March 1999

RAIL CITY HISTORICAL MUSEUM
Regular price: Adults $3, seniors $2
With coupon: Adults $1.50, seniors $1
Valid April 1998 through March 1999
Maximum discount 4 persons per coupon

RAILROAD AND PIONEER MUSEUM
Regular price: Adults $2, seniors and children $1
With coupon: Adults $1, seniors and children $ .50
Valid April 1998 through March 1999

RAILSWEST RAILROAD MUSEUM
Regular price: Adults $3, seniors $2.50, children $1.25
With coupon: Adults $2.50, seniors $2, children $1
Valid April 1998 through March 1999
Maximum discount 2 persons per coupon

ROADSIDE AMERICA
With coupon: Buy one admission get
equal price admission free
Valid April 1998 through March 1999
Group rates excluded

C-6

NEW HOPE & IVYLAND RAILROAD
NEW HOPE, PA
GUIDE TO TOURIST RAILROADS AND MUSEUMS
1998 GUEST COUPON

NATIONAL RAILROAD MUSEUM
GREEN BAY, WI
GUIDE TO TOURIST RAILROADS AND MUSEUMS
1998 GUEST COUPON

OIL CREEK & TITUSVILLE RAILROAD
TITUSVILLE, PA
GUIDE TO TOURIST RAILROADS AND MUSEUMS
1998 GUEST COUPON

NORTH CAROLINA TRANSPORTATION MUSEUM
SPENCER, NC
GUIDE TO TOURIST RAILROADS AND MUSEUMS
1998 GUEST COUPON

ORANGE EMPIRE RAILWAY MUSEUM
PERRIS, CA
GUIDE TO TOURIST RAILROADS AND MUSEUMS
1998 GUEST COUPON

OLD COLONY & FALL RIVER RAILROAD MUSEUM
FALL RIVER, MA
GUIDE TO TOURIST RAILROADS AND MUSEUMS
1998 GUEST COUPON

PHOENIX & HOLLY RAILROAD
CANBY, OR
GUIDE TO TOURIST RAILROADS AND MUSEUMS
1998 GUEST COUPON

OSCEOLA & ST. CROIX VALLEY RAILWAY
OSCEOLA, WI
GUIDE TO TOURIST RAILROADS AND MUSEUMS
1998 GUEST COUPON

RAILROAD AND PIONEER MUSEUM
TEMPLE, TX
GUIDE TO TOURIST RAILROADS AND MUSEUMS
1998 GUEST COUPON

RAIL CITY HISTORICAL MUSEUM
SANDY CREEK, NY
GUIDE TO TOURIST RAILROADS AND MUSEUMS
1998 GUEST COUPON

ROADSIDE AMERICA
SHARTLESVILLE, PA
GUIDE TO TOURIST RAILROADS AND MUSEUMS
1998 GUEST COUPON

RAILSWEST RAILROAD MUSEUM
COUNCIL BLUFFS, IA
GUIDE TO TOURIST RAILROADS AND MUSEUMS
1998 GUEST COUPON

Guide to Tourist Railroads and Museums
1998 GUEST COUPONS

ROCKHILL TROLLEY MUSEUM
With coupon: Buy one admission get
equal price admission free
Valid April 1998 through March 1999
Maximum discount 1 person per coupon

ST. LOUIS, IRON MOUNTAIN & SOUTHERN RAILWAY
Regular price: Adults $12.50, children $6
With coupon: Adults $11, children $5
Valid April 1998 through March 1999

SEASHORE TROLLEY MUSEUM
Regular price: Adults $8, seniors $6, children $4.50
With coupon: Adults $6, seniors $4, children $3
Valid April 1998 through March 1999

SHELBURNE MUSEUM
With coupon: Buy one admission get
equal price admission free
Valid April 1998 through March 1999

SPIRIT OF TRAVERSE CITY TRAVERSE CITY PARKS AND RECREATION
With coupon: Buy one admission get
equal price admission free
Valid April 1998 through March 1999
Maximum discount 2 persons per coupon

STOURBRIDGE LINE RAIL EXCURSIONS
With coupon: $1 off admission
Valid April 1998 through March 1999
Maximum discount 2 persons per coupon

TIOGA SCENIC RAILROAD
With coupon: One half-price ticket when a second ticket
of equal value is purchased.
Valid April 1998 through March 1999
Saturday or Sunday only. One per family.
Not valid for dinner theater.

TOLEDO, LAKE ERIE & WESTERN RAILWAY AND MUSEUM
With coupon: Buy one admission get
equal price admission free
Valid April 1998 through March 1999

TOONERVILLE TROLLEY
Regular price: Adults $18, seniors $17, children $9
With coupon: Adults $17, seniors $17, children $8
Valid April 1998 through March 1999
Maximum discount 6 persons per coupon

TRAINLAND OF ORLANDO
With coupon: $1 off admission
Valid April 1998 through March 1999
Maximum discount 6 persons per coupon

TRAINLAND U.S.A.
With coupon: Buy one admission get
equal price admission free
Valid April 1998 through March 1999
Maximum discount 2 persons per coupon

TROLLEY CAR 36
With coupon: Buy one admission get
equal price admission free
Valid April 1998 through March 1999

VERMONT RAIL EXCURSIONS MIDDLEBURY, VT GUIDE TO TOURIST RAILROADS AND MUSEUMS 1998 GUEST COUPON	**TROLLEY MUSEUM OF NEW YORK** KINGSTON, NY GUIDE TO TOURIST RAILROADS AND MUSEUMS 1998 GUEST COUPON
VIRGINIA MUSEUM OF TRANSPORTATION ROANOKE, VA GUIDE TO TOURIST RAILROADS AND MUSEUMS 1998 GUEST COUPON	**VIRGINIA & TRUCKEE RAILROAD CO.** VIRGINIA CITY, NV GUIDE TO TOURIST RAILROADS AND MUSEUMS 1998 GUEST COUPON
WABASH, FRISCO & PACIFIC STEAM RAILWAY ST. LOUIS, MO GUIDE TO TOURIST RAILROADS AND MUSEUMS 1998 GUEST COUPON	**VALLEY VIEW MODEL RAILROAD** UNION, IL (MCHENRY COUNTY) GUIDE TO TOURIST RAILROADS AND MUSEUMS 1998 GUEST COUPON
WASHINGTON PARK & ZOO RAILWAY PORTLAND, OR GUIDE TO TOURIST RAILROADS AND MUSEUMS 1998 GUEST COUPON	**WALKERSVILLE SOUTHERN RAILROAD** WALKERSVILLE, MD GUIDE TO TOURIST RAILROADS AND MUSEUMS 1998 GUEST COUPON
WHITEWATER VALLEY RAILROAD CONNERSVILLE, IN GUIDE TO TOURIST RAILROADS AND MUSEUMS 1998 GUEST COUPON	**WEST COAST RAILWAY** SQUAMISH, BC, CANADA GUIDE TO TOURIST RAILROADS AND MUSEUMS 1998 GUEST COUPON
CHATTANOOGA CHOO CHOO CHATTANOOGA, TN GUIDE TO TOURIST RAILROADS AND MUSEUMS 1998 GUEST COUPON	**YAKIMA VALLEY RAIL AND STEAM MUSEUM** TOPPENISH, WA GUIDE TO TOURIST RAILROADS AND MUSEUMS 1998 GUEST COUPON

Minnesota, St. Paul

TRAINS AT BANDANA SQUARE BY TWIN CITY MODEL RAILROAD CLUB, INC.

Model railroad
O scale

LARRY VANDEN PLAS

Display: Over 3,000 square feet of O scale operating railroad, featuring a panorama of railroading in Minnesota during the 1940s and 1950s, when steam and diesel shared the rails. The display is located in Bandana Square, the restored Northern Pacific Como Shops that were once used to maintain passenger cars.

Schedule: Year round: Sundays, 12 to 5 p.m.; Tuesdays through Fridays, 11 a.m. to 7 p.m.; Saturdays, 10 a.m. to 6 p.m. Closed major holidays.

Admission/Fare: $1.00; families $3.00.

Locomotive/Rolling Stock: Former Northern Pacific F9; former Grand Trunk Western 0-8-0 locomotives; former Chicago & North Western wooden combine, boxcar, and caboose are displayed outdoors.

Special Events: Night Trains, Saturdays between Thanksgiving and end of year.

Nearby Attractions/Accommodations: Como Park with zoo, lake, and amusement park. Children's Museum. Holiday Inn Express.

Location/Directions: Bandana Square, second floor, NE corner. Off Energy Park Drive between Lexington and Snelling Avenues.

Site Address: Bandana Square, 1021 Bandana Blvd. E., St. Paul, MN
Mailing Address: Bandana Square, Box 26, 1021 Bandana Blvd., St. Paul, MN 55108
Telephone: (612) 647-9628
E-mail: tcmrc@mtn.org
Internet: www.mtn.org/tcmrc

Minnesota, Stillwater

MINNESOTA ZEPHYR LIMITED
Diesel, scheduled
Standard gauge

MINNESOTA ZEPHYR LIMITED

Museum/Ride: The *Minnesota Zephyr* dining train steeps passengers in the ambience of 1940s railroad travel. The 3½-hour journey begins on the Stillwater & St. Paul Railroad, built more than 120 years ago and later acquired by the Northern Pacific Railroad. The 7-mile line first parallels the St. Croix River, then swings west through Dutchtown along scenic Brown's Creek, climbing 250 feet on grades up to 2.2 percent. The tracks pass open fields to the Oak Glen Country Club, the summit area, then head onward to Duluth Junction. The *Zephyr* stops at the junction to prepare for the return to Stillwater. Stillwater Depot, which opened in 1993, features displays about the history of Stillwater and the logging and rail industry.

Schedule: Year round: Mondays through Saturdays, 7:30 p.m; Sundays and afternoon trips, 12 p.m. Call or write for more information.

Admission/Fare: $58.50 for excursion and dinner. Semi-formal attire requested. Reservations required.

Locomotive/Rolling Stock: Two 1951 diesel-electric engines: no. 788, a 1,750-horsepower FP9, and no. 787, a 1,500-horsepower F7; five dining cars.

Location/Directions: Follow Highway 36 east from the Twin Cities to Stillwater.

American Express

Site Address: 601 N. Main Street, Stillwater, MN
Mailing Address: PO Box 573, Stillwater, MN 55082
Telephone: (612) 430-3000 and (800) 992-6100
Internet: mnzephyr.com

Minnesota, Two Harbors

LAKE COUNTY HISTORY AND RAILROAD MUSEUM
Diesel, scheduled, railway museum
Standard gauge

LAKE COUNTY HISTORY AND RAILROAD MUSEUM

Museum: Visit our turn-of-the-century railroad depot with exhibits relating to the early railroad, logging, and shipping history of the area. The "3-Spot," former Duluth & Iron Range 2-6-0 no. 3, the first engine on the D&IR; a 2-8-8-4, former D&IR no. 229 is also on display. Visitors can also see the *Edna G.*, the last coal-fired tug on the Great Lakes; ore-loading docks; and Great Lakes ore boats.

Schedule: Mid-May through mid-October: daily, 9 a.m.-5 p.m.

Admission/Fare: Adults $2.00; children 9-17 $1.00.

Locomotive/Rolling Stock: 1943 steam engine with coal car no. 229 DM&IR "The Mallet"; steam engine with coal car D&IR Baldwin; 1883 Burnham Parry M4 no. 6649; D&IR no. 251 flatbed car and no. 22 caboose.

Special Events: Summer Solstice Party, longest day of year. Heritage Days, mid-July. Folk Festival, mid-July. Steam Train Days, August.

Nearby Attractions/Accommodations: Lighthouse, *Edna G.* Tugboat, ore docks, Sandpaper Museum.

Location/Directions: Downtown Two Harbors.

Site Address: Waterfront Drive and South Avenue, Two Harbors, MN
Mailing Address: PO Box 313, Two Harbors, MN 55616
Telephone: (218) 834-4898

Minnesota, Willmar

KANDIYOHI COUNTY HISTORICAL SOCIETY
Steam, museum

Museum: This historical center is located in the former Great Northern Division of Willmar. Summer guests can climb into the cab of the majestic 2523. The center also features a Great Northern depot built at the turn of the century, railroad exhibits, and other attractions.

Schedule: Summer: weekdays, 9 a.m. to 5 p.m. and weekends, 1 to 5 p.m. Winter: weekdays, 9 a.m. to 5 p.m.

Admission/Fare: Free.

Locomotive/Rolling Stock: Great Northern 2523 P2 class Baldwin.

Nearby Attractions/Accommodations: Little Crow Lake Region, resorts and motels, fishing.

Site Address: 610 N. Business 71, Willmar, MN
Mailing Address: 610 NE Highway 71, Willmar, MN
Telephone: (320) 235-1881

Mississippi, Vaughan — CASEY JONES MUSEUM

Museum: Casey Jones was an engineer on the Illinois Central Railroad who was killed in a collision at Vaughan, Mississippi, on April 30, 1900. Jones would have been forgotten but for a ballad written by Wallace Saunders, a friend of his who was an engine wiper. The song became enormously popular, and Casey Jones became part of American folklore. The Mississippi Bureau of Recreation and Parks operates a museum at Vaughan in a depot moved there from Pickens, a few miles north.

Schedule: Call or write for information.

Admission/Fare: Call or write for information.

Locomotive/Rolling Stock: 0-6-0; hardware; artifacts.

Nearby Attractions/Accomodations: Holmes County State Park.

Location/Directions: I-55 exit 133, east for one mile. Vaughan is 33 miles north of Jackson.

Site Address: 10901 Vaughan Road, No. 1, Vaughan, MS
Mailing Address: 10901 Vaughan Road, No. 1, Vaughan, MS 39179
Telephone: (601) 673-9864

Missouri, Belton

BELTON, GRANDVIEW & KANSAS CITY RR CO.
THE "LEAKY ROOF" ROUTE

Diesel, scheduled
Standard gauge

DAVID HOLLAND

Museum/Ride: Two former Frisco static steam locomotives (2-10-0) no. 1632 and (2-8-0) no. 5, several freight and passenger cars representing various midwestern railroads. Last remaining trackage (56# rail) from the former Kansas City, Clinton & Springfield "Leaky Roof" Railroad. Interpretive displays housed in cases in the former Norfolk & Western baggage express car no. 873. Railroad-related videos shown continuously in the former Santa Fe instruction/theater car no. 80. Train ride is approximately five miles round trip.

Schedule: Mid-May through October 1: weekends and holidays, departs at 2 p.m., ticket sales 1 p.m. Group specials available. Call or write.

Admission/Fare: Museum–free. Train–adults $5; children age 3 and under free if not occupying a seat.

Locomotive/Rolling Stock: 1956 former B&O GP9 no. 102; 1920 former Erie, Delaware & Lackawanna open-window commuter coach no. 4364; 1972 former Missouri Pacific wide-vision cupola caboose no. 13562.

Special Events: Pumpkin Patch Express, October. Wild West Days. Hobo Days. Call or write for information.

Nearby Attractions/Accommodations: Belton Museum, Dunn's Cider Mill, Mac's Country, lodging.

Location/Directions: About 8 miles south of I-435/I-470 and Hwy 71.

Site Address: 502 Walnut, Belton, MO
Mailing Address: 502 Walnut, Belton, MO 64012-2516
Telephone: (816) 331-0630

Missouri, Branson   **BRANSON SCENIC RAILWAY**
                                             Standard gauge

Ride: This railway operates a 40-mile, 1¾-hour round trip through the Ozark foothills over the former Missouri Pacific White River Route, now owned by the Missouri & North Arkansas Railroad. Most trips take passengers south into Arkansas, across Lake Taneycomo and two high trestles and through two tunnels. The original 1906 Branson depot houses the railway's ticket office, waiting room, gift shop, and business offices.

Schedule: March, November, December: Wednesdays through Saturdays, 9 and 11:30 a.m., 2 p.m. April through September: Mondays through Saturdays, 9 and 11:30 a.m., 2 p.m. Memorial Day to Labor Day: 9, 11:30 a.m., 2 and 5 p.m. October: Sundays through Saturdays, 9 and 11:30 a.m., 2 and 5 p.m. Closed Sundays except Memorial Day weekend, July 4, Labor Day, October. Closed Thanksgiving. Dinner train–May through December: Saturdays, 5 p.m.

Admission/Fare: Adults $18.50; seniors $17.50; student 14-18 $13.50; children 4-12 $8.75. Group rates available.

Locomotive/Rolling Stock: No. 83, F9PH, BSR, former B&O Railroad; no. 4265, GP30M, BSR, former B&O Railroad; and more.

Special Events: Craft shows, Troop Train, Holiday Train, shopping.

Nearby Attractions/Accommodations: Lake Taneycomo, campgrounds.

Location/Directions: Downtown Branson, ¾ mile east of U.S. 65.

Site Address: 206 E. Main Street, Branson, MO
Mailing Address: 206 E. Main Street, Branson, MO 65616
Telephone: (417) 334-6110 and (800) 2TRAIN2
Fax: (417) 336-3909

Missouri, Branson

SILVER DOLLAR CITY THEME PARK
Steam, scheduled

SILVER DOLLAR CITY

Ride: The Silver Dollar Steam Train is a ride running throughout the day, taking guests on a fun-filled tour through the Ozark's wooded hills.

Schedule: April 11 through December 30: departures every 30 minutes.

Admission/Fare: Free with paid admission to theme park.

Locomotive/Rolling Stock: 1938 engine no. 13 Orenstein 2-4-0, Koppel, Germany; 1934 engine no. 43 Orenstein 2-4-0, Koppel, Germany; 1940 engine no. 76 2-4-0, Germany.

Special Events: Silver Dollar Sing-Along Steam Train (caroling rides), November and December.

Location/Directions: Highway 76, approximately 5 miles west of Branson.

Site Address: HCR 1, Box 791, Branson, MO
Mailing Address: HCR 1, Box 791, Branson, MO 65616
Telephone: (800) 952-6626 and (417) 338-2611
Internet: www.silverdollarcity.com

Missouri, Eureka   **SIX FLAGS OVER MID-AMERICA**
Steam, scheduled
36" gauge

SIX FLAGS OVER MID-AMERICA

Ride: The narrow gauge Six Flags Railroad was built and first operated in 1971. It consists of one 25-ton steam locomotive, a tender, four passenger cars, and a caboose. The engine is a propane-fueled steam locomotive manufactured by Crown Metal Company.

Schedule: Runs continously around park, stopping at two stations.

Admission/Fare: Park admission required.

Locomotive/Rolling Stock: One 25-ton narrow gauge steam locomotive; open passenger cars.; enclosed caboose.

Location/Directions: I-44 and Allentown Road, west of St. Louis.

Site Address: Eureka, MO
Mailing Address: PO Box 60, Eureka, MO 63025
Telephone: (314) 938-5300

Missouri, Glencoe
(Wildwood, MO)

WABASH FRISCO & PACIFIC RAILWAY
"THE UNCOMMON CARRIER"

Steam, scheduled
12" gauge

DAVID J. NEUBAUER

Ride: A 2-mile, 30-minute round trip over a former Missouri Pacific right-of-way along the scenic Meramec River through wooded areas and over three bridges.

Schedule: May through October: Sundays, 11:15 a.m. to 4:15 p.m.

Admission/Fare: $2; children under age 3 ride free. No reservations.

Locomotive/Rolling Stock: Eight steam locomotives; two diesel locomotives; 35 cars comprising two eight-car trains.

Special Events: Member's Day, September.

Nearby Attractions/Accommodations: Musuem of Transportation, Union Pacific and Burlington Northern Santa Fe mainlines, Eureka, Missouri.

Location/Directions: Twenty-five miles west of St. Louis. I-44 (Eureka), exit 264, north on Route 109 for 3½ miles to Old State Road, make two right turns to depot on Washington Street and Grand Avenue.

*Coupon available, see coupon section.

Radio Frequency: 151.955

Site Address: Foot of Washington and Grand Avenue, Wildwood, MO
Mailing Address: 1569 Ville Angela Lane, Hazelwood, MO 63042-1630
Telephone: (314) 587-3538 and (314) 351-9385
Fax: (314) 554-3260
E-mail: malachi_owens_jr@ue.com
Internet: http://home.stlnet.com/~shahriary/wfp

Missouri, Jackson

ST. LOUIS, IRON MOUNTAIN & SOUTHERN RAILWAY
Steam, scheduled
Standard gauge

ST. LOUIS, IRON MINE & SOUTHERN RAILWAY

Ride: Steam-powered train takes passengers on their choice of three different round trips over a former Missouri Pacific branch line: a 10-mile, 1¼-hour sightseeing trip to Gordonville; a 20-mile, 2-hour dinner trip to Dutchtown.

Schedule: April through October: Gordonville trip–Saturdays, 11 a.m., 2 p.m. and Sundays, 1 p.m. Summer: add Wednesdays and Fridays, 1 p.m. Delta train–April through October (once a month) on Saturday, 5 p.m. Dutchtown trip (dinner train)–Saturdays, 4 or 5 p.m. Group rates and weekday charters available. Breakfast trains and candlelight dinners also.

Admission/Fare: Adults $12.50; children $6; dinner $24.50 to $37.

Locomotive/Rolling Stock: No. 5, 1946 Porter 2-4-2, former Central Illinois Public Service, former Crab Orchard & Egyptian; no. 300, 1926 Alco 2-6-0, former Augusta Railway; no. 911, 1952 Baldwin-Lima-Hamilton diesel-electric, former Pittsburg Plate Glass Co.;1945 New York Central coach no. 4452, former Baltimore & Ohio; open-air observation car (former piggyback car); two bay-window cabooses.

Nearby Attractions/Accommodations: Bollinger Mill and covered bridge, Trail of Tears State Park, Veteran's War Memorial, The Oliver House Historic Home, Old McKendree Chapel, Trisha's Bed and Breakfast.

Location/Directions: Four miles from Cape Girardeau.

*Coupon available, see coupon section.

Site Address: 252 E. Jackson Blvd., Jackson, MO
Mailing Address: PO Box 244, Jackson, MO 63755
Telephone: (573) 243-1688 and (800) 455-RAIL
Internet: www.rosecity.net/trains

Missouri, St. Joseph

PATEE HOUSE MUSEUM
Railway museum

COURTESY OF PATEE HOUSE MUSEUM

Museum: The 1860 Headquarters for the Pony Express, where visitors can climb aboard the Hannibal-St. Joseph steam locomotive and the mail car, which are located inside the museum.

Schedule: Call or write for information.

Admission/Fare: Adults $3.00; seniors $2.50; students under age 18 $1.50; under age 6 are free with family.

Locomotive/Rolling Stock: 1892 Baldwin 4-4-0 no. 35, reconstructed in 1933-34 to resemble H&StJ no. 35.

Special Events: Pony Express/Jesse James Weekend, first weekend in April. See gun shootouts, Pony Express reinactors, and crafts.

Nearby Attractions/Accommodations: Home of Jesse James and a doll museum.

Location/Directions: From Highway 36 take the 10th Street exit, follow 10th Street north to right on Mitchell, and left at 12th Street.

P * ☕ ⛪ ✉ M

Site Address: 12th and Penn, St. Joseph, MO
Mailing Address: 12th and Penn, Box 1022, St. Joseph, MO 64502
Telephone: (816) 232-8206
Fax: (816) 232-8206

Missouri, St. Louis **AMERICAN RAILWAY CABOOSE HISTORICAL EDUCATIONAL SOCIETY, INC. (A.R.C.H.E.S.)**
Cabooseum
Standard gauge

RICHARD A. EICHHORST

Display: The Caboose Museum has at least one of their 30 "cabeese" on display at any given time. While a permanent location is being planned, the equipment is stored at ten different locations in Missouri and Illinois. Some of these cabooses are on loan to other rail museums. In addition to the interpretive center that is open to the public, ARCHES is an international association with members in 33 states and Canada. The members are compiling *Catalog of Captive Cabeese*, which lists the location of cabooses in North America that are no longer in active service.

Schedule: April 5, May 3, June 7, July 5, August 2, September 6, and October 4: 1 to 4 p.m.

Admission/Fare: Donations appreciated.

Cabooses: A&S; B&O; C&O; C&NW; CC; CGW; C&NW; Essex Terminal, Frisco, IC, Manufacturers, N&W, RI, Southern, TRRA, and Union Pacific.

Special Events: Caboose Chili Cook-off, Caboose Chase excursions, Santa Special on MetroLink, Rail Caboose tours.

Location/Directions: Varies, call or write for information.

St. Louis & Kirkwood, MO / Alton, IL

Site Address: St. Louis, MO
Mailing Address: PO Box 2772, St. Louis, MO 63116
Telephone: (314) 752-3148

Missouri, St. Louis

HOLIDAY CRUISIN' RAILS
CANADIAN SUNRISE RAILS
Diesel, scheduled

JONATHAN WOOD

Ride: Rail Cruisin' is more fun and entertainment than you can imagine. Special attendants, excellent food, and careful attention to detail make this an outstanding site to visit. Travel at speeds of 65 to 80 mph over excellent trackage, on day or overnight trips. The business car is all original, just as it was when it served Canadian National's last president.

Schedule: Year round. Call or write for more information.

Admission/Fare: $99.99 for the basic trip; fares vary with cruise choice.

Locomotive/Rolling Stock: Amtrak; Canadian National president's business car no. 100 Bonaventure.

Special Events: Spirit of Christmas (Kansas City and Springfield, Illinois), Show Me Express (Jefferson City), The Land of Lincoln (Springfield, Illinois), International Cork University, Great Escapes to the Unknown, Romance Run Away, Mardi Gras Blow Out, Family Memories Tour, and charter services.

Nearby Attractions/Accommodations: Museum of Transportation, Six Flags, St. Louis Arch, riverboats, Meramec Caverns, Missouri Botanical Gardens, Anheuser-Busch Brewery/Clydesdale Stables, Fairmont Park (horse racing), Purina Farms, St. Louis Blues, St. Louis Cardinals, St. Louis Sports Hall of Fame, and the National Bowling Hall of Fame.

Location/Directions: Downtown St. Louis, near Kiel Center.

Site Address: 550 South 16th Street, St. Louis, MO
Mailing Address: 3621 NW 43rd, Oklahoma City, OK 73112-6359
Telephone: (405) 942-2222
Fax: (405) 942-0123

Missouri, St. Louis

MUSEUM OF TRANSPORTATION
Railway museum
Standard gauge

MUSEUM OF TRANSPORTATION

Museum: The museum houses one of the largest and best collections of transportation vehicles in the world, according to the Smithsonian Instution. With over 70 locomotives, the museum has one of the most complete collections of American rail power, and its collection of automobiles, buses, streetcars, aircraft, horsedrawn vehicles, and river boat material reflects the ever-changing nature of transportation.

Schedule: Year round: daily, 9 a.m. to 5 p.m. Closed Thanksgiving, Christmas, and New Year's Day.

Admission/Fare: Adults $4; seniors and children 5-12 $1.50.

Locomotive/Rolling Stock: Thirty-five steam locomotives; 29 internal combustion locomotives; 9 electric locomotives; 23 passenger cars; 54 freight cars.

Special Events: Annual Transportation Celebration, first weekend in August.

Nearby Attractions/Accommodations: St. Louis Arch, Grant's Farm, Science Center, Zoo, Magic House.

Location/Directions: From I-270 exit Dougherty Ferry Rd., west for ½ mile, left on Barrett Station.

[♿] [P] [🚌] [✳] [☕] [📷] [⛩] [⛪] M [🚂] Kirkwood

Site Address: 3015 Barrett Station Rd., St. Louis, MO
Mailing Address: 3015 Barrett Station Rd., St. Louis, MO 63122
Telephone: (314) 965-7998
Fax: (314) 965-0242

Missouri, Springfield

FRISCO RAILROAD MUSEUM
Railway museum
Standard gauge

FRISCO RAILROAD MUSEUM

Display: This museum, located at station 238 on the Frisco's former Lebanon Subdivision, Eastern Division, is housed in a building originally constructed by the Frisco Railway in 1943 as a Centralized Traffic Control command center. It is the only facility in the country devoted exclusively to the preservation and display of the history and memorabilia of the Frisco Railway. The facility displays more than 2,000 items of Frisco and Frisco-related memorabilia, representing a wide range of operations, equipment, and services. In addition, it has the largest archive of historical, technical, and photographic information about the Frisco currently available to the public through its "Frisco Folks" membership program.

Schedule: Tuesday through Saturday, 10 a.m. to 5 p.m.

Admission/Fare: Adults $2.00; children under 12 $1.00. Group discounts.

Locomotive/Rolling Stock: Caboose no. 1159; boxcar no. 10055; side-door caboose no. 1156; no. 1551 diner-lounge "Oklahoma City" available for meetings, banquets, parties, special events. All former Frisco.

Special Events: Frisco Days, April; Christmas Open House, featuring large collection of train-related ornaments, held 2 weeks before Christmas.

Location/Directions: At 543 East Commercial Street. Take exit 80 A/B off I-44, travel south on business 65 1.3 miles to Commercial Street (third light), then travel west 1.3 miles.

[&] [P] [🚌] [✳] [☕] [🍽] [🚻] [📷] [🎨] M

Site Address: 543 East Commercial Street, Springfield, MO
Mailing Address: 543 East Commercial Street, Springfield, MO 65803
Telephone: (417) 866-SLSF (7573)
E-mail: amunhotep@aol.com
Internet: www.crl.com/~acorley/frisco/frisco.html

Montana, Lewistown

CHARLIE RUSSELL CHOW-CHOO DINNER TRAIN
Diesel, scheduled
Standard gauge

CHERIE NEUDICK

Ride: A 3½-hour ride through a half-mile long tunnel, over three trestles, and past an abundance of wildlife. A full course prime rib dinner is served. Also, a train robbery and other entertainment.

Schedule: June through September: Saturdays.

Admission/Fare: $69.00; New Year's Eve train $99.00.

Locomotive/Rolling Stock: Five Budd-built NSSR passenger cars; diesel locomotive.

Nearby Attractions/Accommodations: Two golf courses, historical sites, water slide, third largest fresh water spring in the world, mountains.

Location/Directions: Highway 87.

Site Address: 408 NE Main, Lewistown, MT
Mailing Address: PO Box 818, Lewistown, MT
Telephone: (406) 538-5436
Fax: (406) 538-5437
E-mail: lewchamb@lewistown.net
Internet: www.lewistown.net

Nebraska, Fremont

FREMONT & ELKHORN VALLEY RAILROAD
NATIONAL RAILWAY HISTORICAL SOCIETY
NEBRASKA CHAPTER

Ride: Take a ride through history on a 30-mile round trip from Fremont to Hooper over rails laid in 1869. Ride on cars built in 1924 and 1925. Enjoy the scenic Elkhorn Valley.

Schedule: May through November: weekends, 1 p.m. Group excursions by appointment.

Admission/Fare: Adults $11.00; seniors $9.90; children 4-11 $6.00; under age four are free.

Locomotive/Rolling Stock: EMD no. 1219 locomotive; no. 1938 Burlington RPO baggage car; 1925 "Lake Bluff" passenger car; 1927 "Fort Andrew" passenger car; 1957 flat car.

Special Events: Civil War reenactments, Memorial Day weekend, third week in August, and July 4. John C. Freemont Days, second weekend of July. Harvest Days, second and third week of October. Halloween activities, last weekend in October and Halloween night. December, Santa Runs (reservations required).

Nearby Attractions/Accommodations: Railway Museum, May Museum, Old Poor Farm, antique shopping, Motor Plex, historical Main Street.

Location/Directions: Approximately 35 miles west of Omaha. Highway 275 exit Military Avenue, travel west through Fremont, turn north on Somers Avenue.

[P] [bus] [*] [coffee] [π] [locomotive] [bridge] M arm

Site Address: 1835 N. Somers Avenue, Fremont, NE
Mailing Address: PO Box 191, Fremont, NE 68026
Telephone: (402) 727-0615
Fax: (402) 727-0615
E-mail: fevr@geocities.com
Internet: www.geocities.com/heartland/hills/4184/fevr.html

Nebraska, Fremont

FREMONT DINNER TRAIN
Diesel, scheduled
Standard gauge

BRUCE EVELAND

Ride: Relive the 1940s on a 30-mile round trip aboard restored 1940s era cars. Fine dining experience in air-conditioned and heated cars.

Schedule: April through October: Fridays and Saturdays, 7:30 to 10:45 p.m.; Sundays, 1:30 to 4:45 p.m. November through March: Saturdays, 6:30 to 9:45 p.m.

Admission/Fare: Adults: Sundays, $37.95, evenings $42.95; children: Sundays, $19.95, evenings $22.95.

Locomotive/Rolling Stock: N&W power car no. 410; two converted cars, former CN; one converted car, former IC; one partially converted car, former Milwaukee.

Special Events: Murder Mysteries, Melodramas, Valentine's Day, July 4th, Halloween, New Year's Eve.

Nearby Attractions/Accommodations: Museum and antique shop district.

Location/Directions: Forty miles northwest of Omaha.

[P] 👤 🚂 ✉

Site Address: 1835 N. Somers Avenue, Fremont, NE
Mailing Address: 650 N. "H," Fremont, NE 68025
Telephone: (402) 727-8321 and (800) 942-7245
Fax: (402) 727-0915
Internet: www.geocities.com/heartland/hills/4184/fevr.html

Nebraska, Goehner

CHIPPEWA NORTHWESTERN RAILWAY CO.
Steam, scheduled
4¾" gauge

SCOTT BLAIR

Ride/Museum: The Chippewa Northwestern Railway Company is located on the grounds of the Seward County Historical Society's Museum. The museum has a fine assortment of historical items from midwest farming. Free train rides are given to the public (see schedule below).

Schedule: Train–May through September: second and fourth Sundays, 1:30 to 4:30 p.m. Museum–May through October: Thursdays and Sundays, 1:30 to 4:30 p.m.

Admission/Fare: Free.

Locomotive/Rolling Stock: One-inch scale–4-6-2; 4-4-2; 2-6-0; 2-8-2; 4-8-2; F7a.

Special Events: Goehner's Heritage Days, second weekend in June. Chippewa's Fall Steam Rush, first weekend in October.

Location/Directions: Twenty-five miles west of Lincoln. I-80, exit 373, one mile north on west side of the highway.

Site Address: Seward County Historical Society Museum, Goehner, NE
Mailing Address: Chippewa NW Railway Co., PO Box 6837, Lincoln, NE 68506
Telephone: (402) 489-4458 and (402) 523-4055
E-mail: jc13803@navix.net

Nebraska, Omaha

OMAHA HENRY DOORLY ZOO RAILROAD
Steam, scheduled
30" gauge

Ride: The zoo operates two live steam locomotives on 2½-miles of track through the grounds. The panoramic train ride highlights a number of the zoo's animals. The Union Pacific Engine House allows for state-of-the-art railroad.

Schedule: Memorial Day through Labor Day: daily, 11 a.m. to 5 p.m. April through Memorial Day and Labor Day through October 31, weekends only.

Admission/Fare: Zoo admission: adults $7.75; seniors $5.75; children $3.75. Train fare: adults $2.50; children $1.50.

Special Events: Ice Cream Safari, June 28; Critter Ride (bike around zoo), July 20.

Nearby Attractions/Accommodations: Rosenblatt Baseball Stadium (home of Omaha Royals), Omaha Community Playhouse, Omaha Children's Museum, The Old Market, Central Park Mall.

Location/Directions: I-80, exit 13th Street south, east on Bert Murphy Avenue. Adjacent to Rosenblatt Stadium.

Site Address: 3701 S. 10th Street, Omaha, NE
Mailing Address: 3701 S. 10th Street, Omaha, NE 68107
Telephone: (402) 733-8401
Fax: (402) 733-7868

Nebraska, Omaha

UNION PACIFIC COLLECTION
Railroad display, museum, model railroad

UNION PACIFIC COLLECTION

Display: Exhibits will tell the story of Union Pacific. Current exhibits include uniforms, china, model trains, and the construction of the railroad.

Schedule: Call or write for information.

Admission/Fare: Call or write for information.

Locomotive/Rolling Stock: No. 1243 Union Pacific; UP sleeping car National Command.

Special Events: Railroad Days.

   &boxed; P ✳ ⛪ M 🚂

Site Address: 801 South 10th Street, Omaha, NE
Mailing Address: 1416 Dodge, Omaha, NE 68179
Telephone: (402) 271-3305
Fax: (402) 271-6460
Internet: www.uprr.com

Nebraska, Omaha

WESTERN HERITAGE MUSEUM
History museum

Display: This museum, housed in Omaha's old Union Station, features Omaha history exhibits, including a Union Pacific engine, passenger car, caboose, and streetcar.

Schedule: Call or write for information.

Admission/Fare: Call or write for information.

Site Address: 801 S. 10th Street, Omaha, NE
Mailing Address: 801 S. 10th Street, Omaha, NE 68108
Telephone: (402) 444-5071

Nevada, Carson City **NEVADA STATE RAILROAD MUSEUM**
Railway museum
Standard and narrow gauge

GEORGE A. FORERO, JR.

Display: The Nevada State Railroad Museum houses over 50 pieces of railroad equipment from Nevada's past and is considered one of the finest regional railroad museums in the country. Included in the collection are 5 steam locomotives and several restored coaches and freight cars. The bulk of the equipment is from the Virginia & Truckee Railroad, America's richest and most famous short line. Museum activities include operation of historic railroad equipment, hand car races, lectures, an annual railroad history symposium, changing exhibits, and a variety of special events.

Schedule: Year round: daily, 8:30 a.m. to 4:30 p.m.

Admission/Fare: $2.00; under age 18 are free.

Locomotive/Rolling Stock: No. 25, 1905 Baldwin 4-6-0; no. 18, "Dayton," 1873 Central Pacific 4-4-0; and no. 22, "Inyo," 1875 Baldwin 4-4-0; all former V&T. No. 1, "Glenbrook," 1875 Baldwin narrow-gauge 2-6-0, former Carson & Tahoe Lumber & Fluming Co.; no. 8, 1888 Cooke 4-4-0, former Dardanelle & Russellville; no. 1, "Joe Douglass," 1882 Porter narrow gauge 0-4-2T, former Dayton, Sutro & Carson Valley. Coaches nos. 3, 4, 8, 11, 12, 17 & 18, express/mail nos. 14 & 21, caboose-coaches nos. 9, 10 & 15, and eleven freight cars, all former V&T; more.

Location/Directions: Highways 50 and 395, at the south end of town.

[&] [P] [bus] [*] [mail] M arm TRAIN

Site Address: 2180 South Carson Street, Carson City, NV
Mailing Address: 2180 South Carson Street, Carson City, NV 89710
Telephone: (702) 687-6953
Internet: pages.prodigy.com/jbryant/nevrr.htm

Nevada, East Ely

NEVADA NORTHERN RAILWAY MUSEUM
Steam, diesel, scheduled
Standard gauge

JACK SWANBERG

Display: Keystone Route–A 14-mile, 1½-hour round trip to the historic mining district of Keystone, passing downtown Ely, tunnel No. 1, the ghost town of Lane City, and Robinson Canyon. Highline Route–A 22-mile, 1½-hour round trip with exciting overviews of the scenic Steptoe Valley, high in the foothills. Displays consist of steam, diesel, and electric locomotives; 1907 steam rotary snowplow; 1910 Jordan spreader; more than 60 pieces of antique passenger, freight, and work equipment; general offices; depot; machine shops; roundhouse.

Schedule: Memorial Day through Labor Day: Saturdays.

Admission/Fare: Call or write for information.

Locomotive/Rolling Stock: No. 40, 1910 Baldwin 4-6-0, Nevada Northern Railway; no. 93, 1909 Alco 2-8-0; no. 105, Alco RS-2, and no. 109, Alco RS-3, both former Kennecott Copper Co.

Location/Directions: In eastern Nevada on U.S. 93.

Site Address: East Ely Depot, 1100 Avenue A, East Ely, NV
Mailing Address: PO Box 150040, East Ely, NV 89315
Telephone: (702) 289-2085
Internet: www.artcom.com/museums/nv/mr/89315-00.htm

Nevada, Las Vegas

EUREKA & PALISADE RAILROAD
Steam, unscheduled
36" gauge

DANIEL MARKOFF

Display: Occasional public display and operation on historical narrow gauge.

Schedule: To be announced.

Admission/Fare: Call or write for details.

Locomotive/Rolling Stock: 1875 Baldwin Locomotive Works 4-4-0 American "Eureka."

Special Events: Call or write for details.

P

Site Address: Las Vegas, NV
Mailing Address: 820 S. 7th Street, Suite A, Las Vegas, NV 89101
Telephone: (702) 383-6893

Nevada, Virginia City

VIRGINIA & TRUCKEE RAILROAD CO.
Steam, scheduled
Standard gauge

VIRGINIA & TRUCKEE RAILROAD CO.

Ride: A 5-mile round trip from Virginia City to the town of Gold Hill through the heart of the historic Comstock mining region. A knowledgeable conductor gives a running commentary of the area and of the 126-year-old railroad.

Schedule: May 23 through October 18.

Admission/Fare: Adults $4.50; children 5-12 $2.25; children under age 4 ride free; all-day pass $9.00.

Locomotive/Rolling Stock: 1916 Baldwin 2-8-0 no. 29, former Longview Portland & Northern; 1907 Baldwin 2-6-2 no. 8, former Hobart Southern; 1888 Northwestern Pacific combine and coach; former Tonopah & Tidewater coach; former Northern Pacific caboose; 1919 0-6-0 no. 30, former Southern Pacific.

Special Events: Party and Night train, once a month during season.

Nearby Attractions/Accommodations: Historic Virginia City, mines, mansions.

Location/Directions: Twenty-one miles from Reno, 17 miles from Carson City.

*Coupon available, see coupon section.

Site Address: Washington and "F" Streets, Virginia City, NV
Mailing Address: PO Box 467, Virginia City, NV 89440
Telephone: (702) 847-0380

New Hampshire, Bretton Woods

THE MOUNT WASHINGTON COG RAILWAY
Scheduled rides
4'8"gauge

THE MOUNT WASHINGTON COG RAILWAY

Ride: Climb aboard the World's first mountain climbing cog railway to the summit of Mount Washington, the highest peak in the Northeast. Rain or shine, this three-hour round trip journey on one of eight enclosed and heated coaches is a truly unique vacation experience for all ages. Visit our new Base Station with musuem, restaurant and gift shop. National Historic Engineering Landmark built in 1869.

Schedule: May through early November: call for schedule. Reservations recommended.

Admission/Fare: Adults $39.00; seniors $35.00; children 6-12 $26.00; under age 6 are free unless occupying a seat.

Locomotive/Rolling Stock: Seven coal-fired steam engines; seven enclosed heated coaches; one speeder.

Nearby Attractions/Accommodations: The Mount Washington Hotel & Resort, over 12 family attractions within 30 miles, outlet shoppping, and hiking.

Location/Directions: Located in the heart of New Hampshire's White Mountains at the base of the Presidential Mountain Range. I-93, exit 35, route 3N, Route 302E to Cog Railway Base Road. Site is located 165 miles from Boston, Massachusetts, and 105 miles from Manchester, New Hampshire.

Site Address: Route 302, Bretton Woods, NH
Mailing Address: Route 302, Bretton Woods, NH 03589
Telephone: (800) 922-8825 and (603) 278-5404
Fax: (603) 278-5830

New Hampshire, Intervale

HARTMANN MODEL RAILROAD, LTD.
Model railroad display

HARTMANN MODEL RAILROAD, LTD.

Museum/Ride: Housed in two buildings, each 8,000 square feet, is a railroad display for all ages. This site features many operating layouts, from G to Z scales, including a replica of Crawford Notch, New Hampshire, in the mid 1950s to early 1960s. Visitors can see several other detailed operating layouts with trains winding through tunnels, over bridges, and past miniature stations and buildings, and Thomas the Tank Engine operates by a light-sensor system. Also on display are about 5,000 model locomotives and coaches, American and European. Come and see our operating outdoor railroad and take a ride with us.

Schedule: Year round: daily, 10 a.m. to 5 p.m.

Admission/Fare: Adults $5.00; seniors $4.00; children 5-12 $3.00; group rates available.

Location/Directions: Four miles north of North Conway.

Site Address: Town Hall Road and Route 302/16, Intervale, NH
Mailing Address: PO Box 165, Intervale, NH 03845
Telephone: (603) 356-9922
Fax: (603) 356-9958

New Hampshire, Lincoln

HOBO RAILROAD
Diesel, scheduled
Standard gauge

ALLAN POMMER

Ride: A 1.25-hour train ride in a woodsy setting along the Pemigewasset River on former Boston & Maine track. On most trips passengers glimpse a variety of wildlife, including a golden eagle, ducks, a blue heron, beavers, and other small creatures. Passengers may also enjoy lunch or dinner on the train. The Hobo Picnic Lunch is a unique specialty, served in a souvenir hobo bindle stick. Fine dining is also offered on the 7:00 p.m. train aboard the "Cafe Lafayette," a restored Dome Pullman dining car.

Schedule: Call or write for information.

Admission/Fare: Call or write for information.

Locomotive/Rolling Stock: No. 1008, 1949 Alco S-1, former Portland Terminal; no. 959, 1949 Alco S-1, former North Stratford; four modified motors, former Erie & Lackawanna; modified Pullman day coach, former New York Central; two kitchen cars, former U.S. Army; several Budd cars; more.

Location/Directions: I-93 exit 32. On Kancamagus Highway, in the heart of the scenic White Mountains.

Radio frequencies: 160.47 and 161.55

Site Address: Kancamagus Highway, Lincoln, NH
Mailing Address: PO Box 9, Lincoln, NH 03251
Telephone: (603) 745-2135

212

New Hampshire, Lincoln **WHITE MOUNTAIN CENTRAL RAILROAD**
Steam, scheduled
Standard gauge

CHET BRICKET

Display/Ride: A facsimile of an 1890s railroad station, a wooden caboose, boxcars, and flatcars. Other exhibits include a fire museum, an Americana museum, a haunted house, an antique photo parlor, a 1920s-era garage, an illusion building, "Merlin's Mansion," and much more. Enjoy a 2-mile, 30-minute ride through the scenic White Mountains, leaving from the beautiful depot at Clark's Trading Post. The train crosses a 120-foot covered bridge and climbs a 2 percent grade into the woods.

Schedule: Late June through Labor Day: daily, 10 a.m. to 4 p.m.

Admission/Fare: $7.00 per person ages 6 years and up.

Locomotive/Rolling Stock: No. 4, 1927 2-truck Heisler, former International Shoe Co.; no. 6, Climax, former Beebe River Railroad; no. 3, former East Branch & Lincoln.

Nearby Attractions/Accommodations: Loon Mountain gondola, Lost River.

Location/Directions: I-93 exit 33 south.

Site Address: Clark's Trading Post, Route 3, Lincoln, NH
Mailing Address: Box 1, Lincoln, NH 03251
Telephone: (603) 745-8913

New Hampshire, Meredith — CAFE LAFAYETTE DINNER TRAINS

SOMMERFELD PHOTO

Ride: Gourmet dining excursions along the shore of scenic Lake Winnipesaukee, Meredith, and Paugus Bays.

Schedule: July through October. Call for details.

Admission/Fare: Adults $38.95; children 4-11 $19.95; age 3 and under $5 minimum.

Locomotive/Rolling Stock: 1924 Pullman dining car, former NYC; 1923 Pennsylvania Railroad caboose.

Nearby Attractions/Accommodations: M.V. Mount Washington, New Hampshire's lakes region. Call or write for accommodation information.

Location/Directions: I-93, exit 23 (route 104 east) for 8 miles, left on route 3 for ¾ miles, left after bridge over railroad tracks.

*Coupon available, see coupon section.

Site Address: Winnipesaukee Railyard, Meredith, NH
Mailing Address: RR1 Box 85, Lincoln, NH 03251
Telephone: (603) 745-3500 and (800) 699-3501 (outside NH)
Fax: (603) 745-9850

New Hampshire, Meredith	**WINNIPESAUKEE SCENIC RAILROAD**
	Diesel, scheduled
	Standard gauge

GEORGE A FORERO, JR.

Ride/Display: This line operates 1- and 2-hour excursions over former Boston & Maine track between Meredith and Lakeport. Passengers view unsurpassed scenery along the shores of New Hampshire's largest lake, Lake Winnipesaukee, in the comfort of climate-controlled coaches. Dining service is available during the summer, and the Ice Cream Parlor Car offers a make-your-own-sundae bar aboard the train. Fall foliage tours are 3-hour round trips to Plymouth. An 1893 former B&M baggage car serves as the ticket office; cabooses and other rolling stock are also on exhibit.

Schedule: Call or write for information.

Admission/Fare: Call or write for information.

Locomotive/Rolling Stock: No. 2, 1943 44-ton General Electric, former U.S. Government; no. 1186, 1952 Alco S-3, former B&M; five Budd RDC-1 coaches; 1893 baggage car, former B&M, serving as ticket office; cabooses; more.

Location/Directions: In the Lakes Region of New Hampshire, with boarding at Meredith or Weirs Beach. Free parking at Meredith, just off route 3.

P ✳ ☕ 👤 ⛩   Radio frequencies: 160.47 and 161.55

Site Address: Meredith, NH
Mailing Address: PO Box 9, Lincoln, NH 03251
Telephone: (603) 745-2135 and (603) 279-5253

New Hampshire, North Conway

CONWAY SCENIC RAILROAD
Steam, scheduled
Standard gauge

D.T. WALKER

Ride/Display: Train rides of varying duration from one hour originate at North Conway's historic 1874 Railroad Station. "Valley Train" travels south to Conway over former Boston & Maine Railroad branchline through farmlands in the Mount Washington Valley and west over former Maine Central Mountain Subdivision to Bartlett. "Notch Train" provides excursion service west from North Conway through spectacular Crawford Notch to Crawford Depot and Fabyan Station. Museum of railroad memorabilia within the 123 year old Victorian North Conway Station. Original Roundhouse and Operating Turntable highlight rail yard, where many pieces of rolling stock are displayed.

Schedule: Call or write for information.

Admission/Fare: Call or write for information.

Locomotive/Rolling Stock: No. 7470, 1921 Grand Trunk 0-6-0, former Canadian National; no. 15, 1945 44-ton General Electric, former Maine Central; no. 1055, 1950 Alco-General Electric S-4, former Portland Terminal Co.; more.

Location/Directions: The depot faces the village park. North Conway is on routes 16 and 302 in New Hampshire's Mount Washington Valley.

*Coupon available, see coupon section.

Radio frequency: 161.250

Site Address: North Conway, NH
Mailing Address: PO Box 1947, North Conway, NJH 03860
Telephone: (603) 356-5251

216

New Hampshire, Wolfeboro Falls

KLICKETY KLACK MODEL RAILROAD
Model railroad

KLICKETY KLACK MODEL RAILROAD

Display: This is the largest operating HO model railroad in New England. This railroad represents over 70,000 hours of work and is housed in a building that is 30 x 76 feet. Watch trains think for themselves as operating orders are received from the 3-color block signals; stopping on red, slowing down on yellow, or going through a green with no change of speed. This is called ATC (Automatic Train Control). Eight trains are operating simultaneously on the main lines. There are over 30 controls that you can operate. Equipment is from 1800s to present.

Schedule: July 1 through September 2: Tuesdays through Saturdays, 10 a.m. to 5:30 p.m. September 3 through June 30: Thursdays through Saturdays, 10 a.m. to 5 p.m. Closed the last week in April.

Admission/Fare: Adults $4.00; children 3-12 $3.00.

Location/Directions: At the junction of routes 28 and 109A.

Site Address: Wolfeboro Falls, NH
Mailing Address: PO Box 205, Wolfeboro Falls NH 03896
Telephone: (603) 569-5384

New Jersey, Cape May

CAPE MAY SEASHORE LINES
Diesel, scheduled
Standard gauge

JOE OSCIAK

Ride: The Seashore Lines offers a 20-mile, 1¼-hour round trip on the former Reading Company's famous steel speedway to the Jersey seashore.

Schedule: Call or write for schedule.

Admission/Fare: Call or write for fares.

Locomotives/Rolling Stock: Eight Budd RDC1s, former Pennsylvania-Reading Seashore Lines; two RDC9s, former Boston & Maine; Alco/EMD RS3m, former Pennsylvania Railroad; EMD GP9, former PRR; P-RSL P70 coaches, former PRR.

Nearby Attractions/Accommodations: Victorian Cape May City, Wildwood Beaches, Boardwalk and Amusement Piers, Cape May Light House, Cape May-Lewes Ferry, Cape May County Park and Zoo, historic Cold Spring Village, Mid-Atlantic Center for the Arts, and Middle Township Performing Arts Center.

Special Events: Railroad Days, July. Halloween Trains, October. The Santa Express, December.

Location/Directions: 4-H Fairgrounds Station–Route 675, Cape May Court House. Cape May Court House Station–Route 615/Mechanic Street. Cold Spring Station–Route 9, Cold Spring. Cape May Rail Terminal–Lafayette Street, Cape May City.

[P] Radio frequency: 161.160

Site Address: Rio Grande, NJ
Mailing Address: PO Box 152, Tuckahoe, NJ 08250-0152
Telephone: (609) 884-2675
Fax: (609) 567-5847

New Jersey, Farmington

THE NEW JERSEY MUSEUM OF TRANSPORTATION, INC.
Diesel, steam, scheduled
36" gauge

GEORGE A FORERO, JR.

Ride: The ride is 12 minutes, two times around a 3,300-foot loop track. Equipment from museum collection is on display.

Schedule: Steam train–June through September: weekends. Diesel train–April, May, and October: weekends; July and August, weekdays. 12 to 4:30 p.m., departures every 30 minutes.

Admission/Fare: $2.00; special events–$2.50; Christmas $3.00.

Locomotive/Rolling Stock: Surry, Sussex & Southampton no. 26, 1920 Baldwin 2-6-2; Ely-Thomas Lumber Co. no. 6, 1927 Lima Class B Shay; Cavan & Leitram Railway (Ireland) no. 3L, 1887 Robert Stevenson 4-4-0T; U.S. Army no. 7751, 1942 GE 25 ton diesel-electric; U.S. Steel no. 45, 1950 GE 50 ton diesel-electric; Newfoundland Railway (CN) no. 502, 1902 wood coach; Central Railroad of NJ no. 91155 1874/1903 caboose.

Special Events: Civil War Re-enactment: Father's Day. Railroaders' Day, Sunday after Labor Day. Christmas Express, four weekends after Thanksgiving, 12 to 3 p.m.

Nearby Attractions/Accommodations: Allaire State Park, including Historic Allaire Village, nature center, playground campgrounds. North Jersey Coast shore attractions.

Location/Directions: Route 524, Wall Township, 2 miles west of Garden State Parkway exit 98, 2 miles east of I-195 exit 31.

[P] [✲] [☕] [🎋] [✉] M arm TRAIN

Site Address: Allaire State Park, Route 524, Wall Township, NJ
Mailing Address: PO Box 622, Farmingdale, NJ 07727
Telephone: (732) 938-5524

New Jersey, Flemington

NORTHLANDZ GREAT AMERICAN RAILWAY, DOLLHOUSE MUSEUM, & ART GALLERY
Model railroad display

NORTHLANDZ

Display: A spectacular adventure on this one-mile indoor tour through a miniature world. The 135 trains and 8 miles of track are just the beginning. Twenty-five years went into sculpting 35-foot mountains and building 40-foot bridges. Marvel at the thousands of hand crafted buildings and over 10,000 freight cars. Considered to be the world's largest miniature railway, The Great American Railway is truly unique to the world. Also, a dollhouse museum and theater pipe organ. Outdoors visit the 36" gauge railroad.

Schedule: Year round: daily 10 a.m. to 6 p.m.

Admission/Fare: Adults $12.75; seniors $11.50; children $8.75.

Locomotive/Rolling Stock: Mostly HO, some LGB and Lionel.

Special Events: Christmas Show, and many year round festivals.

Nearby Attractions/Accommodations: Black River and Western Tourist Railroad, outlet shopping.

Location/Directions: Western New Jersey. Two miles north of Flemington Traffic Circle, right on Highway 202.

Site Address: 495 Highway 202, Flemington, NJ
Mailing Address: 495 Highway 202, Flemington, NJ 08822
Telephone: (908) 782-4022
Fax: (908) 782-5131
Internet: www.northlandz.com

New Jersey, Flemington-Ringoes

BLACK RIVER & WESTERN RAILROAD
Steam, diesel, scheduled

SEAN SIMON

Display: The Black River & Western is a steam excursion train that carries passengers to three of the most attractive destinations in Hunterdon County, New Jersey. From Flemington, home of Liberty Village with its more than 100 designer and brand name outlets, through rural scenic Ringoes, and to Lambertville, where visitors can enjoy hours of antiquing within easy walking distance of New Hope, which is across the bridge over the Delaware River.

Schedule: Flemington/Ringoes run–Year round: weekends, add weekdays during the summer. Lambertville run–May to October: Sundays, dinner trains available. Groups and charters available.

Admission/Fare: Call or write for information.

Locomotive/Rolling Stock: 1937 Alco 2-8-0 no. 60; 1956 EMD GP9 no. 752; 1950 EMD GP7 no. 780; nos. 320-323 commuter cars, former Central of New Jersey; nos. 301-305 "Wyatt Earp" cars, former Delaware, Lackawanna & Western; caboose no. 645, former Maine Central; wreck crane no. 197, former Long Island; more.

Special Events: Numerous. Call or write for information.

Location/Directions: The Flemington Depot is in the center of town near Liberty Village. Ringoes Depot is located on County route 579, ¾-mile from the junction of Highways 31 and 202.

P ✳ ☕ 🚻 ✉

Site Address: Flemington and Ringoes, NJ
Mailing Address: 4 Stockton Road, Stockton, NJ 09559
Telephone: (908) 782-9600
Internet: spiritof76.com/blackrr.html

New Jersey, Hazlet

HAZLET TRAIN STOP
Model railroad display

HAZLET TRAIN STOP

Display/Museum: A large prewar and postwar train collection on display and a 30 x 30 foot operating layout.

Schedule: Summer: Wednesday through Saturday, 10 a.m. to 5 p.m.; Winter: Tuesday through Saturday, 10 a.m. to 6 p.m., and Sunday 1 to 5 p.m.

Admission/Fare: Adult $3.00; student $1.00; children (under age 10) $.50.

Locomotive/Rolling Stock: Lionel, MTH, Marklin, LGB, Thomas the Tank Engine, HO, N, and Z.

Nearby Attractions/Accommodations: Boardwalk, ocean bathing.

Location/Directions: Garden State Parkway Route 353, exit 117, second traffic light turn right, past railroad tracks turn right.

[♿] [P] [✳] [✉] [MasterCard] [VISA]

Site Address: 25 Brailley Lane, Hazlet, NJ
Mailing Address: 25 Brailley Lane, Hazlet, NJ 07730
Telephone: (732) 264-7429 or (732) 494-7329
Fax: (732) 888-7750 or (732) 494-6756
E-mail: HTS2250@aol.com

New Jersey, Whippany

WHIPPANY RAILWAY MUSEUM
Railway museum
Standard gauge

STEVE HEPLER

Display: Visit the Whippany Railway Museum, headquarted in the restored 1904 freight house of the Morristown & Erie, with its outstanding collection of railroad artifacts and memorabilia. Take a leisurely stroll through a railroad yard lost in time, complete with fieldstone depot, coal yard, wooden water tank and historic rail equipment. The museum also features one of the largest operating Lionel layouts in the area. Educational and fun for all ages.

Schedule: April through October: Sundays, 12 to 4 p.m.

Admission/Fare: Museum–adults $1.00; children under age 12, 50 cents. Special event train fare–adults $7.00; children under age 12 $4.00.

Locomotive/Rolling Stock: Morris County Central no. 4039, an 0-6-0 built in 1942 by the American Locomotive Company; Railbus no. 10 built in 1918 by the White Motor Company for the Morristown & Erie RR; more.

Special Events: Easter Bunny Express, Santa Claus Special, many more events throughout the season. Call or write for details.

Nearby Attractions/Accommodations: Morris Museum, Gen. Washington's headquarters, Jockey Hollow National Historic Site, Hanover Marriott (Whippany), Ramada Hotel (E. Hanover), Parsippany Hilton (Parsippany).

Location/Directions: At the intersection of route 10 west and Whippany Road in Morris County.

P ✱ ⊼ 🚂 ✉ arm TRAIN 🚆 Newark & Metropark Sta.

Radio frequency: 160.230

Site Address: 1 Railroad Plaza, Whippany, NJ
Mailing Address: PO Box 16, Whippany, NJ 07981-0016
Telephone: (973) 887-8177
E-mail: paultup@interactive.net
Internet: www.interactive.net/~paultup/wrym.html

New Mexico, Alamogordo

TOY TRAIN DEPOT
Diesel, scheduled
16" gauge
Model railroads

TTD, INC.

Display/Ride: Over 1,200 feet of model railroad track bring back memories of life as it was in the steam era. A guided tour of ten layouts, Z through G gauge, domestic and import model displays. All housed in a refurbished 1898 Southern Pacific depot. The 16" gauge train ride departs every 30 minutes.

Schedule: Year round: Wednesdays through Sundays, 12 to 5 p.m. and other times by appointment.

Admission/Fare: Museum–adults $2.00; children age 12 and under $1.50. Train–adults $2.00; children age 12 and under $1.50.

Locomotive/Rolling Stock: Two G16 ⅛ scale F7s with three cars each.

Special Events: Cottonwood Festival, Labor Day weekend. Railroad Days, Cloudcroft, New Mexico Balloon Rally.

Nearby Attractions/Accommodations: Alameda Park and Zoo, White Sands National Monument, Sunspot Observatory, ISHF Space Hall, Trinity Site.

Location/Directions: At the north end of Alameda Park on highway 54/70. Take U.S. 70 north from I-10 in El Paso, Texas, south from I-40 in Santa Rosa, New Mexico, or east from I-25 in Las Cruces, New Mexico.

Site Address: 1991 N. White Sands Blvd., Alamogordo, NM
Mailing Address: 1991 N. White Sands Blvd., Alamogordo, NM
Telephone: (505) 437-2855
Internet: www.quikpage.com/T/toy

New Mexico, Chama	**CUMBRES & TOLTEC SCENIC RAILROAD**
Colorado, Antonito	*Steam, scheduled*
	36" gauge

ALEX MAYES

Ride: Steam trains travel over highly scenic former Denver & Rio Grande Western narrow-gauge trackage. The 64-mile line crosses Cumbres Pass (elevation 10,015 feet) and goes through spectacular Toltec Gorge, over high bridges, and through two tunnels. Passengers may choose to ride either the Colorado Limited from Antonito to Osier, Colorado, via Toltec Gorge or the New Mexico Express from Chama, New Mexico, to Osier via Cumbres Pass or ride the full length of the trip.

Schedule: Mid-May through mid-October: daily, departs Chama 10:30 a.m. to 4:30 p.m., departs Antonito 10 a.m. to 5 p.m.

Admission/Fare: Round trip: adults $34.00; children under 12 $17.00. Through trips from either terminal with return by van: adults $52.00, children $27.00. Reservations recommended for all trips.

Locomotive/Rolling Stock: Nos. 463, 484, 487, 488, 489, 497, 1925 Baldwin 2-8-2s, former D&RGW.

Special Events: Big Horn Tent Camp, Pony Express Race, Great Beat the Train over the Mountain Bicycle Race, dinner train.

Nearby Attractions/Accommodations: Ghost Ranch Museum/Georgia O'Keefe, Heron Lake, El Vado Lake.

Location/Directions: Stations at Chama, NM and Antonito, CO.

*Coupon available, see coupon section.

Site Address: 500 Terrace Avenue, Chama, NM
Mailing Address: PO Box 789, Chama, NM 87520
Telephone: (505) 756-2151 and (888) CUMBRES
Fax: (505) 756-2694

New Mexico, Clovis

CLOVIS DEPOT MODEL TRAIN MUSEUM
Railroad display, museum

PHIL WILLIAMS

Museum/Display: Exhibits include restored Depot dorm area and dispatcher/telegraph operator positions. Displays depict the history of the railroad in Clovis and along the "Belen Cutoff." The model railroads tell the story of toy trains in the U.S. and Great Britain and of the history of the railroad in Australia, Great Britain, and the U.S. Southwest. Live BNSF train operations on the mainline and in the yard can be viewed from our platform. We provide guided tours of Depot Museum and model railroad displays including running of trains and other hands-on displays.

Schedule: June through August: daily, 12 to 5 p.m. September through May: Wednesdays through Sundays, 12 to 5 p.m. Closed Easter, Thanksgiving, Christmas, and New Year's Eve.

Admission/Fare: Adults $3.00; children 12 and under $1.00; families $7.00.

Locomotive/Rolling Stock: Fairmont Railway motor car.

Nearby Attractions/Accommodations: Blackwater Draw Museum, Blackwater Draw Archaeological site, Norman Petty Studios.

Location/Directions: In a restored ATSF passenger depot adjacent to BNSF mainline, two blocks west of Main Street on U.S. 60/84.

*Coupon available, see coupon section.

Site Address: 221 West First Street, Clovis, NM
Mailing Address: 221 West First Street, Clovis, NM 88101
Telephone: (505) 762-0066

New Mexico, Santa Fe

SANTA FE SOUTHERN RAILWAY
Diesel mixed
Standard gauge

ERICH BROCK

Display: Mixed train departs five times per week on an 18-mile former Santa Fe branch line. Train operates Santa Fe to Lamy and return. Includes 1½-hour layover at the historic landmark, Legal Tender Restaurant.

Schedule: Year round.

Admission/Fare: Call or write for information.

Locomotive/Rolling Stock: GP16, no. 93, former L&N no. 1850; no. 1158, former CNJ Coach; no. 144, former GN Coach; no. 4014, former SP Coach; no. 1370 "Acoma," former AT&SF Superchief.

Lamy, NM

Site Address: 410 South Guadalupe Street, Santa Fe, NM
Mailing Address: 410 South Guadalupe Street, Santa Fe, NM 87501
Telephone: (505) 989-8600
Fax: (505) 983-7620

New York, Arcade

ARCADE & ATTICA RAILROAD
Steam, scheduled
Standard gauge

PETER SWANSON

Display/Ride: The A&A, a common-carrier railroad that has been in existence since 1881, offers a 15-mile, 2-hour round trip over the historic trackage to Curriers. Open-end steel coaches and combination cars from the Delaware, Lackawanna & Western Railroad. A 16 x16 foot HO model railroad is displayed in the Arcade Depot.

Schedule: Memorial weekend through October: weekends and holidays, 12:30 and 3 p.m. July through August: Wednesdays, 12:30 and 3 p.m.; Fridays 1 p.m.. First three weekends in October:12, 2, and 4 p.m. Fridays, 12 p.m.

Admission/Fare: Adults $8.50; seniors $7.50; children 3-11 $5.00; children under age 3 are free.

Locomotive/Rolling Stock: 1917 Baldwin 4-6-0 no. 14, former Escanaba & Lake Superior; 1920 Alco (Cooke) 2-8-0 no. 18, former Boyne City Railroad.

Special Events: Civil War Train Capture, Children's Trains, Murder Mystery Runs, Special Fall Foliage Runs, Christmas Trains, and Winter Runs.

Nearby Attractions/Accommodations: Letchworth State Park, The Farm Craft Village, Wyoming Gas Light Village, Byrncliff Resort, Hillside Inn, Glen Iris Inn.

Location/Directions: In western New York, midway between Buffalo and Olean. Train departs from Arcade Depot in center of town, at routes 39 and 98.

Site Address: 278 Main Street, Arcade, NY
Mailing Address: PO Box 246, Arcade, NY 14009
Telephone: (716) 496-9877
Fax: (716) 492-0100

New York, Dunkirk

ALCO BROOKS RAILROAD DISPLAY
Railway display
Standard gauge

HISTORICAL SOCIETY OF DUNKIRK

Display: The ABRD, located at the Chautauqua County Fairgrounds since 1987, owns an original Alco-Brooks steam locomotive, a wood-sided boxcar housing displays of Chautauqua County commerce and railroads along with a gift shop, and a restored wooden caboose. Other items of interest at the site are a Nickel Plate work car, an Erie Railroad concrete telephone booth, a New York Central harp switch stand, a Pennsylvania Railroad cast-iron crossing sign, a DAV&P land line marker, and an operating crossing flasher.

Schedule: June 1 through August 31: Saturdays, 1 to 3 p.m. weather permitting. Open daily during special events or by appointment.

Admission/Fare: Donations appreciated.

Locomotive/Rolling Stock: 1916 Alco-Brooks 0-6-0 no. 444, former Boston & Maine; Delaware & Hudson 22020 wood-sided boxcar; New York Central 19224 wooden caboose.

Special Events: Chautauqua Co. Antique Auto Show & Flea Market, May 16-18. Chautauqua Co. Fair, July 27 through August 2.

Nearby Attractions/Accommodations: Dunkirk Historical Museum, Dunkirk Lighthouse, Chautauqua Institution, Sheraton Harborfront Hotel.

Location/Directions: Chautauqua Co. Fairgrounds, I-90 exit 59.

P 🚌 ✱ ✉ M 🚂 Dunkirk

Site Address: Chautauqua Co. Fairgrounds, 1089 Central Ave., Dunkirk, NY
Mailing Address: Hist. Soc. of Dunkirk, 513 Washington Ave., Dunkirk, NY 14048
Telephone: (716) 366-3797

New York, Gowanda

NEW YORK & LAKE ERIE RAILROAD
Diesel, scheduled
Standard gauge

KEVIN ARGUE

Ride: This railroad operates excursions over former Erie Railroad trackage: "The Flyer" makes a 20-mile, 2¾-hour round trip to South Dayton over a steep grade and through the Old Stone Tunnel built in 1860. The Murder Mystery and The Blue Diamond Dinner Trains make a 30-mile 4-hour round trip to Cherry Creek, and feature four-course dinners. Intermediate station stops are made at both stations. The depot in South Dayton was featured in the motion pictures, "The Natural" and "Planes, Trains, & Automobiles."

Schedule: "The Flyer"–June 14 through Octobr 18: weekends, 1 p.m. July and August: Wednesdays, 12 p.m. also. Murder Mystery Dinner Train–February through November: third Saturday of each month and October 31, December 12, and 31. Blue Diamond Dinner Train–to be announced. Group tours–May through October: select weekdays. Write or call for complete schedule and rates.

Admission/Fare: "The Flyer"–adults $9.00; seniors $8.00; children 3-11 $4.00. Dinner trains vary. Call or write for information.

Locomotive/Rolling Stock: 1964 Alco C425 no. 1013, former N&W, more.

Special Events: Peter Cottontail Express, Great Train Robbery, Kids Day, Ghost & Goblin Party Train, Teddy Bear's Picnic, Santa Train, and more.

Location/Directions: Turn off routes 62 and 39 at S. Water to Commercial.

Site Address: 50 Commercial Street, Gowanda, NY
Mailing Address: PO Box 309, Gowanda, NY 14070
Telephone: (716) 532-5716
Fax: (716) 532-9128

New York, Greenport and Riverhead

RAILROAD MUSEUM OF LONG ISLAND
Railway museum

RAILROAD MUSEUM OF LONG ISLAND

Museum/Display: Greenport–visit a restored 1890s Long Island Railroad depot. Exhibits plus track car inside with snowplow and caboose outside. Riverhead–houses balance of collection including steam engine no. 39.

Schedule: Greenport–May through December: weekends, noon to 5 p.m. Riverhead–year round: Saturdays (weather permitting).

Admission/Fare: Donations appreciated.

Locomotive/Rolling Stock: LIRR G5S steamer no. 39; Alco RS3 diesel; all aluminum double-deck passenger car no. 200; LIRR cabooses (2); 1910 RPO; 1925 combine; 1907 snowplow; 1928 baggage express; 1928 baggage mail.

Special Events: Santa weekend in Greenport, December; annual benefit dinners; open house.

Nearby Attractions/Accommodations: Greenport–bed and breakfasts, motels, wineries. Riverhead–bed and breakfasts, motels, Splish Splash, Tanger Mall.

Location/Directions: Greenport–via Route 25 or LIRR, 4th Street at the tracks. Riverhead–via LIRR, LIE, or Route 25 to Griffing Avenue, opposite LIRR station.

[P] [🚌] [✳] [🌀] [📷] [✉]

Site Address: Greenport–4th St. at the tracks. Riverhead–opposite LIRR station.
Mailing Address: PO Box 726, Greenport, NY 11944
Telephone: (516) 477-0439 and (516) 727-7920
Internet: rmlipres@aol.com

New York, Kingston

TROLLEY MUSEUM OF NEW YORK
Electric, scheduled
Standard gauge

THE TROLLEY MUSEUM OF NEW YORK

Display: This museum was established in 1955 and moved to its present location in 1983, becoming part of the Kingston Urban Cultural Park. A 2½-mile, 40-minute round trip takes passengers from the foot of Broadway to Kingston Point, with stops at the museum in both directions. A gas-powered railcar operates on private right-of-way and in-street trackage along Rondout Creek to the Hudson River over part of the former Ulster & Delaware Railroad main line. An exhibit hall features trolley exhibits and a theater.

Schedule: May 23 through October 12: weekends and holidays, noon to 5 p.m. Last ride departs at 4:30 p.m. Charters available. Call or write for more information.

Admission/Fare: Adults $3.00; children $2.00. Donations welcome.

Locomotive/Rolling Stock: Eleven trolleys; eight rapid transit cars; Whitcomb diesel-electric; Brill model 55 interurban.

Special Events: Shad Festival, May 2-3; Mother's Day, May 10, (moms ride free); Father's Day, June 21 (dads ride free); Santa Days, December 5-6.

Nearby Attractions/Accommodations: Hudson River Maritime Museum, Senate House, Catskill Mountains, Urban Cultural Park.

Location/Directions: In the historic Rondout Waterfront area of Kingston. Call or write for directions or see map on web page.

*Coupon available, see coupon section.

Radio Frequency: 462.175

Site Address: 89 East Strand, Kingston, NY
Mailing Address: PO Box 2291, Kingston, NY 12402
Telephone: (914) 331-3399
Internet: www.mhrcc.org/kingston/kgntroll.html/

New York, Mt. Pleasant

CATSKILL MOUNTAIN RAILROAD
Diesel, scheduled
Standard gauge

GEORGE A. FORERO, JR.

- **Ride:** This railroad, which operates over trackage of the former Ulster & Delaware Railroad (later the Catskill Mountain branch of the New York Central), offers a 6-mile, 1-hour round trip to Phoenicia along the scenic Esopus Creek, through the heart of the beautiful Catskill Mountains. Tourists, inner-tubers, and visitors interested in canoeing or fishing may ride one way or round trip; round-trip passengers may stay at Phoenicia to visit shops and restaurants and return on a later train.
- **Schedule:** May 23 through September 13: 11 a.m. to 5 p.m. September 19 through October 12: noon to 4 p.m. Trains leave hourly.
- **Admission/Fare:** Round trip: adults $6.00; children 4-11 $2.00; under age 4 are free. One way: adults $4.00; children 4-11 $2.00; under age 4 are free.
- **Locomotive/Rolling Stock:** No. 1, "The Duck," 1942 Davenport 38-ton diesel-mechanical, former U.S. Air Force; no. 2, "The Goat," H.K. Porter 50-ton diesel-electric, former U.S. Navy; no. 2361, 1952 Alco RS-1, former Wisconsin Central (Soo Line).
- **Special Events:** Fall Foliage Trains and others; call for schedule.
- **Location/Directions:** New York State Thruway, exit 19 (Kingston), and travel west 22 miles on Route 28 to the railroad depot in Mt. Pleasant.

Site Address: Mt. Pleasant, NY
Mailing Address: PO Box 46, Mt. Pleasant, NY 12481
Telephone: (914) 688-7400

New York, Old Forge

ADIRONDACK SCENIC RAILROAD
Diesel, scheduled
Standard gauge

MATTHEW GIARDINO

Ride: Scenic 1-hour tours from Old Forge and day trips from Utica to Old Forge.

Schedule: Daily except Fridays, scenic 1-hour tours depart from Old Forge. Tri-weekly service from Utica after July 15, 1998. Call for schedules.

Admission/Fare: Call for package prices. Group rates available. Private car charters on a 1928 "Rail Baron" available for weekends, $2,500 and up.

Locomotive/Rolling Stock: New York Central no. 8223 Alco RS-3 diesel; Alco C-420, former Lehigh Valley no. 408; SW-1 diesel; intercity cars, former CN; commuter cars; open-air observation cars.

Special Events: Train Robbery on scenic train; Mystery Expresses.

Nearby Attractions/Accommodations: F.X. Matt Brewery, Historic Mohawk Valley, Adirondeck Adventures.

Location/Directions: Route 28 in Old Forge. Main Street in Utica.

Site Address: Route 28, Old Forge, NY
Mailing Address: PO Box 84, Thendara, NY 13472
Telephone: (315) 369-6290 or (315) 369-6472
Fax: (315) 369-2479
E-mail: train@telenet.net

New York, Owego

TIOGA SCENIC RAILROAD
Diesel, scheduled
Standard gauge

THOMAS TRENCANSKY

Display/Ride: Experience the beautiful landscape of the Southern Finger Lake region while enjoying fine dining on board the train. A 1¾-hour round trip from Owego to Newark Valley over tracks of the former Southern Central, constructed beginning in 1868 to connect southern New York with the Great Lakes.

Schedule: May through October: weekends, 12 and 3 p.m.

Admission/Fare: Excursions–adults $8.00; seniors $7.50; children 3-11 $5.00. Meals–lunch $14.00 and $22.00; dinner $28.00. Dinner theater available. Call or write for more information.

Locomotive/Rolling Stock: Tioga Scenic Railroad SW1, EMD locomotive no. 40, 600 hp.

Special Events: Many throughout the season. Call or write for information.

Nearby Attractions/Accommodations: Tioga Park (country western theme park), Econo Lodge, Treadway Inn.

Location/Directions: Twenty miles west of Binghamton, route 17, exit 64.

*Coupon available, see coupon section.

Site Address: 25 Delphine Street, Owego, NY
Mailing Address: 25 Delphine Street, Owego, NY 13827
Telephone: (607) 687-6786
Fax: (607) 687-6817
Internet: www.railroad.net/tsrr

New York, Phoenicia

EMPIRE STATE RAILWAY MUSEUM
Railway museum

EMPIRE STATE RAILWAY MUSEUM

Museum: The depot, preserved in its original condition, was added to the National Registry of Historic Places in 1995. Museum members have restored the station and are raising funds to begin restoration of four historic pieces of rolling stock: circa 1923 flatcar No. 7704 and 54-inch, wooden-sided, end-door boxcar, both former Central Vermont; 1912 four-wheel wood-bodied bobber caboose, former Pennsylvania Railroad; and 1890s express Railway Post Office car, former Boston & Maine. Visitors can board the train of the Catskill Mountain Railroad at Mt. Pleasant and ride to the museum in Phoenicia. Displays consist of archival photographs, films, and artifacts of the Ulster & Delaware and other regional branch lines. Membership includes free copy of this book and quarterly newsletters.

Schedule: Memorial Day through Columbus Day: weekends and holidays, 11 a.m. to 4 p.m.

Admission/Fare: Suggested donation–adults $3.00; seniors and students $2.00; children under age 12 $1.00; families $5.00.

Locomotive/Rolling Stock: Rolling stock described below is being restored in Phoenicia. No. 23, 1910 Alco 2-8-0, former Lake Superior & Ishpeming; 1915 Pullman dining car "Lion Gardiner," stored in Kingston.

Special Events: Santa Claus Special, Members Picnic, and others.

Site Address: Off High Street, Phoenicia, NY
Mailing Address: PO Box 455, Phoenicia, NY 12464
Telephone: (914) 688-7501
Internet: www.esrm.com

New York, Riparius

RIVERSIDE STATION
DELAWARE AND HUDSON DEPOT
Railway museum

RIVERSIDE STATION

Museum: Nestled in the Adirondack Mountains of upstate New York along the Hudson River is the Riverside Train Depot, a former Delaware & Hudson station built in 1913, filled with railroad memorabilia and pictures. This depot replaced a smaller Adirondack Company railway station that was built in 1870. The station was restored to its original charm in 1995 and consists of a ticket agent's office, waiting room, and baggage room. The baggage room is how home to a gift shop/train store. In the old waiting room you can relax and enjoy train videos that are shown continuously. In the yard there is a vintage caboose that now serves as a refreshment stand. Williams Old General Store can be seen in the background.

Schedule: May through October. Call or write for more information.

Admission/Fare: Free.

Locomotive/Rolling Stock: Vintage caboose operates as snack bar and ice cream shop.

Special Events: Annual Whitewater Derby, first weekend in May.

Nearby Attractions/Accommodations: Loon Lake, Friends Lake, Schroon Lake, and Lake George.

Location/Directions: Route 8 at Hudson River, 7 miles west on route 8 from northway exit 25.

Site Address: Riparius, NY
Mailing Address: PO Box 4, Riparius, NY 12862
Telephone: (518) 494-7221 and (518) 494-4581

New York, Rochester

NEW YORK MUSEUM OF TRANSPORTATION
Railway Museum

JIM DIERKS

Museum/Ride: Site includes rail and road vehicles, related artifacts, an 11 x 21 foot model railroad, a video/photo gallery. A 2-mile ride connects with the Rochester & Genesee Valley Railroad Museum, departing every half-hour.

Schedule: Museum: year round, Sundays, 11 a.m. to 5 p.m. Groups by appointment. Ride: May through October, weather permitting.

Admission/Fare: Adults $5.00; seniors $4.00; students (5-15) $3.00. Includes entry to NYMT, Rochester & Genesee Valley Railroad Museum, and ride.

Locomotive/Rolling Stock: Nine area trolleys and interurbans; 0-4-0 steam locomotive; antique trucks, car, buggies and much more. Call or write for details.

Special Events: Transportation Day, mid-May; Antique Trade Show, July; Railroad Days, August.

Nearby Attractions/Accommodations: Arcade & Attica Railroad, Genesee County Museum, George Eastman House Museum of Photography.

Location/Directions: NY State Thruway, exit 46, south 2 miles on I-390, exit 11. Route 251 west 1½-miles, right on East River Road, 1 mile to museum entrance.

Radio Frequency: 160.440

Site Address: 6393 East River Road, Rush, NY
Mailing Address: PO Box 136, W. Henrietta, NY 14586
Telephone: (716) 533-1113
Internet: http://www.history.rochester.edu/class/rrmuseum/museum.html

New York, Rochester

ROCHESTER & GENESEE VALLEY RAILROAD MUSEUM
Railway museum
Standard gauge

CHRISTOPHER HAUF

Museum/Ride: The museum, housed in a restored 1908 Erie Railroad station, displays railroad artifacts from western New York railroads. On outdoor tracks are a number of railroad cars and diesel locomotives open for display. Museum has tours and track car rides.

Schedule: May through October: Sundays, 11 am. to 5 p.m. Visits at other times by appointment.

Admission/Fare: Adults $5.00; seniors $4.00; children 5-15 $3.00.

Locomotive/Rolling Stock: 1946 GE 80-ton diesel, former Eastman Kodak; 1953 Alco RS-3, former Lehigh Valley; 1953 Alco S-4, former Nickel Plate; 1941 GE 45-ton, former Rochester Gas & Electric; Fairbanks-Morse H12-44, former U.S. Army.

Nearby Attractions/Accommodations: Strong Museum, Eastman House, Genesee Country Museum, Frontier Stadium, New York Museum of Transportation.

Location/Directions: I-390 exit 11. Take route 251 west to East River Road, turn right, travel two miles to museum entrance.

Site Address: 6393 East River Rd, Henrietta, NY
Mailing Address: PO Box 664, Rochester, NY 14603
Telephone: (716) 533-1431 and (716) 533-1113
Fax: (716) 425-8587
E-mail: mikeb86393@aol.com
Internet: www.rochester.ny.us/railmuseum.html

New York, Roscoe

ONTARIO & WESTERN
ROSCOE O&W RAILWAY MUSEUM
Railway museum

ROSCOE O&W RAILWAY MUSEUM

Ride/Display: This museum was established under the charter of the Ontario & Western Railway Historical Society in 1984 in a former Erie Railroad caboose. The O&W railway festival, first held in August of that year, has since become an annual event. The museum complex consists of a restored O&W caboose, watchman's shanties, and the O&W station motif building. The museum contains displays of O&W memorabilia and other railroadiana, as well as local-history displays that show the impact of the O&W on community life, hunting, fishing, farming, tourism, and local industry. The museum is maintained and operated by members of the Roscoe NYO&W Railway Association. The Archives Center of the history of the Ontario & Western Railway is located in Middletown, New York.

Schedule: Memorial weekend through Columbus Day: Saturday and Sunday, 11 a.m. to 3 p.m. July and August: Wednesday, Saturday, and Sunday, 11 a.m. to 3 p.m.

Admission/Fare: Donations welcomed.

Special Events: Call or write for details.

Location/Directions: Railroad Avenue.

Site Address: Railroad Avenue, Roscoe, NY
Mailing Address: PO Box 305, Roscoe, NY 1776-0305
Telephone: (607) 498-5500

New York, Salamanca

SALAMANCA RAIL MUSEUM
Railway museum

SALAMANCA RAIL MUSEUM ASSOCIATION

Museum: Fully restored BR&P depot and freight house. Artifacts and photographs tell the history of railroads in western New York and Pennsylvania. For children, the museum grounds offer the permanent display of a boxcar, a crew camp car, and the chance to explore two cabooses.

Schedule: April through December: Mondays through Saturdays, 10 a.m. to 5 p.m. and Sundays, 12 to 5 p.m. Closed Mondays in April, October, November, and December.

Admission/Fare: Donations appreciated.

Locomotive/Rolling Stock: B&O caboose; P&WV caboose; Erie crane crew car; Conrail boxcar; Jordan spreader; DL&W electric commuter coach.

Nearby Attractions/Accommodations: Allegany State Park, Seneca Iroquois National Museum, Holiday Valley Summer-Winter Resort, Chautauqua Institution.

Location/Directions: Downtown Salamanca on New York route 17/US route 219.

Site Address: 170 Main Street, Salamanca, NY
Mailing Address: 170 Main Street, Salamanca, NY 14779
Telephone: (716) 945-3133

New York, Salem

NORTHEAST RAIL
BATTEN KILL RAILROAD
Diesel, scheduled
Standard gauge

GEORGE LERRIGO

Ride: On this line, the *Batten Kill Rambler* takes passengers on a scenic, 2-hour and 10-minute, 13-mile round trip along the Batten Kill River. An hour layover allows exploration of Shushan, New York with two museums. At secluded River Park, a picnic park is available by prior arrangement.

Schedule: Call or write for information.

Admission/Fare: Call or write for information.

Locomotive/Rolling Stock: No. 605, 1950 Alco; no. 4116, 1952 Alco still in pinstripes; nos. 2106 and 2108, former New York Central; no. M403, former Pennsylvania Reading Seashore Lines.

Special Events: Children's Theater at River Park. Civil War Homecoming Reenactment. Halloween Train. Santa Trains. Call or write for specific dates and times.

Location/Directions: I-87 to Route 29, at Saratoga Springs east to Salem. Left on Route 22, north to village and station.

[&] [P] [🚌] [✳] [🎏] [⛪] [✉] M 🚂 Saratoga Springs and Albany Rennsselaer

Radio frequency: 160.905

Site Address: 232 Main Street, Salem, NY
Mailing Address: 1 Elbow Street, Greenwich, NY 12834
Telephone: (518) 854-3787 and (518) 692-2191 reservations

New York, Sandy Creek

RAIL CITY HISTORICAL MUSEUM
Railway museum

BOB GROMAN

Museum: Site of the first steam-operating railroad museum in the U.S. Housed in the former RWO&NYC depot from Deer River, New York, the Rail City Historical Museum contains an extensive collection of steam-era photographs, displays of railroad timetables, brochures, posters, artifacts and a unique railroad gift shop.

Schedule: June 22 through Labor Day: daily, Mondays through Saturdays, 10 a.m. to 5 p.m. and Sundays 11 a.m. to 5 p.m. May, June, September, through mid-October: weekends only.

Admission/Fare: Adults $3.00; seniors $2.00; children under age 13 are free with an adult. Group rates available.

Special Events: Rail City Day, September. 19. Call or write for schedule.

Nearby Attractions/Accommodations: Lake Ontario shoreline, charter trout and salmon fishing, Southwick Beach State Park, Sackett's Habor Battlefield (1812), Elms Golf Course, Salmon River Fish Hatchery, Lindsey Corner Restaurant, Deer Creek Motel, and Port Lodge Motel.

Location/Directions: Fifty miles north of Syracuse. I-81 exit 37 (Sandy Creek) west to Main Street (route 11), north on Ellisburg Road, west on Hadley Road, north on route 3, travel ½ mile to museum on left.

P 🚌 ㍻ ✉ M arm

Site Address: Route 3 "Seaway Trail," Sandy Creek, NY
Mailing Address: 162 Stanley Drive, Sandy Creek, NY 13145
Telephone: (315) 387-2932 and (315) 387-5720
Fax: (315) 387-5720 (May-October) and (315) 635-6250 (November-April)

New York, Syracuse

NEW YORK, SUSQUEHANNA & WESTERN RAILWAY CORP.
Steam, diesel, scheduled
Standard gauge

NYS&W

Ride: This line offers two trips: a scenic, 44-mile, 2 hour round trip between Syracuse and Tully, NY, over former Lackawanna Railroad trackage with steam and/or diesel locomotives; and a 5-mile City Express shuttle service between Syracuse University, Armory Square, and Carousel Center with restored rail diesel cars.

Schedule: Call or write for information.

Admission/Fare: Call or write for information.

Locomotive/Rolling Stock: No. 142 2-8-2; Nos. M5, M7, M8; BuddRDCs; Alco C430s; nos. 520524, 1947 long distance coaches, former NYC; more.

Location/Directions: West Jefferson Street off South Clinton Street in Armory Square, downtown Syracuse.

Site Address: West Jefferson Street, Syracuse, NY
Mailing Address: PO Box 1245, Syracuse, NY 13201
Telephone: (800) FOR TRAIN (367-8724) and (315) 424-1212

New York, Utica — CHILDREN'S MUSEUM

CHILDREN'S MUSEUM

Schedule: September through June: Tuesdays through Sundays, 10 a.m. to 4:30 p.m. July and August: 10 a.m. to 3:30 p.m.

Admission/Fare: $2.50. Members are free.

Locomotive/Rolling Stock: Engine; dining car; caboose.

Special Events: Kidstock Christmas on Main Street.

Nearby Attractions/Accommodations: Train station next door, restaurants.

Location/Directions: Thruway exit 31, follow Genesee Street, take Broad Street exit, left on Railroad Street, left on Main Street.

P ◐ ✉ M

Site Address: 311 Main Street, Utica, NY
Mailing Address: 311 Main Street, Utica, NY 13502
Telephone: (315) 724-6129 and (315) 724-6128
Fax: (315) 724-6120 (call first)

North Carolina, Blowing Rock

TWEETSIE RAILROAD
Steam, scheduled
36" gauge

TWEETSIE RAILROAD

Ride: The Tweetsie Railroad is a theme park centered on a three-mile train ride. Visitors can enjoy the train show, live entertainment, rides, mountain crafts, and a petting zoo.

Schedule: Call or write for information.

Admission/Fare: Call or write for information.

Locomotive/Rolling Stock: No. 12, 1917 Baldwin 4-6-0, former Tennessee & Western North Carolina; no. 190, 1943 Baldwin 2-8-2, former White Pass & Yukon.

Location/Directions: Between Boone and Blowing Rock on U.S. 221-321. Take Mile Post 291 exit off the Blue Ridge Parkway.

Site Address: Blowing Rock, NC
Mailing Address: PO Box 388, Blowing Rock, NC 28605
Telephone: (704) 264-9061

North Carolina, Bonsal

NEW HOPE VALLEY RAILWAY
Diesel, scheduled
Standard gauge

GARY LACKEY

Ride: Eight-mile round trip over 4 miles of the original Norfolk Southern Railway's Durham Branch on a diesel-powered train with open cars and cabooses. Other equipment and displays at this site.

Schedule: May through December: first Sunday of month, departures at 12, 1, 2, 3, and 4 p.m.

Admission/Fare: Adults $5.00; children $3.00.

Locomotive/Rolling Stock: 80-ton GE and Whtcomb; 45-ton GE; 50-ton Whitcomb; Heisler steam engine under restoration; cabooses, freight cars.

Special Events: Halloween Train, Santa Claus Train.

Nearby Attractions/Accommodations: Jordan Lake, camping, fishing, boating, Shearon Harris Nuclear Power Plant tours, Ramada Inn in Apex, North Carolina.

Location/Directions: Eight miles south of Apex on SR 1011. In Bonsal turn right on Daisey Street, 300 feet on left.

P 🚌 ✳ ☕ ✉ M arm 🚆

Site Address: 102 Daisey Street, Bonsal, NC
Mailing Address: PO Box 40, New Hill, NC 27562
Telephone: (919) 362-5416
E-mail: nhury67@netpath.net
Internet: pages.prodigy.com/n/c/m/ncrrm/index.htm

North Carolina, Dillsboro

FLOYD McEACHERN HISTORICAL TRAIN MUSEUM
Railway museum

FLOYD MCEACHERN HISTORICAL MUSEUM

Museum/Display: More than 3,000 articles of railroad memorabilia spanning more than 140 years of railroad history are on display at this 5,000 square foot site. O scale model trains operate on 1,800 feet of a beautifully landscaped layout. There is an extensive collection of model trains dating back to the early 1900s. A video booth playing four features: "The Making of the Fugitive," "Riding on Steam Engine no. 1702," "History of the Railroad," and "The Railway and the Community."

Schedule: Year round: Sundays, 10:30 a.m. to 5:00 p.m. Mondays through Saturdays, 8:30 a.m. to 5:00 p.m.

Admission/Fare: Adults $3.00; children $2.00.

Nearby Attractions/Accommodations: Bed & breakfasts, whitewater rafting.

Location/Directions: On Front Street behind the Great Smoky Mountain Railway ticket office.

Site Address: 40 Depot Street, Dillsboro, NC
Mailing Address: PO Box 180, Dillsboro, NC 28725
Telephone: (704) 586-4085

North Carolina, Dillsboro **GREAT SMOKY MOUNTAINS RAILWAY**
Steam, diesel, scheduled
Standard gauge

GREAT SMOKY MOUNTAINS RAILWAY

Ride: This railway offers a choice of five scenic round-trip excursions ranging from 2½- to 7-hours over its 67 miles of track from Dillsboro to Andrews. The Great Smoky Mountains Railway takes you through a beautiful corner of eastern America along river gorges, across fertile valleys and through tunnels pickaxed out of a granite mountain by convict laborers.

Schedule: March 31 through December 31: schedule varies with season. Lunch, dinner, and rail-raft trips are available. Call or write for schedule.

Admission/Fare: Adults $18.95 and up; children under age 13 $9.95 and up. Reservations recommended. Excursion trains depart from Dillsboro, Bryson City, and Andrews.

Locomotive/Rolling Stock: No. 1702, 1942 Baldwin 2-8-0, former U.S. Army; nos. 711 & 777, EMD GP7s; nos. 210 & 223, EMD GP35s.

Site Address: Dillsboro, NC
Mailing Address: PO Box 397, 119 Front Street, Dillsboro, NC 28725
Telephone: (704) 586-8811 and (800) 872-4681

North Carolina, Hamlet

NATIONAL RAILROAD MUSEUM AND HALL OF FAME
Railway museum

NATIONAL RAILROAD MUSEUM AND HALL OF FAME

Museum/Display: The purpose of the museum is to recreate that time when railroads were the main source of long-distance travel and passenger train service was at its zenith.

Schedule: Year round: Saturdays 10 a.m. to 5 p.m.; Sundays 1 to 5 p.m.; other times by appointment.

Admission/Fare: Donations appreciated.

Locomotive/Rolling Stock: Caboose no. 5241, former Seaboard Air Lines; Locomotive no. 1114 SDP 35, former SAL; replica of engine "Tornado"; motor car.

Special Events: Seaboard Festival, last Saturday in October.

Nearby Attractions/Accommodations: CSX classification yard, Pinehurst Golf Capital, beach, mountains several hours drive.

Location/Directions: Highway 74 east. Located in the historical, Victorian, old Seaboard Air Lines depot.

[&] [P] [bus] [*] [camera] [crossing] [church] [envelope] [train] M

Radio frequency: 160.590

Site Address: 2 Main Street, Hamlet, NC
Mailing Address: 2 Main Street, Hamlet, NC 28345

North Carolina, Spencer

NORTH CAROLINA TRANSPORTATION MUSEUM AT HISTORIC SPENCER SHOPS
Transportation museum
Standard gauge

JIM WRINN

Museum/Ride: Spencer Shops was the largest railroad repair facility on the Southern Railway; more than 2,500 people were employed in the 57-acre complex. The massive backshop, 37 stall roundhouse, and nine other major buildings are being restored to chronicle the history of transportation in North Carolina. The museum features an exhibits on railroading, 60 pieces of rolling stock, and a 3-mile, 25-minute train ride.

Schedule: November through March: Tuesdays through Saturdays 10 a.m. to 4 p.m. and Sundays 1 to 4 p.m. April through October: Sundays 1 to 5 p.m. and Mondays 9 a.m. to 5 p.m.

Admission/Fare: Steam train–adults $4.00; seniors and children 3-12 $3.00. Diesel train–adults $3,50; seniors and children 3-12 $2.50.

Locomotive/Rolling Stock: No. 604, 1926 Baldwin 2-8-0, former Buffalo Creek & Gauley no. 4; no. 542, 1903 2-8-0, no. 6900, EMD E8, and no. 6133, EMD FP7, all former SR; no. 1925, 1925 Lima 3-truck Shay, former Graham County Railroad; no. 1616, AS-416 diesel, former Norfolk Southern; no. 620, EMD GP9 diesel, former Norfolk & Western.

Special Events: Rail Days, Antique Auto Show, Antique Truck Show, Steamfest.
Nearby Attractions/Accommodations: North Carolina Zoo, boating, hiking.
Location/Directions: I-85 exit 79 (Spencer). Follow signs to museum.
*Coupon available, see coupon section.

Radio frequency: 160.695

Site Address: 411 S. Salisbury Avenue, Spencer, NC
Mailing Address: PO Box 165, Spencer, NC 28159
Telephone: (704) 636-2889
Fax: (704) 639-1881
Internet: www.ci.salisbury.nc.us/nctrans/index.htm

North Carolina, Wilmington

WILMINGTON RAILROAD MUSEUM
Railway museum

CHARLES KERNAN

Museum: Recapture the essence of railroad days as you climb aboard a 1910 steam locomotive, wander through a bright red caboose, explore extensive artifacts and photographs, or visit our model train displays.

Schedule: April 1 through October 31: Mondays through Saturdays, 10 a.m. to 5 p.m. Sundays, 1 to 5 p.m. Closed Mondays, November through March.

Admission/Fare: Adults $3.00; seniors/military $2.00; children 6-12 $1.50; under age 5 are free; museum members are free.

Locomotive/Rolling Stock: 1910 Baldwin steam locomotive; two cabooses.

Special Events: Annual Model Railroad Show. Father's Day Weekend.

Nearby Attractions/Accommodations: Battleship N.C., Cape Fear Museum, Coast Line Inn.

Location/Directions: Highway 17 to downtown Wilmington, near Water Street.

Site Address: 501 Nutt Street, Wilmington, NC
Mailing Address: 501 Nutt Street, Wilmington, NC 28401
Telephone: (910) 763-2634
Fax: (910) 763-2634 (call first)

North Dakota, West Fargo

BONANZAVILLE, U.S.A.
Railway display
Standard gauge

R.A. YOUNG

Museum: A 15-acre pioneer village made up of 42 museums representing life in the Red River Valley between 1880 and 1920.

Schedule: Memorial weekend through late October: daily, 9 a.m. to 5 p.m.

Admission/Fare: Adult $6.00; student $3.00; under age 6 are free.

Locomotive/Rolling Stock: Rome locomotive 4-4-0; Northern Pacific wood caboose no. 1628; Burlington Northern, former Midland Continental; wood russell plow, former NP; NP steel 80-ton heavy-weight passenger coach, no. 1360.

Special Events: Pioneer Days, third weekend in August.

Nearby Attractions/Accommodations: Cass County Campground, Sunset Motel, Days Inn.

Location/Directions: I-94, exit 343 to West Fargo.

*Coupon available, see coupon section.

Site Address: I-94 and exit 343, West Fargo, ND
Mailing Address: PO Box 719, North Fargo, ND 58078
Telephone: (701) 282-2822
Fax: (701) 282-7606
E-mail: bvillel@juno.com

Ohio, Bellevue

MAD RIVER & NKP RAILROAD SOCIETY
Railway museum
Standard gauge

DENNIS BRANDAL

Display: Museum has hands-on adventure with samples of small-town railroading history.

Schedule: Memorial Day through Labor Day: daily, 1 to 5 p.m. May, September, and October: weekends only.

Admission/Fare: Adults $2.00; children 2-12 $1.00; under age 2 are free.

Locomotive/Rolling Stock: Alco RSD 12 NKP no. 329; EMD GP30 NKP no. 900; FM H1244 Milw no. 740.

Special Events: Excursions and tours throughout the year. Call for information.

Nearby Attractions/Accommodations: Cedar Point Amuseument Park, Sorrowful Mother Shrine.

Location/Directions: Two blocks south of downtown. Follow our green signs.

Site Address: 253 Southwest Street, Bellevue, OH
Mailing Address: 233 York Street, Bellevue, OH 44811-1377
Telephone: (419) 483-2222
E-mail: madriver@onebellevue.com
Internet: www.onebellevue.com/madriver/

Ohio, Carrollton

CARROLLTON-ONEIDA-MINERVA RAILROAD
ELDERBERRY LINE

Diesel, scheduled
Standard gauge

Ride: Travel 14 miles between Carrollton and Minerva through areas of light industry, farmland, marshland, and forest. One-hour layover in Minerva.

Schedule: Memorial Day through October: Fridays, 5:30 p.m.; Saturdays and Sundays, 10 a.m and 2 p.m. Train departs Carrollton.

Admission/Fare: Adults $10; children 2-12 $7.00. Group rates available.

Locomotive/Rolling Stock: 1952 Alco RS-3 locomotive; 1926 Es New Jersey coach; three 1937 coaches, former Canadian.

Nearby Attractions/Accommodations: Atwood Lake Resort, sailing lake, fishing, Pro-football Hall of Fame nearby.

Location/Directions: Site is 100 miles south of Cleveland, 25 miles south of Canton, and 60 miles west of Pittsburgh, PA.

Site Address: 203 Second Street, Carrollton, OH
Mailing Address: 220 Wayne Avenue, Carrollton, OH 44615
Telephone: (330) 627-2282 and (800) 956-4686

Ohio, Cincinnati

RAILWAY EXPOSITION CO.
"Hands-on" railroad musuem
Standard gauge

RAILWAY EXPOSITION CENTER

Museum: Take a 40-minute guided tour through selected interiors of over 80 available locomotives, freight cars, and passenger cars.

Schedule: May through October: weekends 12:30 to 4:30 p.m. Closed holidays. Call for a recorded message.

Admission/Fare: Adults $4.00; children ages 10 and under $2.00.

Locomotive/Rolling Stock: PRR streamlined and Pullman heavyweight train sets.

Special Events: Call for recorded message.

Nearby Attractions/Accommodations: Kings Island Amusement Park, Cincinnati Reds/Bengals. USAF Museum (Dayton).

Location/Directions: Three miles south of Cincinnati, near I-275 and Kentucky route 17.

Site Address: 315 W. Southern Avenue, Covington, KY
Mailing Address: PO Box 15065, Covington, KY 41015
Telephone: (606) 491-7245

Ohio, Conneaut

CONNEAUT RAILROAD MUSEUM
Railway museum
Standard gauge

DALE W. BROWN

Display: Displays antique exhibits of the Steam Era. The Conneaut station, built by the Lake Shore & Michigan Southern in 1900, is adjacent to Conrail (former New York Central) tracks. Inside are extensive displays of timetables, passes, lanterns, old photos, builder's plates, telegraph instruments, and models of locomotives, cars, and structures. An HO scale model railroad operates during regular hours. On display outside are a train, section cars, track equipment, and a ball signal. On the station platform are baggage trucks, hand carts, and old trunks. A stready parade of Conrail trains passes the station.

Schedule: Memorial Day through Labor Day: daily, 12 to 5 p.m.

Admission/Fare: Donations appreciated.

Locomotive/Rolling Stock: No. 755, 1944 Lima 2-8-4, former Nickel Plate. A 90-ton hopper car and a wooden caboose, both former Bessemer & Lake Erie.

Location/Directions: In the old New York Central station at Depot and Mill streets, north of U.S. 20 and I-90. Blue-and-white locomotive signs point the way to the museum.

[&] [P] [✻] [🕂] [✉] M

Site Address: Conneaut, OH
Mailing Address: PO Box 643, Conneaut, OH 44030
Telephone: (216) 599-7878
Internet: www.suite224.net/conneaut/rrmuseum.html

Ohio, Dayton

CARILLON HISTORICAL PARK
Museum
Steam, scheduled

CARILLON HISTORICAL PARK

Museum: Outdoor history museum with transportation emphasis. Tour 20 buildings including an 1894 railroad station, a 1907 watchtower, canal lock and two bridges. Twice each month scheduled rides are given on the small scale live steam railroad.

Schedule: May 1 through October 31: Tuesdays through Saturdays, 10 a.m. to 6 p.m. and Sundays 1 to 6 p.m.

Admission/Fare: Adults $2.00; children 6-17 $1.00; members are free.

Locomotive/Rolling Stock: 1835 B&O no. 1; 1912 Alco with tender; 1900 HK Porter; 1909 Lima fireless; 1903 railroad car; 1904 interurban; caboose.

Special Events: Annual Steam Festival Weekend.

Nearby Attractions/Accommodations: U.S. Air Force Museum, Dayton Aviation Heritage National Historical Park, Marriott, Holiday Inn.

Location/Directions: I-75 exit 51, east on Edwin Moses Blvd., right over bridge, right on Patterson Blvd., right on Carillon to entrance.

Site Address: 2001 S. Patterson Blvd., Dayton, OH
Mailing Address: 2001 S. Patterson Blvd., Dayton, OH 45409
Telephone: (937) 293-2841 and (937) 293-3412 (weekends)
Fax: (937) 293-5798

Ohio, Dennison

THE DENNISON RAILROAD DEPOT MUSEUM
Steam, diesel, scheduled Railway museum

RUSTY FOX

Museum/Ride: Restored 1873 Pennsylvania Railroad station, once the site of a World War II canteen that served more than one million GIs. The depot was part of a complex begun in the mid-1860s by the Pittsburgh, Cincinnati & St. Louis Railroad; at its peak, the Dennison yards and shops employed 3,000 workers. Depot restaurant includes a "Canteen Restaurant" with a unique 1940s themed atmosphere and family dining; Exhibit includes a large N scale layout of Dennison during its heyday; original waiting rooms (men's and women's) filled with railroad displays; a ticket booth; a baggage room; a Railway Express building and office; a 1950 former Norfolk & Western caboose. This museum sponsors excursions ranging from 1-hour to all-day trips, through an arrangement with the Columbus & Ohio River Railroad in Coshocton.

Schedule: Year round: daily, 11 a.m. to 5 p.m. Closed Mondays.

Admission/Fare: Adults $3.00; seniors $2.50; children 7-18 $1.75; under age 7 are free.

Locomotive/Rolling Stock: 1946 Thermos Bottle engine; 1920s B&O flatcar; tank car; two passenger cars; 1940 Nickel Plate caboose; more.

Special Events: Train rides. Forties Fest, first weekend in October.

Nearby Attractions/Accommodations: Amish country, Roscoe Village.

Location/Directions: At the junction of routes 250, 36, and 800.

*Coupon available, see coupon section.

Site Address: 400 Center Street, Dennison, OH
Mailing Address: PO Box 11, Dennison, OH 44621
Telephone: (614) 922-6776
Fax: (614) 922-0105
Internet: web1.tusco.net/rail

Ohio, Hebron

BUCKEYE CENTRAL SCENIC RAILROAD
Diesel, scheduled
Standard gauge

BUCKEYE CENTRAL SCENIC RAILROAD

Ride: We offer a scenic 1½-hours round trip excursion through the rolling countryside of central Ohio on historic rail in vintage passenger coaches powered by a classic diesel locomotive. Our mission is to preserve, maintain, and operate vintage railroad equipment and provide scenic train rides to that we may share with you a small part of this Great American Heritage that means so much to us.

Schedule: Memorial Day through mid-October: departures at 1 and 3 p.m. Trip time 1½-hours.

Admission/Fare: Adults $6.00; children 2-11 $5.00; under age 2 are free if not occupying a seat. Charter trains available.

Special Events: Haunted Halloween Trains: October 22-25, 29-November 1; Thursdays and Sundays, 7 p.m. and Fridays and Saturdays, 7 and 9 p.m. Santa Christmas Specials: December 5-6, 12-13, 4:30 and 6:30 p.m.

P 🚌 ✳ ☕ 🎪 ✉ M

Site Address: 5475 National Road SE, Hebron, OH
Mailing Address: PO Box 242, Newark, OH 43058-0242
Telephone: (614) 366-2029
Internet: www.infinet.com/~pcaravan

Ohio, Independence   **CUYAHOGA VALLEY SCENIC RAILROAD**
Diesel, scheduled
Standard gauge

Ride: The CVSR in Northeastern Ohio runs through the hear of Cuyahoga Valley National Recreation Area. Each trip is a different adventure filled with fun, excitement, natural beauty, and historic sites. Ride comfortably in vintage climate-controlled coaches built between 1939 and 1940. The coaches originally saw passenger service on the NYC and Santa Fe Railroads. Destinations included Peninsula, Hale Farm and Village, Quaker Square, Inventure Place, Canal Visitor Center, and more.

Schedule: Varies. Call or write for information.

Admission/Fare: Varies. Call or write for information.

Locomotive/Rolling Stock: Alco FPA 4s nos. 15 and 6777; Alco FPA 4s nos. 4088 and 4099, former Delaware & Hudson.

Location/Directions: I-77 exit 155 (Rockside Road), travel east one mile. The train departs from the parking area on Old Rockside Road in Independence.

Cleveland and Akron

Site Address: Independence, OH
Mailing Address: PO Box 158, Peninsula, OH 44264-0158
Telephone: (800) 468-4070
Internet: members.aol.com/cvsrail/index.html

Ohio, Jefferson

AC&J SCENIC LINE RAILWAY
Diesel, scheduled
Standard gauge

AC&T SCENIC LINE

Ride: Take a one-hour, 12-mile round trip over the last remaining portion of the New York Central's Ashtabula to Pittsburgh "High Grade" passenger mainline. Ride in vintage passenger cars pulled by first generation diesel.

Schedule: Father's Day weekend through October: weekends, 12:30, 2, and 3:30 p.m.

Admission/Fare: Adults $7.00; seniors $6.00; children 3-12 $5.00; under age 3 are free when not occupying a seat.

Locomotive/Rolling Stock: No. 107, 1950 Alco S-2 diesel, former Nickel Plate and Fairport, Painesville & Eastern; no. 518, 1951 Alco S-2 diesel, former Erie and former Centerior Energy plant switcher (Ashtabula).

Special Events: Spring and Fall Murder Mystery Trains.

Nearby Attractions/Accommodations: Ashtabula, Conneaut, Geneva-on-the-Lake, Pymatuning Resort area, Cleveland, Erie.

Location/Directions: I-90 from east/west exit Ohio 11 south, to Ohio 46 south to Jefferson, left at second light on E. Jefferson Street to tracks. Or north on route 11, exit 307 west to Jefferson, right at second light to tracks.

Site Address: East Jefferson Street, Jefferson, OH
Mailing Address: PO Box 517, Jefferson, OH 44047-0517
Telephone: (440) 576-6346
Fax: (440) 576-8848

Ohio, Jefferson

JEFFERSON DEPOT, INC.
Railroad museum

JEFFERSON DEPOT

Museum: Historic restored 1872 Lake Shore & Michigan Southern Railroad Station and 1918 caboose.

Schedule: Memorial Day through Labor Day: Sundays, 1 to 4 p.m. Other days by appointment. Available for group tours, meetings, reunions, weddings.

Admission/Fare: Suggested donation: adults $1.00; children are free.

Special Events: Strawberry Festival and Craft Bazaar, fourth weekend in June. Antique car show.

Nearby Attractions/Accommodations: AC&J Railroad scenic tours, Buccaneer Campsites.

Location/Directions: From I-90 go south on route 11 to route 46 south to Jefferson. Museum is located between E. Walnut and E. Jefferson Streets.

*Coupon available, see coupon section.

[P] [*] [📷] [⛪] [✉] M

Site Address: 147 E. Jefferson Street, Jefferson, OH
Mailing Address: PO Box 22, Jefferson, OH 44047
Telephone: (440) 293-5532 and (352) 343-8256

Ohio, Lebanon

TURTLE CREEK VALLEY RAILWAY
Diesel, electric, scheduled
Standard gauge

Ride: A one hour train ride through the historic Turtle Creek Valley in southwestern Ohio. Two-hour rides on Sunday afternoons.

Schedule: April through December: weekends. May through October: weekends, Wednesdays, and Fridays. Closed November 21 and 22.

Admission/Fare: Adults $9.00; seniors $8.00; children 3-12 $5.00. Specialty trips are higher.

Locomotive/Rolling Stock: 1950 GM GP7 1500 horsepower; Pullman commuter coaches nos. 101, 102, 103, and 104; gondola no. 100.

Special Events: Mystery Ride-n-Dine events, summer ice cream socials, fall foliage rides, train rides with Santa.

Nearby Attractions/Accommodations: Kings Island, beach, Fort Ancient, The Golden Lamb Inn, Miami Valley Dinner Theater, Renaissance Festival, Blue Jacket Drama, golf, vineyards, canoeing, harness racing.

Location/Directions: I-75 exit 29; I-71 North exit 32; I-71 South exit 28.

Site Address: 198 South Broadway, Lebanon, OH
Mailing Address: 198 South Broadway, Lebanon, OH 45036
Telephone: (800) 48-TRAIN and (513) 398-8584
Fax: (513) 933-8219

Ohio, Marietta

HARMAR STATION
Historical Model Railroad Museum

MITCH CASEY

Museum/Display: Visit Harmar Station and see one of America's most complete private collections of authentic toy electric trains. Harmar Station features more than 1,500 linear feet of multilevel track with as many as 15 trains operating simultaneously. Over 200 vintage locomotives are on display.

Schedule: Year round: daily, 11 a.m. to 5 p.m.

Admission: $5; children under 4th grade free with paying adult; families $15.

Special Events: Sternwheel Festival, weekend after Labor Day.

Nearby Attractions/Accommodations: Butch's Cola Museum, Children's Toy and Doll Museum, Valley Gem Sternwheel, Showboat Becky Thatcher, Rossi Pasta Factory, Lee Middleton Original Doll Factory, Fenton Art Glass Company, Historic Lafayette Hotel.

Location/Directions: I-77 and Ohio Route 7.

*Coupon available, see coupon section.

[♿] [P] [🚌] [✳] [✉]

Site Address: 220 Gilman Street, Harmar Village, Marietta, OH
Mailing Address: 220 Gilman Street, Marietta, OH 45750
Telephone: (614) 374-9995 and (614) 373-5176
Fax: (614) 373-7808
E-mail: mttachamber@ee.net
Internet: www.win.net/~utumno/harmarstation.html

Ohio, Maumee

MAUMEE VALLEY HISTORICAL SOCIETY
Museum

MAUMEE VALLEY HISTORICAL SOCIETY

Display: The depot is part of a five-building museum complex. Guided tours cover the entire complex. The depot and caboose are authentically furnished. Railroad memorabilia on display.

Schedule: Wednesdays through Sundays, 1 to 4 p.m.

Locomotive/Rolling Stock: Caboose and baggage car.

Special Events: Model train exhibit in caboose.

Nearby Attractions/Accommodations: Toledo Zoo, Museum of Art.

Location/Directions: The museum is on River Road in downtown Maumee and can be reached easily from U.S. routes 20 and 24.

Site Address: 1031 River Road, Maumee, OH
Mailing Address: 1031 River Road, Maumee, OH 43537
Telephone: (419) 893-9602
Fax: (419) 893-3108

Ohio, Nelsonville

HOCKING VALLEY SCENIC RAILWAY
Steam, scheduled
Standard gauge

HOCKING VALLEY SCENIC RAILWAY

Ride: This historic railroad offers a 12-mile round trip to Haydenville and a 25 mile round trip to Logan with a visit to an 1860s settlers village at Robbins Crossing. The train operates over a former Chesapeake & Ohio route that was once an original Hocking Valley Railway. Listed on the National Register of Historic Places.

Schedule: Memorial Day weekend through mid-November: weekends and holidays, 12 p.m. from Haydenville (1½-hour trip), 2:30 p.m. from Logan (2¼-hour trip).

Admission/Fare: Haydenville–adults $7.50, children 2-11 $4.75. Logan–adults $10.50, children 2-11 $7.25.

Locomotive/Rolling Stock: No. 33, 1916 Baldwin 2-8-0; no. 5833, 1952 EMD GP7, former Chesapeake & Ohio; no. 7318, 1942 General Electric; no. 3, 1920 Baldwin 0-6-0.

Special Events: Logan: Santa Trains, November 28-29, December 5-6, 12-13, 19-20, 11:15 a.m. and 2:15 p.m. Reservations recommended.

Nearby Attractions/Accommodations: Hocking Hills Area State Park, Robbins Crossing Museum, Stuarts Opera House ca. 1879, Historic Dew Hotel, Nelsonville Public Square.

Location/Directions: Southeastern Ohio on Route 33, 60 miles southeast of Columbus in Hocking Hills region.

Site Address: 33 Canal Street, Nelsonville, OH
Mailing Address: PO Box 427, Nelsonville, OH 45764
Telephone: (614) 470-1300 and (800) 967-7834
Fax: (614) 753-1152

Ohio, Olmsted Township

TROLLEYVILLE, U.S.A.
Electric, scheduled
Standard gauge

RICHARD FUNK

Museum/Ride: Streetcars and miscellanous railroad equipment on display. Museum in the 1875 restored B&O Berea Depot. Ride on over 2½ miles of track.

Schedule: May through November: weekends. June through September: Wednesdays and Fridays.

Admission/Fare: $5.00 adults; seniors $4.00; children $3.00; under age 2 are free.

Locomotive/Rolling Stock: Twelve streetcars; 13 interurban; three work cars and locomotives; two boxcars; two cabooses.

Special Events: Easter Egg Hunt, Murder Mysteries, Halloween, Christmas Festival of Lights.

Nearby Attractions/Accommodations: Swings 'n Things.

Location/Directions: I-48, exit 6A, 2 miles south.

Site Address: 7100 Columbia Road, Olmsted Twp., OH
Mailing Address: 7100 Columbia Road, Olmsted Twp., OH 44138
Telephone: (440) 235-4725
Fax: (440) 235-6556
E-mail: cperry8599@aol.com

Ohio, Orrville

ORRVILLE RAILROAD HERITAGE SOCIETY
Diesel, irregular
Standard gauge

RICHARD JACOBS

Display: This museum is a restored former Pennsylvania Railroad Depot and an unrestored N5C caboose and switch block tower.

Schedule: Museum–May through September: Saturdays, 10 a.m. to 4 p.m. or by appointment. Train: Excursion Saturdays.

Admission/Fare: Donations appreciated.

Locomotive/Rolling Stock: 1951 EMD F9 cab unit no. 82C; two B units; six Budd passenger coaches.

Special Events: Depot Days, June 13-14. Christmas Open House, November 27-28.

Nearby Attractions/Accommodations: Gateway to Amish Country of Wayne and Holmes Counties.

Location/Directions: On State Route 57, 3 miles north of U.S. 30 and 12 miles south of I-76.

Site Address: 145 Depot Street, Orrville, OH
Mailing Address: PO Box 11, Orrville, OH 44667
Telephone: (330) 683-2426 and (330) 682-4327
Fax: (330) 682-2426

Ohio, Sugarcreek

OHIO CENTRAL RAILROAD
Steam, diesel, scheduled
Standard gauge

DAVID PETRIE

Ride: The Ohio Central, a 70-mile-long working railroad, operates the diesel- and steam-powered Sugarcreek Service, a one-hour round trip over former Wheeling & Lake Erie trackage in the Amish country known as the "Switzerland of Ohio."

Schedule: Monday-Saturday, May 2-October 26, 11:00 a.m., 12:30, 2, and 3:30 p.m. Extra trains added, Saturdays, July, August, and October, 5 p.m.

Admission/Fare: Adults $7.00; children 3-12 $4.00; children under age 3 are free.

Locomotive/Rolling Stock: No. 1551, 1912 Montreal 4-6-0, former Canadian National; no. 13, 1920 Alco 2-8-0, former Buffalo Creek & Gauley; no. 3 1926 Alco 0-4-0T, former Southern Wood Preserving Co.; no. 1293 1948 SLW 4-6-2, former Canadian Pacific; no. 71 1950 EMMD SW7, former Montour Railroad.

Special Events: Swiss Festival, October 2-3. Double Header Steam trips. Fall Foliage trips. Murder Mystery Train. Other all-day excursions. Call or write for schedules.

Site Address: 111 Factory Street, Sugarcreek, OH
Mailing Address: PO Box 179, Sugarcreek, OH 44681
Telephone: (330) 852-4676
Fax: (330) 852-2989

Ohio, Waterville and Grand Rapids

TOLEDO, LAKE ERIE & WESTERN RAILWAY
Diesel, scheduled
Standard gauge

GEORGE A. FORERO, JR.

Ride/Display: Each ride is a 20-mile round trip over the lines of the Nickel Plate between the historic towns of Waterville and Grand Rapids. Come and witness a spectacular view from our 900-foot-long bridge over the Maumee River, Providence Metropark, Ludwig Mill, and the Miami & Erie canal boat ride.

Schedule: May through October: Wednesdays through Sundays and holidays. Send SASE for hours or call.

Admission/Fare: Round trip–adults $8.00; seniors $7.00; children 3-12 $4.50. One-way trips and charters available.

Locomotive/Rolling Stock: 1946 no. 112 Alco S2; 1948 no. 5109 Alco S4; B&O chair car nos. 401 and 403; New York Central nos. 405, 407, 408; more.

Special Events: Roch de Beouf Festival (Waterville), early September. Apple Butter Festival (Grand Rapids), October. Garage Sale Days. Call or write for details.

Nearby Attractions/Accommodations: Volmar's Amusement Park, Isaac Ludwig Grist/Saw Mill, Miami & Erie mule-pulled canal boat rides.

Location/Directions: Waterville–US 23/I-475 to west on US 24/Anthony Wayne Trail, north on route 64, to Sixth Street, right turn. Grand Rapids–State route 64, west on route 578 over bridge, right on route 65, left on Wapakoneta Road, right on Third Street. Follow signs for Warehouse Antique Mall.

Site Address: 49 N. Sixth Street, Waterville, OH
Mailing Address: PO Box 168, Waterville, OH 43566
Telephone: (419) 878-2177
Internet: www.meettoledo.org (see Conventions/Vistor's page)

Ohio, Worthington

OHIO RAILWAY MUSEUM
Electric, scheduled
Standard Gauge

DAVE BUNGE PHOTO

Museum/Ride: Museum with 2-mile round trip on historic Trolley-Interurban cars.

Schedule: May through October: Sundays, 1 to 5 p.m.

Admission/Fare: Adults $3.00; seniors $2.00; children $1.00.

Locomotive/Rolling Stock: N&W no. 578 Pacific Steam; OPS no. 21 interurban; passenger cars, street cars, and interurbans.

Special Events: Ghost Trolley, Santa Trolley, State Fair, Twilight Trolleys.

Nearby Attractions/Accommodations: Columbus Zoo, Center of Science and Industry, hotels, and restaurants.

Location/Directions: I-71 exit Route 161, one mile west to Proprietors Road, turn north.

Site Address: 990 Proprietors Road, Worthington, OH
Mailing Address: Box 777, Worthington, OH
Telephone: (614) 885-7345
Internet: members.aol.com/orm578/page/ormhome.htm

Oklahoma, Bartlesville (Ramona)

THE TRAIN HOUSE
Model railroad

Display: Trains, trains, and more trains running everywhere! Exhibits include an outdoor G scale garden railroad, a 28' x 48' Lionel layout, HO and N scale layouts, and a wagon-train ride through the park. Hobby shop features trains and accessories in all scales.

Schedule: Year round: 10 a.m. to 5 p.m. During the holiday season hours are 10 a.m. to 8 p.m.

Admission/Fare: Donations appreciated.

Special Events: Main Line Train Show, July 11. Holiday lights display and wagon-train ride over two acres, November 28 through December 30.

Nearby Attractions/Accommodations: Osage Hills State Park, restaurants, motels, Bartlesville, Oklahoma (15 miles).

Location/Directions: U.S. 75 to County Road 27, east 2 miles to stop sign, north 1½ blocks to entrance.

Site Address: Route 1, Box 488, Ramona, OK
Mailing Address: Route 1, Box 488, Ramona, OK 74061
Telephone: (918) 336-5821

Oklahoma, Choctaw

CHOCTAW CABOOSE MUSEUM
Railway museum

Museum: An old wooden railway caboose has been converted into a museum that displays local history items and photographs.

Schedule: Memorial Day through Labor Day: Saturdays 10 a.m. to 4 p.m. and Sundays 2 to 5 p.m. Other times by appointment.

Admission/Fare: Free.

Locomotive/Rolling Stock: Caboose.

Location/Directions: On Highway 62. Choctaw is east of Oklahoma City.

Site Address: Henney Road and NE 23rd Street, Hwy. 62, Choctaw, OK
Mailing Address: 2701 N. Triple XXX Road, Choctaw, OK 73020-8402
Telephone: (405) 390-2771

Oklahoma, Enid   **RAILROAD MUSEUM OF OKLAHOMA**
Railway museum

Museum: Visit our rail yard with engines, cars, and cabooses. China, silverware, bells, lights, whistles, lanterns and much more on display. Also operating HO and N gauge layouts.

Schedule: Year round: Tuesday through Friday, 1 to 4 p.m. Saturdays, 9 a.m. to 1 p.m. Sundays, 2 to 5 p.m. and by appointment.

Admission/Fare: Donations appreciated.

Locomotive/Rolling Stock: 1965 GE 50-ton locomotive; Frisco Mt. Baldwin 4-8-2 no. 1519; seven cabooses; other rolling stock.

Nearby Attractions/Accommodations: Holiday Inn, Mid-Western Motel, many museums.

Location/Directions: Next to BN-SF mainline.

♿ P 🚌 📷 ⛩ ✉ arm M VIA

Site Address: 702 N. Washington, Enid, OK
Mailing Address: 702 N. Washington, Enid, OK 73701
Telephone: (405) 233-3051

Oklahoma, Hugo

HUGO HERITAGE RAILROAD
Diesel, scheduled
Standard gauge

CHOCTAW COUNTY HISTORICAL SOCIETY

Ride/Display: This operation offers a 2½-hour round trip from Hugo (Circus City, U.S.A.) to points north and south, including Paris, Texas. A museum, located in the former 1915 Frisco depot, is the largest left on Frisco's southwest lines. Displays include an HO gauge model railroad on a mountain layout, railroad artifacts, turn-of-the-century memorabilia, rare photographs, and a working Harvey House restaurant.

Schedule: April through November: Saturdays.

Admission/Fare: Adults $18.00; children $10.00.

Locomotive/Rolling Stock: Commuter coaches, 80'; GP38 locomotive.

Special Events: Railroad Days, October. Grants Bluegrass Festival, August.

Nearby Attractions/Accommodations: Mt. Olive Cemetary, Ft. Towson, Rosehill Cemetary, motels, restaurants.

Location/Directions: Site is located 181 miles from Oklahoma City, OK, and 130 miles from Dallas, TX, and 23 miles from Paris, TX.

[P] 🚌 ❋ ☕ 📷 ⛱ 🚂 ✉ M

Site Address: 309 N. "B" Street, Hugo, OK
Mailing Address: 502 W. Duke, Hugo, OK 74743
Telephone: (405) 326-6630
Fax: (405) 326-6655

Oklahoma, Tulsa   **SUNBELT RAILROAD MUSEUM**
                                                       Musuem

Museum: Displays include railroad mementos, an operating telegraph station, and a library.

Schedule: Year round: Saturdays, except holidays.

Admission/Fare: Donations appreciated.

Nearby Attractions/Accommodations: Food and lodging in downtown Tulsa.

Location/Directions: Near downtown Tulsa.

[P] [*] [✉] M

Site Address: 1323 E. 5th Street, Tulsa, OK
Mailing Address: PO Box 470311, Tulsa, OK 74147-0311
Telephone: (918) 584-3777
E-mail: slsf4500@aol.com
Internet: members.aol.com/slsf4500

Oklahoma, Waynoka

WAYNOKA HISTORICAL SOCIETY
Railroad museum, model railroad display

WAYNOKA HISTORICAL SOCIETY

Museum: Museum is housed in the former Santa Fe Depot, next door to the Harvey House. Buildings are to be restored with over $500,000; architects currently working on plans. Located on BNSF main line from Chicago to Los Angeles–many trains daily. Railroad memorabilia; Transcontinental Air Transport exhibit; German prisoner-of-war paintings; local history; Harvey House display; railways Ice Plant display; John Holbird mural.

Schedule: First weekend after Easter through Labor Day: 2 to 4 p.m. Other times by appointment.

Admission/Fare: Free.

Special Events: Alumni Reunion. Snake Hunt, first Sunday after Easter. Rodeo, August.

Nearby Attractions/Accommodations: Little Sahara State Park, Trails Inn, Little Sahara Motel.

Location/Directions: Two blocks west of Highway 281 on Waynoka Street.

Site Address: Waynoka Street & Cleveland Street, Waynoka, OK
Mailing Address: PO Box 193, Waynoka, OK 73860
Telephone: (405) 824-1886 and (405) 824-5871
Fax: (405) 824-7331

Oklahoma, Yukon

YUKON'S BEST RAILROAD MUSEUM
Railway museum

JACK B. AUSTERMAN

Museum: The museum contains an extensive display of railroad antiques and artifacts of the Rock Island Line and other railroads.

Schedule: Year round by chance or appointment. Call or write for information.

Admission/Fare: Free.

Locomotive/Rolling Stock: Rock Island boxcar no. 5542; caboose no. 17039; Mo Pac caboose no. 13724; UP caboose no. 25865.

Location/Directions: On historic Route 66. Main Street, across from "Yukon's Best Flour" wheat elevator.

P 🚌 🎋 ✉

Site Address: Third and Main Streets, Yukon, MO
Mailing Address: 1020 W. Oak Street, Yukon, MO 73099
Telephone: (405) 354-5079

Oregon, Canby　　　　　　　　**PHOENIX & HOLLY RAILROAD**
Diesel, scheduled
Standard gauge

Ride: Visitors can ride through acres of flowers at the Flower Farmer and enjoy a 1¾-mile ride witha stopover at the petting zoo (July through September).

Schedule: May through September: Saturdays, 11 a.m. to 9 p.m. and Sundays 11 a.m. to 6 p.m. October: open daily, pumpkin patch.

Admission/Fare: Adults $2.50; children age 12 and under $1.75. Groups, weekdays by appointment.

Locomotive/Rolling Stock: Diesel locomotive purpose-built; gondolas; caboose.

Special Events: Pumpkin Run (to pumpkin patch), month of October.

Nearby Attractions/Accommodations: Swan Island, Canby Ferry, state park.

Location/Directions: I-5 to Canby, north on Holly to site.

*Coupon available, see coupon section.

Site Address: 2512 N. Holly, Canby, OR
Mailing Address: 2512 N. Holly, Canby, OR 92013
Telephone: (503) 266-3581
Fax: (503) 263-4027
Internet: trainweb.com/mall/phoenix&holly

Oregon, Hood River

MOUNT HOOD RAILROAD AND DINNER TRAIN
Diesel, scheduled
Standard gauge

MOUNT HOOD RAILROAD

Ride: Built in 1906, the train is a link between two of Oregon's most spectacular natural wonders–the awe-inspiring Columbia River Gorge and the foothills of dramatic, snowcapped Mt. Hood, the state's highest peak. For special occasions, take the dinner train, "The Four Course Dinner with a Thousand Views."

Schedule: April through December: Excursion train–10 a.m. and 3 p.m. Brunch train–11 a.m. Dinner train–5:30 p.m.

Admission/Fare: Excursion train–adults $22.95; seniors $19.95; children $14.95. Brunch train–$55.00. Dinner train–$67.50.

Locomotive/Rolling Stock: Two 1950 GP9s; historic Pullmans from 1920 to 1930.

Nearby Attractions/Accommodations: Mt. Hood, Columbia River National Scenic Area, biking, hiking, wind surfing, golf, historic hotels.

Location/Directions: Sixty miles east of Portland on I-84, exit 63 right to Cascade Street, left to parking lot.

Site Address: 110 Railroad Avenue, Hood River, OR
Mailing Address: 110 Railroad Avenue, Hood River, OR 97031
Telephone: (800) TRAIN-61 and (541) 386-3556
Fax: (541) 386-2140

Oregon, Portland

SAMTRAK
Diesel, irregular
Standard gauge

SAMTRAK

Ride: Climb aboard the open-air car or caboose pulled by "Big Red" for a rone-hour round trip scenic ride along the Willamette River over former Portland Traction Electric Line.

Schedule: May through mid-June: weekends, 11 a.m. to 4 p.m. Mid-June through Labor Day: Tuesdays through Sundays, 11 a.m. to 5 p.m. September: weekends, 11 a.m. to 4 p.m. October 1-13: weekends, 12 to 4 p.m.

Admission/Fare: $4.00; children 1-4 $2.00.

Locomotive/Rolling Stock: GE 45-ton diesel no. 450; GE 25-ton diesel no. 2501; open-air passenger car; restored former Simpson Timber Logging caboose no. 900.

Nearby Attractions/Accommodations: on the south end–Oaks Amusement Park, an amusement park since 1902; north end–Oregon Museum of Science and Industry; south end–boarding station located in OMSI parking lot (1945 SE Water Avenue).

Site Address: 9001 SE McBrod Street (rail yard)
Mailing Address: PO Box 22548, Portland, OR 97269
Telephone: (503) 653-2380
Fax: (503) 659-6546

Oregon, Portland

WASHINGTON PARK & ZOO RAILWAY
Steam, diesel, scheduled
30" gauge

GEORGE BAETJER/WASHINGTON PARK & ZOO RAILWAY

Ride: A 4-mile round trip around the zoo and through forested hills to Washington Park, passing the elephant enclosure for a close-up view of the zoo's world-famous pachyderm herd and overlooking the Alaska Tundra exhibit. The stop at Washington Park station offers a panoramic view of Mount Hood, the city of Portland, and Mount St. Helens, and passengers may obtain a stopover pass there to visit the Rose Test Gardens and the Japanese Garden, located nearby.

Schedule: May 23 through September 7: daily. Trains depart at frequent intervals.

Admission/Fare: Round trip–adults $2.75; seniors and children 3-11 $2.00; under age 3 are free. Zoo admission required.

Locomotive/Rolling Stock: 4-4-0 No. 1, replica of Virginia & Truckee "Reno"; *Zooliner*, replica of General Motors *Aerotrain;* diesel-powered *Oregon Express;* diesel powered switcher and fire train; streamlined cars and open coaches; two trains are wheelchair-accessible. The train is one of the last registered Postal Railway Stations in the United States.

Nearby Attractions/Accommodations: Portland Rose Test Gardens, Japanese Gardens.

Location/Directions: Zoo is located two miles west of Portland City Center, on U.S. Highway 26.

*Coupon available, see coupon section.

Radio frequency: 151.655

Site Address: 4001 SW Canyon Road, Portland, OR
Mailing Address: 4001 SW Canyon Road, Portland, OR 97221
Telephone: (503) 226-1561
Fax: (503) 226-6836

Oregon, Redmond

CROOKED RIVER DINNER TRAIN
Steam, unscheduled
Electric, scheduled
Standard gauge

Ride: Look for cattle, coyotes and cowboys, as you ride through Central Oregon's beautiful rimrock-lined high desert country aboard the Crooked River Railroad Company Dining Train. At your dinner car table, you'll travel over 38 scenic miles of track (round trip) through the historical Crooked River Valley. Don't miss the Friday western dinner shows, the Saturday Western Murder Mystery theater, or our lavish Sunday Champagne Brunch or Sunday Suppers featuring the James Gang and a live action train robbery. Or for special summer fun, enjoy our Cowboy Breakfast, where train robberies occur when you least expect them.

Schedule: Year round: Saturdays, 6 to 9 p.m. Sundays, 11 a.m. to 2 p.m. or 1 to 4 p.m. Schedule varies, special train rides on select dates.

Admission/Fare: Saturdays–adults $69.00; children 4-12 $32.00; infants $16.00. Sundays–adults $59.99.

Locomotive/Rolling Stock: Milwaukee Road coach; Burlington baggage car.

Special Events: Halloween, Thanksgiving, Santa Claus trains, New Year's Eve.

Nearby Attractions/Accommodations: Smith Rock State Park, golfing, resorts.

Location/Directions: Site is 1½ miles north of Redmond on Highway 97. Take right at flashing yellow light and follow O'Neil Highway for ¼ mile over railroad tracks. Train on left.

*Coupon available, see coupon section.

Site Address: 4075 NE O'Neil Way, Redmond, OR
Mailing Address: PO Box 387, Redmond, OR 97756
Telephone: (541) 548-8630
Internet: www.crookedriverrailroad.com/dinnertrain/main.cfm

Oregon, Sumpter Valley

SUMPTER VALLEY RAILROAD
Steam, scheduled
36" gauge

Ride: A ten-mile round trip from McEwen Station to the historic ining town of Sumpter.

Schedule: Memorial Day through September: McEwen–weekends and holidays, 10 a.m., 12:30, and 3 p.m. Sumpter–weekends and holidays, 11:30 a.m., 2, and 4:40 p.m.

Admission/Fare: Adults–round trip $9.00, one-way $6.00; children 6-16 6.50/4.50; families $22.00/$15.00.

Locomotive/Rolling Stock: 1920 Alco 2-8-2; 1915 Heisler; 18-ton Plymouth diesel.

Special Events: Moonlite rides, hobo stew, and music, July 4.

Nearby Attractions/Accommodations: Sumpter Dredge State Heritage Area.

Location/Directions: Highway 7, 22 miles southwest of Baker City off I-84.

Site Address: Dredge Loop Road, Sumpter Valley, OR
Mailing Address: PO Box 389, Baker City, OR 97814
Telephone: (541) 894-2268

Pennsylvania, Altoona

ALTOONA RAILROADER'S MEMORIAL MUSEUM
Railway museum
Standard gauge

PETER D. BARTON

Museum: The museum tells the stories of the people who laid track, built the locomotives, and guided trains across the Allegheny Ridge. Located in the former PRR Master Mechanics Building (in 1998), visitors will experience what it was like to live and work in a community that was a company—the Pennsylvania Railroad.

Schedule: Open year round. Summer beginning first Sunday in April: daily, 10 a.m. to 5 p.m.; Winter beginning last Sunday in October: daily, 10 a.m. to 4 p.m. Closed Mondays.

Admission/Fare: Adults $8.50; seniors $7.75; children (3-12) $5.00. Group rates and school packages available.

Locomotive/Rolling Stock: G-G-1 no. 4913; 1918 Vulcan 0-4-0 switcher Nancy; two diesel locomotives; the Loretto.

Special Events: Horn & Whistle Fair, June; Altoona Railfest, October. Call events line for more information.

Nearby Attractions/Accommodations: Horseshoe Curve National Historic Landmark. Call for free visitors guide (800)84-ALTOONA.

Location/Directions: I-99 (formerly Route 220), 17th Street exit, Downtown Altoona.

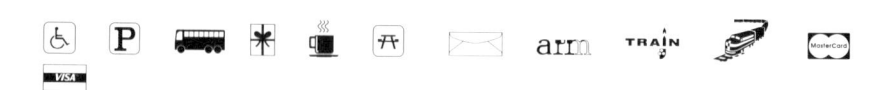

Site Address: 1300 9th Avenue, Altoona, PA
Mailing Address: 1300 9th Avenue, Altoona, PA 16602
Telephone: (814) 946-0834 and (888) 4-ALTOONA
Fax: (814) 946-9457
Internet: http://www.railroadcity.com

Pennsylvania, Altoona

HORSESHOE CURVE
NATIONAL HISTORIC LANDMARK
Railway display

RAILROADER'S MEMORIAL MUSEUM

Display: The Curve's story is now told at the modern interpretive Visitor Center, located in a picturesque setting. A seven-minute film describes the role of Pennsylvania transportation in America's move to the West. Guests may ride to track elevation aboard a single-track funicular or walk the 194 stairs. It is located on Conrail's busy East-West Main Line with more than 50 trains passing each day. Trains climbing or descending the 1.8 percent grade can be viewed and photographed safely from the trackside park.

Schedule: Open year round. Summer beginning first Sunday in April: daily, 10 a.m. to 5 p.m.; Winter beginning last Sunday in October: daily, 10 a.m. to 4 p.m. Closed Mondays.

Admission/Fare: Adults $3.50; seniors $3.00; children (3-12) $1.75. Group rates and school packages available.

Locomotive/Rolling Stock: Former Pennsylvania Railroad GP9, No. 7048 on display at track elevation.

Nearby Attractions/Accommodations: Altoona Railroaders Memorial Museum. Free visitors guides (800) 84-ALTOONA.

Location/Directions: Kittanning Point Road, State Route 4008. Follow Heritage Route signs.

Site Address: Altoona, PA
Mailing Address: 1300 9th Avenue, Altoona, PA 16602
Telephone: (814) 941-7960

Pennsylvania, Ashland

PIONEER TUNNEL COAL MINE & STEAM TRAIN
Steam, scheduled
Narrow gauge

PIONEER TUNNEL COAL MINE & STEAM TRAIN

Ride: Scenic ride along the Mahanoy Mountain behind an old fashioned steam locomotive of the 0-4-0 type built in 1927 by the Vulcan Iron Works of Wilkes Barre, PA. Guides tell the story of strip mining, bootlegging and the Centralia Mine Fire. Also available is a tour of a real anthracite coal mine in open mine cars pulled by a battery operated mine motor. Mine guides show and tell the fascinating story of anthracite coal mining.

Schedule: Mine tours–April, May, September, October: weekends 11 a.m., 12:30, 2 p.m. Memorial Day through Labor Day: daily, 10 a.m. to 6 p.m. Steam train–April: for groups by reservation only. Memorial Day through Labor Day: daily, 10 a.m. to 6 p.m. May, September, October: weekends, 10 a.m. to 6 p.m.

Admission/Fare: Steam train–adults $3.50; children under age 12 $2.00. Mine–adults $6.00; children under age 12 $3.50. Group discounts available.

Locomotive/Rolling Stock: A spare "Lokie" of the 0-4-0 type built by Vulcan Iron Work; two battery powered mine motors.

Special Events: 6th Annual Pioneer Day, August 22.

Nearby Attractions/Accommodations: PA Museum of Anthracite Mining.

Location/Directions: I-81 exit 36W (Frackville). Follow route 61 north to Ashland.

Site Address: 19th & Oak Streets, Ashland, PA
Mailing Address: 19th & Oak Streets, Ashland, PA 17921
Telephone: (717) 875-3850
Fax: (717)875-3301
Internet: www.easternpa.com/pioneertunnel

Pennsylvania, Bellefonte

BELLEFONTE HISTORICAL RAILROAD
Diesel, scheduled
Standard gauge

W.M. RUMBERGER

Ride/Display: Scheduled and special trips over the 60-mile Nittany & Bald Eagle Railroad to Lemont, Vail (Tyrone), and Mill Hall. Regular service includes stopovers at Lemont, Bellefonte, Curtin Village, and Julian Glider Port. Fall foliage and railfan runs cover up to 120 miles; all-inclusive restaurant runs to Tyrone are also offered. The Bellefonte Station, a restored former Pennsylvania Railroad structure built in 1888, houses an operating N-gauge layout of the Bellefonte-Curtin Village route, as well as historical photos and memorabilia of area railroading. A snowplow and caboose under restoration are displayed beside the station.

Schedule: May 30 through September 30: weekends and holidays. October: special runs. Call or write for information.

Admission/Fare: Adults $6.00 and up; children 3-11 $3.00 and up.

Locomotive/Rolling Stock: No. 9167, 1952 RDC-1, and 1962 No. 1953; air-conditioned passenger cars. Can be configured for meal service.

Special Events: Spring, Fall, Christmas trains.

Nearby Attractions/Accommodations: Curtin Village, Julian Glider Port, Penn State University, historic Bellefonte.

Location/Directions: Central Pennsylvania, a short distance from I-80.

Site Address: The Train Station, Bellefonte, PA
Mailing Address: The Train Station, Bellefonte, PA 16823
Telephone: (814) 355-0311 and (814) 355-2392

Pennsylvania, Cresson

ALLEGHENY PORTAGE RAILROAD NATIONAL HISTORIC SITE
Railway display
Standard gauge

ALLEGHENY PORTAGE RAILROAD

Display: This site was established in 1964 to commemorate the first railroad to cross the Allegheny Mountains, in 1834. The Portage Railroad, considered a technological wonder of its day, played a role in opening the interior of the United States to trade and settlement. Today's park, covering fifteen hundred acres, preserves remains of this railroad and reveals its interesting story. The visitor center features a twenty-minute motion picture and exhibits that help tell the story of the railroad. A new feature is the Engine House 6 Exhibit Building, which protects the remains of the original engine house and includes a full-sized model of a stationary steam engine. The Lemon House, a tavern during the days of the railroad, has been restored to its nineteenth-century appearance.

Schedule: Visitor Center and Lemon House–Memorial Day through Labor Day: daily, 9 a.m. to 6 p.m.; rest of the year, 9 a.m. to 5 p.m. Ranger-guided train tours–June through October: Thursdays through Saturdays, call for information. Closed Christmas Day.

Admission/Fare: Adults $2.00; children under age 17 are free.

Locomotive/Rolling Stock: A full-sized model of the 1837 steam locomotive "Lafayette" is on display in the Visitor Center.

Location/Directions: Off the Gallitzin exit of U.S. 22, between Altoona and Cresson.

Site Address: Cresson, PA
Mailing Address: PO Box 189, Cresson, PA 16630
Telephone: (814) 886-6150 and (814) 495-4643 tour information
E-mail: www.nps.gov/alpo/

Pennsylvania, Cressona

MINE HILL & NORTHERN RAILROAD PRESERVATION SOCIETY
Standard gauge

DAVID GAMBLE

Display: A collection of privately owned, full scale railroad equipment undergoing various stages of restoration. Members focus on anthracite railroads of northeastern Pennsylvania, but other railroads are also represented.

Schedule: By appointment only.

Admission/Fare: Donations appreciated.

Locomotive/Rolling Stock: LV 95116 caboose; CNJ 91516 caboose; RDG 94070 caboose; EL 319 caboose; NH 622 caboose; HRCX 5830 shop car; private car "Anthracite," former NYC coach.

Special Events: Rust-busters annual summer picnic.

Nearby Attractions/Accommodations: Pioneer Tunnel Coal Mine and Anthracite Technological Musuem at Ashland, Pennsylvania. Reading Company Technical and Historical Society at Leesport, Pennsylvania. Eckley Miner's Village at Hazelton, Pennsylvania.

Location/Directions: West Cressona yard is located in Cressona on routes 901 and 183, a short distance north of Schuylkill Haven and south of Pottsville, near the heart of the Southern Anthracite Field. The site is about 40 miles north of Reading and 45 miles east of Harrisburg.

Site Address: Cressona, PA
Mailing Address: c/o Heritage Railcar, PO Box 334, Palmyra, PA 17078-0334
Telephone: (717) 838-3143

Pennsylvania, Gettysburg

GETTYSBURG SCENIC RAIL TOURS
Diesel, scheduled
Standard gauge

AL SAUER

Ride: Travel into history as you ride through the First Day's Battlefield of Gettysburg National Military Park. Ride behind Vintage F-units along this beautiful former Reading Railroad line.

Schedule: April through October: call or write for schedule; daily in July and August. Groups and charters welcome.

Admission/Fare: Varies by trip length and special events.

Locomotive/Rolling Stock: Two F7s nos. 81A and 81C, former Milwaukee Road; double-deck open air car; 1920s vintage open window coaches.

Special Events: Civil War Train Rides, Lincoln Weekend, Easter Bunny Train, Santa Claus Train, dinner trips, Fall Folliage Excursion, and Spring Blossom Excursion. Call or write for dates.

Nearby Attractions/Accommodations: Gettysburg National Military Park, Eisenhower Farm, SK: Liberty, and numerous hotels and fine restaurants.

Location/Directions: From Harrisburg, Baltimore, or Washington D.C. take route 15 to US 30 west to North Washington Street.

Site Address: 106 North Washington Street, Gettysburg, PA
Mailing Address: 106 North Washington Street, Gettysburg, PA 17325
Telephone: (717) 334-6932
Fax: (717) 334-4746

Pennsylvania, Greenville

GREENVILLE RAILROAD PARK AND MUSEUM
Railroad display
Standard gauge

IAN SCOTT FORBES

Display/Museum: Engine 604, the last of its kind, was one of nine of the largest switch engine ever built for the Union Railroad in 1936. When the locomotives were retired in 1960 only one, the Greenville Engine, was saved.

Schedule: May through first weekend in June (includes Memorial Day), September, and October: weekends 12 to 5 p.m. June through Labor Day: daily except Mondays: 12 to 5 p.m.

Admission/Fare: Donations appreciated.

Locomotive/Rolling Stock: No. 304/604 1936 Baldwin locomotive; B&LE caboose no. 1895; Wheeling & Lake Erie caboose no. 0205; Union Pacific caboose no. UP 25437; 1952 B&LE iron ore-pellet car no. 20567.

Nearby Attractions/Accommodations: Greenville Erie Canal Musuem, Kidd's Mill Covered Bridge, Pymatuning State Park.

Location/Directions: I-79 to route 358, or I-80 to route 18, or route 58.

Site Address: 314 Main Street, Greenville, PA
Mailing Address: 314 Main Street, Greenville, PA 16125
Telephone: (412) 588-4009
Internet: www.quikpage.com/G/greenvillerr

Pennsylvania, Hamburg

BLUE MOUNTAIN & READING RAILROAD
Steam, diesel, scheduled

Ride: The Blue Mountain & Reading began operating freight service over a former Pennsylvania Railroad line between Temple and South Hamburg, Pennsylvania, 13 miles, in September 1983. On July 13, 1985, steam-powered passenger trains returned to the line. Trains make the 26-mile round trip in 1.5 hours.

Schedule: Call or write for information.

Admission/Fare: Call or write for information.

Locomotive/Rolling Stock: 1928 Baldwin 4-6-2 no. 425, former Gulf, Mobile & Northern; 1952 EMD E8A nos. 5706 and 5859, former Pennsylvania Railroad; more.

Special Events: Numerous. Call or write for information.

Nearby Attractions/Accommodations: Wanamaker, Kempton & Southern, Roadside America, Crystal Cave, Crystal Springs Golf Course, Hawk Mountain Sanctuary, outlet malls.

Location/Directions: Temple Station–north of Reading on Tuckerton Road between route 61 and U.S. 222. Hamburg Station–on route 61 at Station Road, one mile south of exit 9A off I-78.

Site Address: Hamburg, PA
Mailing Address: PO Box 425, Hamburg, PA 19526
Telephone: (610) 562-2102

Pennsylvania, Honesdale

BIG BEAR FARM
Steam, scheduled
24" gauge

HOWARD J. WALTON

Ride/Display: A half-mile ride (eventually to be a one-mile loop) on a two-foot-gauge railroad through forest and pasture, where deer and other animals roam. Steam engines, gas engines, precision models, coal-mining equipment, an antique reciprocating-saw display, antique tractors, and other mechanical antiques, as well as a former Delaware & Hudson battery-powered coal-mine locomotive, a 1920 wooden Central Vermont caboose, and other railroad artifacts. Also located here is a performing-bear show, a game farm, and a museum.

Schedule: Call or write for information.

Admission/Fare: Adults $5.50; children $3.50.

Locomotive/Rolling Stock: 1922 Kraus steam engine; 1936 Whitcomb gas locomotive; gondolas.

Nearby Attractons/Accommodations: Ponderosa Pines Campground.

Location/Directions: Eight miles north of Honesdale. Take route 6 west through Honesdale to route 170 north, then follow signs for Big Bear Farm and the Ponderosa Pines Campground.

*Coupon available, see coupon section.

Site Address: RD 3, Honesdale, PA
Mailing Address: RD 3 Box 1352, Honesdale, PA 18431
Telephone: (717) 253-1794

Pennsylvania, Honesdale

STOURBRIDGE LINE RAIL EXCURSIONS
Diesel, scheduled
Standard gauge

GEORGE A. FORERO, JR.

Ride: A 50-mile round trip from Honesdale to Hawley and Lackawaxen, through scenic Wayne and Pike counties along the Lackawaxen River, closely following the route of the old Delaware & Hudson Canal.

Schedule: Late March through mid-December: weekends.

Admission/Fare: Vary depending on event.

Locomotive/Rolling Stock: 1949 EMD BL2 no. 54, former Bangor & Aroostook.

Special Events: Bunny Train, Great Train Robbery, Dinner Theater, Bavarian Festival, Fall Foliage, Halloween, Santa Express. Call or write for information.

Location/Directions: Northeastern Pennsylvania, 24 miles from Scranton.

*Coupon available, see coupon section.

Site Address: 303 Commercial Street, Honesdale, PA
Mailing Address: 303 Commercial Street, Honesdale, PA 18431
Telephone: (717) 253-1960
Fax: (717) 253-1517

Pennsylvania, Kempton

WANAMAKER, KEMPTON & SOUTHERN, INC.
Steam, scheduled
Standard gauge

WANAMAKER, KEMPTON & SOUTHERN, INC.

Ride/Display: A six mile, 40-minute round trip through scenic Pennsylvania Dutch country over part of the former Reading Company's Schuylkill & Lehigh branch. Restored stations relocated from Joanna and Catasauqua, Pennsylvania; original circa 1874 Wanamaker station; operating HO-gauge model layout.

Schedule: May through October: Sundays. July, August, October: Saturdays. Departures at 1, 2, 3, 4 p.m.

Admission/Fare: Adults $4.50; children 3-11 $2.50; age 2 and under ride free.

Locomotive/Rolling Stock: No. 2, 1920 Porter 0-4-0T, former Colorado Fuel & Iron; no. 65, 1930 Porter 0-6-0T, former Safe Harbor Water Power; no. 7258 1942 GE diesel electric 45-ton, former Birdsboro Corp.; coaches nos. 1494 & 1474 and combine no. 408, all former Reading Company; coach no. 582, former Lackawanna; assorted freight cars and caboose, former Lehigh & New England; steel and wood cabooses, former Reading.

Special Events: Mother's Day Special, Father's Day Special, Sandman Special, Kids' Fun Weekend, Harvest Moon Special, Halloween Train, Santa Claus Special. Write for schedule.

Location/Directions: Depot is located at Kempton on routes 143 or 737, a short distance north of I-78. The site is 20 miles west of Allentown and 30 miles north of Reading.

[P] [✻] [☕] [⊼] TRAIN

Site Address: Kempton, PA
Mailing Address: PO Box 24, Kempton, PA 19529
Telephone: (610) 756-6469

Pennsylvania, Kutztown

EAST PENN RAIL EXCURSIONS, INC.
Diesel, scheduled
Standard gauge

WALTER M. MATUCH

Ride: Train excursion.

Schedule: Easter, June 6 through September 7, October, Thanksgiving through Christmas: weekends and holidays only. Trains depart 12 and 2 p.m.

Admission/Fare: Adults: $8.00; seniors $7.00; children 2-12 $4.00; under age 2 are free.

Locomotive/Rolling Stock: GE 44-ton no. 57, former NY Dock; passenger cars nos. 838, 869, 834, former Reading; caboose no. 91545, former CRR-NJ.

Special Events: Easter Bunny, April 4-5, 12. Uncle Sam, July 4-5. Railroad Days, August 1-2. Santa Claus, November 29 through December 20.

Nearby Attractions/Accommodations: Crystal Cave, Hawk Mountain Bird Sanctuary, Mid-Atlantic Air Museum. WKTS Steam Train. Kutztown University.

Location/Directions: Kutztown is located between Allentown and Reading off U.S. 22, Main Street.

Site Address: 110 Railroad Street, Kutztown, PA 19530
Mailing Address: PO Box 148, Kutztown, PA 19530-1048
Telephone: (610) 683-9202

Pennsylvania, Lewisburg

WEST SHORE RAIL EXCURSIONS
Diesel, scheduled
Standard gauge

REUBEN S. BROUSE

Ride/Display: This operation offers two narrated rides. The Lewisburg & Buffalo Creek Railroad is a 1½-hour round trip over the former Reading Railroad through Victorian Lewisburg, past Bucknell University, and along the Susquehanna River and the cliffs of the Buffalo Mountains to the village of Winfield. The West Shore Railroad is a 2½-hour round trip over the former Reading & Pennsylvania Railroad through the scenic Amish and Mennonite farms of the Buffalo Valley to Victorian Mifflinburg. A dinner train is available. Delta Place Station displays engines, passenger cars, a dining car, several cabooses, a train station, and scales.

Schedule: April, May: weekends, 2 p.m. June through August: weekends, 11:30 a.m. and 2 p.m. June 24 through August 26: Wednesdays, 11:30 a.m., 2 and 6 p.m. September, October: weekends, 2 p.m. Dinner train–May through October: first Saturdays. Mother's and Father's Day. Closed Mondays.

Admission/Fare: Adults $8.00 and up; seniors $7.00 and up; children ages 1-12 $4.00 and up. Dinner trains $30.00 per person.

Locomotive/Rolling Stock: Steel coaches; cabooses; dining car.

Special Events: Motor Car and Hand Railcar Show, Antique Machinery, Easter, Cartoon Express, July 4, Fall Foliage, Halloween, Christmas; more.

Location/Directions: Two miles north of Lewisburg.

Site Address: RR 3, Box 154, Route 15 North, Lewisburg, PA
Mailing Address: RR 3, Box 154, Route 15 North, Lewisburg, PA 17837
Telephone: (717) 524-4337
Fax: (717) 5243-7282

Pennsylvania, Marienville

KNOX & KANE RAILROAD
Steam, diesel, scheduled
Standard gauge

GEORGE A. FORERO, JR.

Ride: This line offers one round trip each operating day to Kane and the Kinzua Bridge over a former Baltimore & Ohio branch line. Passengers may board at Marienville for a 96-mile, 8-hour trip or at Kane for a 32-mile, 3½-hour trip. The 2,053-foot-long, 301-foot-high Kinzua Bridge, built in 1882 to span the Kinzua Creek Valley, was at the time the highest bridge in the world. It is on the National Register of Historic Places and is a National Historic Civil Engineering Landmark.

Schedule: June and September: Friday through Sunday. July and August: Tuesday through Sunday. Early October: Wednesday through Sunday. Depart Marienville 8:30 a.m.; depart Kane 10:45 a.m.

Admission/Fare: From Marienville: adults $20.00; children $13.00. From Kane: adults $14.00; children $8.00. Advance reservations suggested. Box lunches available by advance order, $3.75.

Locomotive/Rolling Stock: No. 38, 1927 Baldwin 2-8-0, former Huntington & Broad Top Mountain; No. 44, Alco diesel; No. 58, Chinese 2-8-2 built in 1989; Porter Switcher No. 1; steel coaches; open cars; two snack and souvenir cars.

Location/Directions: In northwestern Pennsylvania, about 20 miles north of I-80.

Site Address: Marienville, OH
Mailing Address: PO Box 422, Marienville, PA 16239
Telephone: (814) 927-6621

Pennsylvania, Middletown

MIDDLETOWN & HUMMELSTOWN RAILROAD
Diesel, scheduled
Standard gauge

MIDDLETOWN & HUMMELSTOWN RAILROAD

Ride: An 11 mile, 1¼-hour round trip along the Swatara Creek. Live narration and live music performed on all trains. Free yard tour each day.

Schedule: Seasonal. Call or write for information.

Admission/Fare: Varies. Call or write for information.

Locomotive/Rolling Stock: GE 65-ton nos. 1 and 2; Alco T6 no. 1016; CN 2-6-0 no. 91; former Lackawanna coaches; various trolleys.

Special Events: Dinner trains, Santa and Easter Bunny trains, Picnic trains. Call for details and reservations.

Nearby Attractions/Accommodations: Hershey Park, Pennsylvania Dutch Country, Gettysburg Battlefield, Indian Echo Caverns.

Location/Directions: On Race Street adjacent to Hoffer Park, 20 minutes from Hershey, three blocks from Amtrak's Middletown Station.

Site Address: Race Street Station, Middletown, PA
Mailing Address: 136 Brown Street, Middleton, PA 17057
Telephone: (717) 944-4435
Fax: (717) 944-7758

Pennsylvania, New Freedom

NORTHERN CENTRAL RAILWAY
Diesel, scheduled
Standard gauge

NORTHERN CENTRAL RAILWAY

Ride: Passengers enjoy fine dining, dancing, and entertainment on a 3½-hour excursion through the scenic Codorus Creek Valley.

Schedule: Year round: weekends and some weekdays.

Admission/Fare: Dinner train $34.99 to $49.99; coach $9.00 or $5.00 one-way; bike rack $3.00.

Locomotive/Rolling Stock: An extensive collection of air-conditioned streamlined, lightweight passenger cars from the 40s and 50s.

Special Events: Railroad Heritage Days Festival, June 20, 21. Other special trains, call or write for details.

Nearby Attractions/Accommodations: Stewartstown–Naylor Winery; Shrewsbury–Kolter House.

Location/Directions: I-83 to exit 1, follow Pennsylvania Route 851 west to New Freedom. Turn left on Penn Street, 1 block to the tracks.

Site Address: 117 North Front Street, New Freedom, PA
Mailing Address: 117 North Front Street, New Freedom, PA 17349
Telephone: (800) 94-TRAIN and (717) 235-4000
Fax: (717) 235-5609
Internet: www.classicrail.com/ncry

Pennsylvania, New Hope

NEW HOPE & IVYLAND RAILROAD
Steam, diesel, scheduled
Standard gauge

NEW HOPE & IVYLAND RAILROAD

Ride: A 50-minute narrated round trip through the rolling hills and valleys of Bucks County. The train travels over the famous "Perils of Pauline" trestle and along the Delaware Canal.

Schedule: Year round: weekends. Mid-May through November: daily. Dinner train, Saturdays; Brunch train, Sundays.

Admission/Fare: Adults $8.50; seniors $7.50; children 2-11 $4.50; under age 2 $1.50.

Locomotive/Rolling Stock: No. 40, 1925 Baldwin 2-8-0, former Lancaster & Chester; no. 3028, 1946 Alco 4-8-4, former National de Mexico; no. 614, 1948 Lima 4-8-4, former C&O; no. 2198, 1963 EMD GP-30, former Pennsy; no. 9423, EMD SW-1.

Special Events: Santa Express, Thanksgiving through Christmas.

Nearby Attractions/Accommodations: Mule barge rides, paddle boats, shopping, hotels.

Location/Directions: West Bridge Street, Route 179. Convenient access from I-95.

*Coupon available, see coupon section.

Site Address: 32 West Bridge Street, New Hope, PA
Mailing Address: 32 West Bridge Street, New Hope, PA 18938
Telephone: (215) 862-2332
Fax: (215) 862-2150

Pennsylvania, North East

LAKE SHORE RAILWAY HISTORICAL SOCIETY, INC.
Railway museum
Standard gauge

RAY L. WAY

Museum: A restored New York Central passenger station built by Lake Shore & Michigan Southern Railway in 1899 houses an extensive collection of displays. The museum is adjacent to Conrail and Norfolk Southern mainlines.

Schedule: May 23 through September 7: Wednesdays through Sundays, holidays, 1 to 5 p.m. September 12 through October 25: weekends, 1 to 5 p.m.

Admission/Fare: Donations appreciated.

Locomotive/Rolling Stock: NYC U25B no. 2500; CSS&SB "Little Joe" electric locomotive no. 802; Heisler fireless 0-6-0; passenger and freight cars.

Special Events: Christmas-at-the-Station, December 5-6. Wine Country Harvest Festival, September 26-27. Call or write for additional special events.

Nearby Attractions/Accommodations: Peek 'n Peak Resort, Presque Isle State Park, Lake Erie beaches and marinas.

Location/Directions: At Wall and Robinson Streets. Fifteen miles east of Erie, 2 miles north of I-90 exit 11, three blocks south of U.S. 20.

[&] [P] [🚌] [✳] [☕] [📷] [🚂] [✉] [🚆] M

Site Address: 31 Wall Street, North East, PA
Mailing Address: PO Box 571, North East, PA 16428-0571
Telephone: (814) 825-2724

Pennsylvania, Northbrook

BRANDYWINE SCENIC RAILWAY
Diesel, scheduled
Standard gauge

ANTHONY DIYENNA

Ride: One hour, 15-mile narrated round trips operating both northbound and southbound from Northbrook Station through the scenic and historic Brandywine River Valley along the former Reading Wilmington & Northern Branch. Ninety-minute, 21-mile round trips offered in the Spring and Fall.

Schedule: Palm Sunday weekend through Christmas: weekends and holidays, 11 a.m., 1 and 3 p.m. Rails-to-the-River trips–Memorial Day weekend through Labor Day weekend: 9:30 a.m. and 1 p.m.

Admission/Fare: Adults $8.00; seniors $7.00; children 2-12 $6.00; under age 2 are free. Special events slightly higher. Group rates and caboose rentals available.

Locomotive/Rolling Stock: 1924 Pullman-built steel open-window coaches, former Delaware, Lackawanna & Western; and more.

Special Events: Bunny Train Express, Spring Thaw, Fall Foliage, North Pole Express, Good Old Summertime, Murder Mysteries, Family Fun, Concert Trains, and Sandy Flash Robberies. Call or write for dates.

Nearby Attractions/Accommodations: Brandywine River Museum, Brandywine Battlefield Park, Longwood Gardens, Valley Forge Park.

Location/Directions: On Northbrooke Road, ½ mile north of route 842, six miles west of West Chester, Pennsylvania. One hour west of Philadelphia.

*Coupon available, see coupon section.

Site Address: 1810 Beagle Road, Northbrooke, West Chester, PA
Mailing Address: PO Box 403, Pocopson, PA 19366-0403
Telephone: (610) 793-4433
Fax: (610) 793-5144

Pennsylvania, Philadelphia

THE FRANKLIN INSTITUTE SCIENCE MUSEUM
Model railroad display, railroad display
Standard gauge

THE FRANKLIN INSTITUTE SCIENCE MUSEUM

Display: The centerpiece of Railroad Hall is a Baldwin Locomotive Works No. 60000, a 3-cylinder 4-10-2 built in 1926 and moved to the Franklin Institute in 1933. Two other locomotives share the room: Reading's Rocket of 1838 and a Reading 4-4-0 built in 1842. New to the exhibit is a G gauge model railroad that viewers can operate; it includes full-size signals actuated by the trains and a video hookup between the locomotive and a monitor in a half-size cab. The remainder of the museum collection covers the larger subject of U.S. industrial technology and science. There are models, films and quizzes on videodiscs, and a giant walk-through heart. The Franklin Institute is at 20th Street and The Parkway in downtown Philadelphia, within walking distance of Suburban Station.

Schedule: Year round: daily, 9:30 a.m. to 5 p.m.

Admission/Fare: Call or write for information.

Location/Directions: Center city Philadelphia.

[&] [P] [✱] [☕] [⓴] [🚻] [M] [🚂] 30th Street, ¼ mile away

Site Address: 222 N. 20th Street, Philadelphia, PA
Mailing Address: 222 N. 20th Street, Philadelphia, PA 19103
Telephone: (215) 448-1176
Fax: (215) 448-1235
E-mail: ewilner@fi.edu
Internet: sln.fi.edu/

Pennsylvania, Rockhill Furnace

EAST BROAD TOP RAILROAD
Steam, scheduled
36" gauge

JOHN J. HILTON

Ride/Display: The East Broad Top Railroad, chartered in 1856, is the last operating narrow-gauge railraod east of the Mississippi. The road hauled coal, freight, mail, express, and passengers for more than 80 years. Today the East Broad Top offers passengers a ten ile, 50-minute ride through the beautiful Aughwick Valley with its own preserved locomotives; the ride takes passengers from the historic depot at Rockhill Furnace to the picnic grove, where the train is turned. On display are the railroad yard with shops, operating roundhouse, and turntable. Dates, times, and fares are subject to change. Call or write for latest information.

Schedule: June through October: weekends.

Admission/Fare: Adults $9.00; children $6.00.

Locomotive/Rolling Stock: 1911 Baldwin locomotive 2-8-2 no. 12; 1912 Baldwin locomotive 2-8-2 no. 14; 1914 Baldwin locomotive 2-8-2 no. 15; 1918 Baldwin locomotive 2-8-2 no. 17; all original East Broad Top Railroad.

Special Events: Fall Spectacular, Columbus Day Weekend.

Location/Directions: Pennsylvania Turnpike exit Willow Hill or Fort Littleton.

Site Address: Rockhill Furnace, PA
Mailing Address: PO Box 158, Rockhill Furnace, PA 17249
Telephone: (814) 447-3011
Fax: (814) 447-3256

Pennsylvania, Rockhill-Orbisonia

ROCKHILL TROLLEY MUSEUM
Electric, scheduled
Standard gauge

JOEL SALOMON

Ride/Display: A nonprofit, educational museum incorporated in 1962, the Rockhill Trolley Museum is composed of volunteers who preserve, restore, and maintain a collection of two dozen electric rail vehicles, about twelve of which are in operating condition. Trolleys operate over dual-gauge trackage on the former Shade Gap Branch of the East Broad Top Railroad for a 2-mile, 20-minute round trip. Standard-gauge streetcars meet narrow-gauge steam trains.

Schedule: May through October: weekends and holidays, 11:30 a.m. to 4:30 p.m. Weekday bus groups by arrangement.

Admission/Fare: Adults $3.00; children 2-12 $1.00. Group rates available.

Locomotive/Rolling Stock: No. 163, 1924 Brill curveside car, former York Railways (Pennsylvania); no. 172, 1929 "Toonerville" type, former Porto, Portugal; more.

Special Events: Fall Spectacular, Columbus Day weekend. Santa, December 12.

Nearby Attractions/Accommodations: Raystown Lake, Altoona Railroader Museum.

Location/Directions: Twenty miles north of exit 13 of PA turnpike, adjacent to East Broad Top Railroad.

*Coupon available, see coupon section.

Site Address: Rockhill Furnace, PA
Mailing Address: 460 Paul Avenue, Chambersburg, PA 17201-3773
Telephone: (717) 263-3943 and (814) 447-9576 weekends

Pennsylvania, Schenley

KISKI JUNCTION RAILROAD
Diesel, electric, scheduled
Standard gauge

Ride: Ride along the Kiski River from Schenley to Bagdad on the former Pennsylvania Canal.

Schedule: By reservation only.

Admission/Fare: Adults $7.00; seniors $6.00; children 4-12 $4.00.

Locomotive/Rolling Stock: 1943 Alco S1 no. 7153.

Nearby Attractions/Accommodations: Tour Ed Mine.

Location/Directions: Two miles north of Leechburg on route 66. Turn west on Schenley Road for four miles.

[P]

Site Address: Box 48, Schenley, PA
Mailing Address: Box 48, Schneley, PA 15682
Telephone: (412) 295-KJRR
Fax: (412) 295-5588

Pennsylvania, Scottdale

LAUREL HIGHLANDS RAILROAD
Steam, scheduled

LAUREL HIGHLANDS RAILROAD

Ride: The Laurel Highlands railroad offers a variety of rides along 62 miles of trackage from the former Pennsylvania and B&O Railroads. The Youngwood Historical Society maintains a railroad museum, also a hobby shop at both layovers.

Schedule: First weekend in May through Halloween: weekends and holidays. Call or write for schedule.

Admission/Fare: Adults $7/$8/$12; children 5-11 $5/$6/$9.

Locomotive/Rolling Stock: 1934 HK Porter 2-4-0; 1926 Jersey Central coaches.

Special Events: Scottdale Coal and Coke Festival, September. Civil War re-enactments, train robberies, Halloween Spook Nights, Santa Trains.

Nearby Attractions/Accommodations: Coal and Coke Museum, West Overton Museum, Seven Springs Mountain Resort, Zephyr Glen Bed and Breakfast, Pine Wood Acres Bed and Breakfast.

Location/Directions: Turnpike exit 8 (New Stanton) south on route 119 south, to route 819 south, to Sheetz Convenience Store (next to parking lot).

[P]

Site Address: Scottdale, PA
Mailing Address: 25 South Broadway, Scottdale, PA 15683
Telephone: (412) 887-4568

Pennsylvania, Scranton

STEAMTOWN NATIONAL HISTORIC SITE
Railway museum
Standard gauge

NPS PHOTO: KEN GANZ

Ride/Display: A 27-mile round-trip steam excursion will operate between Scranton and Moscow, Pennsylvania, beginning Memorial Day weekend through the first weekend of November. The site's visitor facilities include two museums, a theater, a visitor center, restored portions of the roundhouse, and a bookstore. Roundhouse tours, locomotive shop tours, preservation shop tours, and various additional programs will be offered. Many locomotives and cars are on display in the buildings and in the historic Delaware, Lackawanna & Western Railroad yards.

Schedule: Year round: daily, 9 a.m. to 5 p.m. Closed Thanksgiving, Christmas, and New Year's Day.

Admission/Fare: Call or write for information.

Locomotive/Rolling Stock: Many steam locomotives; three operate. Electric trailers; suburban and day coaches; combines; business car; troop sleeper. Railway Post Office car, boxcars, cabooses, gondolas, hoppers, snowplows, baggage cars, and tank car.

Location/Directions: Entrance is off West Lackawanna Avenue.

Site Address: Scranton, PA
Mailing Address: 150 S. Washington Avenue, Scranton, PA 18503
Telephone: (717) 340-5200

Pennsylvania, Shartlesville

ROADSIDE AMERICA
Model railroad

ROADSIDE AMERICA

Display: Roadside America, an idea born in June 1903, is a childhood dream realized. From day to day and almost without interruption, this indoor miniature village has grown to be the largest and most beautiful of its type. More than 60 years in the making by Laurence Gieringer, it is housed in a new, modern, comfortable, air-conditioned building and covers more than 8,000 square feet of space. The display includes 2,570 feet of track for trains and trolleys and 250 railroad cars. O gauge trains and trolleys run among the villages.

Schedule: July 1 through Labor Day: weekdays, 9 a.m. to 6:30 p.m.; weekends, 9 a.m. to 7 p.m. September 6 through June 30: weekdays, 10 a.m. to 5 p.m.; weekends, 10 a.m. to 6 p.m.

Admission/Fare: Adults $4.00, senior citizens $3.75, children $1.50.

Location/Directions: I-78, exit 8, between Allentown and Harrisburg.

*Coupon available, see coupon section.

Site Address: Shartlesville, PA
Mailing Address: P.O. Box 2, Shartlesville, PA 19554
Telephone: (215) 488-6241

Pennsylvania, Stewartstown

STEWARTSTOWN RAILROAD
Diesel, scheduled
Standard gauge

RAY MCFADDEN

Ride: A seven mile, one hour round trip between Stewartstown and the rural village of Tolna, in the Deer Creek Valley.

Schedule: May through September: Sundays and holidays. Call or write for schedule.

Admission/Fare: Adults $7.00; children 3-11 $4.00. Special trains slightly higher.

Locomotive/Rolling Stock: No. 9 35-ton Plymouth ML8 Plymouth 1943 Stewartstown Railroad; no. 10 44-ton diesel, FE 1946, former Coudensport and Port Allegany.

Special Events: Easter Bunny special, April. Country breakfast trains, June through November. Civil war re-enactments, October. Santa Claus special, December.

Location/Directions: I-83 exit 1 (Shrewsbury) travel four miles east to Stewartstown.

*Coupon available, see coupon section.

Site Address: 21 W. Pennsylvania Avenue, Stewartstown, PA
Mailing Address: PO Box 155, Stewartstown, PA 17363
Telephone: (717) 993-2936

Pennsylvania, Strasburg

CHOO CHOO BARN TRAINTOWN U.S.A.
Model railroad display

FRED M. DOLE

Display: This is a fantastic model railroad exhibit of Lancaster County with 17 operating O-gauge trains, 135 moving figures and vehicles, plus incredibly detailed hand-built scenery. See Lancaster County's Amish Country come to life on this 1700 square foot operating miniature village. Watch Amishmen at a barn raising. Stop by the 3-ring circus complete with aerial acts and operating amusement rides. Model railroad supplies, books, videos, train novelties, and Thomas the Tank Engine and Friends superstore next door.

Schedule: April 4 through May 31: daily, 10 a.m. to 5 p.m. June 1 through September 6: daily, 10 a.m. to 6 p.m. September 7 through January 3: daily, 10 a.m. to 5 p.m. Admission stops 30 minutes prior to closing.

Admission/Fare: Adults $4.00; children 5-12 $2.00; under age five are free.

Special Events: Canned Food Fridays, December 4, 11, 18. Admission is a can of food which benefits local church food banks.

Nearby Attractions/Accommodations: Strasburg Railroad, Railroad Museum of Pennsylvania, National Toy Train Museum, Gast Classic Motorcars, Pennsylvania Dutch Amish farmland.

Location/Directions: Located on route 741 east of Strasburg, .25 mile west of the Strasburg Railroad. Strasburg is located three miles south of U.S. route 30.

*Coupon available, see coupon section.

Site Address: Route 741 East, Strasburg, PA
Mailing Address: PO Box 130, Strasburg, PA 17579
Telephone: (717) 687-7911
Fax: (717) 687-6529
E-mail: choo2barn@aol.com
Internet: www.800padutch.com/choochoo.html

Pennsylvania, Strasburg

THE NATIONAL TOY TRAIN MUSEUM
Model railroad museum
Toy trains and accessories

NATIONAL TOY TRAIN MUSEUM

Display: Housed in a beautiful replica of a Victorian railroad station, this museum has one of the finest collections inthe world of toy trains, dating from 1880 to the present. The collection includes items from such manufacturers as Ives, Lionel, American Flyer, LGB, and Marklin. Five operating layouts feature O, S, G, HO, and Standard gauge trains. A video on train subjects plays continuously. TCA national headquarters.

Schedule: May 1 through October 1: daily. April, November, and December: weekends and holidays. 10 a.m. to 5 p.m.

Admission/Fare: Adults $3.00; seniors $2.75; children 5-12 $1.50. Group discounts available.

Nearby Attractions/Accommodations: Strasburg Railroad, Railroad Museum of Pennsylvania, Choo Choo Barn.

Location/Directions: From the Strasburg Station, travel east on route 741, turn north onto Paradise Lane past the Red Caboose Motel.

Site Address: 300 Paradise Lane, Strasburg, PA
Mailing Address: PO Box 248, Strasburg, PA 17579
Telephone: (717) 687-8976
Fax: (717) 687-0742
E-mail: toytrain@traincollectors.org
Internet: www.traincollectors.org

Pennsylvania, Strasburg

RAILROAD MUSEUM OF PENNSYLVANIA
Railway museum

RAILROAD MUSEUM OF PENNSYLVANIA

Museum: The museum displays one of the world's finest collections of over 75 steam, electric, and diesel-electric locomotives, passenger and freight cars, and related memorabilia. The 90,000-square-foot building covers six tracks, which exhibit equipment dating from 1825 to 1992.

Schedule: April, May, June, September, and October: Mondays through Saturdays, 9 a.m. to 5 p.m.; Sundays, noon to 5 p.m. July and August: Mondays through Thursdays, 9 a.m. to 5 p.m.; Fridays and Saturdays, 9 a.m. to 7 p.m.; Sundays noon to 5 p.m. November, December, January, February, and March: Tuesdays through Saturdays, 9 a.m. to 5 p.m.; Sundays, noon to 5 p.m.

Admission/Fare: Adults 13-59 $6.00; seniors $5.50; students 6-12 $4.00; families $16.00.

Locomotive/Rolling Stock: See above.

Special Events: Reading Company Weekend, July 3-5. Circus Days, August 13-16. Pennsy Days, September 12-13. Halloween Lantern Tours, October 24. Home for the Holidays, December 12.

Nearby Attractions/Accommodations: Strasburg Railroad National Toy Train Museum, Choo-Choo Barn, Historic Strasburg Inn.

Location/Directions: Ten miles east of Lancaster on Route 741.

Site Address: 300 Gap Road, Route 741 East, Strasburg, PA
Mailing Address: PO Box 15, Strasburg, PA 17579
Telephone: (717) 687-8628 and (717) 687-8629
Fax: (717) 687-0876
E-mail: frm@redrose.net
Internet: www.rrhistorical.com

Pennsylvania, Strasburg

STRASBURG RAILROAD
Steam, scheduled
Standard gauge

JOHN E. HELBOK

Ride/Display: A nine mile, 45-minute round trip from Strasburg to Paradise. Train travels through lush farmlands and turns around adjacent to the Amtrak main line. The Strasburg Rail Road, one of the oldest and busiest steam tourist railroads in the country, displays a large collection of historic cars and locomotives.

Schedule: April through October: daily. Dinner Train Service–July through August: Thursdays through Sundays, 7 p.m.; September through October, May, and June: weekends. Call for reservations and information. Complete timetables are sent upon request.

Admission/Fare: Adults $7.75 and up; children $4.00 and up. Group rates available.

Locomotive/Rolling Stock: Open-platform wooden combine and coaches; "Hello Dolly" open observation car; first-class service including food and beverages aboard parlor "Marian." Lunch served on full-service diner "Lee Brenner" on hourly trains. No. 31, 1908 Baldwin 0-6-0 & no. 89, 1910 Canadian 2-6-0, former Canadian National; no. 90, 1924 Baldwin 2-10-0, former Great Western; more.

Special Events: Easter Bunny trains, Easter weekend. Halloween ghost trains, October 31. Santa Claus trains, November 28 thorugh December 20, weekends.

Location/Directions: On Route 741 in Pennsylvania Dutch country, a short distance from Lancaster.

Radio frequency: 161.235

Site Address: Route 741, Strasburg, PA
Mailing Address: PO Box 96, Strasburg, PA 17579
Telephone: (717) 687-7522
E-mail: srrtrain@800padutch.com
Internet: www.800padutch.com/srr.html

Pennsylvania, Titusville

OIL CREEK & TITUSVILLE RAILROAD
Diesel, scheduled
Standard gauge

BEVERLY SNYDER

Ride: A 27-mile, 2½-hour round trip over former Pennsylvania Railroad trackage through the Oil Creek Valley, birthplace of the oil industry. The train makes its way through Oil Creek State Park, passing Petroleum Centre and Drake Well Park.

Schedule: School Runs–May 12-14 & 19-20: Tuesdays-Thursdays, depart Perry Street 11:00 a.m.; depart Drake Well 11:15 a.m.; depart Rynd Farm 12:15 p.m. (12: 15 is one-way). Regular Season–June13-September 27: weekends and July-August: Wednesdays-Sundays, depart Perry Street 2:00 p.m.; depart Drake Well 2:15 p.m.; depart Rynd Farm 3:30 p.m. (3:30 is one-way). Fall Runs–September 30-October 31: Wednesdays-Fridays, see Regular Season schedule. Weekends: depart Perry Street 11:45 a.m. and 3:15 p.m.; depart Drake Well 12 and 3:30 p.m.; depart Rynd Farm 1:15 and 4:30 p.m.

Admission/Fare: Adults $10.00; seniors $9.00; children 3-17 $6.00. One-way, group, car-rental, and train-rental rates available.

Locomotive/Rolling Stock: 1947 Alco S-2 no. 75, former South Buffalo Ry.

Special Events: Many, call or write for details.

Nearby Attractions/Accommodations: Drake Well Musem and more.

Location/Directions: Titusville train station–I-80 exit Route 8. Rynd Farm–3½ miles north of Oil City on Route 8.

*Coupon available, see coupon section.

Site Address: 409 S. Perry Street, Titusville, PA
Mailing Address: PO Box 68, Oil City, PA 16301
Telephone: (814) 676-1733
Fax: (814) 677-2192
Internet: www.usachoice.net/oct-railroad

Pennsylvania, Washington

PENNSYLVANIA TROLLEY MUSEUM
Electric, scheduled
5'-2½" gauge, standard gauge

JIM CROUCH, JR.

Ride: A 3-mile round trip trolley ride, carbarn guided tour, "Pennsylvania's Trolley Neighborhoods" exhibit, theater, and gift shop.

Schedule: April through December: weekends, 11 a.m. to 5 p.m. Memorial Day through Labor Day and December 26-31: daily, 11 a.m. to 5 p.m.

Admission/Fare: Adults $5.00; seniors $4.00; children 2-15 $3.00. Group rates available with advance reservations.

Locomotive/Rolling Stock: New Orleans Streetcar Named Desire; trolley from Pittsburgh, Johnstown, and Philadelphia.

Special Events: Trolley Fair, June 27-28. Pumpkin Patch Trolley, October 10-11, 17-18. Santa Trolley, November 27-29, December 5-6, 12-13.

Nearby Attractions/Accommodations: Meadowcroft Museum of Rural Life, LeMoyne House, Ladbroke Meadows Racetrack.

Location/Directions: I-79 to exit 8 (Meadow Lands), follow signs. Thirty miles southwest of Pittsburgh.

Site Address: 1 Museum Road, Washington, PA
Mailing Address: 1 Museum Road, Washington, PA 15301-6133
Telephone: (724) 228-9256
Fax: (724) 228-9675
E-mail: ptm@pa-trolley.org
Internet: www.pa-trolley.org

Pennsylvania, Wellsboro

TIOGA CENTRAL RAILROAD
Diesel, scheduled
Standard gauge

RICHARD L. STOVING

Ride: A 24-mile round trip through beautiful country with excellent scenic views, or enjoy a 42-mile round trip on our elegant dinner train.

Schedule: May 9 through October 18: weekends, departures at 11 a.m., 1, and 3 p.m. Dinner train–May 16 through October 18: Saturdays, 5:30 p.m.

Admission/Fare: Adults $10.00; seniors $9.00; children 6-12 $5.00. Dinner train–$28.00 per person.

Locomotive/Rolling Stock: Alco S2; RS1; RS3u; PRR P70; CNR coaches, club car; diner car.

Special Events: Railfan weekend, October 24-25. Other special trains. Call or write for information.

Nearby Attractions/Accommodations: Pennsylvania "Grand Canyon," Wellsboro.

Location/Directions: Three miles north of Wellsboro on State 287. Wellsboro is on U.S. 6.

[P] 🚌 ✳ ☕ 👤 🚂 ✉ M

Site Address: Wellsboro, PA
Mailing Address: PO Box 269, Wellsboro, PA 16901
Telephone: (717) 724-0990

Pennsylvania, Williamsport

LYCOMING COUNTY HISTORICAL SOCIETY & MUSEUM
History museum
Toy trains

Display: The Shempp toy-train collection is one of the finest in the country. More than 337 complete trains, one hundred individual engines (twelve are one-of-a-kind), and two working model layouts are on display. Exhibit includes items in L, TT, N, OO, HO, O, and 1 gauges; Lionel, American Flyer, Marx, Ives, and American Model Train Company pieces; an American Flyer Mayflower; a copper-and-gold-finished GG1; and American Flyer S-gauge displays.

Schedule: May 1 through October 31: Tuesdays through Fridays, 9:30 a.m. to 4 p.m.; Saturdays, 11 a.m. to 4 p.m.; Sundays, 1 to 4 p.m. November 1 through April 30: Tuesdays through Fridays, 9:30 a.m. to 4 p.m.; Saturdays, 11 a.m. to 4 p.m. Closed major holidays.

Admission/Fare: Adult $3.50; seniors, AARP/AAA $3.00; children $1.50.

*Coupon available, see coupon section.

Site Address: 858 West Fourth Street, Williamsport, PA
Mailing Address: 858 West Fourth Street, Williamsport, PA 17701-5824
Telephone: (717) 326-3326

Rhode Island, Newport
Connecticut, Essex

DINNER TRAINS OF NEW ENGLAND
Diesel, scheduled

NEWPORT DINNER TRAIN

Ride: Experience a scenic train ride while dining on fine cusine such as our award-winning baby back ribs.

Schedule: May through November/December: Thursday-Friday, lunch; Friday-Sunday, dinner.

Admission/Fare: $39.95 plus tax and gratuity. First class add $5.00. Entertainment additional charge.

Locomotive/Rolling Stock: Newport G.E. 1943 diesel.

Special Events: Murder Mystery or Barber Shop Quartets.

Nearby Attractions/Accommodations: Newport–Historic downtown, mansions. Essex–Gilette Castle.

Location/Directions: Newport, Rhode Island–19 America's Cup Avenue. Essex, Connecticut–Route 9 exit 3.

Site Address: Call for either Newport or Essex.
Mailing Address: PO Box 1081, Newport, RI 02840
Telephone: (800) 398-RIBS and (401) 841-8700
Fax: (401) 841-8724

South Carolina, Rockton

SOUTH CAROLINA RAILROAD MUSEUM
Railway museum
Standard gauge

MATT CONRAD

Display: This museum offers a 6-mile, 45-minute round trip between Rockton and Greenbrier on a portion of the museum's 12-mile long rail line, which was originally operated by the Rockton-Rion Railway. As track rebuilding progresses, the trip will be extended; please write for further details. Founded in 1973, the museum features exhibits in some of its pieces of rolling stock. Guided tours, which include the interior of the former Seaboard office car "Norfolk" dining car no. 3157 and Railway Post Office car no. 27 are also given.

Schedule: May 2 through October 17: first and third Saturday of each month, 9:30 a.m. to 3:30 p.m. Charter trips available.

Admission/Fare: Adults $4.75; children 2-16 $2.75. First class $8.00. Open-air car add $1.00. Infants not occupying seat ride free.

Locomotive/Rolling Stock: No. 44, 1927 Baldwin 4-6-0, former Hampton & Branchville; no. 76, 1949 45-ton Porter diesel, and no. 82, 1941 45-ton General Electric, both former U.S. Army Transportation Corps; more.

Special Events: Easter Bunny Train, April 11. Railfan Weekend, April 18-19. Caboose Day, July 4. Motor and Gang Car Day, August 15. Santa Train, November 28-29, December 5.

Nearby Attractions/Accommodations: Zoo, Days Inn, Ramada Inn.

Location/Directions: Junction of Highways 34 and U.S. 321.

P 🚌 ✳ ☕ 📷 🏛 ✉ M arm TRAIN 🚂

Site Address: 230 Industrial Park Road, Winnsboro, SC
Mailing Address: PO Box 7246, Columbia, SC 29202
Telephone: (800) 968-5909 and (803) 796-8540
E-mail: imconrad@infoave.net
Internet: www.webtelpro.com/nscrm

South Dakota, Hill City

BLACK HILLS CENTRAL RAILROAD
Steam, scheduled
Standard gauge

SOUTH DAKOTA DEPT. OF TOURISM

Ride: Passengers can take a two-hour round trip journey between Hill City and Keystone Junction. Experience a ride from the past as you travel through the Black Hills seeing the old mine sights and Harney Peak.

Schedule: Mid-May through early October: daily. Trains added during summer season. Call or write for information.

Admission/Fare: Adults $15.00; children 4-14 $9.00; age 3 and under are free. Group rates available for parties of 20 and up.

Locomotive/Rolling Stock: 1923 Baldwin 2-6-2 no. 104 saddle tank; 1919 Baldwin 2-6-2 no. 7; 1880s-1910 passenger cars.

Special Events: Railroad Days, last weekend of June.

Nearby Attractions/Accommodations: Mt. Rushmore and Crazy Horse monuments.

Location/Directions: Highway 16/385, 24 miles south of Rapid City or Keystone, Highway 16A.

Site Address: 222 Railroad Avenue, Hill City, SD
Mailing Address: PO Box 1880, Hill City, SD 57745
Telephone: (605) 574-2222
Fax: (605) 574-4915
E-mail: office@1880train.com
Internet: www.1880train.com

South Dakota, Madison

PRAIRIE VILLAGE
Steam, diesel, irregular
Standard gauge, 24" gauge

DAVE SANFORD

Display/Museum/Ride: Prairie Village is a collection of turn-of-the-century buildings assembled from area towns. There are many steam engines on display, along with gas tractors and all types of farm equipment. Passengers may take a two-mile ride around the grounds; part of the loop is from the original Milwaukee line that ran from Pipestone, Minnesota, to Wessington Springs, South Dakota. One-third of a mile of 24-inch-gauge track surrounds the old Wentworth, South Dakota, depot.

Schedule: Museum–May 2 through September 29: daily, 9 a.m. to 6 p.m. Train–Sundays, Railroad Days, and Jamboree.

Admission/Fare: Museum–$5.00. Train–$3.00.

Locomotive/Rolling Stock: No. 29, 0-6-0, and no. 11, 0-4-0; former REA/Santa Fe express refrigerator car converted to coach; 1909 former C&NW combination coach/baggage car no. 7403 (with original seats and lights); coaches, former Deadwood Central; and more.

Special Events: Railroad Days, June. Fall Jamboree, August 21-23.

Nearby Attractions/Accommodations: Lake Herman State Park.

Location/Directions: Two miles west of Madison. From Sioux Falls, take I-29 north to the Madison/Coleman exit, then travel west on highway 34.

Site Address: Highway 34, Madison, SD
Mailing Address: PO Box 256, Madison, SD 57042-0256
Telephone: (800) 693-3644 and (605) 256-3644

South Dakota, Milbank

WHETSTONE VALLEY EXPRESS
Diesel, irregular
Standard gauge

WHETSTONE VALLEY EXPRESS

Display/Ride/Museum: A 20-mile, 2½-hour round trip from Milbank to Corona over a former Milwaukee Road branch. Dinner is available. The train is operated by the common carrier Sisseton Milbank Railroad in conjuction with the Whetstone Valley Railroad Historical Society.

Schedule: May 1 thorugh October 15.

Admission/Fare: Adults $14.00; children $7.00. Dinner is additional.

Locomotive/Rolling Stock: 1954 EMD SW1200 no. 627; 1953 EMD SW1200 no. 561.

Special Events: Train Festival, August 7-9.

Nearby Attractions/Accommodations: Hartford Beach State Park.

Location/Directions: Site is 126 miles north of Sioux Falls or 180 miles west of Minneapolis or 126 miles south of Fargo.

Fargo, ND   M   Radio frequency: 466.950

Site Address: Lake Farley Depot, Milbank, SD
Mailing Address: PO Box 631, Milbank, SD 57252
Telephone: (605) 432-5505 and (800) 675-6656
Fax: (605) 432-9463

Tennessee, Chattanooga

CHATTANOOGA CHOO CHOO
Railway display

CHATTANOOGA CHOO-CHOO

Display: Opened in 1909 as the Southern Railway's Terminal Station, this depot welcomed thousands of travelers during the golden age of railroads. Today, the restored station is the heart of the Chattanooga Choo Choo Holiday Inn, a 30-acre complex with a full range of entertainment. Forty-eight passenger cars are part of the 360-room hotel; three passenger cars serve as a bar, formal restaurant, and meeting/banquet room.

Schedule: Season 1–Sundays through Saturdays, 10 a.m. to 8 p.m. Season 2–Mondays through Saturdays, 6 to 10 p.m. Call or write for current scehdule.

Admission/Fare: Adults $2.00; children $1.00; under age 6 are free.

Locomotive/Rolling Stock: Five to eight trains running in museum.

Special Events: Victorian Holidays Open House, December.

Nearby Attractions/Accommodations: Tennessee Aquarium, IMAX Theater, Southern Belle Riverboat, Rock City, Ruby Falls.

Location/Directions: I-24 exit 178, take South Broad Street split and follow signs to Choo Choo.

*Coupon available, see coupon section.

Site Address: Chattanooga Choo Choo Holiday Inn
Mailing Address: 1400 Market Street, Chattanooga, TN 37402
Telephone: (423) 266-5000
Fax: (423) 265-4635
E-mail: choochoo.com
Internet: www.choochoo.com

Tennessee, Chattanooga

LOOKOUT MOUNTAIN INCLINE RAILWAY

Ride: A ride unlike any other! The thrill of riding "America's Most Amazing Mile" has delighted guests for a century. As the Incline climbs Lookout Mountain, Chattanooga's surrounding mountains and valleys come alive as the trolley style railcars carry you cloud high. The breathtaking 72.7 percent grade of the track near the top gives the Incline the unique distinction of being the steepest passenger railway in the world. See centennial exhibits depicting the history of one of Chattanooga's most unusual landmarks. Displays include rare photographs and points of interest on the mountain from late 1800s to present.

Schedule: Year round making 3 or 4 trips per hour. Memorial Day weekend through Labor Day: daily, 8:30 a.m. to 10 p.m. April, May, September, and October: daily, 9 a.m. to 6 p.m. November through March: daily, 10 a.m. to 6 p.m. Closed Christmas Day.

Admission/Fare: Round trip: adults $8.00; children 3-12 $4.00. One way–adults $7.00; children 3-12 $3.00. Group rates available.

Nearby Attractions/Accommodations: Rock City, Ruby Falls, Battles for Chattanooga, Tennessee Aquarium, IMAX 3D Theater, Creative Discovery Museum, Chattanooga Riverboat, Tennessee Valley Railroad.

Location/Directions: The Lower Station and free parking are located at the foot of Lookout Mountain near I-24, just three blocks south of Highways 11, 41, 64, and 72 on Highway 58. Follow Incline signs.

Site Address: 3917 St. Elmo Avenue, Lookout Mountain, TN
Mailing Address: 827 East Brow Road, Lookout Mountain, TN 37350
Telephone: (423) 821-4224 and (423) 629-1411
Fax: (423) 821-9444 and (423) 698-2749

Tennessee, Chattanooga

TENNESSEE VALLEY RAILROAD
Steam, scheduled
Standard gauge

STEVEN R. FREER

Display: A 6-mile, 45-minute round trip, much on original ET&G roadbed, across Chickamauga Creek and Tunnel Boulevard and through 986-foot-long Missionary Ridge Tunnel to East Chattanooga Depot, where a shop, turntable, displays, and active steam-locomotive repair shop are located. Tour of caboose, display car, theater car, diner, Pullmans, and various steam and diesel locomotives; Grand Junction Depot; large gift shop; audio-visual show; outside exhibits.

Schedule: May, September, and October: daily, 10 a.m. to 1:30 p.m. June through August: daily, 10 a.m. to 5 p.m. April through November: Sundays, 12 to 5 p.m.

Admission/Fare: Adults $8.50/$13.50; children 3-12 $4.50/$9.50. Group rates and charters available.

Locomotive/Rolling Stock: No. 610, 1952 Baldwin 2-8-0, and nos. 8669 and 8677, Alco RSD-1 diesels, former U.S. Army; no. 349, 1891 Baldwin 4-4-0, former Central of Georgia; no. 509, 1910 Baldwin 4-6-0, former Louisiana & Arkansas; no. 630, 1904 Alco 2-8-0, and no. 4501, 1911 Baldwin 2-8-2, both former Southern Railway; no. 913, Alco RS-1, former Hartford & Slocomb; no. 36, Baldwin VO1000, former U.S. Air Force; ACT-1, DOT experimental electric train; and more.

Location/Directions: I-75 exit 4, Highway 153, 1.5 miles west.

Radio frequency: 160.425

Site Address: 4119 Cromwell Road, Chattanooga, TN
Mailing Address: 4119 Cromwell Road, Chattanooga, TN 37421-2119
Telephone: (423) 894-8028
Fax: (423) 894-8029
Internet: www.chattanooga.net/rail

Tennessee, Cowan

COWAN RAILROAD MUSEUM
Railway museum

COWAN RAILROAD MUSEUM

Display: The former station is now a museum housing a re-creation of a turn-of-the-century telegraph operator's office, various artifacts, and an HO scale model of the Cowan Pusher District. Nearby the CSX line from Nashville to Chattanooga (once Nashville, Chattanooga & St. Louis, later Louisville & Nashville) climbs over Cumberland Mountain south of Cowan. The grades are steep enough to require helpers in each direction; they are added to southbound trains at Cowan.

Schedule: May 1 through October 31: Thursdays through Saturdays, 10 a.m. to 4 p.m.; Sundays 1 to 4 p.m.

Admission/Fare: Donations appreciated.

Location/Directions: I-24 exit 135, travel west 12 miles on U.S. 41A/64.

    [&] [P] M

Site Address: Cowen, Tennessee
Mailing Address: PO Box 53, Cowan, TN 37318
Telephone: (615) 967-7365

Tennessee, Jackson

CASEY JONES MUSEUM AND TRAIN STORE
Railway museum

DON LANCASTER

Museum: A historic home and railroad museum.

Schedule: Year round: daily, 8 a.m. to 9 p.m. Closed Easter, Thanksgiving, and Christmas.

Admission/Fare: Adults $3.50; seniors $3.00; children 6-12 $2.50; children age 5 and under are free.

Locomotive/Rolling Stock: HO and O27 model train display.

Special Events: Year round, varies. Call or write for information.

Nearby Attractions/Accommodations: Old Country Store Restaurant with gift shop, Adventure Golf, motel.

Location/Directions: I-40 exit 80A onto 45.

[P]

Site Address: Casey Jones Village, Jackson, TN
Mailing Address: 56 Casey Jones Lane, Jackson, TN
Telephone: (901) 668-1222
Fax: (901) 664-7782
E-mail: casey@aeneas.net
Internet: www.caseyjonesvillage.com

Tennessee, Knoxville

SOUTHERN APPALACHIA RAILWAY MUSEUM
Railway museum
Standard gauge

CHRIS WILLIAMS

Display: This museum is dedicated to the preservation of freight and passenger equipment native to the region.

Schedule: Anytime by appointment.

Admission/Fare: Donations appreciated.

Locomotive/Rolling Stock: 1949 Budd coach no. 827; 1949 Pullman sleeper car no. 2206 "Roanoke Valley"; 1926 Pullman dining car no. 3164; 1942 St. Louis Car Company baggage car no. 543; 1928 RPO American Car and Foundry no. 34; caboose X261; 1947 Budd coach no. 664 "Fort Oglethorpe," former Central of Georgia; caboose no. 6487, former Louisville & Nashville; caboose no. 9990, former Oneida & Western; boxcar, former Boston & Maine.

Special Events: Operating train beginning in 1998. Call for schedule.

Location/Directions: Middlebrook Industrial Park.

P 📷 ✉ M

Site Address: Knoxville, TN
Mailing Address: PO Box 5870, Knoxville, TN 37928
Telephone: (423) 588-2160

Tennessee, Nashville

BROADWAY DINNER TRAIN
Diesel, scheduled
Standard gauge

BROADWAY DINNER TRAIN

Display/Ride: Each car is unique, some dating back as far as 1939. We have plaques in each car designating which railroad(s) that particular car once ran on, and any other pertinent information or specifications on each car. Ride the 2½-hour rail excursion through middle Tennessee. A four-course meal is served each Thursday, Friday and Saturday evening. Five entrees to choose from. Live entainment nightly featuring Nashville singer/songwriter.

Schedule: Year round: Thursdays, Fridays, and Saturdays, 7 p.m. departure.

Admission/Fare: $49.95

Locomotive/Rolling Stock: Two EMD E8 locomotives, nos. 5764 and 6802; Cummin diesel generator in a restored RPO post office car.

Special Events: Murder Mysteries, children's excursions. Call or write for schedule. We cater to corporate and tour groups.

Location/Directions: In Nashville. I-40 to exit 209B (Broadway Demonbreun). Take Broadway to dead end at Riverfront Park. Train is to the right of park, behind Nashville Thermal Transfer plant.

Site Address: 108 First Avenue South, Nashville, TN
Mailing Address: 108 First Avenue South, Nashville, TN 37201
Telephone: (615) 254-8000 and (800) 274-8010
Fax: (615) 254-5855

Tennessee, Nashville

TENNESSEE CENTRAL RAILWAY MUSEUM
Diesel, irregular
Standard gauge

Display/Ride: Our excursion train trips are designed to provide the general public with the chance to experience traditional American passenger train travel during the post-WWII years. The museum operates trips each year between Nashville and Watertown, Tennessee; and Columbia and Lawrenceburg, Tennessee. Our display consists of the rolling stock we have acquired over the past six years.

Schedule: Museum–9 a.m. to 3 p.m. or by appointment. Train–Spring and Fall, periodic trips. Call or write for detailed information.

Admission/Fare: $10 to $50.

Locomotive/Rolling Stock: Nashville & Eastern locomotives SW8 TCRX no. 52.

Special Events: Watertown Mile Long Yard Sale, April.

Nearby Attractions/Accommodations: Broadway Dinner Train, downtown Nashville, Opryland.

Location/Directions: I-65 to exit 209B (Broadway), east to 1st Avenue, south onto 1st Avenue South.

P † ♦ ☐ M arm

Site Address: 108 1st Avenue South, Nashville, TN
Mailing Address: 709 N. Lake Circle, Brentwood, TN 37027-7844
Telephone: (615) 781-0262
Internet: www.hsv.tis.net/~bgaddes/tcrm/tcrm.htm

Tennessee, Pigeon Forge

DOLLYWOOD ENTERTAINMENT PARK
Steam, scheduled
Narrow gauge

RICHARDS & SOUTHERN

Display: The *Dollywood Express*, located in the Village area of Dollywood, takes visitors on a 5-mile journey through this scenic park, known as "the friendliest town in the Smokies." As passengers ride on the authentic, coal-fired steam train, they can catch a glimpse of the different areas of Dollywood: Daydream Ridge, Rivertown Junction, The Village, Craftsman's Valley, Country Fair, Showstreet, Jukebox Junction, and the Dollywood Boulevard. The *Dollywood Express* also takes visitors through replicas of a typical turn-of-the-century mountain village and logging community. During Christmas Festivals, the train is decorated with lights and features a special Christmas message for visitors.

Schedule: Thirty-minute rides every hour during park operating hours.

Admission/Fare: Adults $26.99; seniors $22.99; children 4-11 $18.99.

Locomotive/Rolling Stock: "Klondike Katie," a 1943 Baldwin 2-8-2, former U.S. Army no. 192; "Cinderella," a 1939 Bladwin 2-8-2, former U.S. Army no. 70; open-air passenger cars.

Special Events: Harvest Celebration, October. Smoky Mountain Christmas Festival, mid-November, December. School field trips.

Nearby Attractions/Accommodations: Numerous restaurants, lodging, shopping, and attractions in Pigeon Forge area.

Location/Directions: Call for directions.

Site Address: 1020 Dollywood Lane, Pigeon Forge, TN
Mailing Address: 1020 Dollywood Lane, Pigeon Forge, TN 37863-4101
Telephone: (423) 428-9488 and (800) DOLLYWOOD

Tennessee, Townsend

LITTLE RIVER RAILROAD AND LUMBER COMPANY
Railroad museum

LITTLE RIVER RAILROAD AND LUMBER CO. MUSEUM

Display: The museum is located on the original site of the Little River Lumber Company sawmill, housed in the original Walland Depot, which was moved to this site. The Little River Company logged huge tracts in what is now the Great Smoky Mountains National Park. Inside exhibits include over 200 vintage photos with text describing logging and railroad operations in detail, a history of trainwrecks, and the full locomotive roster. The Little River was known for its innovative locomotives, including the first 2-4-4-2 and the smallest Pacific ever built. Outside, Shay no. 2147 is displayed along with a vintage wood caboose and assorted logging and milling equipment.

Schedule: April, May, and September: weekends. June through August, and October: daily. November through March: by appointment only.

Admission/Fare: Donations appreciated.

Locomotive/Rolling Stock: Little River Shay no. 2147.

Location/Directions: Highway 321, near the entrance to the Great Smoky Mountains National Park. Approximately 18 miles east of Maryville and 15 miles southwest of Pigeon Forge.

*Coupon available, see coupon section.

[P] [🚌] [✳] [📷] [✉] M

Site Address: 7747 E. Lamar Alexander Parkway, U.S. 321, Townsend, TN
Mailing Address: PO Box 211, Townsend, TN 37882
Telephone: (423) 448-2211
Fax: (423) 448-2312

Texas, Austin

AUSTIN & TEXAS CENTRAL RAILROAD
Steam, scheduled
Standard gauge

GEORGE A. FORERO, JR.

Ride: Regular steam excursion service through 33 miles of the scenic Texas Hill Country.

Schedule: Hill Country Flyer–March through November: Saturdays and Sundays, 10 a.m.; December: 2:30 p.m. Departures from Cedar Park. Twilight Flyer–selected Saturdays, 7 p.m.

Admission/Fare: Adults $24/$38; children age 13 and under $10/$19.

Locomotive/Rolling Stock: Southern Pacific 2-8-2 no. 786; six PRR P70 day coaches; three air-conditioned parlor sleepers.

Special Events: Special Christmastime schedule. Call or write for information.

Nearby Attractions/Accommodations: Highland Lakes, State Capitol, LBJ Library and Museum, wineries, Vanishing Texas River Cruise.

Location/Directions: Intersection of U.S. 183 and FM 1431 in Cedar Park, 19 miles northwest of downtown Austin.

Radio frequency: 160.550

Site Address: 401 E. Whitestone Blvd., Cedar Park, TX
Mailing Address: Box 1632, Austin, TX 78767
Telephone: (512) 477-8468 (reservations) and (512) 477-6377 (office)
Fax: (512) 477-8633
Internet: www.main.org/flyer

Texas, Dallas

AGE OF STEAM RAILROAD MUSEUM
Railway museum
Standard gauge

BOB LAPRELLE

Display: Operated by the Southwest Railroad Historical Society since 1963, this museum offers a nostalgic journey back to the days of steam locomotives and name passenger trains, featuring some of the world's largest steam, diesel-electric, and electric locomotives. A superlative collection of heavyweight passenger equipment includes meticulously restored dining car "Goliad," former Missouri-Kansas-Texas; business car "Texland," former Fort Worth & Denver; and parlor-club car no. 3231, former Santa Fe. Other exhibits include chair and Pullman cars, vintage freight cars and cabooses, Dallas's oldest surviving train station, and many railroad artifacts. Come blow the steam locomotive whistles and enjoy one of the nation's foremost railroad collections. Former Santa Fe "doodlebug" M-160 and former Western Railroad VO-1000 no. 1107 operate periodically within the museum site. Also on display is Santa Fe Tower 19, a Texas landmark interlocking tower built in 1903.

Schedule: Wednesdays through Sundays, 10 a.m. to 5 p.m.

Locomotives/Rolling Stock: "Big Boy" no. 4018, 1942 Alco 4-8-8-4 and "Centennial" no. 6913, EMD DDA40X, both former Union Pacific; no. 1625, 1918 Alco 2-10-0, former Eagle-Picher Mining Co.; and more.

Admission/Fare: Adults $3.00; children under age 13 $1.50.

Location/Directions: Two miles east of downtown. I-30 westbound, exit 47A right onto Exposition Avenue, left on Party Avenue.

Site Address: 1105 Washington Street, Fair Park, Dallas, TX
Mailing Address: PO Box 153259, Dallas, TX 75315-3259
Telephone: (214) 428-0101
Fax: (214) 426-1937
Internet: www.startext.net/homes/railroad

Texas, Dallas

McKINNEY AVENUE TRANSIT AUTHORITY
Electric, scheduled
Standard gauge

ALLAN H. BERNER

Ride: Four restored trolleys operate on 2.7 miles of track from downtown Dallas through the historic Uptown area.

Schedule: Year round: Sundays through Thursdays, 10 a.m. to 10 p.m.; Fridays and Saturdays, 10 a.m. to 12 a.m.

Admission/Fare: Adults $1.50; seniors $ .50; children 2-12 $1.00.

Locomotive/Rolling Stock: 1906 Portugal Brill no. 122, former Porto; 1913 Dallas Stone & Webster no. 186; 1920 Dallas Birney no. 636; 1925 W2 no. 369, former Melbourne, Australia.

Nearby Attractions/Accommodations: Hard Rock Cafe, art galleries, antique shops, numerous restaurants with sidewalk cafe dining.

Location/Directions: Operates from downtown Dallas Arts District to the Historic Uptown Area. From the DART St. Paul Light Rail Station walk four blocks north.

Site Address: Car Barn at McKinney Avenue and Bowen Street, Dallas, TX
Mailing Address: 3153 Oak Grove Avenue, Dallas, TX 75204
Telephone: (214) 855-0006
Fax: (214) 855-5250

Texas, Grapevine/Fort Worth

TARANTULA TRAIN
Steam, scheduled

TARANTULA TRAIN

Ride: Travel over 21 miles of the Cotton Belt Railroad, linking Grapevine and Fort Worth's historic stockyards or take a ten-mile trek over a real working freight railroad that runs alongside the famous Chisholm Trail.

Schedule: Year round: daily.

Admission/Fare: Grapevine to Stockyards–adults $19.95; children $9.95. Stockyards to 8th Avenue–adults $10.00; children $5.50. Senior discounts on Wednesdays. Group rates available.

Locomotive/Rolling Stock: Cooke Locomotive Works 4-6-0 1896 steam locomotive no. 2248; 1925 day coaches nos. 206, 207, 208, 209, former Strasburg Railroad; 1927 touring coaches no. 1808, 1819, former Wabash.

Special Events: Grapevine–Main Street Days and Grapefest. Stockyards–Chisholm Train Days and Pioneer Days. Train–Sweetheart Express, July 4 and Murder on the Tarantula.

Nearby Attractions/Accommodations: Grapevine–Camping at Lake Grapevine, near DFW Airport, wineries, Heritage Center, restaurants, specialty shops. Stockyards–Cowtown Coliseum, Stockyards Hotel, Billy Bob's, shops, saloons, Miss Molly's Bed and Breakfast.

Location/Directions: Grapevine–Hwy 114 or 121, north on Main Street. Stockyards–I-35W to westbound Northeast 28th Street, south on N. Main, left on Exchange Avenue.

Radio frequency: 160.215

Site Address: Cotton Belt Depot, 707 S. Main Street, Grapevine, TX
Site Address: Stockyards Station, 140 E. Exchange Ave., Fort Worth, TX
Mailing Address: 140 E. Exchange Avenue, Fort Worth, TX 76106
Telephone: (800) 952-5717 and (817) 625-RAIL
Fax: (817) 740-1119

Texas, Houston

GULF COAST RAILROAD MUSEUM
Gulf Coast Chapter, National Railway Historical Society
Railway museum

DAVID M. SEE

Display: This museum, located near the Union Pacific's Sunset Route in northeastern Houston, features historic locomotives and passenger and freight cars of regional significance, many in operable condition.

Schedule: March 28 through November 1: Saturdays, 11 a.m. to 4 p.m. and Sundays 1 to 4 p.m. Group tours available at other times by appointment.

Admission/Fare: Adults $3.00; children under age 13 $1.50.

Locomotive/Rolling Stock: Texas-Mexican Baldwin DS44-750 no. 510; MKT coach "New Braunfels"; ATSF Pullman "Verde Valley"; KCS tavern-lounge-observation "Good Cheer"; CM&O parlor car "Alton"; ATSF RPO no. 3401; MKT caboose no. 6; SP bay window caboose no., 4696; SP&P heavyweight baggage car no. 50; ATSF end-door baggage express car no. 1890.

Special Events: National Model Railroad Month Open House, November.

Nearby Attractions/Accommodations: Six Flags Astroworld, Waterworld, Anheuser-Busch Brewery, Hampton Inn.

Location/Directions: Abot 1.5 miles north of McCarty Drive (U.S. Highway 90) off North Loop 610.

[♿] [P] [🚌] [✻] [☕] [📷] [✉] M [🚆]

Radio frequency: 464.150

Site Address: 7390 Mesa Drive, Houston, TX
Mailing Address: PO Box 457, Houston, TX 77001-0457
Telephone: (713) 631-6612
Internet: www.neosoft.com/gulfcoast

Texas, Rusk and Palestine

TEXAS STATE RAILROAD
Steam, scheduled
Standard gauge

BILL LANGFORD

Ride: Established in 1896, the Texas State Railroad now carries visitors on a 4-hour, 50-mile round trip across 24 bridges as it travels through the heart of the east Texas rolling pine and hardwood forest. Victorian-style depots are located in Rusk and Palestine.

Schedule: March through November: weekends. June and July: Thursdays through Sundays.

Admission/Fare: Round trip–adults $15.00; children $9.00. One-way–adults $10.00; children $6.00.

Locomotive/Rolling Stock: No. 201, 1901 Cooke 4-6-0, former Texas & Pacific no. 316; no. 300, 1917 Baldwin 2-8-0, former Texas Southeastern no. 28; no. 400, 1917 Baldwin 2-8-2, former Magma Arizona no. 7; no. 500, 1911 Baldwin 4-6-2, former Santa Fe no. 1316; no. 610, 1927 Lima 2-10-4, former Texas & Pacific no. 610.

Special Events: Murder on the Dis-Oriented Express, Great Texas Train Race, Special Dogwood Excursion, Civil War and World War II re-enactments.

Nearby Attractions/Accommodations: Rusk–nation's longest foot bridge. Palestine–National Scientific Balloon Base.

Location/Directions: Highway 84, 2 miles west of downtown Rusk, 3 miles east of downtown Palestine.

Site Address: 2503 W. 6th, Rusk, TX
Mailing Address: Box 39, Rusk, TX 78785
Telephone: (800) 442-8951 and (903) 683-2561
Fax: (903) 683-5634
Internet: www.tpwd.state.tx.us/park/railroad/railroad.html

Texas, San Antonio

TEXAS TRANSPORTATION MUSEUM
Railway museum

TEXAS TRANSPORTATION MUSEUM

Museum/Ride: Passengers enjoy a ⅓-mile caboose ride on the "Longhorn & Western Railroad" behind a 60-ton diesel. The track is being extended one mile. Santa Fe business car No. 404; heavyweight Pullman "McKeever"; Missouri Pacific transfer caboose; Union Pacific caboose; Southern Pacific station from Converse, Texas, with railroad displays and pictures; G gauge garden railroad; 5,000-square-foot display building with 100-foot-long HO model railroad; transportation toy display; fire trucks; antique automobiles and carriages; technology display.

Schedule: Train–Saturdays and Sundays, 12:30 to 3:30 p.m. departures every 45 minutes. Museum–Thursdays, Saturdays, and Sundays, 9 a.m. to 4 p.m.

Admission/Fare: Adults $3.00; children under age 12 $1.00.

Locomotive/Rolling Stock: Moscow Camden & St. Augustine no. 6; GE 44-ton no. 7071; Baldwin no. 4035 U.S. Army.

Nearby Attractions/Accommodations: San Antonio

Location/Directions: Site is located 2½-miles north of Loop 410, take Bwy or Wetmore exit, north of intersection of Starcrest and Wetmore.

Site Address: 11731 Wetmore Road, San Antonio, TX
Mailing Address: 11731 Wetmore Road, San Antonio, TX 78247
Telephone: (210) 490-3554

Texas, Temple

RAILROAD AND PIONEER MUSEUM
Railway museum

FRED M. SPRINGER

Display: Early Santa Fe and Missouri-Kansas-Texas station equipment and furniture, including a working telegraph for train orders. The museum houses a large collection of railroad artifacts and displays of woodworking, ranching, farming, blacksmithing, and local history. Also displayed is a large collection of railroad timetables and passes, photographs, and papers from around the world.

Schedule: Year round: Tuesdays through Fridays, 1 to 4 p.m. and Saturdays, 10 a.m. to 4 p.m.

Admission/Fare: Adults $2.00; seniors and children age 5 and older $1.00.

Locomotive/Rolling Stock: No. 3423, 1921 Baldwin 4-6-2, former Santa Fe; no. 2301, 1937 Alco, the oldest surviving Santa Fe diesel. Steel caboose no. 1556, former Gulf, Colorado & Santa Fe; three section cars; steel caboose no. 140, former MKT; handcar, caboose, and boxcar, all former Missouri Pacific; World War II Pullman troop sleeper; an MKT (Glover Glade) Pullman sleeper (1917).

Special Events: Texas Train Festival, third weekend in September.

Location/Directions: I-35 exit Avenue H.

*Coupon available, see coupon section.

Site Address: 710 Jack Baskin, Temple, TX
Mailing Address: PO Box 5126, Temple, TX 76505
Telephone: (254) 298-5172
Fax: (254) 298-5171
E-mail: mirving@ci.temple.tx.us

Texas, Wichita Falls

WICHITA FALLS RAILROAD MUSEUM
Railway museum
Standard gauge

DAVID H. GAINES

Museum: The museum is preserving the railroad history of Wichita Falls, Texas, and the surrounding area. Artifacts, displays, and the Wichita Falls Model Railroad Club HO gauge layout are housed in the historic Route Building. The museum's yard is located on the site of the Wichita Falls Union Passenger Station and is adjacent to the Burlington Northern Santa Fe's (former Fort Worth & Denver) Forth Worth to Amarillo mainline.

Schedule: Year round: Saturdays, 12 to 4 p.m. and by appointment (unless temperature is below 32 degrees F or precipitation is falling).

Admission/Fare: Donations appreciated. Fee for special events.

Locomotive/Rolling Stock: FW&D 2-8-0 no. 304; MKT NW-2 no. 1029, FW&D RPO baggage no. 34; CB&Q power combine no. 7300; more.

Special Events: Zephyr Days Railroad Festival, last weekend in September. Depot Square Heritage Days, early October.

Nearby Attractions/Accommodations: Kell House Museum, Wichita Falls Police and Fire Museum, Texas Tourist Information Center, Econo Lodge, Holiday Inn Hotel & Suites, Sheraton Four Point.

Location/Directions: Located on the east side of downtown Wichita Falls. From Holliday or Broad Streets, take 8th Street toward downtown. The museum's gate will be to the right at the end of the street.

P 🚌 ✳ ☕ 📷 TRAIN M

Site Address: 501 8th Street, Wichita Falls, TX
Mailing Address: PO Box 4242, Wichita Falls, TX 76308-0242
Telephone: (940) 723-2661 and (940) 692-6073

Utah, Heber City

HEBER VALLEY RAILROAD
Steam, diesel, scheduled
Standard gauge

STEVEN W. BELMONT

Ride: Visitors can choose a one-hour or 3½-hour excursion across farmland, along a lake shore, and descend into the breathtaking Provo Canyon. See history in motion.

Schedule: May through September: daily. October, December through March: weekends. Closed November and April.

Admission/Fare: One-hour train–$8.00. 3½-hour train–$17.00.

Locomotive/Rolling Stock: 1907 Baldwin 2-8-0; NW2 dielsel MRS1; Davenport 44-ton diesels; coaches.

Special Events: Blue Grass Express Train/Blue Grass music, summer.

Nearby Attractions/Accommodations: Park City Ski Resort, Alpine Forest, Cascade Springs, Provo River rafting.

Location/Directions: U.S. 40 to Heber City, six blocks west of town.

*Coupon available, see coupon section.

Site Address: 450 South 600 West, Heber City, UT
Mailing Address: PO Box 609, Heber City, UT 84032
Telephone: (801) 654-5601 and (801) 581-9980
Fax: (801) 654-3709
E-mail: kenm@shadowlink.net
Internet: www.hebervalleycc.org/hbrvlyrr.html

Utah, Ogden

OGDEN UNION STATION
Railroad display, museum, model railroad display

OGDEN UNION STATION

Display: Ogden Union Station is composed of four indoor museums, model railroad, classic cars, Browning firearms, and natural history—there is also an art gallery. Outside are three actual locomotives. The model railways are done in realistic scenes behind glass enclosures. The classic cars are in roped off area. Gems and minerals are in glass case with descriptions of what they are. Browning guns are in separate classifications behind glass.

Schedule: Memorial Day to Labor Day. Call or write for more information.

Admission/Fare: Call or write for information.

Locomotive/Rolling Stock: The Spencer S. Eccles center is our rolling stock. The most powerful locomotive built is a gas turbine called "Big Blow." Also The Centennial is the largest diesel produced.

Special Events: Numerous. Call or write for information.

Site Address: 2501 Wall Avenue, Ogden, UT
Mailing Address: 2501 Wall Avenue, Ogden, UT 84401
Telephone: (801) 629-8535
Fax: (801) 629-8555

Utah, Promontory

GOLDEN SPIKE
NATIONAL HISTORIC SITE
Railway museum
Standard gauge

GOLDEN SPIKE NATIONAL HISTORIC SITE

Display: This is the spot where the famous Golden Spike ceremony was held on May 10, 1869, completing the nation's first transcontinental railroad. Exact operating replicas of the original locomotives are on display; these locomotives run to the Last Spike Site on their own power each morning (from April to the second weekend in October) and return to the enginehouse in late afternoon. In the Visitor Center are color movies and many exhibits. Park rangers are on hand to explain the importance of the railroad and the significance of the ceremony of 1869.

Schedule: May 25 through September 2: daily, 8 a.m. to 6 p.m. September 3 through May 24: 8 a.m. to 4:30 p.m. Closed Thanksgiving, Christmas, and New Year's Day.

Admission/Fare: Adults: $3.50; cars $7.00.

Locomotive/Rolling Stock: Full-sized operating replicas of Union Pacific 4-4-0 no. 119; and Central Pacific 4-4-0 no. 60, "The Jupiter."

Special Events: Annual Celebration, May 2. Annual Railroader's Festival, second Saturday in August. Annual Railroader's Film Festival and Winter Steam Demonstration, December 27-29.

Location/Directions: Thirty-two miles west of Brigham City, via Highways 13 and 83 through Corinne.

Site Address: Promontory, UT
Mailing Address: PO Box 897, Brigham City, UT 84302
Telephone: (801) 471-2209

Vermont, Bellows Falls

GREEN MOUNTAIN RAILROAD
GREEN MOUNTAIN FLYER
Diesel, scheduled
Standard gauge

GREEN MOUNTAIN RAILROAD

Ride: Climb aboard and experience a journey into Vermont's rich history and scenic splendor. Ride the two-hour, 26-mile excursion in fully restored open-window coaches from the former Rutland and Jersey Central railroads.

Schedule: June 27 through September 7: Tuesdays through Sundays. September 19 through October 18: daily. October 3-4, 10-11, 17-18: Ludlow foliage specials. October 3-4, 10-11: fall sunset specials.

Admission/Fare: Round trip–adults $11.00; children 3-12 $7.00. One-way–adults $7.00; children $5.00. Under age 3 are free when not occupying a seat.

Locomotive/Rolling Stock: Alco RS 1 no. 405, former Rutland; EMD GP9 no. 1850, former Chesapeake & Ohio; EMD GP9 no. 1848, former Bangor & Aroostook; EMD GP9 no. 1851, former Norfolk Southern.

Special Events: Valentine's Day, February 14. Sugar on Snow, March 21. Easter Bunny, April 11. Mother's Day, May 10. Memorial weekend, May 23-25. Ludown Limited, July 4. Rutland Express, September 12. Santa Express, December 13, 19, 20.

Nearby Attractions/Accommodations: Basketville, Santa's Land, Vermont Country Store, Bellows Falls Fish Ladder.

Location/Directions: I-91 exit 5 to Bellows Falls route 5, north 3 miles.

*Coupon available, see coupon section.

Site Address: 8 Depot Street, Bellows Falls, VT
Mailing Address: PO Box 498, Bellows Falls, VT 05101
Telephone: (802) 463-3069 and (802) 463-9531
Fax: (802) 463-4084
E-mail: railroads@souer.net
Internet: www.virtualvermont.com/greenmountainrr.

Vermont, Middlebury

VERMONT RAIL EXCURSIONS
Diesel, scheduled
Standard gauge

Ride: Passengers enjoy a 35-mile ride through the scenic west side of Vermont along Lake Champlain through farmland and small towns. Watch for trestles, wildlife, and bison.

Schedule: May 24 through June 22: weekends. June 24 through September 1: Tuesdays through Sundays. September 2 through October 26: Thursdays through Tuesdays. Routes–Tuesdays: Middlebury to Rutland. Wednesdays through Sundays: Middlebury to Burlington.

Admission/Fare: Round trip–adults $12.00; seniors $10.00; children 3-12 $7.00.

Locomotive/Rolling Stock: 1971 VTR locomotive no. 205; "Dreammaker" no. SRXT000400; "Mollyocket" no. SRXT000700; "Mahoosuc" no. SRXT000600.

Special Events: Sundown Leisure Trips, special parties, charter trips, group tours.

Nearby Attractions/Accommodations: Lake Champlain, Shelburne Museum, lake cruises, Middlebury Inn, Morgan Horse Farm.

Location/Directions: Burlington–on the waterfront. Middlebury–Exchange Street.

*Coupon available, see coupon section.

Site Address: Exchange Street, Middlebury, VT
Mailing Address: PO Box 243, Middlebury, VT 05753
Telephone: (800) 707-3530 and (802) 388-0193
Fax: (802) 388-0189
Internet: www.sugarbush-vt-express.com

Vermont, Shelburne

SHELBURNE MUSEUM
Museum, railway display
Standard gauge

SHELBURNE DEPOT

Museum: This museum displays an extensive and internationally renowned collection of Americana housed in 37 historic buildings on a 45-acre site. The railroad exhibit features the restored 1890 Shelburne depot with a Central Vermont steam locomotive and the private car "Grand Isle." Nearby is former Woodstock Railroad steam inspection car "Gertie Buck." There is also a wooden replica of Baldwin's "Old Ironsides" of 1832 and a collection of railroad memorabilia. Other exhibits at the museum include a 220-foot sidewheel steamer, the *Ticonderoga*, which was moved overland from Lake Champlain, and collections of antiques, quilts, carriages, art, decoys, and tools.

Schedule: Late May through late October: daily, 10 a.m. to 5 p.m.

Admission/Fare: Adults $17.50; children 6-14 $7.00.

Locomotive/Rolling Stock: Locomotive no. 220; railcar Grand Isle.

Special Events: Lilac Festival, May. Apple Days, October. Celebrations of the Season, December.

Nearby Attractions/Accommodations: Vermont Teddy Bear Factory, Shelburne Farms.

Location/Directions: Site is located on route 7, 7 miles south of Burlington.

*Coupon available, see coupon section.

Site Address: Route 7, Shelburne, Vermont
Mailing Address: PO Box 10, Shelburne, VT 05482
Telephone: (802) 985-3346
Fax: (802) 985-2331
Internet: shelburnemuseum.org

Virginia, Fairfax Station

FAIRFAX STATION RAILROAD MUSEUM
Railway display

Museum: A restored Southern Railway depot rich in Civil War and local history. Clara Barton was a nurse here after the Second Battle of Manassas.

Schedule: Year round: Sundays, 1 to 4 p.m.

Admission/Fare: Adults $2.00; children $1.00; families $5.00.

Locomotive/Rolling Stock: Caboose N&W 518606.

Special Events: Annual Model Train Display, first weekend in December. Annual Civil War Day, Quilt Show, Art Show.

Nearby Attractions/Accommodations: Washington D.C., museums, Manassas Museum, Fairfax City Museum.

Location/Directions: Three miles south of Fairfax. Located ¼ mile from corner of route 123 (Ox Road) and Fairfax Station Road.

Site Address: 11200 Fairfax Station Road, Fairfax Station, VA
Mailing Address: PO Box 7, Fairfax Station, VA 22039
Telephone: (703) 425-9225 and (703) 278-8833
E-mail: ox6525@aol.com
Internet: www.fairfax-station.org/

Virginia, Fort Eustis   **U.S. ARMY TRANSPORTATION MUSEUM**
                                   Railway display

U.S. ARMY TRANSPORTATION MUSEUM

Museum: This military-history museum displays items of transportation dating from 1776 to the present. Inside the 15,000-square-foot museum are dioramas and exhibits; on five acres outside are rail rolling stock, trucks, jeeps, amphibious marine craft, helicopters, aircraft, and an experimental hovercraft.

Schedule: Year round: Tuesdays through Sundays, 9 a.m. to 4:30 p.m. Closed Mondays and federal holidays.

Admission/Fare: Free.

Locomotive/Rolling Stock: Steam locomotive 2-8-0 no. 607; steam locomotive 0-6-0 no. V-1923; ambulance ward car no. 87568; steam wrecking crane; 40-T and 50T flatcars; caboose; Berlin duty train cars.

Nearby Attractions/Accommodations: Colonial Williamsburg, Busch Gardens, Virginia Beach.

Location/Directions: I-64 exit 250A.

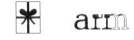

Site Address: Building 300, Washington Blvd., Fort Eustis, VA
Mailing Address: Building 300, Washington Blvd., Fort Eustis, VA 23604
Telephone: (757) 878-1182 and (757) 878-1183
Fax: (757) 878-5656
E-mail: BOWERB@eustis-EMH.1.Army.Mil

Virginia, Manassas

HISTORIC MANASSAS, INC.
1998 RAILWAY FESTIVAL
Presented by the Washington Post

MARK MILLIGAN

Display: Attend this once-a-year festival and see living history, railroadiana vendors, modular exhibits in G, O, HO, and N scales, live railroad-related music, and excursion rides. Call or write for free brochure.

Schedule: June 6, 1998, 10 a.m. to 4 p.m.

Admission/Fare: Free.

Locomotive/Rolling Stock: Full-size rail cars on exhibit, modern and antique.

Nearby Attractions/Accommodations: Historic Old Town Manassas, The Manassas Museum, hotels, shops, and restaurants.

Location/Directions: I-66 to route 28, south to Old Town Manassas.

Site Address: Manassas, VA
Mailing Address: 9431 West Street, Manassas, VA 20110
Telephone: (703) 361-6599
Fax: (703) 361-6942

Virginia, Richmond **OLD DOMINION RAILWAY MUSEUM**
Railway museum

OLD DOMINION RAILWAY MUSEUM

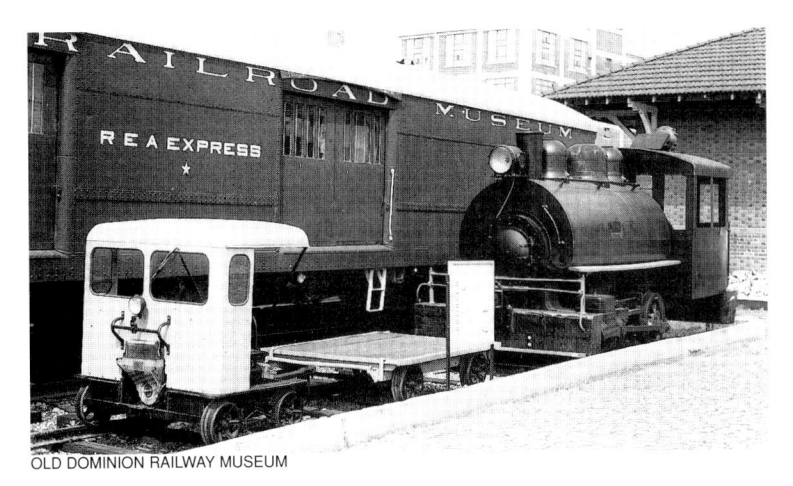

Display: This museum's collection includes a caboose, freight equipment, and track-maintenance equipment; a Richmond, Fredericksburg & Potomac baggage car contains exhibits on telegraphy, passenger depots, the Railway Express Agency, and railroad workers.

Schedule: Year round: Saturdays, 11 a.m. to 4 p.m. and Sundays, 1 to 4 p.m.

Admission/Fare: Donations appreciated.

Locomotive/Rolling Stock: Porter saddletank 0-4-0; 1959 boxcar and 1969 caboose, both former Seaboard; 1937 baggage car, former RF&P; track-inspection car.

Special Events: Floodwall Guided Walking Tours, second Sunday of each month.

Nearby Attractions/Accommodations: Downtown Richmond tourist area, Richmond Floodwall Promenade.

Location/Directions: Downtown in the former Southern Railway Hull Street station.

P 🚌 ✳ 📷 ✉ M arm 🚂

Site Address: 102 House Street, Richmond, VA
Mailing Address: PO Box 8583, Richmond, VA 23226
Telephone: (804) 233-6237
Fax: (804) 745-4735
Internet: www.odcnrhs.org/

Virginia, Roanoke

VIRGINIA MUSEUM OF TRANSPORTATION
Railway museum
Standard gauge

VIRGINIA MUSEUM OF TRANSPORTATION, INC.

Display: See the largest diesel collection in the United States, a 4-tier O gauge model layout, archives, and antique trolleys, buses, and cars.

Schedule: Year round: Sundays, 12 to 5 p.m.; Mondays through Saturdays, 10 a.m. to 5 p.m. January and February: closed Mondays.

Admission/Fare: Adults $5.25; seniors $4.20; children $3.15.

Locomotive/Rolling Stock: No. 611, J Class 4-8-4, former Norfolk & Western; no. 4, 1910 Baldwin class SA 0-8-0, former Virginian Railway; no. 6, 1897 Baldwin class G-1 2-8-0, former N&W; no. 763, 1944 Lima class S-2 2-8-4, former Nickel Plate; no. 1, Celanese 0400 fireless locomotive; many diesels, City of Roanoke trolley, and D.C. Transit trolley; IT Presidential Business car, N&W Safety Car No. 418, N&W Dynamometer Car, Southern "Glen Summit" sleeping car, Southern "Lake Pearl" sleeping car, N&W Class PG passenger car.

Special Events: Railway Festival, Columbus Day weekend in October. Spring Railfair, May.

Nearby Attractions/Accommodations: Science museum, zoo, art museum, explore park, hotels, convention center, Blue Ridge Parkway.

Location/Directions: I-581 exit 5, downtown Roanoke.

*Coupon available, see coupon section.

Site Address: 303 Norfolk Avenue, Roanoke, VA
Mailing Address: 303 Norfolk Avenue, Roanoke, VA 24016
Telephone: (540) 342-5670
Fax: (540) 342-6898
Internet: www.vmt.org

Virginia, Williamsburg

AMERICA'S RAILROADS ON PARADE
Model railroads
O, HO, S gauges

DAVE FRARY

Display: Broadway-designed layouts with computer lighting, collectibles, animations, hands-on exhibits, and over 30 (multiple scale) simultaniously operating model trains.

Schedule: Year round: daily, 10 a.m. to 6 p.m.

Admission/Fare: Adults $5.00; seniors/college students $3.50; children 3-18 $2.50; under age 3 are free; families $12.00 maximum. All day re-entry.

Locomotive/Rolling Stock: All eras from 1830s to present day represented by over 2,000 rotating model trains in operation.

Special Events: Special trains, displays, and discounts on all holidays.

Nearby Attractions/Accommodations: Busch Gardens, Mike's Trainland, Colonial Williamsburg, Army Transportation Museum, Marriott (2), Best Western, Holiday Inn, Ramada Inn, Hampton Inn (2), Quality Inn.

Location/Directions: I-64 exit 242A to route 60 east, next to Busch Gardens in the village shops at Kingsmill.

*Coupon available, see coupon section.

Site Address: 1915 Pocahontas Trail, Suite A4, Williamsburg, VA
Mailing Address: 1915 Pocahontas Trail, Suite A4, Williamsburg, VA 23185
Telephone: (757) 220-8725
Internet: www.trains.ontheline.com

Washington, Anacortes

ANACORTES RAILWAY
Steam, scheduled
18" gauge

THOMAS THOMPSON JR.

Display/Ride: Railroad artifacts and photographs are displayed in the depot; Tangley air calliope. The railway offers a ¾-mile scenic train ride from the historic Great Northern Depot to downtown Anacortes along the city's waterfront and tree-lined parkways. In operation since 1986, this family-owned tourist line is one of the world's smallest narrow-gauge passenger railroads (as distinguished from a miniature railway). Turntables at each end of the line rotate the locomotive for its return trip. Limited cab rides are allowed.

Schedule: June 14 through Labor Day: weekends and holidays, noon to 4:30 p.m. (frequent departures).

Admission/Fare: $1.00

Locomotive/Rolling Stock: Forney-type steam locomotive, rebuilt from a 1909 H.K. Porter compressed-air 0-4-0 mining locomotive, fueled with fir bark; seven steel flatcars formerly used at the Asarco Smelter in Tacoma; one gondola, wood-sided for ballast service.

Special Events: Anacortes Arts and Crafts Festival, August 2 and 3.

Nearby Attractions/Accommodations: Maritime Museum, an art gallery in depot, and the ferry to the San Juan Islands.

Location/Directions: 7th Street and R Avenue. Take R Avenue exit to narrow gauge railway crossing, turn right.

Seattle, Everett
Mt. Vernon, Burlington

Site Address: 7th Street and R Avenue, Anacortes, WA
Mailing Address: 387 Campbell Lake Road, Anacortes, WA 98221
Telephone: (360) 293-2634

Washington, Carnation　　　　**REMLINGER FARMS RAILROAD**
Steam, scheduled
24" gauge

REMLINGER FARMS RAILROAD

Ride: An approximately 15-minute ride that travels around the farm and along the Tolt River. For all ages.

Schedule: June 15 through September: Tuedays-Sundays, 11:00 a.m. to 3 p.m.

Admission/Fare: $2.00; Fall Harvest Festival, adults $7.00; children 12 and under $8.00.

Locomotive/Rolling Stock: Crown locomotive 4-4-0 modified; three covered excursion cars.

Special Events: Fall Harvest Festival: October weekends, 10 a.m. to 4 p.m. Includes steam train rides, pony rides, puppet shows, pioneer village, farm animals, pirate adventure, giant slides, and hay jump. All activities for one price.

Nearby Attractions/Accommodations: McDonald Park.

Location/Directions: Site is one mile south of Carnation, off Highway 203.

Site Address: 32610 NE 32nd Street, Carnation, WA
Mailing Address: PO Box 177, Carnation, WA 98014
Telephone: (425) 333-4135
Fax: (425) 333-4373

Washington, Cashmere — **CHELAN COUNTY HISTORICAL SOCIETY PIONEER VILLAGE AND MUSEUM**

CHELAN COUNTY HISTORICAL SOCIETY

Museum: Visitors can see a caboose, dining car, ticket office, and section house, plus a pioneer village with over 20 furnished buildings and a historical museum.

Schedule: March through October: daily, 9:30 a.m. to 5 p.m. Closed Mondays.

Admission/Fare: Adults $3.00; seniors and students $2.00; children 5-12 $1.00; families $5 maximum.

Locomotive/Rolling Stock: Great Northern wooden caboose x494; 1926 Pullman diner.

Special Events: Family Days, first Saturday of each month. Founders Day, last weekend in June. Apple Days, first weekend in October.

Nearby Attractions/Accommodations: Aplets and Cotlets Candy Kitchen, Ohme Gardens, Leavenworth's Bavarian Village, Wenatchee River County Park.

Location/Directions: Cashmere is located between Leavenworth and Wenatchee on Highway 2. Take Cottage Avenue exit.

*Coupon available, see coupon section.

Site Address: 600 Cottage Avenue, Cashmere, WA
Mailing Address: PO Box 22, Cashmere, WA 98815
Telephone: (509) 782-3230

Washington, Chehalis

CHEHALIS-CENTRALIA RAILROAD ASSOCIATION
Steam, scheduled
Standard gauge

CENTRALIA *DAILY CHRONICLE*

Display: A 12-mile, 1¾-hour round trip over ex-Weyerhaeuser trackage (former Milwaukee Road) between South Chehalis and Millburn, under contract with the Mt. Rainier Scenic Railroad. An extended trip to Ruth (nine miles west of Chehalis), offered on Saturdays, passes through scenic rural farmlands and a river valley. Selected Saturdays feature dinner train on the 5:00 p.m. trip. Call for information. Restored Union Pacific C-5 cabooses serve as the ticket office and gift shop.

Schedule: May 24 through September 1: weekends and holidays. Depart Chehalis, 1 and 3 p.m. Ruth trip–Saturdays, depart Chehalis 5 p.m.

Admission/Fare: Round trip–adults $7.00; children 3-16 $5.00. Ruth trip–adults $11.00; children $9.00.

Locomotive/Rolling Stock: No. 15, 1916 Baldwin 90-ton 2-8-2, former Cowlitz, Chehalis & Cascade, former Puget Sound & Cascade no. 200. This engine had been displayed for 30 years in a local park; restoration was completed in 1989 by Mt. Rainier Scenic Railroad shop and volunteers from Lewis County; Z-frame 40-foot wood boxcar used as shop/supply car, and more.

Location/Directions: Midway between Seattle, Washington, and Portland, Oregon. Chehalis–I-5 to exit 77. Turn west to first street south (Riverside Road). Proceed ¼ mile to Sylvenus Street. Turn left one block to railroad tracks.

Radio frequency: 161.385 and 160.635

Site Address: 1100 Sylvenus Street, Chehalis, WA
Mailing Address: 1945 S. Market Blvd., Chehalis, WA 98532
Telephone: (360) 748-9593

Washington, Dayton

DAYTON HISTORICAL DEPOT
Railway museum

DAYTON HISTORICAL DEPOT SOCIETY

Museum: Railroad memorabilia dedicated to the pioneers of Dayton.

Schedule: Year round: Tuesdays through Saturdays, 9 a.m. to 5 p.m.

Admission/Fare: $1.00.

Special Events: Festival at Depot, July 18-19. Homespun Christmas.

Nearby Attractions/Accommodations: County Courthouse, 89 historical houses and buildings on National Historic Register.

Location/Directions: Located one block off Main Street, down 2nd Street.

Site Address: 222 Commercial Street, Dayton, WA
Mailing Address: PO Box 1881, Dayton, WA 99328
Telephone: (509) 382-2026

Washington, Elbe

MT. RAINIER SCENIC RAILROAD
Steam, scheduled
Standard gauge

J. S. DAVID WILKIE

Ride: A 14-mile, 1½-hour round trip over a secluded right-of-way, over former Milwaukee Road trackage, on the south slope of Mt. Rainier. The train goes through farms, forests, and tree farms, over rivers and creeks, up hills and down. There is a 20-minute layover at Mineral Lake. Passengers may stay there to visit or picnic and return on a later train. The *Cascadian Dinner Train* makes a 4-hour round trip to Eatonville (26-mile trip), and offers a five-course prime rib dinner, prepared and served aboard a restored Union Pacific dining car and lounge/observation car.

Schedule: June 15 through Labor Day: daily. Memorial Day through September: weekends. Departures at 11 a.m., 1:15, and 3:30 p.m. Dinner train: spring and fall, 1 p.m.; summer, 5:30 p.m.

Admission/Fare: Adults $9.50; seniors $8.50; juniors 12-17 $7.50; children under 12 $6.50. Dinner train: $55.00. Reservations required.

Locomotive/Rolling Stock: A 1924 Porter 2-8-2 no. 5, former Port of Grays Harbor; a 1928 Climax 3-truck no. 10, former Hillcrest Lumber Co.; two commuter coaches; dining car, former Union Pacific; and many more.

Special Events: Christmas Train, first three weekends in December, Railfan Photo Specials, spring or fall weddings, charters, movies, commercials.

Location/Directions: Forty-two miles southeast of Tacoma on Highway 7.

*Coupon available, see coupon section.

Tacoma   Radio frequency: 161.385 and 160.635

Site Address: Highway 7, Elbe, WA
Mailing Address: PO Box 921, Elbe, WA 98330
Telephone: (360) 569-2588
Fax: (360) 569-2438

Washington, Friday Harbor **MODEL TRAIN MUSEUM (MTM)**
Scheduled, electric/600 volt, standard gauge

Museum: Large layout of operating model trains featuring G, O, S, HO, and N gauges.

Schedule: Summer: daily, 10 a.m. to 5 p.m.

Admission/Fare: Donations appreciated.

Locomotive/Rolling Stock: Lionel, MTH, Weaver, K-Line.

Nearby Attractions/Accommodations: Whale Museum, Button Fly Museum, numerous bed and breakfasts.

Location/Directions: By ferry out of Anacortes, by plane, or by boat.

Site Address: 260 Spring Street West, Friday Harbor, WA
Mailing Address: PO Box 4372, Friday Harbor, WA 98250
Telephone: (360) 378-3061
Fax: (360) 378-3749

Washington, Renton SPIRIT OF WASHINGTON DINNER TRAIN
Scheduled
Standard gauge

Ride: Experience the nostalgia of passenger rail as you ride and dine in our luxurious, vintage rail cars. The Spirit of Washington Dinner Train takes you on a 3½-hour excursion that showcases scenic views of the Puget Sound regions. The 45-mile round trip is enhanced by scenery of Lake Washington, the Olympic Mountains, the Seattle skyline and Mount Rainier. You'll dine in comfort and elegance as your journey takes you to Woodinville's beautiful Columbia Winery. There, you'll sample fine Northwest wines and enjoy a tour of the winery before returing to the depot.

Schedule: Call or write for information.

Admission/Fare: Regular Seating–$57.00 dinner; $47.00 lunch/brunch. Dome Seating–$69.00 dinner; $59.00 lunch/brunch. Also available for conventions, corporate parties, weddings and special events up to 370.

Locomotive/Rolling Stock: Former Santa Fe coaches and dome lounge; former Reading Crusade observation car; former Milwaukee Road Super Dome.

Nearby Attractions/Accommodations: Seattle, Puget Sound.

Location/Directions: I-405 exit 2 (Route 162, Renton/Rainier Avenue), travel north to South 3rd Street, turn right, turn right again on Burnett Avenue South for one block to depot.

[P] [*] [()]

Site Address: Renton, WA
Mailing Address: PO Box 835, Renton, WA 98057
Telephone: (206) 227-RAIL and (800) 876-RAIL
Internet: www.pattismith.com/spirit/

Washington, Seattle   **AMERICAN ORIENT EXPRESS RAILWAY CO.**
UNITED STATES AND CANADA
Diesel, scheduled
Standard gauge

JACK PARSONS, TCS EXPEDITIONS

Ride: Travel aboard the deluxe American Orient Express private train on five- to 10-day trips throughout the U.S. and Canada. The train's 15 beautifully restored carriages are from the streamliner era of the 1940s and 50s. Gourmet meals are served at tables set with china, silver, crystal, and linen. There are two club cars with baby grand pianos and a historic observation car at the end of the train. Sightseeing excursions are included, and guest lecturers accompany each trip.

Schedule: March through October.

Admission/Fare: Trips range from $1,290.00 to $4,990.00 per person.

Locomotive/Rolling Stock: Two Amtrak locomotives.

Site Address: Varies.
Mailing Address: 2025 First Avenue, Suite 830, Seattle, WA 98121
Telephone: (888) 759-3944 and (206) 441-2725
Fax: (206) 727-7309
E-mail: tcsexp@wolfenet.com

Washington, Snoqualmie

PUGET SOUND RAILWAY HISTORICAL ASSOCIATION
Diesel, scheduled
Standard gauge

PUGET SOUND RAILWAY HISTORICAL ASSOCIATION

Display/Ride: The group offers a ride between Snoqualmie and North Bend. The 1890 Snoqualmie Depot houses the Northwest Railway Museum. Wood and heavy-weight steel cars are pulled by Alco or Fairbanks-Morse diesel locomotives.

Schedule: Train–May through September: weekends. October: Sundays. Museum–year round: Thursday through Monday, 10 a.m. to 5 p.m.

Admission/Fare: Train–adults $7.00; seniors $6.00; children $5.00. Museum–no charge.

Locomotive/Rolling Stock: No. 201, Alco RSD-4 former Kennecott Copper Corp.; no. 1 Fairbanks H12-44 former Weyerhaeuser Timber Co.; miscellaneous rolling stock.

Special Events: Santa Train, November 28, 29 and December 5, 6, 12, 13.

Location/Directions: I-90, westbound exit 27 or eastbound exit 32.

Site Address: 38625 SE King Street, Snoqualmie, WA
Mailing Address: PO Box 459, Snoqualmie, WA 98065
Telephone: (425) 746-4025 or (425) 888-3030
Fax: (425) 888-9311

Washington, Toppenish

YAKIMA VALLEY RAIL AND STEAM MUSEUM
Diesel, scheduled
Standard gauge

HAROLD K. CHANDLER

Ride/Display: This museum operates freight and passenger service on the former Northern Pacific White Swan branch line. Passenger excursions are 20-mile round trips from Harrah to White Swan. The 1911 former NP railroad depot in Toppenish serves as the museum and gift shop. The freight house has been converted to an engine house, where steam locomotive No. 1364 is being restored. The former NP section foreman's house is adjacent to the depot.

Schedule: Train: April-October; Saturdays & Sundays, 1:00 p.m. Museum: daily, summer; weekends, winter. Train: adults $5.00, children $3.00, family $20.00. Museum: adults $2.00, senior citizens & children (under 18) $1.00. Charters available.

Locomotive/Rolling Stock: No. 1364, 1902 Baldwin 4-6-0, former NP; No. B-2070, 1953 120-ton Alco, former U.S. Army. Two 1920s P70 heavyweights, former PRR; No. 588, 1947 coach, former NP; combine, former New Haven.

*Coupon available, see coupon section.

Site Address: 10 Asotin Avenue, Toppenish, WA
Mailing Address: PO Box 889, Toppenish, WA 98948
Telephone: (509) 865-1911

Washington, Yakima   **YAKIMA ELECTRIC RAILWAY MUSEUM**
Electric, scheduled
Standard gauge

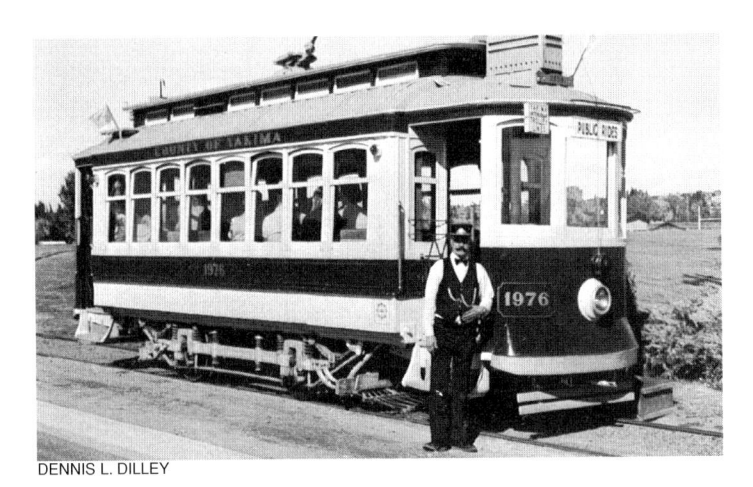

DENNIS L. DILLEY

Ride/Musuem: A 90-minute round trip though city streets, past orchards, and along the Naches River and the shoulder of Yakima Ridge through Selah Gap, over a route established by the former Yakima Valley Transportation Company in 1907. Guided tours of the Car Barn Museum can be requested during public ride hours.

Schedule: May through mid-October: weekends and holidays. Depart Yakima at 10 a.m., 12, 2, and 4 p.m. Depart Selah at 11 a.m., 1, and 3 p.m.; and July through August: Fridays, 7 p.m. Call for Friday night confirmation.

Admission/Fare: Train–adults $4.00; seniors $3.50; children 6-12 $2.50; under age 6 are free with paying adult; families $12.00. Charters available. Museum–donations appreciated.

Locomotive/Rolling Stock: Line Car "A," 1909 Niles 26-ton boxcab converted to line-car use in 1922 (in continuous service since 1909); freight motor no. 298, General Electric 50-ton steeple-cab; nos. 21 & 22, 1930 double-truck Brill Master Units that originally operated in Yakima from 1930 to 1947; nos. 1776 & 1976, single-truck Brill cars from Oporto, Portugal (the same type that operated in Yakima from 1907-1929); others.

Location/Directions: Passengers board at the Yakima Electric Railway Museum Shop at 3rd Avenue and Pine or at the Selah Terminal.

P ✳ ☕ 🏛 ✉ M arm

Site Address: 306 W. Pine, Yakima, WA
Mailing Address: PO Box 649, Yakima, WA 98907
Telephone: (509) 575-1700 and (800) 995-4836
Fax: (509) 453-5088

West Virginia, Cass

CASS SCENIC RAILROAD STATE PARK
Steam, scheduled
Standard gauge

CASS SCENIC RAILROAD

Display: Complete with two switchbacks and a ruling grade of 9 percent, this is the only place in North America where geared locomotives still get a workout. Passengers choose either a 22-mile, 4½-hour round trip to Bald Knob's saddle or an 8-mile, 1½-hour trip to Whittaker Station.

Schedule: Regular season–May 23 through September 7: daily, 10:50 a.m., 1 and 3 p.m. Bald Knob tours: daily except Mondays, 12 p.m. Fall season–September 11-13, 18-20 and October 22-25, 31, November 1. Special Fall Color season–September 26 through October 18: Whittaker tour daily, Bald Knob tour–daily except Mondays. Whittaker Station Dinner Train–mid June through September, most Saturdays, 5:30 p.m. Charters–May through October.

Admission/Fare: Adults $10.00 and up; children $6.00 and up; under age 5 are free. Prices vary with event. Group rates available. Reservations recommended.

Locomotive/Rolling Stock: No. 2 1928 Pacific Coast Shay; no. 4 1922 70-C Shay; no. 5 1905 80-C Shay; no. 6 1945 150C Shay; and more.

Special Events: Spring Railfan Weekend, May 15-17. Other railfan charters during Spring and Fall; call for information.

Nearby Attractions/Accommodations: Cass State Park with on-site accommodations including 13 former mill town rental dwellings, a bed and breakfast.

*Coupon available, see coupon section.

Site Address: Route 66, Cass, WV
Mailing Address: PO Box 107, Cass, WV 24927
Telephone: (304) 456-4300 and (800) CALL-WVA
Fax: (304) 456-4641
E-mail: cassrr@neumedia.net
Internet: www.neumedia.net/~cassrr/

West Virginia, Durbin

DURBIN & GREENBRIER VALLEY RAILROAD
Gasoline, mechanical, scheduled
Standard gauge

DURBIN & GREENBRIER VALLEY RAILROAD

Ride: A 5-mile round trip along the Greenbrier River. The train departs from an orginal 1903 C&O depot and travels through unspoiled scenery in eastern West Virginia.

Schedule: April 1 through September 20: Thursdays through Mondays, 9 a.m. and 12 to 6 p.m. September 21 through November 10: daily except Wednesdays, 8 a.m. to 6 p.m.

Admission/Fare: Adults $5.00; seniors and children 6-12 $4.00; age five and under are free. Group rates and charters are available.

Locomotive/Rolling Stock: 1940 20-ton Whitcomb; open and closed cars; caboose.

Special Events: Civil War Battle Re-enactment, first week of October and last week of April. Durbin Days Celebration, July 17-20.

Nearby Attractions/Accommodations: Monongahela National Forest, Snowshoe Ski Resort, Cass Scenic Railroad, Seneca Rocks National Recreation Area, National Radio Astronomy Observatory.

Location/Directions: U.S. route 250, 38 miles south of Elkins and 20 miles north of Cass.

*Coupon available, see coupon section.

Site Address: East Main Street, Durbin, WV
Mailing Address: PO Box 44, Durbin, WV 26264
Telephone: (304) 456-4935
Fax: (304) 456-4935

West Virginia, Harpers Ferry

HARPERS FERRY TOY TRAIN MUSEUM AND JOY LINE RAILROAD
Railway museum
16" gauge

HARPERS FERRY TOY TRAIN MUSEUM & JOY LINE RAILROAD

Museum/Ride: Passengers ride ¼-mile track aboard a 1953 train traveling over a trestle and past an authentic railroad station brought to Harpers Ferry from Hagerstown, Maryland. The museum houses pre-World War II toy trains.

Schedule: April through October: weekends and holidays.

Admission/Fare: $1.00.

Locomotive/Rolling Stock: Two F7s; miniature steam train; more.

Special Events: Halloween Train.

Nearby Attractions/Accommodations: Harpers Ferry National Park.

Location/Directions: One mile west of Harpers Ferry National Park, on Bakerton Road.

*Coupon available, see coupon section.

Site Address: Bakerton Road, Harper's Ferry, WV
Mailing Address: Route 3, Box 315, Harper's Ferry, WV 25425
Telephone: 9304) 535-2521 and (304) 535-2291

West Virginia, Huntington

COLLIS P. HUNTINGTON RAILROAD HISTORICAL SOCIETY, INC.
Museum and rail excursions

JEAN CHAPMAN

Museum: Museum and rail excursion.

Schedule: Memorial Day through Labor Day: Sundays, 1 to 4 p.m. By appointment year round.

Admission/Fare: Donations appreciated.

Locomotive/Rolling Stock: C&O no. 1308 steam locomotive; two C&O coaches; C&O caboose; operating hand car; dome car; boxcar; and baggage car.

Special Events: Annual New River Train Excursions, October. One-day 300 mile round trips.

Nearby Attractions/Accommodations: Pilgrim Glass, Blenko Glass, Huntington Museum of Art, Radio Museum, CSX and NS mainlines.

Location/Directions: 14th Street, west at Ritter Park just off U.S. route 60 and I-64.

*Coupon available, see coupon section.

Site Address: 7th Avenue & 9th Street, Huntington, WV
Mailing Address: 1429 Chestnut Street, Kenova, WV 25530
Telephone: (304) 453-1641 and (606) 327-7735
Fax: (606) 324-3218
E-mail: railtwo@aol.com

West Virginia, Huntington

MOUNTAIN STATE MYSTERY TOURS
Mainline rail excursions

DIANA BISHOP

Ride: Excursions of varying lengths to destinations with interactive theater on selected dates.

Schedule: Year round.

Admission/Fare: $59 and up.

Locomotive/Rolling Stock: Modern Amtrak Superline equipment.

Special Events: The Official West Virginia State Fair Train. New River Fall Foliage Excursions. Santa Express.

Nearby Attractions/Accommodations: Pilgrim Glass, Blenko Glass, Radio Museum.

Location/Directions: Downtown Huntington, 10th Street & 8th Avenue.

*Coupon available, see coupon section.

Site Address: 1050 8th Avenue, Huntington, WV and other points
Mailing Address: PO Box 8254, Huntington, WV 25705
Telephone: (304) 529-6412 tickets and (800) 225-5982 information

West Virginia, Kingwood

WEST VIRGINIA NORTHERN RAILROAD
Diesel, scheduled; future steam
Standard gauge

BOB ROBINSON

Ride: Ride the rails on the 22-mile trip through two switchbacks and up the mountainside to Tunnelton.

Schedule: May through October: weekends and holidays, 11 a.m. and 3 p.m.

Admission/Fare: Adults $12.00; children $6.00.

Locomotive/Rolling Stock: Original diesels; 1920s passenger coaches; two cabooses.

Special Events: Fall Foliage Tours, Buckwheat Festival.

Nearby Attractions/Accommodations: Restaurants, hotels, historic district of Kingwood.

Location/Directions: I-68, south on route 26 to Kingwood.

Site Address: 156 Sisler Street, Kingwood, WV
Mailing Address: PO Box 424, Kingwood, WV 26537
Telephone: (800) 253-1065 and (304) 329-3333
Internet: www.wvnr.com

West Virginia, Romney

POTOMAC EAGLE
SCENIC RAIL EXCURSIONS
Diesel, scheduled
Standard gauge

DAVID W. CORBITT

Ride: Diesel-powered, open-window coach train takes passengers on a 3-hour round trip through the beautiful West Virginia wilderness. Passengers ride the rails along the clear and tranquil waters of the Potomac River's South Branch and watch for American bald eagles that have returned to this remote valley and made it their home.

Schedule: May 16 through June 27: Saturdays, 1 p.m. July 4 through September 6: weekends, 10 a.m. and 2 p.m. September 12 through September 27: Saturdays, 10 a.m. and 2 p.m. and Sundays 1 p.m. September 28 through October 25: Mondays through Fridays, 1 p.m. and weekends, 10 a.m. and 2 p.m.

Admission/Fare: Coach–adults $18.00-$20.00; seniors $16.00-$18.00; children 3-12 $10.00-$12.00. First Class Club Car $38.00-$44.00.

Locomotive/Rolling Stock: GP9s, former Baltimore & Ohio; F units, former CSX; 1920s open-window coaches, former CN; 1950s era lounge car, former C&O.

Special Events: All-day round trips to Romney/Petersburg: May 30, June 27, July 25, August 29, September 26, October 3 and 24. Memorial Day, July 4, and Labor Day events.

Location/Directions: Train departs Wappocomo Station, one mile north of Romney on route 28.

Site Address: Route 28, Romney WV
Mailing Address: Station Agent, PO Box 657, Romney, WV 26757
Telephone: (800) 22-EAGLE
Fax: (304) 485-5901
Internet: wvweb.com/www/potomac_eagle/

Wisconsin, East Troy

EAST TROY ELECTRIC RAILROAD
WISCONSIN TROLLEY MUSEUM
Electric, scheduled
Standard gauge

SCOTT PATRICK

Ride: The museum offeres 10-mile round trip trolley rides over their original 1907 trolley line. The museum also offers dinner and afternoon tea trains on America's only all-electric dinner train in regular service. Photos, videos, and historic exhibits are on display in the museum's depot.

Schedule: Trolleys–May 23 through October 25: Saturdays, Sundays, holidays, 11:30 a.m. to 4 p.m. June 17 through August 14: Wednesdays through Fridays, 11 a.m. and 1 p.m. Dinner/tea trains–May 10, June 21 and 28, July 26, August 8, September 13 and 26, October 3, 17, 24, and 31.

Admission/Fare: Trolley–adults $8.00; children 3-11 $4.00. Dinner train–$45.00. Tea train–$22.50.

Locomotive/Rolling Stock: CSS&SB 9, 11, 24, 35, 111; CTA S105, 4420, 4453; Duluth-Superior Streetcar 253; P&W 64; ETER 21; more.

Special Events: Annual Trolley Festival: May 17, 18. Transportation Heritage Day, June 21. Model Railroad Weekend, September 26-27. Fall Fun Days, September 26 through October 25.

Nearby Attractions/Accommodations: Located 45 minutes from Milwaukee and 30 minutes from Lake Geneva resort area. Elegant Farmer, Wisconsin's largest farm market. Many historic attractions, restaurants, two hotels, and a campground in East Troy area.

Location/Directions: I-43 and Highway 20, 35 miles southwest of Milwaukee.

Site Address: 2002 Church Street, East Troy, WI
Mailing Address: PO Box 556, Waukesha, WI 53187-0556
Telephone: (414) 548-3837
Fax: (414) 548-0400

Wisconsin, Eau Claire

CHIPPEWA VALLEY RAILROAD ASSOCIATION
Steam, diesel
16" gauge

CHIPPEWA VALLEY RAILROAD

Ride/Display: A ½-mile ride through the woods of Carson Park, Eau Claire, Wisconsin. Depot, roundhouse, turntable, Soo Line Pacific no. 2719, 4-6-2, Alco 1923, National Register, Standard G, under restoration; Chicago & North Western interlocking tower (last operating tower in Wisconsin).

Schedule: Memorial Day through Labor Day: Sundays.

Admission/Fare: Adults $1.00; children $ .50.

Locomotive/Rolling Stock: Two 4-4-0 steam locomotives; miniature train G-16 diesel; Soo line no. 2719 4-6-2 standard display.

M Tomah, WI and Minneapolis, MN

Site Address: Carson Park Drive, Carson Park, Eau Claire, WI
Mailing Address: PO Box 925, Eau Claire, WI 54702
Telephone: (715) 835-7500
Fax: (715) 835-1411
E-mail: steam@discover-net.net

Wisconsin, Green Bay

NATIONAL RAILROAD MUSEUM
Railway museum
Standard gauge

NATIONAL RAILROAD MUSEUM

Ride/Display: Visitors to this museum can take a 20-minute train ride in vintage equipment, enjoy the "Rails to America" theater show, and embark on guided or self-guided tours of the equipment displays. On the train, the uniformed conductor talks about hobo history, the museum, and local points of interest. Established in 1958, this museum holds more than 70 historic locomotives and railroad cars, and more.

Schedule: Museum–daily, 9 a.m. to 5 p.m. Train–May 1 through October 15. Guided tours–May 29 through September 4. Closed Easter, Thanksgiving, Christmas, and New Year's Day.

Admission/Fare: May 1 through October 15: adults $6.00; seniors $5.00; students 6-15 $3.00; children under age six are free; families $16.00. October 16 through April 30: half-price admission. Group rates available.

Locomotive/Rolling Stock: No. 4017 4-8-8-4, former Union Pacific; no. 24 2-8-0, former Lake Superior & Ishpeming; no. 2718, 4-6-2, former Soo Line; more.

Special Events: Boxcar Willie Concert, March. Antique Auto Show, Memorial Day weekend. Railfest. Thomas the Tank and Friends Event. Railroad Memorabilia Show & Auction. Football Train. Pumpkin Train. Special Dinner Train charters. More.

Location/Directions: Highway 172 to Ashland Avenue (business highway 41), travel north to Cormier Avenue and east three blocks.

*Coupon available, see coupon section.

Site Address: 2285 S. Broadway, Green Bay, WI
Mailing Address: 2285 S. Broadway, Green Bay, WI 54304
Telephone: (920) 437-7623
Fax: (920) 437-1291
E-mail: staff@nationalrrmuseum.org
Internet: www.nationalrrmuseum.org

Wisconsin, Laona

CAMP FIVE MUSEUM FOUNDATION, INC.
Logging museum
Steam, scheduled

CAMP FIVE MUSEUM FOUNDATION, INC.

Ride/Display: Camp Five offers visitors a unique mix of history, steam railroading, and ecology. Visitors ride the *Lumberjack Special* steam train to the museum complex; once there, take a guided surrey tour through beautiful forests managed on a perpetual-cycle basis. A hayrack/pontoon ride on the Rat River is also an optional offer. Logging museum with an early-transportation wing and an active blacksmith shop; half-hour steam engine video; nature center with northern Wisconsin wildlife diorama; petting corral; large outdoor display of logging artifacts.

Schedule: Mid-June through August: daily, 11 a.m., 12, 1, and 2 p.m.

Admission/Fare: Adults $14.00; students 13-17 $9.00; children 4-12 $4.75; families $38.00. Group discounts available.

Locomotive/Rolling Stock: 1916 Vulcan 2-6-2; cupola cabooses.

Special Events: Heritage Celebration, August. Fall Color Tours, September and October. The Hayrack/Pontoon Trip through a Natural Wildlife Refuge. Call or write for information.

Location/Directions: West of Laona on Highway 8.

*Coupon available, see coupon section.

Site Address: Highway 8, Laona, WI
Mailing Address: RFD #1, Laona, WI 54541
Telephone: (715) 674-3414 and (800) 774-3414

Wisconsin, Milwaukee

ZOOFARI EXPRESS
MILWAUKEE COUNTY ZOO
Steam, diesel, unscheduled
15" gauge

MIKE NEPPER

Ride: This railroad has operated at the Milwaukee County Zoo since 1958, carrying over 13 million riders. The 1.25-mile trip across zoo property lasts about 8 minutes.

Schedule: Easter through the end of October: daily, usually 10 a.m. to 4 p.m. weather permitting.

Admission/Fare: Zoo admission required–adults $7.50; children 3-12 $5.50; parking $5.00. Train–adults $2.00; children 3-12 $1.00.

Locomotive/Rolling Stock: Sandley light locomotive and rolling stock–coal-fired steam locomotive 4-6-2 no. 1924; coal-fired steam locomotive 4-4-2 no. 1916; diesel hydraulic switcher no. 1958; F2 diesel hydraulic no. 1996; 16 twelve-passenger day coaches nos. 1080-1096.

Nearby Attractions/Accommodations: Wisconsin State Fair Park, Summerfest Grounds, Milwaukee County Stadium, Milwaukee Public Museum, Mitchell Park Domes, Wehr Nature Center, Whitnall Boerner Botanical Gardens, Cool Waters Water Park, Best Western Midway, Holiday Inn Express, Sheraton Inn Mayfair, Excel Inn, many restaurants and area attractions.

Location/Directions: Zoo is located 8 miles west of downtown Milwaukee at the intersection of I-94, I-894, and Highway 45.

Site Address: 10001 W. Bluemound Road, Milwaukee, WI
Mailing Address: 10001 W. Bluemound Road, Milwaukee, WI 53226
Telephone: (414) 771-3040
Fax: (414) 256-5410
Internet: www.omnifest.uwm.edu/zoo/

Wisconsin, New London   **NEW LONDON HISTORICAL SOCIETY**
Railway display

Display: Restored CNW depot complete with railroad artifacts.

Schedule: June through August: first and third Sundays, 1 to 4 p.m. or by appointment.

Admission/Fare: Donations appreciated.

Locomotive/Rolling Stock: Soo Line caboose no. 138; CNW caboose no. 11153.

Special Events: Rail Fest Days, second Sunday in August.

Nearby Attractions/Accommodations: Rainbow Restaurant, Mosquito Hill Nature Center.

Location/Directions: 45N to Bus. 45, High Street east to railroad tracks, north to the depot.

Site Address: 900 Montgomery Street, New London, WI
Mailing Address: 612 W. Beacon Avenue, New London, WI 54961-1322
Telephone: (920) 982-5186 and (920) 982-8557

Wisconsin, North Freedom

MID-CONTINENT RAILWAY HISTORICAL SOCIETY
Steam, scheduled
Standard gauge

WILLIAM RAIA

Ride: Mid-Continent, which has operated steam trains at North Freedom since 1963, is dedicated to preserving turn-of-the-century railroading. Its line and equipment are historic, all a part of the "golden age of railroading." The 7-mile, 50-minute "Experience 1900" round trip takes passengers on a former Chicago & North Western branch line built in 1903 to serve iron mines. Trains depart from a restored 1894 C&NW depot. The museum is nationally known for its wooden passenger and freight cars; restored equipment is displayed in the coach shed. The collection also includes locomotives, snowplows (including a 1912 steam rotary), and steam wreckers. Artifact and photography exhibits are in the depot and the coach shed.

Schedule: Call or write for information.

Admission/Fare: Call or write for information.

Locomotive/Rolling Stock: No. 1385, 1907 Alco 4-6-0, former C&NW; no. 2, 1912 Baldwin 2-8-2, former Saginaw Timber; more.

Special Events: Numerous. Call or write for information.

Location/Directions: In Sauk County, seven miles west of Baraboo. Follow route 136 west to PF, then turn south to North Freedom. The depot is ½-mile west of the four-way stop in North Freedom.

*See advertisement on page A-14.

P ✳ ☕ 🎟 M arm TRAIN

Site Address: North Freedom, WI
Mailing Address: PO Box 358, North Freedom, WI 53951-0358
Telephone: (800) 930-1385
Email: midcon@baraboo.com
Internet: www.mcrwy.com

Wisconsin, North Lake

KETTLE MORAINE RAILWAY
Steam, scheduled
Standard gauge

R.M. HINEBAUGH

Ride: The Kettle Moraine Railway offers a train ride back in time, when life was a little simpler. The train departs an 1889 refurbished depot making an 8-mile round trip, which takes approximately 50 minutes. This nostalgic ride behind a steam engine is both educational and recreational.

Schedule: June through September and Labor Day: Sundays, 12:30, 2:00, and 3:30 p.m. First three weekends in October: Saturdays, 12:30, 2:00, and 3:30 p.m. and Sundays, 11 a.m., 12:30, 2:00 p.m.

Admission/Fare: Adults $8.00; children 3-11 $4.50; under age three ride free unless occupying a seat.

Locomotive/Rolling Stock: EMD gas electric no. 1000; 1917 65-ton Heisler no. 3, former Craig Mt. Railroad; 1943 Davenport gas powered 0-4-0 switcher no. 3.

Special Events: Goblin Express, first three Saturdays in October, 7 p.m. Thomas the Tank Engine. Call or write for information and dates.

Nearby Attractions/Accommodations: Holy Hill, Honey Acres, Hartford Car Museum, Delafield Stagecoach Inn (restored).

Location/Directions: I-94, north on Highway 83 (exit 287), 9 miles to North Lake. Look for signs.

Site Address: Intersection of Highways 83 and VV
Mailing Address: Box 247, North Lake, WI 53064
Telephone: (414) 782-8074

Wisconsin, Osceola

OSCEOLA & ST. CROIX VALLEY RAILWAY
MINNESOTA TRANSPORTATION MUSEUM

Steam, diesel, scheduled
Standard gauge

MORT JORGENSON

Ride: Enjoy the scenic St. Croix River Valley on a 90-minute round trip between Osceola, Wisconsin, and Marine-on-St. Croix, Minnesota, or a 45-minute round trip through rural Wisconsin between Osceola and Dresser. See the restored Osceola Historical Depot, featuring exhibits about railroading and the Osceola area. U.S. Railway Post Office exhibits aboard Northern Pacific triple combine no. 1102.

Schedule: Memorial Day through October: weekends and holidays. Charters available during the week.

Admission/Fare: Marine trip–$8.00 to $12.00; Dresser trip–$5.00 to $9.00.

Locomotive/Rolling Stock: Northern Pacific no. 328 4-6-0 steam locomotive; NP no. 105 LST&T switcher engine; nos. 2604 and 2608 cars, former Rock Island; NP triple combine car no. 1102.

Special Events: Romance on the Rails, June. Fireworks Express, July. Hi/Low Bridge Steam Trip, August. Fall Leaves Trip, September.

Nearby Attractions/Accommodations: Cascade Falls, St. Croix River Aveda Spa, St. Croix Center for the Arts, motels, and campgrounds.

Location/Directions: I-35W north at Forest Lake, Highway 97 east to Highway 45 north, to I-243 across the St. Croix, to Highway 35, south to Depot Road.

*Coupon available, see coupon section.

Site Address: 114 Depot Road, Osceola, WI
Mailing Address: PO Box 176, Osceola, WI 54020
Telephone: (800) 711-2591 and (612) 228-0263
Fax: (715) 294-3330
E-mail: oscvrlwy@win.bnight.net
Internet: www.arc.umn.edu/~wes/mtm/oscv.html

Wisconsin, Platteville

THE MINING MUSEUM AND ROLLO JAMISON MUSEUM

Museum/Ride: The Mining Museum tells the story of lead and zinc mining in the Upper Mississippi Valley. Visitors tour an 1845 lead mine and ride (above ground) in converted ore cars pulled by a 1931 Whitcomb locomotive used in a local zinc mine.

Schedule: May through October: daily. November through April: Mondays through Fridays, self-guided tour areas and office open. Group tours year round with reservation. Train ride weather permitting.

Admission/Fare: Tours–adults $4.00; seniors $3.50; children 5-15 $2.00; under age five are free. Train–$ .50.

Locomotive/Rolling Stock: 1931 Whitcomb locomotive no. 13193.

Special Events: Heritage Day, July 4. Christmas exhibit including toy train layout.

Nearby Attractions/Accommodations: University of Wisconsin-Platteville. Chicago Bears training camp.

Location/Directions: Located at intersection of Main Street and Virginia Avenue, three blocks north of Highway 151.

Site Address: 405 E. Main Street, Platteville, WI
Mailing Address: PO Box 780, Platteville, WI 53818-0780
Telephone: (608) 348-3301
Fax: (608) 348-6098

Wisconsin, Spooner

RAILROAD MEMORIES MUSEUM
Railroad museum

RAILROAD MEMORIES MUSEUM

Display: The old CNW/Omaha depot houses the Railroad Memories Museum which is dedicated to Spooner's railroad heritage and railroading world-wide. There are eight rooms full of artifacts, tools, memorabilia, art, rare uniforms, history, reference books, track inspection vehicles and many working lights, bells, and horns. A VCR provides long-running videos of all aspects of railroading. There is also a G gauge model elevated in the main room, with both a steam freight and a diesel passenger running.

Schedule: Memorial weekend through Labor Day weekend: daily, 10 a.m. to 5 p.m. Groups by appointment.

Admission/Fare: Adults $3.00; children 6-12 $ .50; under age 6 are free.

Special Events: Historical Railroad Days, July 17-18.

Nearby Attractions/Accommodations: Wisconsin Great Northern Railroad excursion train, wood carving museum, Heart O' North Rodeo, State Fish Hatchery (largest Mmusky hatchery in the world).

Location/Directions: In an old CNW depot, downtown, east end of Walnut Street.

Site Address: Front Street, Spooner, WI
Mailing Address: N8425 Island Lake Road, Spooner, WI 54801
Telephone: (715) 635-3325 and (715) 635-7252

Wisconsin, Wisconsin Dells

RIVERSIDE & GREAT NORTHERN RAILWAY
Steam, scheduled
15" gauge

MARSHALL L. "PETE" DEETS

Ride: A beautiful 3-mile ride through the natural Wisconsin Dells countryside along the Wisconsin River.

Schedule: Mid-May to Memorial Day and Labor Day to mid-October: weekends, 10 a.m. to 4 p.m. Memorial Day to Labor Day: daily, 10 a.m. to 6 p.m.

Admission/Fare: Call or write for information.

Locomotive/Rolling Stock: No. 82, 1957 4-4-0, former Milwaukee County Zoo; vertical-boilered "Tom Thumb"; no. 95, SW style diesel.

Nearby Attractions/Accommodations: Mid-Continent Railway Museum, North Freedom, WI.

Location/Directions: Stand Rock Road north to right on County N, go under the bridge, turn left to our parking lot.

[&] [P] [🚌] [✽] M [🚂]

Site Address: N115 County Road N, Wisconsin Dells, WI
Mailing Address: N115 County Road N, Wisconsin Dells, WI 53965
Telephone: (608) 254-6367
Fax: (608) 254-6886
E-mail: rgnrick@aol.com
Internet: members.aol.com/rgnrick/rgn.htm

Wyoming, Cheyenne

WYOMING TRANSPORTATION MUSEUM AND LEARNING CENTER
Transportation museum

WYOMING STATE MUSEUM LIBRARY

Museum: Transportation displays housed in the historic Union Pacific depot.

Schedule: Year round: Tuesdays through Fridays, 9 a.m. to 2 p.m. and other times by appointment. Group tours available.

Admission/Fare: $1.00.

Special Events: Brewer's Festival, Father's Day weekend. Fine Arts Show, last full weekend in July.

Nearby Attractions/Accommodations: Capitol, Wyoming State Museum.

Location/Directions: I-80, Central Avenue exit to 16th Street.

Site Address: Capitol and 15th Street, Cheyenne, WY
Mailing Address: PO Box 704, Cheyenne, WY 82003-0704
Telephone: (307) 637-3376
Fax: (307) 634-9349

Alberta, Calgary   **HERITAGE PARK HISTORICAL VILLAGE**
Steam, electric, scheduled
Standard gauge

HERITAGE PARK HISTORICAL VILLAGE

Ride/Display: With more than 100 restored buildings and exhibits assembled from many parts of western Canada, Heritage Park is an authentic living memorial to pre-1914 western settlement. A visit begins with a 7-minute streetcar ride from the Fourteenth Street entrance over a winding route to the park's main gate. Inside, a steam train operates continuously on a 20-minute schedule. Exhibits include original stations from Bowell, Laggan, Midnapore, and Shepard; water tank; sand tower; six-stall roundhouse; railway car shop; single-track engine shed; no. 76, 1882 business car, used at Last Spike ceremonies on completion of the Canadian Pacific Railway, November 7, 1885; no. 100, 1901 private car, former Dominion of Canada no. 100 (Prime Minister's car); no. 5, 1902 business car "Pacific"; no. 141, 1907 suburban coach; Canadian Pacific wooden colonist cars, coaches; freight cars; work equipment.

Schedule: May 16 through August 31: daily, 9 a.m. to 5 p.m. September through October 11: weekends only.

Admission/Fare: Call or write for information.

Locomotive/Rolling Stock: Extensive collection.

Special Events: Railway Days. Call or write for information.

Nearby Attractions/Accommodations: Calgary Stampede, Calgary Tower.

Location/Directions: Follow Heritage Drive west.

Site Address: 1900 Heritage Drive SW, Calgary, AB
Mailing Address: 1900 Heritage Drive SW, Calgary, AB T2V 2X3
Telephone: (403) 259-1900
Fax: (403) 252-3528
E-mail: heritage@heritagepark.org
Internet: www.heritagepark.ab.ca *or* www.heritagepark.org

Alberta, Edmonton

FORT EDMONTON PARK
Steam, scheduled
Standard gauge

FORT EDMONTON PARK

Display: Nestled in Edmonton's river valley, Fort Edmonton Park is brought to life by costumed staff reenacting life as it was in Edmonton at the 1846 fur trading fort, and on the streets of 1885, 1905, and 1920. The train transports visitors through the Park.

Schedule: May 17 through September 7: daily, Sundays in September.

Admission/Fare: Adults $6.75; seniors and youth 13-17 $5.00; children 2-12 $3.25; families $20.00. Price includes train ride.

Locomotive/Rolling Stock: 1919 Baldwin 2-6-2 no. 107, former Oakdale & Gulf Railway (restored to its 1905 appearance).

Special Events: Call or write for information.

Nearby Attractions/Accommodations: Downtown Edmonton and West Edmonton Mall.

Location/Directions: Edmonton, Alberta.

Site Address: Fox Drive & Whitemud Drive, Edmonton, Alberta
Mailing Address: PO Box 2359, Edmonton, AB Canada T5J 2R7
Telephone: (403) 496-8787
Fax: (403) 496-8797
Internet: www.gov.edmonton.ab.ca/fort

British Columbia, Cranbrook

CANADIAN MUSEUM OF RAIL TRAVEL
Railway museum
Standard gauge

WALTER LANZ

Display: This static display portrays the elegant lifestyle aboard trains of the past. Plans call for five complete train sets, under cover, by 1998. Several pieces for these future consists are now in storage. The centerpiece is an entire set of the Canadian Pacific Railway's 1929 "flag train," the *Trans-Canada Limited,* featuring restored inlaid woods, brass fixtures, plush upholstery, and wool carpets. The 1900-era Elko Station is the visitor center and gift shop. The dining car is often open for tea, coffee, and light refreshments.

Schedule: Summer: daily, 8 a.m. to 8 p.m. Winter: Tuesdays through Saturdays, 12 to 5 p.m.; Shoulder seasons: daily 10 a.m. to 6 p.m.

Admission/Fare: Varies. Grand Tour tickets recommended.

Locomotive/Rolling Stock: "River Rouge" solarium lounge car; day parlor car no. 6751; sleepers "Rutherglen," "Glencassie," "Somerset"; dining car "Argyle"; baggage-sleeper car no. 4489; 1928 business car "British Columbia"; baggage car no. 4481, former CPR with HO train layout; more.

Special Events: School programs, September thorugh May. Christmas dinners.

Nearby Attractions/Accommodations: Fort Steele Heritage Town, Bavarian City, Splash Zone Water Park, camping, lodging, restaurants.

Location/Directions: Downtown Cranbrook, Highway 3/95.

Site Address: 1 Van Horne Street, Cranbrook, BC
Mailing Address: Box 400, Cranbrook, BC V1C 4H9
Telephone: (250) 489-3918
Fax: (250) 489-5744
E-mail: camal@cyberlink.bc.ca
Internet: www.cyberlink.bc.ca/~camal

British Columbia, Duncan

BRITISH COLUMBIA FOREST MUSEUM
Steam, scheduled
36" gauge

BRITISH COLUMBIA FOREST MUSEUM

Museum: The B.C. Forest Museum is located on 100 acres just north of Duncan. The train travels the circumference of the area, showing B.C. Forest heritage. There are also exhibits, demonstrations, and historical collections.

Schedule: May through September: daily, 9:30 a.m. to 6 p.m. First train departs at 10:30 a.m. and last train departs at 5 p.m.

Admission/Fare: Adults $7.00; seniors and students 13-18 $6.00; children 5-12 $4.00; under age 5 are free.

Locomotive/Rolling Stock: Shay locomotive no. 1.

Special Events: National Forestry Week, Mother's Day, Father's Day, Classic Tractors, picnic, Celebration of Steam Weekend, Labor Day Celebration.

Nearby Attractions/Accommodations: Duncan Totem Tours, Native Heritage Centre, Chemainus Murals.

Location/Directions: Located five minutes north of Duncan off Highway 1.

Site Address: 2892 Drinkwater Road, Duncan, BC
Mailing Address: 2892 Drinkwater Road, Duncan, BC Canada V9L 3W8
Telephone: (250) 715-1113
Fax: (250) 715-1170
E-mail: bcfm@islandnet.com
Internet: www.bcforestmuseum.com

British Columbia, North Vancouver

BC RAIL, LTD.
Steam, scheduled
Standard gauge

BC RAIL, LTD.

Ride: BC Rail offers a spectacular 80-mile, six-hour round trip to Squamish including a two-hour stopover there. Heading the train is no. 2860, a stainless-steel-jacketed "Royal Hudson"; resplendent in polished maroon and black, it makes a fine sight at the head of its tuscan-red passenger train. The highly scenic route takes passengers along the coast of Howe Sound where they view the island-dotted sea on one side and coastal mountains on the other. Passage available in standard class or parlor class (a restored vintage dining car). Train-boat option also available.

Schedule: May 30 through September 20: Wednesdays through Sundays, 10 a.m. departure.

Admission/Fare: Adults $46.50; seniors/youth $40.50; children $12.75; under age five are free. Parlor Class $89.75. Reservations required.

Locomotive/Rolling Stock: No. 2860, 1940 Montreal 4-6-4, former Canadian Pacific no. 3716, 1912 Montreal 2-8-0, former CP; power car, 11 coaches, 2 cafe lounge cars, 1 parlor car.

Location/Directions: Located at the foot of Pemberton Street, a 20-minute ride from downtown Vancouver.

[♿] [P] [🚌] [✳] [☕] [✉] [🚂] Vancouver

Site Address: 1311 West First Street, North Vancouver, BC
Mailing Address: PO Box 8770, Vancouver, BC Canada V6B 4X6
Telephone: (604) 631-3500 and (800) 663-8238
Fax: (604) 984-5505
E-mail: passinfo@bcrail.com
Internet: www.bcrail.com

British Columbia, Port Alberni

WESTERN VANCOUVER ISLAND INDUSTRIAL HERITAGE SOCIETY
Steam, scheduled
Standard gauge

BERT SIMPSON

Ride/Display: A 3-mile round trip along the industrial waterfront on MacMillan Bloedel Yard trackage and a historical display and gift shop in the restored 1912 Port Alberni Station.

Schedule: July 1 through Labor Day: weekends and statutory holidays, 11 a.m. to 4 p.m.

Admission/Fare: Adults $3.00; children $2.00.

Locomotive/Rolling Stock: No. 2, "Two Spot," 1912 Lima 42-ton 2-truck Shay; no. 7, 1928 Baldwin 90-ton 2-8-2 ST; no. 11, 1942 General Electric 45-ton diesel-electric; no. 1, 1928 Westminster Iron Works Buda gas switcher; no. 8427, Montreal Locomotive Works/Alco RS-3 diesel; no. 107 1927 Plymouth 8-ton gas switcher; more.

Rolling Stock/Equipment: Two modified cabooses, former Canadian National; early 1900s Victoria Lumber & Manufacturing Co. crew car.

Special Events: Grand Opening Parade of Locomotives and Vintage Trucks, July 1 weekend. Santa Claus Run, Sunday before Christmas.

Nearby Attractions/Accommodations: The Station is the entrance to Harbour Quay, the departure point for the Lady Rose/Frances Barclay cruises down the Alberni Inlet to the Vancouver Island west coast.

Location/Directions: Harbour Quay in Port Alberni on Vancouver Island.

[P] 🚌 ✳ ☕ 🚻 🎨 ✉ M
Radio frequency: 160.305

Site Address: 3100 Kingsway Avenue, Port Alberni, BC Canada
Mailing Address: 3100 Kingsway Avenue, Port Alberni, BC Canada V9Y 3B1
Telephone: (250) 723-2118 station and (250) 724-0346 roundhouse

British Columbia, Prince George

FORT GEORGE RAILWAY
Steam, unscheduled
2' gauge

Display: One-half mile track.

Schedule: May 24 through Labor Day weekend: weekends and holidays, 12 to 4 p.m. Charters available.

Admission/Fare: $1.00; children under age 3 are free.

Locomotive/Rolling Stock: 1912 Steam engine built in Davenport, Iowa; two 25-seat coaches.

Nearby Attractions/Accommodations: City of Prince George.

Location/Directions: Fort George Park.

*Coupon available, see coupon section.

[&] [P] [⊼] VIA

Site Address: Fort George Park, Prince George, BC
Mailing Address: 101 Freeman Street, Prince George, BC Canada V2M 2P6
Telephone: (250) 564-4764

British Columbia, Prince George

PRINCE GEORGE RAILWAY & FORESTRY MUSEUM
Railway museum
Standard gauge

ROY SMITH

Display: This museum houses a large collection of railway buildings, rolling stock, and equipment, complemented by the Fire Hall, housing a 1929 Reo fire truck, a 1948 fire truck, and a horse-drawn fire sleigh. The pioneer building contains a large telephone display and an operating telegraph system. A turn-of-the-century bunkhouse shows how the Yelanka, a local ethnic group, lived while working on the railway. Logging displays include a 1930 band saw, a 1950 gang saw, and several pieces of logging road equipment.

Schedule: Mid-May through September: daily, 10 a.m. to 5 p.m.

Admission/Fare: Adults $3.00; children under age 14 $1.50; family of five $8.00.

Locomotive/Rolling Stock: 1899 caboose; 1906 locomotive; five diesels; 1913 operating steam crane.

Special Events: Steam Days, four times each year. Call or write for dates.

Nearby Attractions/Accommodations: Downtown Prince George.

Location/Directions: Cottonwood Island Park adjacent to CN Rail Yards.

Site Address: River Road, Cottonwood Island, Prince George, BC
Mailing Address: PO Box 2408, Prince George, BC Canada V2N 2S6
Telephone: (250) 563-7351
Fax: (250) 563-7351

British Columbia, Prince Rupert

KWINITSA RAILWAY STATION MUSEUM
Railway museum

KWINITSA RAILWAY STATION MUSEUM

Museum: The Kwinitsa Railway Station Museum is housed in an authentic 1912 Grand Trunk Pacific Railway station. Several rooms are restored to their original state, including the telegrapher's office and living quarters, and the bunkroom for the section crew. This award-winning museum also features exhibits chronicling the early history of Prince Rupert and its role as the terminus of the Grand Trunk Railway. Videos depicting railway construction in 1911 and the operation of this and similar stations along the Skeena River complement the exhibits. In the old waiting room a small gift shop offers books on the railway and souvenirs. The scenic ocean-front location and the adjacent park make this an excellent place to visit.

Schedule: June through September 6: daily, 9 to 12 a.m. and 1 to 5 p.m.

Admission/Fare: Donations appreciated.

Nearby Attractions/Accommodations: Museum of Northern British Columbia.

Location/Directions: Located on the city of Prince Rupert's scenic waterfront at the western terminus of the CNR and Highway 16.

[P] [✱] [⛝] [✉]

Site Address: Prince Rupert, BC
Mailing Address: PO Box 669, Prince Rupert, BC Canada V8J 3S1
Telephone: (250) 624-3207 and (250) 627-1915
Fax: (250) 627-8009

British Columbia, Revelstoke

REVELSTOKE RAILWAY MUSEUM
Railway museum

REVELSTOKE RAILWAY MUSEUM

Display: This new, unique museum was built to honor the builders of the Canadian Pacific Railway. The three galleries in the museum take you through the development, construction, and present day operation of the railway.

Schedule: July, August: daily, 9 a.m. to 8 p.m. May, June, September: daily, 9 a.m. to 5 p.m. April, October, November: Mondays through Fridays, 9 a.m. to 5 p.m. Winter months the museum closes for renovations but opens for personal or group tours by appointment.

Admission/Fare: Adults $5.00; seniors $3.00; students $2.00; families $10.00.

Locomotive/Rolling Stock: Mikado 2-8-2 engine 5468; business car no. 4; flange car; snow plow; more.

Nearby Attractions/Accommodations: Revelstoke Dam on the Columbia River, Piano Museum, Local City Museum, Glacier and Mount Revelstoke National Parks.

Location/Directions: On the Trans Canada Highway, midway between Vancouver, BC and Calgary, AB. It is a gorgeous 3½-hour drive through the Rockies from Banff.

Site Address: 719 Track West, Revelstoke, BC
Mailing Address: PO Box 3018, Revelstoke, BC Canada V0E 2S0
Telephone: (250) 837-6060
Fax: (250) 837-3732
E-mail: railway@junction.net
Internet: railwaymuseum.com

British Columbia, Squamish

WEST COAST RAILWAY HERITAGE PARK

WEST COAST RAILWAY

Display/Ride: See over 60 vintage railway cars and locomotives. Ride on a miniature railway through the park.

Schedule: May through October: daily, 10 a.m. to 5 p.m. Group tours year round and at other times by appointment.

Admission/Fare: Adults $4.50; seniors and children $3.50; families $12.00.

Locomotive/Rolling Stock: No. 551, 65-ton, former PGE; no. 53, former CP; no. 960, former B.C. Electric; 2-8-2 no. 16, former Comox Logging & Railway; nos. 4069 and 4459, both former CP; others. "Bell Island" sleeper no. 2183, former CP; colonist car no. 2514 and observation no. 598, both former CP; cafe-observations nos. 1090 & 1057, both former Great Northern; diner "Dunraven," former Canadian National. Snowplow no. 55365, former CN; Jordan spreader no. 402846 and steam crane no. 414330, both former CP; cabooses nos. 1817 and 1821, former PGE; transfer caboose, former GN; more.

Special Events: Many throughout the year. Call or write for information.

Nearby Attractions/Accommodations: Brittania Mines, windsurfing, Eagle viewing, lodging.

Location/Directions: Located 2 miles (3 km) north of downtown Squamish, follow Railway Heritage Park signs on Highway 99.

*Coupon available, see coupon section.

Site Address: 39645 Government Road, Squamish, BC
Mailing Address: Box 2790, Stn. Terminal, Vancouver, BC Canada V6B 3X2
Telephone: (604) 898-9336 and (800) 722-1233
Fax: (604) 898-9349
Internet: www.wcra.org

British Columbia, Surrey

BEAR CREEK MINIATURE TRAIN
Diesel, steam, unscheduled
15" gauge

J. COWAN

Ride: A ⅝-mile, 8-minute ride in Bear Creek Park's forest and gardens, through a tunnel and over a trestle.

Schedule: January through November: daily, 10 a.m. to dark. December: 10 a.m. to 9 p.m. for Christmas lights.

Admission/Fare: Adults $2.00; seniors and children $1.50. Group discounts available.

Locomotive/Rolling Stock: 1967 Dutch-built steam engine based on Welsh mining design; 1988 Alankeef diesel locomotive; covered British antique coaches.

Special Events: Winterfest light display, December. Canada Day, July 1.

Nearby Attractions/Accommodations: Bear Creek Park is a 160-acre park with picnic facilities, art center, playground, water park, skate bowl, five-acre landscaped garden, walking trails, and sports fields.

Location/Directions: Twelve miles from U.S. border via King George Highway, 20 miles from downtown Vancouver.

Site Address: 13750 88th Avenue, Surrey, B.C.
Mailing Address: 13750 88th Avenue, Surrey, B.C. V32W 3L1
Telephone: (604) 501-1232 and (604) 594-2404
Fax: (604) 594-2331

British Columbia, Vancouver   **ROCKY MOUNTAINEER RAILTOURS**
Electric, scheduled
Standard gauge

ROCKY MOUNTAINEER RAILTOUR

Ride: Rocky Mountaineer Railtours is a two-day, all daylight train tour operating between May and October. Beginning in Vancouver, Calgary, Banff or Jasper, the train travels east- and westbound through the spectacular scenery of British Columbia, Alberta and the Canadian Rockies. All *GoldLeaf Dome* and *Signature Service* guests enjoy two days onboard the Rocky Mountaineer, overnight accommodations in Kamloops, breakfast and lunch daily with exemplary service and magnificent views. This tour can be combined with a variety of independent package tours and customized group programs.

Schedule: Call or write for information.

Admission/Fare: Call or write for information.

Locomotive/Rolling Stock: Nos. 800, 804, 805, 806, and 807 General Motors GP40-2 locomotives.

Passenger Cars: Seventeen Dayniter 44-seat coaches, 1954 Canadian Car and Foundry, rebuilt 1972 and 1985-88; 20 cafe coaches; 48-seat no. 5749; 1949 Pullman, four 72-seat bi-level dome coaches; Rader Railcar.

Site Address: Vancouver, BC Canada
Mailing Address: 1150 Station St., First Floor, Vancouver, BC Canada V6A 2X7
Telephone: (604) 606-7200 and (800) 665-7245
Fax: (604) 606-7250 reservations

Manitoba, Winnipeg

WINNIPEG RAILWAY MUSEUM
Railway museum

JOHN S. HIGH

Museum: Static display of locomotive (Countess of Dufferin) and numerous railroad displays.

Schedule: April 22 through Labor Day: Fridays, Saturdays, Sundays, and holidays, 12 to 5 p.m. Winter hours: weekends and holidays, 12 to 4 p.m.

Admission/Fare: Free.

Locomotive/Rolling Stock: Steel caboose CNR; Mack rail bus; rail sedan; steel baggage car CNR; CNR combine.

Nearby Attractions/Accommodations: Access to the Forks, Fort Garry Hotel.

Location/Directions: VIA rail station, downtown Winnipeg.

[P] 🚌 ✳ 📷 🏛 M VIA

Site Address: VIA Rail Station, Main and Broadway Streets, Winnipeg, MB
Mailing Address: Box 1855, Winnipeg, MB Canada R3C 3R1
Telephone: (204) 942-4632

Nova Scotia, Louisbourg

SYDNEY & LOUISBURG RAILWAY MUSEUM
Railway museum

S&L RAILWAY HISTORICAL SOCIETY

Museum: The S&L Railway Historical Society operates a three-building complex: the original 1895 station displaying railway artifacts; the original freight shed; and a new roundhouse. During the summer a Ceilidh (community party) is held with local musicians, singers and dancers, a mini-milling frolic, oatcakes, bannoch, and tea.

Schedule: May, June, and September: daily, 9 a.m. to 5 p.m. July, August: daily, 9 a.m. to 7 p.m. Special tours by appointment.

Admission/Fare: Donations appreciated.

Locomotive/Rolling Stock: Two passengers cars, 1881 and 1914; boxcar, tankcar; caboose; small hand cars.

Special Events: Special annual exhibits in the roundhouse. Annual renuion, second Sunday of September. Ceilidh at the roundhouse, second Thursday beginning July 10.

Nearby Attractions/Accommodations: Louisbourg Boardwalk at harbor, The Playhouse (designed after Shakespeare's Globe). Fortress Louisbourg, a 1744 reconstruction of French fortress. Motels, inns, motor home parks, campsites, restaurants, gift shops.

Location/Directions: On Main Street, which is a continuation of route 22 as you come into town.

Site Address: Station Hill, Louisbourg, NS
Mailing Address: PO Box 225, Louisbourg, NS Canada B0A 1M0
Telephone: (902) 733-2720

Ontario, Chatham   **CHATHAM RAILROAD MUSEUM SOCIETY**
Railroad museum

GARY SHURGOLD

Museum: This museum is located in a CN baggage car built in 1955. It was removed from active service in 1982 and was resurrected in its present form in 1989. This museum contains early railroad equipment such as switches, a caboose stove, several model trains, lanterns, and various other memorabilia used in Kent County by the men who made the trains roll.

Schedule: May 1 through September 1: Mondays through Saturdays, 9 a.m. to 5 p.m. Group tours by appointment.

Admission/Fare: Donations appreciated.

Special Events: Railroad Fun Days, call or write for information.

Nearby Attractions/Accommodations: Festival of Nations, July. Waterfront Weekends, all summer. Highland Games, July. Heritage Days, October. Chatham Cultural Centre, Chatham-Kent Museum, Thames Art Gallery, Wild Zone, Best Western Wheels Inn, Comfort Inn, Days Inn, Holiday Express Inn.

Location/Directions: The museum is located north of the 401 Highway on McLean Street, at the intersection of Queen and William Streets.

[P] 🚌 📷 ⛩ ✉ M VIA

Site Address: 2 McLean Street, Chatham, ON
Mailing Address: PO Box 434, Chatham, ON Canada N7M 5K5
Telephone: (519) 352-3097

Ontario, Milton

HALTON COUNTY RADIAL RAILWAY
Electric, scheduled
4'10⅞" gauge

J.D. KNOWLES

Ride/Display: Located on the right of way of the former Toronto Suburban Railway, Canada's first operating railway museum offers a 2-mile ride through scenic woodlands. More than 50 pieces of rolling stock from a variety of electric lines in Ontario. Visitors experience living history by touring our car houses and historically designated Rockwood Station.

Schedule: May, September, October: weekends and holidays. June: Wednesdays through Sundays. July and August: daily. 10 a.m. to 5 p.m.

Admission/Fare: Adults $6.50; seniors $5.50; youth 3-18 $4.50. Groups of 4 or more $1.00 off each ticket. Groups/charters of 20 or more $4.00 per ticket.

Locomotive/Rolling Stock: No. 327, 1893 4-wheel open car (rebuilt 1933); no. 55, 1915 Preston single-truck closed car; no. 2890, 1923 small Peter Witt, Ottawa; no. 2424, 1921 large Peter Witt; and no. 4000, 1938 PCC; all former Toronto Transportation Commission. no. 107, 1912 Montreal & Southern Counties interurban; more.

Special Events: Feature events held the fourth Sunday of June thorugh September and November. Christmas Night Show, first Saturday of December. Call or write for more information.

Location/Directions: Highway 401 exit 312 (Guelph Line) traveling north for 9 miles (15 km).

*Coupon available, see coupon section.

Site Address: 13629 Guelph Line, Milton, ON
Mailing Address: PO Box 578, Milton, ON Canada L9T 5A2
Telephone: (519) 856-9802
Fax: (519) 856-1399
E-mail: streetcar@hcry.org
Internet: www.nl-marketing.com/hcrr

Ontario, Ottawa

NATIONAL MUSEUM OF SCIENCE & TECHNOLOGY
Science museum
Railway displays

MALAK

Museum: The most comprehensive science and technology museum in Canada, this museum features all types of transportation, from Canada's earliest days to the present time. On display in the Steam Locomotives Hall are four huge steam locomotives, a CNR narrow-gauge passenger car from Newfoundland, and a caboose. The visitors have access to two of the cabs, where sound effects give the feeling of live locomotives. The engines are meticulously restored, with polished rods and lighted number boards and class lights.

Schedule: May 1 to Labor Day: daily, 9 a.m. to 6 p.m. Fridays till 9 p.m. October through April: Tuesdays through Sundays, 9 a.m. to 5 p.m. Closed Mondays and Christmas Day.

Admission/Fare: Adults $6.00; seniors and students $5.00; children 6-15 $2.00; children under age 5 are free; family of 2 adults/2 children $12.00. Group rates available.

Locomotive/Rolling Stock: CN6400 4-8-4 Montreal 1936; CP926 4-6-0 1912; CP2858 4-6-4 Royal Hudson, Montreal 1938; CP3100 4-8-4 Montreal 1928; CNR businer car Terra Nova; CNR 76109 caboose.

Location/Directions: Located ten minutes from downtown Ottawa. Queensway (Highway 417) exit St. Laurent south for 2.6 km, left at Lancaster Road (at the lighthouse).

Site Address: 1867 St. Laurent Blvd., Ottawa, ON
Mailing Address: PO Box 9724, Stn. T, Ottawa, ON Canada K1G 5A3
Telephone: (613) 991-3044
Fax: (613) 990-3654
E-mail: scitech@istar.ca
Internet: www.science-tech.nmstc.ca

Ontario, Port Stanley

PORT STANLEY TERMINAL RAIL
Diesel, scheduled
Standard gauge

AL HOWLETT

Ride: Three different rides, all from the station in Port Stanley, on the harbor next to the lift bridge. Trains pass over two bridges and northward for up to 7 miles through the Kettle Creek Valley. Port Stanley is a commercial fishing village on the north shore of Lake Erie. Equipment includes cabooses; heavyweight coaches; open coaches; baggage cars; boxcars; flatcars; hopper cars; a snowplow; tank cars; Burro Cranes; and more. Ticket office and displays are in the former London & Port Stanley station. Open excursion cars; cabooses, former Canadian National, modified into enclosed coaches; standard coaches, former VIA. The "Little Red Caboose" can be chartered for birthday parties and other events with advance reservation.

Schedule: January through April: Sundays. November through December: weekends. May, June, September, October: daily.

Admission/Fare: Adults $8.50-$11.50; children 2-12 $4.75-$6.25.

Locomotive/Rolling Stock: GE converted cabooses 25 and 44-ton.

Special Events: Easter, Teddy Bear, Santa, and Entertainment Trains.

Nearby Attractions/Accommodations: St. Thomas Elgin Railroad Museum.

Location/Directions: Located on the north side of Lake Erie, 25 miles (50km) south of London, Ontario.

Radio frequency: 160.575

Site Address: 309 Bridge Street, Port Stanley, ON
Mailing Address: 309 Bridge Street, Port Stanley, ON Canada N5L 1C5
Telephone: (519) 782-3730
Fax: (519) 782-4385
Internet: www.pstr.on.ca

Ontario, St. Thomas

ELGIN COUNTY RAILWAY MUSEUM
Diesel, irregular
Standard gauge

JIM BOLAND

Museum: Walk through railway history when you visit this site. Several pieces of rolling stock inside 1913 MCRR shops. Also take in our "Railway Wall of Fame."

Schedule: Year round: Mondays, Wednesdays, Saturdays, mornings. May through September: add Sundays, 10 a.m. to 4 p.m.

Admission/Fare: Donations appreciated.

Locomotive/Rolling Stock: Hudson steam locomotive no. 5700; Wabash no. 51; CP no. 8921; L&PS L1 electric Pullman sleeper; more.

Special Events: Railway Nostalgia Weekend, first weekend in May. Railway Heritage Weekend, fourth weekend in August.

Nearby Attractions/Accommodations: Dalewood Conservation Area, Hawk Cliff, Super 8 Motel, New Elgin Motel.

Location/Directions: Exit 401 at Wellington Road South (London). Highway 3 bypass, exit bypass at First Avenue, then south to Wellington Street.

Site Address: Wellington Street, St. Thomas, ON
Mailing Address: RR #6, St. Thomas, ON Canada N5P 3T1
Telephone: (519) 631-0936
E-mail: sjbecrm@elgin.net
Internet: www.ccia.st-thomas.on.ca/elgin_regional_museum.html

Ontario, Sault Ste. Marie

ALGOMA CENTRAL RAILWAY INC.
Scheduled
Standard gauge

ELMER KARS

Display: We operate both tour trains and regular passenger service. Tour trains take you on a one-day wilderness excursion to Agawa Canyon Wilderness Park. Regular passenger train provides service to Hearst, Ontario as well as access to a variety of wilderness lodges.

Schedule: Passenger service train–Year round. Agawa Canyon train–June through mid-October: daily. Snow train–January through mid-March: weekends. Group rentals available.

Admission/Fare: Call for information.

Locomotive/Rolling Stock: Refurbished F9s; refurbished 1950s VIA coaches.

Nearby Attractions/Accommodations: Major hotels located nearby.

Location/Directions: Located in downtown Sault Ste. Marie, minutes from International Bridge.

Site Address: 129 Bay Street, Sault Ste. Marie, ON
Mailing Address: PO Box 130, Sault Ste. Marie, ON Canada P6A 6Y2
Telephone: (705) 946-7300 and (800) 242-9287
Fax: (705) 541-2989

Ontario, Uxbridge/Stouffville

YORK DURHAM HERITAGE RAILWAY
Diesel, scheduled
Standard gauge

JOHN SKINNER, EAGLE VISION PHOTOGRAPHY

Display/Ride: See the newly restored 90-year-old Uxbridge Station with the unique "witch's hat" design. Inside the station is the railway's gift shop and museum. Displays include old photos and railway memorabilia.

Schedule: Victoria Day weekend through Canadian Thanksgiving. Trains run weekends and holidays, 3 time daily.

Admission/Fare: Call or write for information.

Locomotive/Rolling Stock: No. 3612 Alco 1956 diesel; no. 1310 Alco 1951 diese; no. 201 50T (7040) 1950.

Special Events: Stouffville Strawberry Festival.

Location/Directions: Uxbridge Station is located on Railway Lane off Brock Street in Uxbridge. From downtown Toronto take the Don Valley Parkway to 404, exit east on Stouffville side road. Stouffville Station is located on this road which turns into Main Street in Stouffville. Approximately 35 minutes from Toronto.

Site Address: Uxbridge and Stouffville, ON
Mailing Address: PO Box 462, Stouffville, ON L4A 7Z7 Canada
Telephone: (905) 852-3696
Fax: (905) 462-0099 (call first)
Email: quelch.c@sympatico.ca

Ontario, Waterloo

WATERLOO-ST. JACOBS RAILWAY
Diesel, scheduled
Standard gauge

BOB CHAMBERS

Ride: Roll the clock back almost half a century when you step aboard the Fifties Streamliner. Your Day Pass allows you to ride every train operating that day. Get off to explore Canada's largest farmer's market and the factory outlet mall, then board another train to travel to the quaint village of St. Jacobs with its unique shops, crafters, and restaurants.

Schedule: April through December: daily in summer, weekends at other times.

Admission/Fare: Day pass–adults $8.50; seniors and students $7.50; children $5.50. Fares subject to change.

Locomotive/Rolling Stock: FP9A locomotives nos. 6508 and 6520, former CN Rail; ten coaches; two cafe-lounges; combination car; two baggage cars; Super Continental; Daynight coach, former CNR; sleeper Conestogo River, former CNR; more.

Special Events: Maple Syrup Festival Express, Mother's Day, Father's Day, Murder Mystery trains, Waterloo Busker Carnival, Comedy on the Rails, Oktoberfest specials, Halloween Express to Terror, Santa, Festival of Lights.

Nearby Attractions/Accommodations: St. Jacobs offers many attractions.

Location/Directions: Waterloo is 60 miles west of Toronto. From Highway 401, take Highway 8 to Highway 86, north to Bridgeport Road, west on Bridgeport and follow signs to Waterloo Station.

[P] 🚌 ✳ ☕ 🅿 ✉ VIA

Site Address: 10 Father David Bauer Drive, Waterloo, ON
Mailing Address: Box 40103, Waterloo Sq. P.O., Waterloo, ON Canada N2J 4V1
Telephone: (800) 754-1054 and (519) 746-1950
Fax: (519) 746-3521

Quebec, Hull

HULL-CHELSEA-WAKEFIELD STEAM TRAIN
Steam, diesel, scheduled
Standard gauge

MALAK

Ride: Scenic rail tour on board a 1907 steam train from Hull to picturesque Wakefield, Quebec. Located only minutes from Ottawa's downtown and all other major attractions. On board bilingual tour guides and professional musical entertainers throughout the journey. Licensed concession and seat service in spacious, comfortable air-conditioned coaches. The exclusive Sunset Dinner Train offers a fine-dining experience with exceptional service. Enjoy spectacular fall foliage excursions. Or choose a combined river cruise/train journey on the Rail & Sail package.

Schedule: May 9 through October 18.

Admission/Fare: Adults $26.00; children $12.00; dinner train $58.00.

Locomotive/Rolling Stock: 1907 class 2-8-0 Swedish steam; 8-passenger coach; restaurant car; five diners.

Special Events: Sunset Dinner Train, featuring exquisite French cuisine and live entertainment.

Nearby Attractions/Accommodations: City of Ottawa, national museums, major hotels.

Location/Directions: Highway 5 north exit Casino Blvd. One mile from Hull Casino.

Site Address: 165 Deveault Street, Hull, QB
Mailing Address: 165 Deveault Street, Hull, QB Canada J8Z 1S7
Telephone: (819) 778-7246 and (800) 871-7246
Fax: (819) 778-5007
Internet: www.justlooking.com/train.htm

Quebec, Saint Constant

CANADIAN RAILWAY MUSEUM
Railway museum
Standard gauge

KEVIN ROBINSON

Display: Discover the golden era of railways, its brutish workhorses, its lightfooted fillies, and its fiery magnificent queens. Take a ride in the Museum's streetcar, one of the last to run in the streets of Montreal. A collections of more than 130 railway vehicles, one of North America's best, awaits you at the demonstration runs of the John Molson steam locomotive or the Sunday train rides.

Schedule: May 3 through September 6: daily, 9 a.m. to 5 p.m. Weekends and holidays to October 18.

Admission/Fare: Adults $5.75; seniors $4.75; students 13-17 $3.25; children 5-12 $2.75.

Special Events: Steam Weekend, June 20-21. Diesel Weekend, September 12-13. Please confirm.

Location/Directions: Highway 15 exit 42, route 132 to Chateauguay, left at fifth light.

Site Address: 122A Saint-Pierre Street, Saint-Constant, Quebec
Mailing Address: 120 rue Saint-Pierre, Saint-Constant, Quebec Canada J5A 2G9
Telephone: (514) 632-2410 information and (514) 638-1522 administration
Fax: (514) 638-1563
E-mail: mfcd@quebectel.com

Saskatchewan, Carlyle

RUSTY RELICS MUSEUM
Railway museum
Standard gauge

BRENT HUME

Museum: The museum is housed in a CNR station. It features historical, industrial, personal, and household artifacts of the area. Farm machinery, CNR toolshed, CP caboose, one-room country school.

Schedule: Mid-June to Labor Day: daily, 10 a.m. to 5 p.m.

Admission/Fare: Adults $2.00; students $1.00; preschoolers are free.

Special Events: Opening day, June 7.

Nearby Attractions/Accommodations: Moose Mountain Provincial Park, waterslides, golf courses, swimming pool, tennis courts.

Location/Directions: At the junction of Highways 9 and 13, approximately 60 miles north of the U.S. border, and 40 miles west of the Manitoba border.

[P] [✱] [📷] M

Site Address: Railway Avenue, Carlyle, SK
Mailing Address: Box 840, Carlyle, SK Canada S0C 0R0
Telephone: (306) 453-2266

Saskatchewan, Moose Jaw

WESTERN DEVELOPMENT MUSEUM
Steam, scheduled
Narrow gauge

WESTERN DEVELOPMENT MUSEUM

Museum: Display of artifacts of rail, land, air, and water transportation.

Schedule: Year round: daily, 9 a.m. to 6 p.m. January through March: closed Mondays.

Admission/Fare: Adults $4.50; seniors and students $3.50; children $1.50.

Nearby Attractions/Accommodations: Camping, motels, variety of cultural and sporting events.

Location/Directions: Junction of Highways 1 and 2.

Site Address: 50 Diefenbaker Drive, Moose Jaw, SK
Mailing Address: Box 185, Moose Jaw, SK Canada S6H 4N8
Telephone: (306) 693-5989
Fax: (306) 691-0511

Saskatchewan, Saskatoon

SASKATCHEWAN RAILWAY MUSEUM
Railway museum
Standard gauge

SASKATCHEWAN RAILWAY MUSEUM

Museum: Seven acres of railway buildings and rolling stock. Demonstration of Woodings and Fairmont motor cars.

Schedule: Victoria Day through Labor Day: weekends and holidays, 1 to 6 p.m. Other times by appointment.

Admission/Fare: Adults $2.00; children under age 16 $1.00; preschoolers are free.

Locomotive/Rolling Stock: MLW S-3 CP diesel electric, four cabooses; 1913 CP snowplow; Wooding and Fairmont motor cars; 1926 Saskatoon streetcar.

Nearby Attractions/Accommodations: City of Saskatoon, hotels, camping, Western Development Museum.

Location/Directions: Approximately 4 km southwest of Saskatoon, on Highway 7 to Highway 60, then 2 km to museum.

P 🚌 ✳ 📷 ⛩ ✉ M VIA

Site Address: Highway 60, Pike Lake Road, Saskatoon, SK
Mailing Address: Box 19, Site 302, Saskatoon, SK Canada S7K 3J6
Telephone: (306) 382-9855
E-mail: aa741@stn.saskatoon.sk.ca
Internet: aa741@stn.saskatoon.sk.ca

A

AC&J Scenic Line Railway 262
Abilene & Smoky Valley Railroad 127
Adirondack Scenic Railroad 234
Adrian & Blissfield Railroad 158
Age of Steam Railroad Museum 338
Alaska Railroad 8
Alco Brooks Railroad Display 229
Algoma Central Railway, Inc. 409
Allegheny Portage Railroad Natl. Historic Site . .290
Altoona Railroader's Memorial Museum 286
America's Railroads on Parade 357
American Orient Express Railway Co. 366
American Railway Caboose Hist. Education Soc. 195
Anacortes Railway 358
Anderson Steel Flange 125
Arcade & Attica Railroad 228
Arizona Railway Museum 11
Arizona Train Depot 13
Arkansas & Missouri Railroad 20
Arkansas Railroad Museum 19
Austin & Texas Central Railroad 337

B

BC Rail 394
B&O Railroad Museum, The 145
Baltimore Streetcar Museum 146
Bear Creek Miniature Train 401
Bellefonte Historical Railroad 289
Belton, Grandview & Kansas City RR Co. 188
Berkshire Scenic Railway 156
Beverly Historical Society and Museum 153
Big Bear Farm 295
Big South Fork Scenic Railway 135
Black Hills Central Railroad 324
Black River & Western Railroad 221
Blue Mountain & Reading Railroad 294
Bluegrass Railroad Museum 136
Bonanzaville U.S.A. 253
Boone & Scenic Valley Railroad 120
Boothbay Railway Village 140
Brandywine Scenic Railway 305
Branson Scenic Railway 189
British Columbia Forest Museum 393
Broadway Dinner Train 333
Buckeye Central Scenic Railroad 260
Buckleberry Railroad 168

C

Cafe Lafayette Dinner Train 214
California State Railroad Museum 44
California State Railroad Museum-Sacramento . . .45
California Western Railroad 30
Camp Five Museum Foundation, Inc. 380

Canadian Museum of Rail Travel 392
Canadian Railway Museum 414
Cape Cod Railroad 155
Cape May Seashore Lines 218
Carillon Historical Park 258
Carrollton-Oneida-Minerva Railroad 255
Carthage, Knightstown & Shirley Railroad 116
Casey Jones Museum 187
Casey Jones Museum and Train Store 331
Cass Scenic Railroad State Park 370
Catskill Mountain Railroad 233
Charlie Russell Chow-Choo Dinner Train 199
Chatham Railroad Museum Society 405
Chattanooga Choo Choo 327
Chehalis-Centralia Railroad Association 361
Chelan County Historical Society 360
Chesapeake Beach Railway Museum 147
Children's Museum 245
Children's Museum of Indianapolis, The 115
Chippewa Northwestern Railway Co. 202
Chippewa Valley Railroad Association 378
Choctaw Caboose Museum 274
Choo Choo Barn Traintown U.S.A. 314
City of Traverse City Parks and Recreation 172
Clovis Depot Model Train Museum 226
Collis P. Huntington Railroad
    Historical Society 373
Colorado Railroad Museum 63
Conneaut Railroad Museum 257
Connecticut Antique Machinery Association, Inc. .74
Connecticut Trolley Museum 71
Conway Scenic Railroad 216
Corydon Scenic Railroad 110
Cowan Railroad Museum 330
Crooked River Dinner Train 284
Crystal Springs & Cahuenga Valley Railroad ...38
Cumbres & Toltec Scenic Railroad 225
Cuyahoga Valley Scenic Railroad 261
Cypress Gardens 88

D

Danbury Railway Museum 69
Danville Junction Chapter NRHS 104
Dayton Historical Depot 362
Dennison Railroad Depot Museum, The 259
Denver & Rio Grande U.S. Natl. Park Service ...67
Dept. of Transportation Vintage Trolleys 163
DeQuincy Railroad Museum 137
Descanso, Alpine & Pacific Railway 21
Dinner Trains of New England 322
Disneyland Railroad 22
Dollywood Entertainment Park 335
Durango & Silverton Narrow-Gauge Railroad ...61
Durbin & Greenbrier Valley Railroad 371

E

East Broad Top Railroad 307
East Penn Rail Excursions, Inc. 298
East Troy Electric Railroad Wis. Trolley 377
Eldorado Express Railroad 36
Elgin County Railway Museum 410
Ellis Railroad Museum 129
Empire State Railway Museum 236
End-O-Line Railroad Park and Museum 175
Essex Steam Train and Riverboat Ride 72
Eureka & Palisade Railroad 208
Eureka Springs & North Arkansas Railway 17

F

Fairfax Station Railroad Museum 352
Florida Central Adventure Dinner Train 84
Florida Gulf Coast Railroad Museum, Inc. 87
Floyd McEachern Historical Train Museum 248
Folsom Valley Railway 29
Forney Historic Transportation Museum 59
Fort Edmonton Park 391
Fort Fairfield Railroad Museum 141
Fort George Railway 396
Fort Madison, Farmington & Western 124
Fort Wayne Railroad Historical Society 112
Fox River Trolley Museum 105
Franklin Institute Science Museum, The 306
Fremont & Elkhorn Valley Railroad 200
Fremont Dinner Train 201
French Lick, West Baden & Southern Railway ..113
Frisco Railroad Museum 198

G

Galesburg Railroad Museum 98
Georgetown Loop Railroad 62
Gettysburg Scenic Rail Tours 292
Gold Coast Railroad Museum 82
Golden Gate Live Steamers, Inc. 23
Golden Gate Railroad Museum 48
Golden Spike National Historic Site 348
Grand Canyon Railway 15
Great Plains Transportation Museum, Inc. 130
Great Smoky Mountains Railway 249
Green Mountain Railroad/Flyer 349
Greenville Railroad Park and Museum 293
Gulf Coast Railroad Museum 341

H

Halton County Radial Railway 406
Hardin Southern Railroad 132
Harmar Station 265
Harper's Ferry Toy Train Museum 372
Hartmann Model Railroad, LTD 211
Hawaiian Railway Society 93

Hazlet Train Stop 222
Heart of Dixie Railroad Museum 5
Henry Ford Museum and Greenfield Village ...162
Henry Morrison Flagler Museum, The 86
Herber Valley Railroad 346
Heritage Park Historical Village 390
Hesston Steam Museum 114
Historic Huntsville Depot 7
Historic Manassas, Inc. '98 Railway Festival ...354
Historic Pullman Foundation 95
Historic Railroad Shops 91
Hobo Railroad 212
Hocking Valley Scenic Railway 267
Holiday Crusin' Rails 196
Holyoke Heritage Park Railroad, Inc. 154
Hoosier Valley Railroad Museum, Inc. 119
Horseshoe Curve Natl. Historic Landmark 287
Huckleberry Railroad 167
Hugo Heritage Railroad 276
Hull Chelsea Wakefield Steam Train 413

I

Illinois Railway Museum 106
Indiana Transportation Museum 118
Iron Mountain Iron Mine 168
Ironworld Discovery Center 174
Irvine Park Railroad 40

J

Jefferson Depot, Inc. 263
Junction Valley Railroad 159

K

Kandiyohi County Historical Society 186
Kelley Park Trolley 51
Kennesaw Civil War Museum 90
Kentucky Central Railway 134
Kentucky Railway Museum 133
Kettle Moraine Railway 384
Kiski Junction Railroad 309
Klickety Klack Model Railroad 217
Knox & Kane Railroad 300
Kwinitsa Railway Station Museum 398

L

Lahaina, Kaanapali & Pacific Railroad 94
Lake County History and Railroad Museum 185
Lake Shore Railway Historical Society, Inc. 304
Lake Superior & Mississippi Railroad 177
Lake Superior Museum of Transportation 178
Laurel Highlands Railroad 310
LAWS Railroad Museum & Historical Site 25
Leadville, Colorado & Southern Railroad 65
Linden Railroad Museum 117

Little River Railroad 161
Little River Railroad and Lumber Company ... .336
Livingston Junction Cabooses 16
Lookout Mountain Incline Railway 328
Lomita Railroad Museum 35
Louisiana State Railroad Museum 138
Lowell National Historical Park 157
Lycoming County Historical Society
   & Museum 321

M

Mad River & NKP Railroad Society 254
Maine Narrow Gauge Railroad and Museum ... .144
Manitou & Pike's Peak Railway 66
Mason City & Clear Lake Electric Railway .... .121
Maumee Valley Historical Society 266
McKinney Avenue Transit Authority 339
Michigan AuSable Valley Railroad 166
Michigan Railroad History Museum 164
Michigan Star Clipper Dinner Train Coe Rail ... .173
Michigan State Trust for Railway Preservation . .170
Michigan Transit Museum 169
Mid-Continent Railway Historical Society 383
Middletown & Hummelstown Railroad 301
Midland Railway 128
Midwest Central Railroad 126
Mine Hill & Northern Railroad 291
Mining Museum and Rollo Jamison Museum ... 386
Minnesota Trans. Museum, Como-Harriet 180
Minnesota Trans. Museum, Minnehaha Depot ... 181
Minnesota Trans. Museum, Osceola & St. Croix .385
Minnesota Zephyr Limited 184
Model Train Museum 364
Monticello Railway Museum 100
Mount Dora, Tavares & Eustis Railroad 83
Mount Hood Railroad and Dinner Train 281
Mount Rainier Scenic Railroad 363
Mount Washington Cog Railway, The 210
Mountain State Mystery Tours 374
Museum of Alaska Transportation and Industry ... 10
Museum of Science and Industry 96
Museum of Transportation 197
My Old Kentucky Dinner Train 131

N

Napa Valley Wine Train 39
National Capital Trolley Museum 151
National Museum of Science & Technology 407
National New York Central Railroad Museum ... 111
National Railroad Museum 379
National Railroad Museum and Hall of Fame ... 250
National Toy Train Museum 315
Naugatuck Railroad 75
Nevada Northern Railway Museum 207

Nevada State Railroad Museum 206
New Hope & Ivyland Railroad 303
New Hope Valley Railway 247
New Jersey Museum of Transportation, Inc. ... .219
New London Historical Society 382
New York & Lake Erie Railroad 230
New York Museum of Transportation 238
New York, Susquehanna & Western 244
Niles Canyon Railway 53
Niles Depot Museum 31
North Alabama Railroad Museum 6
North Carolina Transportation Museum 251
North Cove Express Dinner Train, The 73
North Shore Scenic Railroad 179
North Star Rail, Inc. 182
Northeast Rail Batten Kill Railroad 242
Northern Central Railway 302
Northern Counties Logging Museum 26
Northlandz 220

O

Ogden Union Station 347
Ohio Central Railroad 270
Ohio Railway Museum 272
Oil Creek & Titusville Railroad 318
Old Colony and Fall River Railroad Museum ... 153
Old Depot Railroad Museum, The 176
Old Dominion Railway Museum 355
Old Pueblo Trolley 14
Omaha Henry Doorly Zoo Railroad 203
Ontario & Western Roscoe O&W 240
Orange Empire Railway Museum 42
Orland, Newville & Pacific Railroad 41
Orrville Railroad Heritage Society 269
Osceola & St. Croix Valley Railway 385

P

Patee House Museum 194
Pennsylvania Trolley Museum 319
Phoenix & Holly Railroad 280
Pike's Peak Historical Street Railway
   Foundation 58
Pioneer Tunnel Coal Mine & Steam Train 288
Pioneer Village and Museum 360
Port Stanley Terminal Rail 408
Portola Railroad Museum 43
Potomac Eagle Scenic Rail Excursions 376
Prairie Village 325
Prince George Railway & Forestry Museum ... 397
Puget Sound Railway Historical Association ... .367

Q

Queen Anne's Railroad 77

R

Rail City Historical Museum 243
Railroad and Pioneer Museum 344
Railroad Memories Museum 387
Railroad Museum of Long Island 231
Railroad Museum of Oklahoma 275
Railroad Museum of Pennsylvania 316
Railroad Museum of S. Florida-Displays, The 79
Railroad Museum of S. Florida-Train Village, The 80
Railswest Railroad Museum 123
Railtown 1897 Sierra Railway Company 34
Railway Exposition Co. 256
Rayville Railroad Museum 101
Redwood Valley Railway Corp. 24
Remlinger Farms Railroad 359
Revelstoke Railway Museum 399
Rio Grande Chapter NRHS 64
Riverside & Great Northern Railway 388
Riverside Station Delaware and Hudson Depot . .237
Roadside America 312
Rockhill Trolley Museum 308
Rocky Mountaineer Railtours 402
Rochester & Genesee Valley Railroad Museum . .239
Royal Gorge Scenic Railway 57
Rusty Relics Museum 415

S

Sacramento Southern Railroad 45
St. Louis, Iron Mountain & Southern Railway . . .193
Salamanca Rail Museum 241
Samtrak 282
San Diego Model Railroad Museum 46
San Diego Railroad Museum 47
San Francisco Cable Car Museum 49
San Francisco Municipal Railway 50
Sandy River Railroad Museum 143
Santa Cruz, Big Trees & Pacific Railway 27
Santa Fe Southern Railway 227
Saskatchewan Railway Museum 417
Seashore Trolley Museum 142
Seminole Gulf Railroad 81
Shelburne Museum 351
Shore Line Trolley Museum 70
Silver Creek & Stephenson Railroad 97
Silver Dollar City Theme Park 190
Six Flags Over Mid-America 191
Ski Train, The 60
Skunk Train, The 30
Smithsonian Institution 76
Society for the Preservation of Carter Railroad . . .32
Society for the Preservation of SS City of Milw .165
Sonora Short Line Railway 54
South Carolina Railroad Museum 323
South Coast Railroad Museum 33

Southeastern Railway Museum 89
Southern Appalachia Railway Museum 332
Southern Michigan Railroad Society 160
Spirit of Washington Dinner Train 365
Steamtown National Historic Site 311
Stewartstown Railroad .313
Stone Mountain Scenic Railroad 92
Stourbridge Line Rail Excursions 296
Strasburg Railroad 317
Sumpter Valley Railroad 285
Sunbelt Railroad Museum 277
Sydney & Louisburg Railway Museum 404

T

Tarantula Train 340
Tennessee Central Railway Museum 334
Tennessee Valley Railroad 329
Texas State Railroad 342
Texas Transportation Museum 343
Tiny Town Railroad 68
Tioga Central Railroad .320
Tioga Scenic Railroad 235
Toledo, Lake Erie & Western Railway 271
Toonerville Trolley and Riverboat Trips 171
Toy Train Depot 224
Train House, The 273
Train Town 52
Trains at Bandana Square, Twin City MR Club . .183
Trainland of Orlando 85
Trainland U.S.A. 122
Travel Town Museum 37
Trolley Car 36 103
Trolley Museum of New York 232
Trolleyville U.S.A. 268
Turtle Creek Valley Railway 264
Tweetsie Railroad 246

U

U.S. Army Transportation Museum 353
Union Depot Railroad Museum 99
Union Pacific Collection 204

V

Valley View Model Railroad 107
Verde Canyon Railroad 12
Vermont Rail Excursions 350
Virginia & Truckee Railroad Co. 209
Virginia Museum of Transportation 356

W

Wabash Frisco & Pacific Railway 192
Walker Transportation Collection 152
Walkersville Southern Railroad 150
Wanamaker, Kempton & Southern, Inc. 297

Washington Park & Zoo Railway 283
Waterloo St. Jacobs Railway 412
Waterman & Western Railroad 108
Waynoka Historical Society 278
West Coast Railway Heritage Park 400
West Shore Rail Excursions 299
West Virginia Northern Railroad 375
Western Development Museum 416
Western Heritage Museum 205
Western Maryland Railway Historical Society ...149
Western Maryland Scenic Railroad 148
Western Vancouver Island Indust. Heritage Soc. .395
Wheels O' Time 102
Whetstone Valley Express 326
White Mountain Central Railroad 213
White Pass & Yukon Route 9
White River Railway 18
Whitewater Valley Railroad 109
Whippany Railway Museum 223
Wilmington Railroad Museum 252
Wilmington & Western Railroad 78
Winnipeg Railway Museum 403
Winnipesaukee Scenic Railroad 215
Wiscasset, Waterville & Farmington Railway ...139
Witchita Falls Railroad Museum 345
Wyoming Transportation Museum 389

Y

Yakima Electric Railway Museum 369
Yakima Valley Rail and Steam Museum 368
Yolo Shortline Railroad Company 55
York Durham Heritage Railway 411
Yosemite Mountain Sugar Pine Railroad 28
Yreka Western Railroad 56
Yukon's Best Railroad Museum 279

Z

Zoofari Express Milwaukee County Zoo 381